GARDENWALKS

*101 of the Best Gardens
from Maine to Virginia
and Recommended Gardens
Throughout the Country*

MARINA HARRISON
LUCY D. ROSENFELD

Illustrations by Lucy D. Rosenfeld

MICHAEL KESEND PUBLISHING · NEW YORK

Copyright 1997 © by Marina Harrison and Lucy D. Rosenfeld
First Publication 1997
Second Printing 1998
Published by Michael Kesend Publishing, Ltd.
1025 Fifth Avenue, New York, NY 10028

Library of Congress Cataloging-in-Publication Data

Harrison, Marina, 1939–
      Gardenwalks: 101 of the best gardens from Maine to
Virginia and gardens throughout the country / by Marina
Harrison and Lucy D. Rosenfeld.
            p.   cm.
      Includes index.
      ISBN 0-935576-52-5
      1. Gardens—Northeastern States—Guidebooks.
2. Gardens—United States—Guidebooks. 3. Northeastern
States—Guidebooks. 4. United States—Guidebooks.
I. Rosenfeld, Lucy D., 1939–   . II. Title.
SB466.U65N755 1997
712' .025'74—dc21   97–397
                                                          CIP

CONTENTS

PREFACE

This book invites garden lovers to join us in a search for beautiful and interesting sights. While we don't pretend to be horticulturists, botanists, or even to have very green thumbs ourselves, we do know an aesthetic treat when we see one.

As you may know from our previous guidebooks, we are inveterate walkers and connoisseurs of exceptional art and scenery. The 101 gardens we have selected in our region provide both natural and aesthetic pleasures. We describe in some detail our favorite gardens, which reflect the melting pot aspects of our nation, ranging in style from the most eccentric personal expressions to the traditional formal elegance found in European and Asian forms. Nor have we overlooked natural and wildflower preserves, which some people consider the best gardens of all. Also included are sculpture and architectural gardens; conservatories and indoor gardens; specialty gardens, such as an all-peony garden; gardens for the disabled; Asian gardens; gardens with great views, whose very settings make them special; and some intriguing private gardens, whose owners graciously invite visitors. You'll also find at the end of each chapter "And in Addition . . .," writeups of other worthy garden sites in the states.

We have tried to introduce you to the various historic, multinational, and artistic garden designs in a section at the beginning of the book called "Thoughts on Garden Styles." At the end of the book is "Choosing an Outing," a guide that will help you select a garden to visit according to style or tradition.

Every garden in this book is open to the public on a more or less regular basis in season; we have not included gardens open only one day a year. While we cannot—in a useful, portable guide—fully describe every choice garden nationwide, we have given a thumbnail sketch of those you should not miss as you travel around the country.

We have spent several years visiting every sort of garden in every season—on beautiful sunny days, as well as in pouring rain. Wherever we have gone, we have been given enthusiastic and helpful suggestions. Many people have directed us to gardens we might have overlooked, and others have recommended books and garden tours, and have even led us to hard-to-find places themselves. Among those we would like to thank are Andy Boose, Bob Rodgers, Cecily Morse, Barbara Merrill, Sophie Rosenfeld and Matthew Affron, Catherine and Ray Stainback, Susan and Phil Harrison, Elena and Mark Morris, and our always willing and enthusiastic husbands, Peter Rosenfeld and Jim Harrison. To Michael Kesend, we extend our thanks for his encouragement and the realization of our vision.

Gardens are, by definition, fragile. As living environments they are subject to the whims and changes of nature—and nurture. As we wrote this book, all the gardens we describe were in good condition and welcomed visitors. We hope you will find them as pleasing and carefully tended as we have.

GLOSSARY

Allée: a stately tree-lined avenue

Arboretum: a place where an extensive variety of trees are cultivated for scientific, educational, or ornamental purposes

Belvedere: a structure such as a summer house situated to command a view

Bosquet: a small grove or thicket

Botanical garden: a place where a wide variety of plants are cultivated for scientific, educational, or ornamental purposes

Butterfly garden: A garden in which flowers are specially chosen to attract butterflies

Classical garden: a formal garden whose aesthetic attitudes and values are embodied in ancient Greek and Roman design

Colonial garden: a garden designed or reconstructed in the colonial American style, with separate sections for flowers, fruit trees, vegetables, herbs, and various outbuildings

Conservatory: a greenhouse in which plants are arranged for aesthetic display and in carefully controlled climatic conditions

Cottage garden: a small, unpretentious garden featuring flowers and vegetables in a casual arrangement

Cup garden: a garden in ancient Chinese tradition, in which an object is framed by its surroundings

Demonstration garden: a garden whose purpose is horticultural education

English garden: a naturalistic garden style first developed in 18th century England, as compared with the more formal French style

Espalier: a fruit tree or shrub trained to grow flat against a wall often in a symmetrical pattern

Folly: a whimsical garden structure that is decorative rather than useful

Formal garden: a garden in which nature is trained to adhere to geometric or other formal decorative principles

Garden rooms: individual, self-contained and separately designed sections of a larger garden

Gazebo: a free-standing roofed structure, usually with open sides, that provides a shady resting place in a garden

Grotto: a small cave or cavern or an artificial structure made to resemble one

Ha-ha: a sunken hedge or moat that serves as a fence without impairing the view

Italianate garden: a garden in the Italian style often featuring classical elements, statuary, and fountains

Knot garden: elaborate planting of greenery, usually thyme or box, following the patterns of knots

Maze: a garden labyrinth: an intricate, deliberately confusing, patterned network of hedges and pathways, designed to entertain

Naturalistic garden: a garden in which the design attempts to imitate nature in its free form rather than to impose form upon it

Orangerie: a sheltered place such as a greenhouse, used particularly in a cold climate, to grow oranges

Parterre: an ornamental flower garden whose beds and paths form a pattern

Pergola: an arbor or passageway with a roof or trellis on which climbing plants are trained to grow

Pleasure garden: a garden such as a flower garden or park, designed purely for enjoyment

Promenade: A place for strolling in a garden

Rock garden: a garden in which rocks and plants are arranged in a carefully designed, decorative scheme, often featuring Alpine plants

Shade garden: a garden featuring plants that grow best in shaded areas

Topiary garden: a garden in which live trees and shrubs are clipped into fanciful shapes

Water garden: a garden in which ponds, streams, and other water elements, as well as plants that grow at water sites, are an integral part of the overall design

Wildflower garden: usually a preserve, in which flowering plants grow in a natural, uncultivated state

Winter garden: a conservatory or other indoor garden that can be enjoyed all year

Zen garden: a garden in the Japanese tradition designed for beauty and contemplation

THOUGHTS ON
GARDEN STYLES

The Asian Garden

A lonely pond in age-old stillness sleeps,
Apart, unstirred by sound or motion till
Suddenly into it a little frog leaps . . .
—*Basho (1644–94)*

Gardens of the Orient were the first to become living artistic statements. Closely aligned with religious beliefs of Buddhism, Taoism, and Shintoism, Chinese and Japanese gardens were places of meditation and renewal. In an attempt to tame nature's wildness, deliberately placed trees and plants were combined with materials of long-lasting value, like wood, sand, and stone. Each element of the garden was symbolic, designed for spiritual awareness as its owners strolled through it.

Chinese "cup gardens"—ranging in size from picturesque lakes surrounded by hills to small stone areas with a bonsai (artificially pruned, miniature tree) in the center—were among the first symbolically designed Asian gardens. The earliest cup garden is believed to have been created by the great landscape painter and poet Wang Wei (A.D. 699–759) during the T'ang Dynasty. It was Wang Wei who first articulated the close relationship of the Chinese garden to art, poetry, and spirituality.

If you look at a traditional scroll painting of a Chinese landscape, in fact, it is hard to know which art is imitating which, for the great Chinese gardens have the ambiance of paintings, while the paintings seem inextricably bound up with the delicately designed traditional garden. Harmonious in design, the Chinese landscape is distinctive, with its careful balance of leaning trees and craggy rocks, arched bridges over reflective water, and gentle flowering plants.

The cup garden was surrounded (like the inside of a cup) by a wall or a hedge, or other barrier in order to provide isolation from the chaos of outside world. Within its boundaries, the cup garden drew the visitor's attention to accents—a particular plant or stone or body of water. The garden's purpose was introspection and privacy, using an artistic design and symbolism to bring close communication and union with nature and its forces.

The symbolic elements and design of ancient Chinese gardens strongly influenced the Japanese, who went on to create elaborate and exquisite gardens of their own. The Japanese stroll garden also became a place for introspection: an orderly, aesthetic environment where balance, beauty, and harmony mirrored the proper harmony of the soul.

There is little that is accidental or uncalculated in a Japanese garden. Carefully placed, asymmetrical plantings such as bamboo and katsurra trees, ferns, delicate iris, and lilies grow among symbolic settings. These important elements range from free-form ponds that reflect the sky, to statuary such as small deities or cranes (representing wisdom and long life), to raked sand (representing the ocean's tides), to carefully placed rocks and small stones (suggesting the earth's natural forms), to tiny islands in the pond (symbolizing clouds). Small buildings such as the familiar Japanese tea house provide a haven of peace and beauty. To the Shintoists, spirits inhabit all natural phenomena, and the Japanese garden suggests no less than heaven on earth.

Southeast Asian gardens share many of the same designs and ideas, but in Thailand and Burma, for example, there is greater freedom from the precise symbolism of the Japanese. Though not as burdened by the meaning of each rock and bamboo shoot, these gardens are also spiritual sanctuaries adorned with sculptured deities, including small Buddhas set amid the greenery and flowers.

The Asian garden stunned and delighted Westerners who traveled to the East. In the seventeenth and eighteenth centuries many aspects of Chinese artistry—including garden design and exotic plants—began to appear in European gardens and subsequently in America.

Today, in addition to many great Chinese and Japanese gardens carefully maintained in the United States, we also find Oriental plantings and landscape design intermixed with the more Western styles of many of our American gardens. Among the elements adopted in our own gardens are numerous exotic trees (ranging from Asian magnolias and rhododendrons to Japanese flowering cherries) and many flowers, including species of jasmine, poppies, azaleas, and lilies.

But even more obvious to our Western eyes are the elements of Asian design that have crept into our own formal and informal gardens: trickling water and delicate lily ponds, small arched bridges and waterfalls, "living still lifes" of stones and foliage so prized in Asian design, and garden areas created for meditation and harmony with nature.

The Colonial Garden

Let every house be placed if the Person pleases in the middle of its plot so that there may be ground on each side for Gardens or Orchards, or fields, so that it may be a green Country Towne . . . and will always be wholesome.

—William Penn

Colonial gardens are an important part of America's cultural heritage, and one of its most delightful. Scattered about our region, from New England to the South, they represent a particular time in our history. Whether authentic seventeenth- and eighteenth-century gardens, replicas, or simply newer interpretations of a basic style, they all share certain characteristics, with some variation. More formal than not (without being necessarily "grand"), they are ordered, geometric, and often symmetrical. Most are enclosed and intimate. Their organized structure reflects the needs and perspectives of a culture that prized order, balance, and economy.

The early settlers had a pragmatic approach to gardening, whether they were facing the harsh winters of Massachusetts, or the milder climate of Virginia. First, it was essential to enclose each household compound to keep out animals, wild or domestic. Within a fence or stone wall was a well-planned arrangement that emphasized function, rather than aesthetics, without compromising overall harmony and charm. The location of the house, its outbuildings and connecting "yards," and planted areas were carefully sited for best drainage and exposure. Each had its specific purpose. Between the house and outbuildings was the "dooryard," where animals were shorn, soap was made, or wool was dyed. This rustic spot was hardly a place for much greenery, except for a few shade trees (which were also useful as places to attach pulleys and lift heavy objects).

Each family maintained a basic garden and orchard to serve its needs. These formal plantings were often wedged in small areas between the house, yards, sheds, barns, meadows, and pastures. At first, necessity dictated planting vegetables and fruit shrubs and trees, rather than flowers. (During the eighteenth century, gardens became less utilitarian and often included decorative plants as well as edibles.) Orchards contained large fruit trees, such as apples, but pears, peaches, apricots, and plums were arranged in borders or espaliers closer to the house. Herbs used for cooking were planted in simple, rectangular plots next to the house, or were sometimes mixed in with other plants. Physicians sometimes kept a "physic garden," or botanic garden, to provide the proper curative herbs for their patients.

On large colonial southern plantations it was especially essential to create kitchen gardens and orchards, as these estates were often isolated from towns and villages. And given a more agreeable climate than that found in New England, plentiful varieties of English plants thrived there. According to Robert Beverly, who in 1705 wrote *History of the Present State of Virginia,* "A Kitchen-Garden don't thrive better or faster in any part of the Universe than there. They have all the Culinary Plants that grow in England, and in far greater perfection, than in England."

Most colonial gardens were arranged in neat, rectangular blocks bordered by boxwood (especially in the South) or other decorative plants. Separating these geometric, cultivated areas were brick or stone paths. The more elaborate gardens might also include a central azalea path aligned with the main door of the house and leading to a vista, stone bench, or statue. On either side of the walk were raised plots (for better drainage) usually arranged in symmetrical fashion. While vegetables and small fruits were kept in designated areas, ornamental plants surrounded the more important walkways. Sometimes edible plants and flowers were mixed in together, creating formal geometric designs.

In New England, especially in the more elegant houses of Boston or Providence, it was common practice to cultivate a garden in front of the house, as well as in back. These tiny "parlor gardens" were sometimes no wider than the house itself and featured decorative shrubs and flowers.

During the eighteenth century Philadelphia became one of the most important garden centers in the country. No doubt this was because of the Quakers' interest in botany and horticulture—not surprising in view of the fact that their austere life-style excluded most other arts and activities. The great horticulturist John Bartram, a Quaker who founded the first botanical garden in the colonies, was largely responsible for generating great interest in plants and gardens. The results of his efforts are still very evident in the historic colonial gardens found in the Philadelphia region.

In Virginia and other parts of the South colonial gardens tended to be larger and more elaborate than in the North. With large-scale introduction of slavery into the southern colonies, manor houses were built, surrounded by often grand landscaped settings. One such place is the Governor's Place in Williamsburg, famous for its elegant eighteenth-century gardens (and a popular tourist attraction to this day). (See page 287.) Another is Gunston Hall, in Lorton, Virginia, an example of a well-designed twentieth-century recreation featuring a stately arrangement of boxwoods growing in neat, geometric hedges.

Thomas Jefferson who, along with George Washington, was one of the most famous colonial gardeners of all, had an abiding interest in horticulture, garden design, and botany—and a fundamental belief that the strength of the country lay in its agrarian society. He surrounded his extraordinary estate, Monticello, with vegetable plots (where he conducted various experiments), flower beds, and orchards. Monticello and Washington's Mount Vernon are examples of the colonial style at its grandest, but, still, they were created in basically the same spirit as the simplest colonial garden, emphasizing the order, harmony, and balance of pleasure and usefulness.

The Conservatory Garden

There is an inherent wonderful fascination in being able, in the middle of winter, to open the window of a salon and feel a balmy spring breeze instead of the raw December or January air. It may be raining outside, or the snow may be falling in soft flakes from a black sky, but one opens the glass doors and finds oneself in an earthly paradise that makes fun of the wintry showers.
—Princess Mathilde de Bonaparte, 1869

The idea of collecting, nurturing, and displaying plants in an enclosed, controlled environment is an ancient one. The first greenhouses may have been built by the Romans to protect the exotic plants they found during their military campaigns in distant lands. Emperor Nero's *specularium* (for so this type of Roman structure was called) contained his much loved cucumbers, which he could thus enjoy throughout the year. Over the course of human history plants have been gathered, arranged, and housed for many reasons—from the most pragmatic to the aesthetic, spiritual, scientific, or even whimsical. And their artificial habitats—from the specularium to the conservatory—have evolved considerably.

The earliest indoor gardens functioned both as places to display plants and to store and protect them from the sometimes harsh European winters. Ornamental plants were admired and often regarded as "trophies" won during victorious battles. (The taste for unusual flora existed at least as far back as ancient Egypt, when royal gardeners were routinely sent to other countries to gather rare species.) Crusaders and later many explorers came home with unfamiliar varieties, which required careful tending in controlled environments.

In sixteenth-century England and France it became fashionable to maintain decorative citrus trees, and *orangeries* came into being. In the elegant estates of the time these winter gardens were *de rigueur*. During the coldest months orange and lemon trees in large tubs were placed in neat rows inside glass-walled chambers, mostly for show. Some were on a very grand scale; indeed, the 9,000-square-foot orangerie at Heidelberg Castle in 1619 included more than 400 trees, many of which were at least 25 feet high!

But the real "botanic" gardens filled with rare plants—both indoor and outdoor—came into being as a result of a new interest in the spiritual and scientific dimensions of the plant kingdom. The Garden of Eden was actually the inspiration for the botanic gardens of the sixteenth century. After the discovery of the New World's natural life, the first notion arose of a *hortus inclusis,* a gathering of all the plants that had been dispersed from that biblical paradise. Exotic plants brought back from voyages around the world formed the basis for the first botanic gardens at Leiden, Padua, and Montpellier. In the next century others were started in Paris, London, and Uppsala, Sweden.

Most of these early gardens were arranged in squares, divided into quadrants representing the four corners of the earth (in those days that meant Asia, Africa, Europe, and America). The quadrants were then divided into parterres, with grass walks dividing them. Each plant was carefully labeled; the botanic garden became a "living encyclopedia" of Creation. (It was believed, in fact, that the visitor who spent time contemplating in such a place, might regain his or her lost innocence and even gain insight into the "mind of God.")

By the seventeenth century, theologians upset this easy method of finding Paradise. (They looked at zoos—established for the same reason—and saw no Peaceable Kingdoms ensuing.) Some great thinkers believed that the natural wilderness was closer to the original than these highly organized settings. And there were problems of a more practical nature: for example, which climate did the Garden of Eden have? Plants from so many different climes could not grow in the same place at the same temperature. The botanic garden as a place of science was created; it featured indoor and outdoor areas devoted to climatic differences, propagation, and the survival of species.

In their capacity as "laboratories" for scientific study, botanic gardens and, particularly, greenhouses, became places to grow plants for medicinal purposes. During the seventeenth and eighteenth centuries botanists traveled to the New World on merchant ships to identify and gather species of possible medicinal or other scientific value. John Bartram, among the most famous of these botanists, discovered many valuable tropical plants in his scientific expeditions abroad. (He was, by the way, a member of Captain James Cook's scientific expedition in 1772.)

The emphasis on greenhouses and imported rarities from all over the world also had an artistic effect: the concept of a "museum" of plants. The early botanic garden became a collection of exotic and fascinating individual plants, set out for easy enjoyment and identification, rather than a larger, overall form of environmental or artistic beauty. (As we will see in the discussions that follow below, these diverse aims have been admirably united in the botanic gardens of today.)

One of the first great botanical gardens in the United States was the Elgin Botanic Garden in New York City, where Rockefeller Center is today. Started in 1801, it occupied a huge area with a conservatory featuring scientifically identified plants. The garden—then in "the wilds" of upper Manhattan—was surrounded by a belt of trees and a great stone wall. Needless to say, it did not survive the city's expansion.

But in 1824 a Belgian horticulturist named André Parmentier came to New York and built the Brooklyn Botanic Garden. One of its most popular aspects was a tower from which visitors could see the gardens and surrounding area with a bird's-eye view. Parmentier's wonderful gardens continue to thrive today and can be visited. (See the Brooklyn Botanic Garden write-up on page 147.)

Another such enterprise was begun, only 29 years after Washington became the capital of the United States (in 1820), when a group of amateur scientists founded a similar enterprise there. Although it lasted for only about 18 years before it ran out of funds, the idea of a national botanic garden was taken up again in 1842.

Plans for a new garden were encouraged by the 1838–42 commercial expedition of Captain Charles Wilkes (the model for Captain Ahab, by the way). He had circumnavigated the globe with 440 men and six ships (one of which must have been needed just to carry home the 10,000 plant variety seeds, dried samples, and live plants he collected from all over the world). A federally funded national botanic garden was finally built, in 1842. In 1849 it was moved to its present location, and it can be visited today in all its splendor.

As indoor gardens have had a variety of functions over the ages, so, too, have they evolved stylistically. The earliest greenhouses contained little glass; indeed, it is likely that Romans used sheets of mica instead to allow the sun to filter in. With improved technology, particularly during the Industrial Age, greenhouses became all-glass structures and took on new shapes. While eighteenth-century orangeries and conservatories had had extensive windows but conventional roofs, in the nineteenth century they began to be built with domed roofs. Theorists had discovered that the form of roof best suited for the admission of the sun's rays was hemispherical. Because of the development of iron frames and glazed roofs it was now possible to build greenhouses that looked like what we now think of as "conservatories" (and what we imagine when we inevitably read about them in Victorian novels). These elegant and fanciful structures culminated with Sir Joseph Paxton's famous Crystal Palace in London, inaugurated as the main attraction at the First International Exhibition in Hyde Park in 1851. Greeted with great enthusiasm, its enormous success helped stimulate the building of conservatories everywhere, including in America. More elaborate than greenhouses, conservatories contained plants primarily chosen for their showy effect.

The Formal and Informal Garden

Romanticism is an idea which needed a classical mind to have it.
—*J.F. Shade, 1898–1959*

Among the fundamental questions that have defined landscape design in America and other Western countries is the issue of formal versus naturalistic gardens. Should a garden focus on structure and architecture or on its plantings? Should it be arranged in geometric patterns, or in a flowing, more random manner reflecting a natural landscape?

The formal approach has its cultural roots in the traditions of Italy and France. Formal gardens in the Italian and French style share important similarities. Both are regarded as architectural extensions of the house; both emphasize structure, symmetry, and classical motifs, such as statues and balustraded terraces; and in both, plants are considered subordinate to the overall design.

The first Italian gardens (as we know them today) appeared during the Renaissance, generally in the regions surrounding Florence and Rome, where some of the most important patrons, sculptors, and architects lived and worked. Villas were built as rural retreats from the city, much like their predecessors in antiquity. Their gardens, linking the house to the surrounding countryside, were designed to be ideal places for contemplating and experiencing nature. At carefully chosen sites, viewers were invited to enjoy sweeping vistas of the formal layout and the countryside beyond.

The ideal Italian Renaissance garden—elegant, proportioned, and symmetrical—represented a harmonious balance between nature and architecture. Here nature was tamed and ordered into neatly clipped evergreens of laurel, box, and yew shaped into elaborate mazes and borders. Stone and marble forms—colonnaded stairways, terraces,

11

and statues depicting allegorical and mythological characters—were essential elements of this style. So, too, was water. The Villa d'Este at Tivoli, with its spectacular fountains, cascades, and basins—and amazing water-powered mechanisms—is one of the most magnificent Renaissance gardens of all.

The Medici family of Florence helped introduce Italian garden designs to France, as did migrating Italian artisans and gardeners. The formal gardens of seventeenth-century France represented a new interpretation of these ideals. To a substantially greater degree than Italian gardens, these totally controlled landscapes symbolized humanity's mastery of the natural world.

Essential to French formal gardens were ornamental garden beds (parterres) fashioned from exquisitely shaped boxwood and yew. These intricate geometric compartments with squares, circles, and ovals were flawless in their symmetrical designs. They could be viewed from the formal reception rooms of the house overlooking them, or along an orderly grid of walkways. Sometimes complementing them were rows of small trees or shrubs shaped into topiary forms. (Topiaries in Italy tended to represent whimsical creatures, while those in France were strictly geometric and abstract.)

Versailles, the great masterpiece of André Le Nôtre, is certainly the most noted garden in the French style. Everything in it was laid out to symbolize the triumph of humanity (more specifically, the Sun King) over nature, from its majestic proportions and perspectives, to the central axis leading to broad vistas, to the grand canals, fountains, and heroic statues.

In contrast to the formality and symmetry of the continental garden, the English Arcadian landscape was a dramatic return to nature. Influenced by romantic landscape painting and the glory of ancient ruins, English garden designers in the eighteenth century sought to recreate a sense of nature's free, wild beauty. Instead of the classical elegance of geometric perspective, orderly planting beds, walkways, and rectangular reflecting pools, the English garden turned to poetic disorder, to free-form designs, even to reconstructed ruins and grottos—in short, to the garden as a metaphor for romantic poetry and art. Its aim was the "picturesque."

"All gardening is landscape painting," remarked the first great English landscape designer, William Kent. It was Capability Brown and Humphrey Repton, however, who created the Arcadian landscapes of the great English country houses. In their designs the garden became landscape, a rolling vista that combined hills and fields, clumps of trees, rushing water, poetic lakes, and everywhere distant views. The flower garden was replaced by the beauties of landscape. There are "three aspects of landscape gardening," wrote William Shenstone, "the sublime, the beautiful, and the melancholy or pensive."

The "English garden" as we know it evolved from these poetic landscapes. The flower garden near the house made a comeback in the nineteenth century, replacing the vast green lawns just beyond the door. With a new emphasis on color and an abundance of apparently (though not at all) disordered plantings in mixed species, the glorious flower beds that we think of as English became popular. This style of informal "cottage garden" swept into fashion and could be seen everywhere—from the terraces of grand houses of Britain to Monet's gardens at Giverny. The return of flower gardens and the Victorian interest in the exotic and the extravagant led to increasing use of imported plants, rare flowers, and "the gardenesque"—a deliberately near-chaotic approach to landscape.

To Americans, gifted with spectacular landscapes of a "natural paradise," most thoughts of French formality seemed irrelevant. As Americans first moved beyond their careful, colonial-style gardens into the realm of larger pleasure gardens, many were surely influenced by the English style. Americans with large estates, as well as those planning the first public parks, tried to incorporate natural landscape wonders into their own garden designs. Picturesque gardens were nestled into areas like the magnificent Palisades along the Hudson River, their dramatic settings adding to both design and ambiance.

As the great era of wealth in the late nineteenth century brought increased travel abroad, America's new rich familiarized themselves with the elegant French and Italian landscape. Castles rivaling those of Europe were constructed in places like Newport or Philadelphia. Surrounding them were great formal gardens, patterned after Versailles or other grand continental wonders. To the owners of the American palaces, the French garden seemed the epitome of grandeur, the free-form English garden a less elegant option.

As you visit gardens today, you'll find distinct examples of both continental formality and the English "picturesque." But in many cases, particularly in gardens designed in the more recent past, you'll see a mixture of styles and influences that is typical of so many of our contemporary arts. Borrowing liberally from the varied ideas of the past, today's gardens might include formality and fountains, as well as free-form planting beds and abstract contemporary sculpture. Exotic plantings, so prized by Victorians, might grow alongside a traditional Roman wall, or a geometric reflecting pool might be edged with contemporary tile. The postmodern emphasis on using elements from diverse sources has not escaped the world of landscape design. Thus, the debate between English informality and continental formality has all but passed into garden history, like the artificial grotto, the ha-ha, and the topiary maze.

The Rock Garden

It may appear at first that the collection of stones, etc., is designed to appear wild and irregular, little Art would be required in its construction; but this is so far from being the case, that perhaps rockwork is more difficult to design and execute than any other kind of garden scenery.
—*Jane Loudon, c. 1930*

We take rock gardens for granted nowadays, enjoying the combination of hard, surprising stone and delicate, careful plantings. Many a rocky American hillside is planted these days with wildflowers and Alpine specialties, and some such gardens are even created from the start.

But the rock garden does not have as long a history as most of the designs and styles of gardens we have described. In fact, the rock garden dates to 1777 when Sir Joseph Banks, a well known British naturalist (and President of the Royal Society some years later), visited Iceland. On a 12-day hike to a volcanic mountain in Iceland, Banks collected the lava from the volcano's last eruption five years before. (He used it for ballast for his ship on the return to Britain.)

When he got home, he presented the hardened lava to the Apothecaries' Garden in Chelsea, where it was combined with piles of stone from the old walls of the Tower of London, discarded bricks, and various other types of stone. Plants began to grow all over this huge and motley mound of rock.

Within 50 years, rock gardens were popular in Britain. Jane and John Loudon, noted writers on all subjects of gardening, described "rockwork" as fragments of rock "thrown together in an artistic manner, so as to produce a striking and pleasing effect, and to serve as a nest or repository" for a variety of plants. Rock gardens are more difficult to design than they look, they warned their readers. As the "cluttered" garden (much like the Victorian parlor) soon replaced the expansive, airy stretches of the previous era, the rock garden with its many composite parts became more and more popular.

Among the early designs in private gardens for rockeries, as they were known, were an imitation Swiss mountain scene made of white marble to simulate snow and a naturalistic rocky hollow made from an abandoned quarry. Plants for these original gardens varied from traditional British ornamental shrubs and flowers to imported specimens, originating from rocky hillsides in other countries.

By midcentury many English rock gardens were devoted entirely to Alpine plants in the Swiss style, even though the plants' native habitat on high, snowy mountains could not easily be transplanted to Britain. Advice proliferated on caring for such plants—described as "low, bushy, and evergreen" and "tiny and elfin"—and on how to design the rockeries. Before long, the rock garden became synonymous with the Alpine garden and a fashionable addition to many a country estate, where miniature mountains, gorges, valleys, waterfalls, and bridges appeared.

The Alpine garden was the subject of intense interest to botanists and gardeners who traveled the world in search of rare plants that adapted well to their stony surroundings. The designs for such gardens were described by Reginald Farrer in "My Rock Garden," who wrote derisively that there were three common ideas for rock gardens: the "Almond Pudding scheme," which has spiky pinnacles of limestone jutting up among the plants; the "Dog's Grave," with a pudding shape but its stones laid flat; and the "Devil's Lapful," which contains cartloads of bald, square-faced boulders dropped about anywhere, with plants dropped in between them. He preferred a naturalistic setting. (And so did many later garden designers, who went so far as to use imitation rocks to create "lifelike" landscapes.)

Today, the Alpine idea is still popular, but it is no longer an imitative or confining design. There is great freedom of idea and layout in the American rock gardens we have visited. Many combine the naturalistic features of a rocky terrain (with the huge boulders common to our part of the world) and a judicious use of stone walls and stairways and other rocky additions. The plantings in these gardens range widely from imported Alpine delicacies to plants that lend themselves to falling over stone walls. Raised beds, stone pools, and tiny waterfalls are among the elements you might find.

The Topiary Garden

And all these [flowers] by the skill of your Gardener, so comelily and orderly placed in your borders and squares and so intermingled, that one looking thereon, cannot but wonder to see, what Nature, corrected by Art, can do.
—*William Lawson,* A New Orchard and Garden, *1618*

Topiary, the ancient art of shaping plants into living sculptures, has brought charm, whimsy, and surprise to many a garden over the centuries. The term comes from the Latin *toparius,* referring to a gardener who specializes in carving plants; for it is such a gardener who, with the skill and vision of an artist, can transform an ordinary landscape into a delightful living tableau, adding both elegance and fun to the landscape. Because of its many possibilities of expression, topiary art has appealed to gardeners of all kinds, including the most eccentric, who find it an amusing outlet for their imaginations.

The topiary tradition comes with a wealth of sculpted plant shapes and designs. Shrubs and trees are pruned, clipped, cut, coaxed, and styled (sometimes on wire frames) into fanciful animals, mythological creatures, or elegant geometric forms. Yew, privet, hemlock, boxwood, and ivy—to name some of the most popular plants used—can be fashioned into peacocks, roosters, dragons, and centaurs as well as pyramids, globes, arches, and decorative scalloped hedges. Some topiary gardens feature entire sequential scenes: for example, a leafy foxhunt or a flotilla of ships. Others are created on an intimate scale and might include potted topiary that can be moved about or brought indoors.

Topiary gardens are not limited to green sculptures, however. There are also espalier gardens, knot gardens, parterres, and mazes. The espalier is a plant trained into an open, flat pattern to create a two-dimensional effect. The branches of shrubs and trees—often fruit trees such as pear, peach, and apple trees—are bent and pruned into intricate, delicate motifs to adorn walls and other vertical surfaces.

Knot gardens are level beds whose designs are made from the intertwining patterns of herbs and hedges. (Today's versions sometimes include flowers and pebbles as well.)

The *parterre* (French for "on the ground") is a variation of the knot garden. Usually on a larger scale, its designs are more fluid, with arabesques, open scrolls, or *fleurs de lis*. Patterns are created by using carefully clipped dwarf hedges, flowers, grass, and colored stones.

The maze—one of the more delightful topiary forms—is like a life-sized puzzle. It is made of a network of connecting hedges and paths intended to amuse through surprise and confusion. In its earlier forms, in eighteenth-century Europe, the maze sometimes included hidden water games and sprays that were meant to catch the unsuspecting visitor by surprise, or well-hidden lovers' benches at the very center.

The history of topiary gardens shows us that, though they were highly popular from Roman times until the eighteenth century, they are much more rare today in contemporary gardens (though in European gardens of the past you will find many restored topiaries).

The earliest recorded topiary garden seems to have come about in ancient Rome. Around A.D. 100 the younger Pliny drew a distinction between the beauties of nature—beloved by the Romans—and the beauties of a cultivated garden. Pliny wrote long letters describing the gardens he had laid out at his Tuscan estate. Distinguishing between art and nature, he commented that the beauty of the landscape was owing to nature, while the beauty of his garden was owed to "art."

In describing in detail his plantings and garden design, Pliny indicated that his gardeners had employed what we know of today as topiary gardens. His paths, he wrote, were lined with boxwood hedges "and in between grass plots with box trees cut into all kinds of different shapes, some of them being letters spelling out the name of the owner or of the gardener who did the work." Interspersed with these topiary delights were white marble statues, obelisks, pillars, and seating areas.

A friend of Emperor Augustus named C. Matius was responsible for the invention of the topiary garden. Matius, according to Pliny's uncle, had invented the cutting of trees into various shapes around 5 B.C. (Don't be surprised by the sophistication of ancient Roman gardening; Romans had been grafting fruit trees, for example, for generations by the time Pliny made his gardens!)

We next hear of the topiary garden in medieval times, when the Flemish, in particular, favored small clipped evergreens (box or yew, as today) trained into tiers. (You can see a somewhat later example of the Flemish topiary in Pieter Breughel's *Spring*.) But unlike the Romans, the Flemish apparently only clipped their evergreens in simple ways, rather than the elaborate designs described by Pliny.

French medieval gardeners developed the espalier in their walled cities where there was little room for orchards. The fact that espaliers required little space and that they bore their fruit early and abundantly was a great asset during those harsh times. Later espaliers became popular as purely ornamental features in French gardens.

Also developed in France in the Middle Ages, by the way, were the first mazes: they were inspired by the medieval belief that a penitent soul might crawl on his hands and knees to imitate the path of earthly travail and thus gain heavenly grace.

Topiary art came thoroughly into fashion in the Italian Renaissance, when all the arts and their illusionary qualities were so admired, and when so many classical and ancient styles were revived. A Renaissance gentleman named Leon Batista Alberti described the principles of garden design in the fifteenth century. Among his many pieces of advice (on a wide range of architectural and landscaping subjects) was to select sites with "a view of cities, land and sea, a spreading plain, and the known peaks of the hills and mountains." He recommended cool shell-covered grottos, groves of fruit trees, and box-bordered paths and topiary work. "The gardeners of ancient times," he said, "flattered their patrons by writing their names in letters formed in box and other odorous herbs." We can see examples of the elaborate gardens of the fifteenth and sixteenth centuries (such as those described by Alberti) in engravings and paintings from France and Italy and England.

In fact, in Queen Elizabeth the First's England in the sixteenth century, topiary designs, knot gardens, and mazes became quite fashionable at the palaces and castles of the aristocracy. At Sudely Castle in Gloucestershire topiary yew hedges included small, doorlike openings for sheltering during England's sudden and frequent rain storms, and Elizabeth's hunting lodge had both a knot garden and flat-cut hedges that are said to have been used for drying "linen, cloathes and yarne!" Among the designs used in Elizabethan gardens were "cockle shells," "beestes," "men armed in the field, ready to give battle," "swift-running grey-hounds," "pretty pyramides," and little turrets with bellies." Later, English gardens featured "outdoor rooms" in which the lawn was the carpet and the topiary the "furniture."

France became a center of formal gardens under the Bourbon kings. In the seventeenth century the art of topiary was apparently *de rigueur* in the great formal settings of the French chateaux. Extravaganzas of all kinds characterized French Baroque court life; not the least of them were the elaborate pavilions and topiary designs. These included living plant decorations in the shapes of animals and people, sailing ships, and birds, as well as complex arrangements based on medieval dance patterns, parterres, three-part patterns, criss-crossed walks, mazes, and other features designed to entertain the lords and ladies who strolled through them.

But the craze for topiary gardens came to an end. In 1728 a French garden architect and writer (Alexandre Le Blond) wrote disparagingly, "at present nobody gives into these trifles (topiary gardens) in France, how well soever they may be kept. . . . We chose rather a plain regularity less clutter'd and confus'd, which indeed looks much more nobel and great." Rousseau's dedication to the principles of naturalism and informality and "the simple life" added to the dislike for the artificial topiary design. Instead a new emphasis on natural beauty replaced the intricate formal gardens of the Baroque.

Visits to stately homes of Britain and chateaux of France will still often include historic topiary gardens and mazes. But in the United States, where we do not have the tradition in our past, they are more of a rarity. However, we have found several for your enjoyment. Read on!

The Walled Garden

A Garden inclosed is my sister, my spouse; a spring shut up, a fountain sealed. Thy plants are an orchard of pomegranates with pleasant fruits.
—*from* The Song of Solomon

Throughout history gardens have been seen as different, idealized worlds in which we create an orderly and beautiful environment cut off from tumultuous reality. Thus, of course, they must be enclosed. Most gardens, in fact, are surrounded in some way—separated from the wild, the urban, the public, the unknown. In this way gardens are like beautifully framed paintings. Such divisions between the wild and intrusive, and the cultivated and the private create the sense of specialness and secrecy that characterizes an enclosed space. The "secret garden" is a concept that is undeniably inviting.

Artificial boundaries for gardens—when they are not naturally surrounded by geographical borders—are most often created by walls, hedges, or fences. Whether the border is formed by high boxwood hedges or medieval stone walls, trellis fences or rows of evergreens, the "framing" of the garden is found all over the world, and throughout garden history.

The walled garden is the most private, for walls—whether of stone or hedge—can be high and impenetrable. Their origins are long in the past, when they kept out human and animal intruders and protected those within. In many cultures the enclosed garden, designed for both useful growing and pleasing contemplation, was a practical or an aesthetic choice. Thus, the enclosed gardens of some civilizations—such as Egyptian and medieval Christian—were also metaphors for religious belief. (Walled gardens of the Middle Ages, for example, were thought to symbolize freedom and beauty with precisely set boundaries.)

Beautiful enclosed gardens can be seen in paintings from Egyptian and Roman walls, in Persian miniatures, and in the cloisters of medieval buildings. Trellis-fenced gardens appear in Renaissance art; the great classical gardens of France and England used both hedges and fences to enclose parts of their elaborate landscape designs. Boxwood, evergreen, and other living borders were common in gardens ranging from ancient Rome to colonial America, their carefully tended shapes creating dense hedgerows and geometric patterns.

Many of these garden boundaries were not just utilitarian borders to surround the plantings, but were integral parts of the garden design. Medieval walls featured carvings, patterned stonework, delicate espaliered trees or climbing plants, and carved stone blossoms reflecting the blooms within the garden. Some of the thick hedge borders of the most complex European gardens were cut into topiary designs, making the garden "walls" fantastic in shape and illusion.

American enclosed gardens date to colonial times, when their walls kept out the frightening wilderness. Many early American gardens have high brick walls and matching paths whose subtle deep red contrasts delightfully with the dark shiny greens of ivy and boxwoods. Versions in the United States of European cloisters and Victorian "cottages" included walled gardens. Our great nineteenth-century estates feature many enclosed garden areas, in which marble and granite not only provide a backdrop for plantings and sculpture, but create both color and texture in themselves. Espaliered fruit trees, climbing roses, ivies, wisteria, and trumpet vines are among the many popular plantings that can be seen covering the walls of enclosed gardens in our area.

Today the walled garden is often in the middle of a city. Urban gardeners use stone or brick walls in imaginative and contemporary ways, sometimes combining sculpture, falling water, and environmental design. Some of the smallest, but most appealing walled gardens today are the "vest-pocket" parks in our cities.

Clearly, the concept of the enclosed garden is still valid; its plantings and design may be symbolic or practical or purely aesthetic, but the walled garden remains the special, magical space, serene and cut off from the world outside.

The Water Garden

Any garden ornament or piece of architecture mirrored in water receives an addition to its dignity by the repetition and continuation of upright line.
—*Gertrude Jekyll, 1901*

Water has embellished gardens around the world since the earliest civilizations. Not only has it been used in gardens for practical reasons, but also for pure pleasure and decoration. The effects of water on the senses are varied and fascinating: it can delight, charm, soothe, cool, stimulate, and excite. Through its magical powers of illusion and reflection, it can create an environment of mystery and even surprise. Natural sources of water—streams, brooks, or water-falls—as well as artful canals, pools, or fountains have been focal points in gardens over the ages.

The Egyptians were among the first who recognized the importance of "decorative water" in garden design. Ancient tomb paintings depict gardens with rectangular pools, lilies, lotus, and papyrus. Not only were these basins of water practical—they were used to irrigate the surroundings—but they were also refreshingly appealing in the parched lands.

The pleasure-loving Romans copied these early models in their own gardens, adding more sophisticated elements, such as elaborate fountains and canals. The fabled garden of Pliny the Younger included (according to his nephew) "a semicircular bench of white marble shaded with a vine which is trained on four small pillars of marble. Water, gushing through several little pipes from under this bench . . . falls on to a stone cistern underneath, from whence it is received into a fine polished marble basin, so artfully contrived that it is always full without overflowing." It seems that at mealtime plates of food were placed on the water, so they could float from one person to the next.

Water, revered by the Persians as the essence of life, was the chief element in their paradise gardens. These magnificent, enclosed oases with fountains, tiled pools, and intricate water channels provided a delicious respite in a torrid climate. Formal and geometric, they usually included rows of stately cypress trees and scented roses, irrigated by underground tunnels.

Water gardens reached some of their highest level of artistry in those created by the Moors of medieval Spain. Such magnificent and lavish gardens as those in the Alhambra were intricately planned by some of the most sophisticated designers of all time. These masterful hydraulic engineers/artists used ingenious techniques to channel precious water from distant mountain springs through elaborate tunnels to palaces and courtyards. The gardens were thus filled with the sight and sound of water continuously flowing (and recycled) through fountains, marbled channels, and basins.

The rest of Europe (which, during the Middle Ages had confined its gardens to relatively modest cloisters with small wells and fountains) saw a rebirth of the water garden during the Renaissance, especially in Italy. Along with a renewed interest in antiquities came a fascination with science and the study of such basic elements as water; water became a central focus of Italian villa gardens. Amid the waters of elegant fountains and graceful pools, and even inside mysterious grottos, Italian designers placed statues depicting mythological characters—ranging from river gods and gorgons to Venus and Neptune surrounded by nymphs and dolphins. Amazing water-powered machines and animated ornaments graced some villa gardens; the fabled Villa d'Este, in Tivoli, one of the most dazzling water gardens of all time (it continues to delight visitors to this day), displayed spectacular aquatic fireworks in addition to its other exquisite garden features.

Fountains were used most lavishly in seventeenth-century French gardens. At Versailles, for example, the master designer André Le Nôtre (along with an army of artists and engineers) channeled water through myriad dams, falls, pools, cascades, and an especially long canal (where mock naval battles were occasionally held to amuse the courtiers). Le Nôtre's designs for Versailles became a standard by which numerous other formal gardens were (and are still) measured.

Romantic English gardens used water in a less artificial way; instead of the grand geometric, formal pools and fountains of the French, they featured meandering streams and rivers surrounded with naturalistic plantings and graceful garden paths. Some of the great Capability Brown's designs called for picturesque garden lakes, created by dammed streams and massive excavations.

Of course, the "natural" use of water—so favored in the Romantic era—had long been featured in the gardens of the Far East. In classical Chinese and Japanese gardens water, regarded as a vital ingredient, appeared almost always in an entirely naturalistic way. But water in Asian gardens also had symbolic significance; for example, both the sight and the sound of water in Japanese gardens is part of the aesthetic importance of their traditional gardens. (See our earlier remarks about Asian gardens.)

Today, water gardens have been inspired by these varied historic and cultural traditions and reinterpreted to accommodate contemporary needs and tastes. As you visit the gardens that feature water designs described below you will perhaps identify some of these stylistic elements.

GARDENS FROM
MAINE TO
VIRGINIA

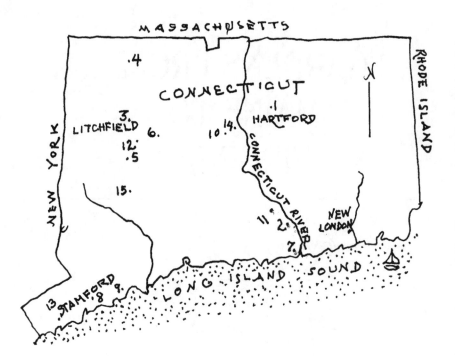

CONNECTICUT GARDENWALKS

1. Coventry: Caprilands Herb Farm
2. East Haddam: Gillette Castle State Park
3. Litchfield: Laurel Ridge Foundation
4. Norfolk: Hillside Gardens
5. North Bethlehem: Bellamy-Ferriday Garden
6. Thomaston: Cricket Hill Garden
7. Waterford: Harkness Memorial State Park
8. Westport: Private Garden of Susan and Robert Beeby

And in Addition . . .

9. Fairfield: Larsen Sanctuary
10. Farmington: Nook Farm
11. Higganum: Sundial Herb Gardens
12. Morris: White Flower Farms
13. New Canaan: Olive W. Lee Memorial Garden
14. Stamford: Old Fort
15. West Hartford: Elizabeth Park
16. Woodbury: Gertrude Jekyll Garden at the Glebe House Museum

CONNECTICUT

Caprilands Herb Farm, Coventry

One of the most enjoyable types of gardens to visit is the eccentric garden. Occasionally people see their gardens as canvases or notebooks in which to present their own visions of color and composition, as well as personal meaning. Such thematic gardens express their owners' views and personalities; sometimes we are lucky enough to find a variety of themes all in one large, very personal garden.

Caprilands Herb Farm is one such place; it is the creation of the redoubtable Adelma Simmons, who for the past 60 or more years has guided its unusual path. On what was once a rock-strewn Connecticut dairy farm (bought by her family in 1929), Miss Simmons has built an irregular series of separate gardens with whimsical names and intriguing quotations propped among the flowers. Typical low stone walls divide the 50-acre landscape. Primarily an herb farm growing some 360 varieties of herbs, Caprilands also includes any number of flowers and shrubs (and weeds too). There is nothing pristine or formal about this landscape—in fact, that is part of its great charm.

While Caprilands began as a venture in growing and selling herbs to the public (and still has a shop in a barn, a large mail-order business, a lecture series by Miss Simmons, a basket shop, a lunch, and high tea restaurant in the colonial-style farmhouse, and clients for its herbs—including such noted chefs as Pierre Bouley), there is little

27

that seems tastelessly commercial here. Instead, the visitor ambles through overgrown paths, seeking the various thematic gardens as identified on old school slates. Bits of wood and statuary adorn the pocket-sized gardens. A map is available at the desk.

Each separate bed has a name and a theme illustrated by the flowers or herbs chosen by Miss Simmons. We understand that these designations are definitely subject to change and that no two visits to Caprilands is the same, due to Miss Simmons' tireless energy and active mind. She, by the way, spends each long day, except for a few holidays, overseeing the gardening and regally receiving curious and admiring visitors from her chair in the shop in the weathered barn (formerly the milk house). There you can purchase herbs and her books—some 50 different titles, including her best-known *Herb Gardening in Five Seasons,* now in its 18th printing. She will autograph them for you. (You may enjoy her impromptu lectures in the barn, as well as her culinary menus in the farmhouse, including salads with edible flowers.)

Among the 30 thematic gardens that caught our attention were the Medieval Garden (in which all the flowers and leaves are silver), the Garden of the Stars (in which plantings are divided into twelve culinary beds based on signs of the Zodiac), the Saints' Garden (adorned with small statuary and planted with symbolic plants such as rosemary and Madonna lilies), the Shakespeare Garden (with appropriate quotations), the Bride's Garden (in which two hearts outlined in brick are filled with symbolic plants representing love throughout history— lemon verbena, forget-me-nots, orange trees), and more practical gardens like the Cook's Garden and the Salad Garden. There are plots devoted to colors—gold, blue, white; and there are gardens for dyeing colors, for potpourri, for flowers that are good for drying or for fragrance, and even for onions.

Most of these small, patterned beds are delightful in their own miniature way. (For the serious visitor a guidebook by Miss Simmons—who is exceptionally knowledgeable about the history and herbal uses for each plant— is available. It identifies the plants and describes the symbolism, preservation, and practical use for each.) For those who prefer the literary relevance, handwritten quotations abound:

> About tansy (*tanecetum*): "on Easter Sunday be the pudding seen/ To which tansy lends her sober green" (from the *Oxford Sausage*).

About onions: "This is every cook's opinion,/ no savory dish without an onion,/ But lest your kissing should be spoiled/ Your onions must be fully boiled" (by John Swift).

About broom: "I'm sent with Broom before/ To sweep the dust behind the door" (Shakespeare, in *Midsummer Night's Dream*).

Caprilands is a particularly interesting garden visit for young naturalists, because they can wander on their own with map or guide in hand and search out hundreds of different plants. The historic, medicinal, and culinary uses are truly fascinating. And for those of us who simply enjoy the color and variety of unusual and surprising plantings, Caprilands is made for exploring.

INFORMATION
Caprilands Herb Farm is open daily except major holidays year-round. We recommend a visit in spring or summer. (In the winter it is open only in the afternoons.) There are numerous special events, including lectures and demonstrations of herbal uses. Telephone: (860) 742-7244.

DIRECTIONS
Caprilands Herb Farm is located at 534 Silver Street in Coventry, between Manchester and Willimantic, just off Route 44. From Hartford take I-84 East to Exit 59, which is Route 384. Go to its end and turn left on Route 44 East. Silver Street is a right-hand exit from Route 44.

Gillette Castle State Park, East Haddam

Gillette Castle is a celebration of eccentricity. Perched high atop one of seven hills (known as the Seven Sisters) overlooking the scenic Connecticut River—and surrounded by 122 acres of woodland—it appears as a grandiose folly from a bygone era. The craggy, hand-built fieldstone castle, terraced gardens, high walls, and woodsy pathways connected by suspended bridges and the remnants of a private outdoor railroad—trestles, tunnels, and all—paint a picture of unusual imagination and whimsy. The fact that the castle is also accessible by ferry—a delightful five-minute boat ride to the east side of the river—adds a touch of romance to this adventure.

The creator of this unique site was William Hooker Gillette, a longtime actor and playwright whose portrayal of Sherlock Holmes finally brought him fame. In 1913, while looking for the ideal place to build his dream home, he was captivated by this picturesque river front location with its sweeping views. Naming the property "Seventh Sister" after the southernmost hill of the region, he began a most ambitious construction project.

Gillette himself designed the 24-room castle, its thick, fortresslike granite walls, and its eclectic interior. He personally supervised the intricate hand-hewn woodwork, stone carvings, and other decorative details. Using his lively imagination and sense of fun, he came up with fanciful ideas—such as making each of the 47 oak doors different from one another, or hanging lighting fixtures with garlands of colored glass salvaged from old bottles, or fashioning doorstops and mantels in catlike shapes. (A lover of cats, he was at one time supposed to have kept 15 on the premises.) It took about five years for his army of 25 workers to complete construction— and well over a million dollars (an extraordinarily impressive sum at the time).

This nonconformist who, according to his contemporaries, had "uncanny inventive ability, a precocious and daring initiative and a total disregard for accepted standards and ways," took great delight in developing the grounds surrounding his castle. A train and locomotive enthusiast, he built for himself and his friends a man-sized railroad that began at the castle and wound around through the forest, making a 3-mile loop. (Although the railroad has since been dismantled, signs of it remain.) He also created intricate walking paths and constructed giant vertical steps, arched stone bridges, wooden trestles, and a goldfish pond. (Many of these oddities can still be found.) The gardens here are just one part of an eccentric and always interesting landscape.

Gillette's will stipulated that the property should not "fall into the hands of some blithering saphead who has no conception of where he is or with what surrounded." Accordingly, after his death the property was acquired by the state. In 1943 Gillette Castle State Park was officially created, and it has attracted thousands of visitors over the years.

Anyone—old and young—will be enchanted by this intriguing site. Children will be fascinated by the looming medieval-like fortress, the old railroad beds, and the many woodsy paths to be explored. There are wonderful hiking trails for those so inclined. Garden lovers and others sensitive to nature's beauties will find the extraordinary views and setting inspiring. Unlike many other grand estates, the castle does not include traditional formal gardens (nothing is "conventional" about this place); it does have, however, unusually inviting terrace gardens and a beautifully maintained conservatory. The terraces, graced by charming flower beds and other contained plantings, offer the most spectacular river and hillside views of all. You will want to linger in these "gardens with a view."

For an entrance fee, you can visit the castle and enjoy its many eccentricities either by guided tour or on your own. On the other hand, you are free to roam the vast grounds, including the terrace gardens at will, perhaps enjoying a picnic at the end of your explorations. Gillette Castle is best seen off season, perhaps on a bright day in early fall, when you might have the place almost to yourself, including the ferryboat.

INFORMATION

Gillette Castle State Park is open daily, Monday through Sunday, from 8 A.M. to sunset. The castle is open daily from Memorial Day through Columbus Day, 10 A.M. to 5 P.M., and weekends only from 10 A.M. to 4 P.M. from Columbus Day through the last weekend before Christmas. There is an admission fee for the castle only. Telephone: (860) 526-2336. The Chester–Hadlyme car ferry operates continuously, from early morning until sunset for a small fee. Alternatively, you can reach the castle via a more roundabout road and bridge.

After your visit, don't miss the charming nearby village of Chester. You will enjoy its elegant shops and sidewalk cafes.

DIRECTIONS

From Interstate 95 go north on Route 9 (near Old Saybrook) to Route 148 east, past Chester. Follow signs to the ferry. As you cross the river, you will see the castle directly in front of you, its unmistakable silhouette looming above.

Laurel Ridge Foundation, Litchfield

Laurel Ridge is without doubt one of the most enchanting and unspoiled spots we have discovered in our many garden ramblings. To reach this little known hillside narcissus garden, you pass through some of northwestern Connecticut's most scenic countryside of rolling hills, winding roads, stone walls, and ponds. Along the way, you even see a working windmill, something of a rarity these days.

The site itself is an open, free, and wild landscape, rather than a traditional garden. Some 10 bucolic acres of gently sloping woodland, fields, and wonderfully aged stone walls overlook a small sparkling lake with two tiny islands. Literally covering the hillside—and on one of the islands—are thousands and thousands of daffodils growing at random, swaying in the soft breezes. In late April and early May, this spectacular sight truly takes your breath away.

Laurel Ridge has none of the usual signs of a public garden—no gates, admission fees, gift shops, or crowds; a small, discreet sign simply indicates the site and asks that you not bring in dogs. After leaving your car by the side of the road, you are on your own to wander about freely, from dawn to dusk. Some rustic stone steps invite you to walk down the slope to simple, meandering paths (created by walkers) leading you up and down and around the lake and beyond. This is a quiet place, where you can enjoy the sounds of nature and have the place practically to yourself.

The first narcissus display was planted in 1941. Over the years the original 10,000 daffodils have naturalized and multiplied. The current owners of the property (who live across the road and up a hill) fortunately have maintained the display, adding thousands of new plants every year—and have very generously shared their exceptional garden with the public. The different varieties create three distinctive color peaks: in late April the overall color scheme is a dark yellow, followed by a softer yellow, and finally, a dreamy white in mid-May.

You will want to linger at Laurel Ridge, perhaps even picnic at a spot of your own choosing (picnicking is allowed, so long as you make sure not to leave anything behind).

INFORMATION
Laurel Ridge, a few miles from the center of Litchfield, is open from dawn to dusk, daily. Plan to visit in late April or during the first two weeks of May, when the daffodils are at their full glory. There is neither telephone nor entrance fee.

DIRECTIONS
From Litchfield Village take Route 118 east to Route 254 for 3 miles. Turn right onto Wigwam Road. Laurel Ridge is located about 1 mile on the left.

Hillside Gardens, Norfolk

Hillside Gardens, in the heart of northwest Connecticut's rural back-roads, is a pleasant combination of perennial display gardens and nursery. Situated on 5 acres surrounding the colonial farmhouse of the owners Fred and Mary Ann McGourty, the site adjoins a state park, which boasts some of the most scenic vistas in the state. This is not your typical commercial nursery—indeed, it is barely notice-able from the road. The ambiance is more that of a country garden than anything else. Plants are arranged in natural looking borders, rather than in standard nursery rows. The gently sloped land has beautiful old stone walls, a 600-foot-long berm, fields, and woods.

Hillside is one of the few perennial gardens in the region that wel-comes visitors on a regular basis. Whether or not you intend to buy from its wide and unusual assortment of perennials, you are free to wander about amid the lovely plantings or consult with the staff on garden questions.

Cultivating this northern site, whose elevation rises to some 1,400 feet, is a quite a challenge. Only hardy plants seem to thrive, and the growing season is relatively short. But, from May through September, the rapid succession of blossoming perennials makes the gardens a delight, particularly during their late July peak. From the first daffodils, primulas, colombines, iris, and peonies of spring, to summer's phloxes, daylilies, foxgloves, and Russian sage, to September's asters, chrysanthemums, and elegant ornamental grass-es, Hillside is a changing tableau of colors.

You will find a visit to Hillside an informative and pleasant expe-rience, which you might wish to combine with a nature walk and picnic in the nearby preserve.

INFORMATION
Hillside Gardens are located at 515 Litchfield Road (Route 272) in Norfolk, Connecticut, 11 miles north of Torrington. Telephone: (860) 542-5345. The gardens and nursery are open from May 1 through September 15, from 9 A.M. to 5 P.M. daily, except holidays. There is no admission fee if you walk about on your own; guided tours are available (for a fee) by previous arrangement.

DIRECTIONS
From New York, take Interstate 684 east to I-84 to Waterbury. Go north on Route 8 to Torrington. Once there, take Route 272 north

for about 11 miles and look for a small sign. The gardens are on your right and parking on your left.

The Bellamy-Ferriday Garden, North Bethlehem

The Bellamy–Ferriday estate combines the best of a Connecticut landscape with a delightful semiformal garden. The mansion and numerous farm buildings (open to the public) sit serenely in their green and rolling landscape of gently sloping fields divided by stone walls, flowering trees, and quiet woods. The 9-acre estate is now contiguous to a much larger preserved forest area for hiking.

The original house was built in 1744 by Joseph Bellamy, the local pastor and director of the first divinity school in America. (He was also known as "the Pope of Litchfield County" for his theological tract called "True Religion Delineated.") His son and heirs and subsequent owners added to the building, making it the fine mansion of today with a Palladian facade, verandas, and great windows. Long a working farm, the estate's simple white eighteenth- and nineteenth-century outbuildings (including an old schoolhouse) are clustered nearby. In 1912 the Ferriday family bought the farm. Mrs. Ferriday and her daughter not only added to the house, but also reshaped the landscape and planted the charming garden that has been restored today.

It was Mrs. Ferriday who put in the great lawn, planted the wall of evergreens that now shield the house from the road, and tended the orchard (first planted in 1750), the lilacs, peonies, roses, and specimen trees. Her daughter Caroline further restored the house and grounds and prepared the estate for preservation. She assured its future by bequeathing it to the Antiquarian and Landmarks Society, whose members have continued the restoration. Today you'll find a colorful collection of blooming shrubs (magnolias, Japanese snowballs, lilacs, and peonies among others) all over the property. (A map is available at the desk.)

Of particular interest to garden lovers, of course, is the formal garden with its rose collection. First designed in 1920, this exceptionally pretty arrangement is next to the house in a sheltered and invitingly terraced and enclosed area. Here in unusually serpentine shaped, yew-edged planting beds are a heady mix of flowers—an informal profusion within formal outlines. A small circular pool with stone edges and a statue add to the romantic aura of this intimate garden.

We found this to be one of the most pleasing gardens we have seen—one certainly to inspire the home gardener—for it is neither of grand size nor exotic in plantings. It is, instead, particularly well conceived, with an unusual eye for color and ambiance. The use of local stones for walls and terraces adds to its harmonious setting within the larger landscape.

INFORMATION
The Bellamy–Ferriday Garden is open only on Wednesdays, Saturdays, and Sundays from 11 A.M. to 4 P.M. from May through October. Telephone: (203) 266-7596. There is an admission fee for touring the house. You will also find a number of special events supporting the restoration. Hiking trails are accessible from the property.

DIRECTIONS
The Bellamy–Ferriday Garden is at 9 Main Street North, Bethlehem. From Route 84 in Connecticut, take Route 6 north to Route 61 north; Bethlehem is at the intersection of Routes 61 and 132 (south of Litchfield).

Harkness Memorial State Park, Waterford

Discovering Harkness Memorial State Park for the first time is an unexpected—and joyful—surprise. You are sure to wonder why it hasn't been on your—or everybody else's—itinerary for all these years. This magnificent public park, on the Connecticut shores overlooking Long Island Sound, may well be one of the better-kept secrets in the region.

The combination of spectacular ocean views, sweeping lawns extending to the sea, fine formal gardens surrounding a romantic Italianate mansion, magnificent old trees, and vast areas for walking along the beach, across fields, and on shaded paths, makes Harkness Park unusually inviting. You can easily see why this site might inspire painters. (In fact, on our last visit we saw some local artists at work, trying to capture the scene.) The contrasting shapes and colors are a feast to the eye—from the intimate garden rooms set off by broad sky, land, and sea to the brilliantly colored flowers, graceful statuary, topiary shapes, and meandering pathways.

The 234-acre estate (100 acres of which have since been developed into a camp for handicapped children) was one of the summer homes of philanthropists Edward and Mary Harkness. Situated on Goshen Point, a promontory where the Pequot Indians once camped, it was named "Eolia," after the mythical wind god. (You'll find the site quite breezy, but pleasantly so.) The elegant—but unpretentious—limestone mansion was built in 1902, its 42 rooms, terraces, and porticoes affording lovely panoramic views. (The mansion is presently closed, awaiting restoration.)

In 1919 the Harkness family hired the well-known landscape designer Beatrix Jones Farrand to refurbish some of the existing gardens surrounding the house. Farrand designed the plantings for the Oriental east garden to complement its stone wall, statues, and pool; she created a picturesque rock garden, with a stone path bordered by beds of wildflowers; and she revamped the Italian west garden. In the latter, using an existing limestone pergola as centerpiece, Farrand planted her trademark perennials grouped by color, from the softest of blues and mauves to intense shades of orange and yellow.

In subsequent years, other landscape designers were called upon to add their artistic touch to the gardens. Marian Coffin, who had worked on so many of Long Island's sumptuous estates, as well as on Winterthur in Delaware, favored a pastel color scheme. She planted flower beds in delicate pinks, lavenders, and whites. The gardens you see today—some of which are yet again undergoing restoration—are an appealing blend of several design styles. Upon Mrs. Harkness's death in 1950, the property was bequeathed to the state of Connecticut to be turned into a public park.

Today's visitor will find Harkness Park a true respite from the bustling outside world. Rarely crowded, it is a treat for garden lovers and walkers of all ages—including children. There is a feeling of informality about the place; you can walk at will from one end of the park to the other, unhampered by the many restrictions found in most public sites. The mile-long beach is easily accessible by foot and a year-round pleasure for anyone, including families. Even off-season it is an ideal spot for kite flying, picnicking, fishing, or just walking.

The gardens are to be savored at a leisurely pace. Contained within a small area around the mansion, they face the ocean. On one side of the house is the Oriental garden, with fountains, statues, and patterned flower beds. An open porch on the other side overlooks the romantic Italian garden. Surrounded by trimmed boxwood hedges, it contains colorful flower beds and the previously mentioned pergola, now covered with grape and wisteria vines. Small pathways lead to the rockery, intriguing with its sunken paths, small patterned plantings, and secluded grotto. Beyond are cutting gardens near a water tower, greenhouses, stables, and extensive lawns.

INFORMATION
Harkness Memorial State Park is at 275 Great Neck Road (Route 213). Open year-round, from 8 A.M. to sunset. There is a small parking fee. During the summer occasional classical music and jazz concerts are held under a tent on the main lawn. Telephone: (860) 443-5725.

DIRECTIONS
From the New York area, take Interstate 95 (the New England Thruway) to Exit 74, and then Route 160 to its end. Make a left onto Route 156 to Route 213 and follow the signs to the park.

Cricket Hill Garden, Thomaston

Cricket Hill Garden could well be subtitled "Peony Heaven" (in fact, the very name of one of its publications), so glorious is its peony collection—and so idyllic. Overlooking a pond, meadows, and woodlands in the picturesque Connecticut highlands, this low-key, rural nursery/display garden can't help but appeal to those sensitive to nature's beauties, whether or not they have a particular love for the peony. What makes Cricket Hill extra special is that it features the Chinese tree peony, a more unusual variety that has inspired Chinese artists and poets since ancient times.

Ideally, you should plan to visit during the last two weeks in May, when the glorious blossoms are at their peak. You will be treated to a blissfully colorful and fragrant tableau of tree peonies interspersed with tulips and other plantings, set on 3 acres of gently sloped, terraced hillside. These peonies (some 100 varieties, we are told) are quite different from the more widely known herbaceous types that are often found in old-fashioned gardens. Ranging in height between 4 and 10 feet when fully grown, they have woody, shrublike stems and generously proportioned leaves. The blossoms (measuring 6 to 12 inches in diameter) form an assortment of cylindrical or rounded shapes, sometimes in the very same plant. The flowers come in the most subtle shades of violet, pink, magenta, yellow, gold, or cream. Tree peonies can live to be quite old, some even reaching more than 100 years (although there are none of this vintage in this relatively new site). Unlike the common herbaceous peonies, they continue to grow profusely from one season to the next and don't simply vanish during the winter months. Some tree peonies produce up to 70 blossoms per year.

Not surprisingly, the owners, creators, and gardeners of Cricket Hill, Kasha and David Furman, are passionate advocates of the Chinese tree peony. They publish valuable information (readily available) on the subject—ranging from a journal to sundry catalogs—and are eager to share their vast knowledge with any willing listener. Topics might include anything from such practical matters as the ideal soil, sun exposure, or suitable climate for cultivating the tree peony to the plant's long history and its importance in traditional Chinese culture.

Records of this most renowned flowering plant of ancient China date as far back as the fourth century A.D. Revered for its extraordinary fragrance and abundant blossoms, the tree peony was grown in profusion in the imperial gardens. It was admired by much of society, including the nobility who would routinely travel great distances with horse and carriage to view it in its many variations. The *mudan*—its name in Chinese—was also a great source of inspiration for poets and painters, as the many traditional painted scrolls attest.

During the T'ang Dynasty, the mudan reached its peak of popularity and graced many gardens. Considered a representation of sensual beauty and wealth, it became the only flower to gain a permanent place in the traditional Chinese garden, along with rocks, water, and trees. In China today you can still find stands of mudan that are hundreds of years old.

The Chinese tree peonies of Cricket Hill are apparently related to those grown in the gardens of China some 13 centuries ago. The Furmans continue to follow the traditional planting methods still being used in China today, as they expand their cultivated areas. A visit to this unusually inviting nursery is an enriching experience; aside from enjoying the beauty and peace of the site, you can learn a great deal. You are free to walk around at will, without pressure to buy, although you might well be tempted to try your hand at starting a collection of your own.

INFORMATION
Cricket Hill Garden is located at 670 Walnut Hill Road in Thomaston, Connecticut, in Litchfield County. The nursery/display gardens are best seen from mid-May through June, Wednesday through Sunday, 10 A.M. to 4 P.M. Telephone: (860) 283-1042.

DIRECTIONS
From Interstate 95 or 84 take Route 8 north to the Thomaston exit (#38). Turn left on Main Street, to Route 254; turn left and continue north for 1/2 mile to a blinking light. Turn left at Walnut Hill Road and continue up the hill for about 1 mile. Cricket Hill Garden is on the right.

Private Garden of Susan and Robert Beeby, Westport

It is always a pleasure to visit a private garden: by definition, you know it won't be crowded or commercial. Susan and Robert Beeby's garden on Connecticut's coastline is not only unspoiled, as you would expect; it is also a beautifully designed garden, combining both new and recreated plantings. A walk along its inviting paths leads from one enchanting spot to the next—from Giverny-like water lily ponds, graceful waterfalls, and Japanese-style rock formations, to banks of wildflowers, trellises adorned with blossoms, and old-fashioned flower beds.

The story of how this garden came to be is intriguing. On this site there once existed the so-called Bedford Gardens, created in 1912 by local philanthropist Edward T. Bedford. A true lover of nature, Bedford was apparently happy to share his gardens with the public, even though they were on his private estate. Until the late 1930s they were a popular destination, attracting thousands of visitors. Unfortunately, Bedford's heirs were unable to keep the gardens open and eventually sold the estate.

When the Beebys bought the property in 1980, there was no sign of the historic gardens. Their many intricate stone structures—pathways, walls, stairways, fountains, decorative pools, and terraces—and vast, sloping lawns—were all buried under piles of weeds and unkempt vines. Even Bedford's mansion and greenhouses had been destroyed.

With tireless diligence, the Beebys cleared the land and—like archeologists—uncovered the lost gardens. Much of the original maze of waterways, stone structures, and greenery has been restored. What had once been banks of rhododendron, andromeda, and boxwood were resurrected; masses of wild daylilies were replanted where they were found to have graced the base of a slope; and the former elaborate water channels, pools, and water-falls were refurbished and integrated with new plantings. (The orig-inal stone piping system is now used only as a decorative feature.)

The gardens extend from the owners' Provence-style house and terrace, one smoothly flowing into the next, up and down the gen-tly sloped terrain. With the help of landscape architect James Bleuer, the Beebys have devised new planting schemes to which they have added artifacts and sculptures collected on their world travels over the years. Among these decorative and artistic touches are a pair of elegant cranes from Thailand standing tall on the edges of both pools, surrounded by masses of flowering shrubbery and rocks.

INFORMATION
To visit the Beebys' private garden, located in the Green Farms sec-tion of Westport, you must phone them first at (203) 255-6463. They will give you the necessary directions.

And in Addition . . .

Fairfield: Larsen Sanctuary of
Connecticut Audubon Society
2325 Burr Street. Telephone: (203) 259-6305.
This site will appeal not only to bird-watchers, but also to those interested in horticulture. You'll find a wide variety of native shrubs and herbaceous plants, as well as a trail specially designed for the blind, with a fine collection of fragrant plants. Open Tuesday through Saturday, 10 A.M. to 5 P.M., Sunday 12 noon to 5 P.M. Fee.

Farmington: Nook Farm
Farmington Avenue. Telephone: (860) 522-9258 and 525-9317.
This historic complex includes the adjoining house and gardens of Harriet Beecher Stowe and Mark Twain. The Stowe garden was

restored from old photographs, and, like its neighbor, is intimate Victorian in style. You can tour both houses for memorabilia and historic anecdotes. Open daily from June 1 through September 1, 10 A.M. to 4 P.M. Fee.

Guilford: William Pinchbeck, Inc.
929 Boston Post Road. Telephone: (860) 453-2186.
The two giant greenhouses (each almost a quarter of a mile long) of this commercial grower contain some 90,000 rose bushes that produce 3 million blooms a year. A prearranged tour here will introduce you to rose gardening on a very grand scale. Open year-round.

Higganum: Sundial Herb Gardens
Brault Hill Road. Telephone: (860) 345-4290.
Along a winding road lined with stone walls and fine old shade trees typical of rural Connecticut, you'll see a pretty courtyard with weathered fences and potted trees next to a charming old barn. Behind are the Sundial Herb Gardens, a rich collection of diverse herbs and topiary plants. Any herb enthusiast won't want to miss this spot. Guided tours are conducted through the well maintained and tidy gardens.

Before or after your visit you can enjoy an English-style tea elegantly served in an intimate tearoom, where you can sample dishes made with some of the herbs grown on the property. Reservations are necessary. The gardens are open on Friday, Saturday, and Sunday in July, August, and September, from 10 A.M. to 5 P.M.

Morris: White Flower Farm
Route 63 (just outside Litchfield). Telephone: (860) 567-8789.
Though primarily a large, commercial nursery, this beautiful spot also features open meadows, stone walls, many flower beds (all plants with identification tags), and fine views. Among the pleasures here: a dwarf evergreen collection that comes from cuttings from the National Arboretum, a greenhouse of tuberous begonias, and a rose garden filled with labeled varieties. Open daily from April through October and weekends in wintertime.

New Canaan: Olive W. Lee Memorial Garden
Chichester Road.
This smallish but unusually pretty woodland garden is planted with daffodils, ferns, laurels, and rhododendrons on hilly terrain with

winding paths. It is especially nice to visit in the spring. There are no facilities.

Stamford: Old Fort
Westover Road. Telephone: (203) 977-4692.

Hidden within rural winding roads high above Stamford is a tiny, eighteenth-century-style enclosed garden at a site called the "Old Fort." The fort itself is gone, but what remains is an idyllic garden with an Italianate balustrade, colorful plantings, and a pretty wisteria trellis. Expanses of lawn surround the Old Fort, adding to its appeal. Children will love this spot. Open daily.

West Hartford: Elizabeth Park
Prospect and Asylum Avenues.

In this well-known urban rose garden you can enjoy thousands of old and new species. Be sure to visit in June, during the peak flowering period. Open daily, sunrise to sunset.

Woodbury: Gertrude Jekyll Garden at the Glebe House Museum
Hollow Road. Telephone: (203) 263-2855.

Gertrude Jekyll was a distinguished English garden designer of some 400 notable sites—almost all of them in Britain. This is the only Gertrude Jekyll garden maintained in the United States. Jekyll is particularly noted for her emphasis on border plantings based on color. The component parts of a Jekyll border—shrubs, annuals, bulbs, perennials, small trees, and even potted plants—were all arranged with an eye toward color patterns. While her "cottage" gardens seemed informal and perhaps accidental, each plant was in fact part of a sophisticated composition in color and architectural design.

Though it is not large, Glebe House's elegant, geometric design and profusion of plantings make it both orderly and lush. Created in 1927 for the opening of the Glebe House Museum (the eighteenth-century house is considered to be the birthplace of the American Episcopal Church), the newly restored site includes a rose allée leading to rose quadrants, a terrace of flowers, a kitchen herb garden, and—Jekyll's specialty—some 600 feet of mixed herbaceous and perennial border. A chart available at the house identifies each of the 90 varieties of plantings and its location, including a giant sycamore tree (thought to be 200 years old and the ninth largest in the state). The blooms are at their best in summer, though the garden can be visited from April through November, Wednesday through Sunday, 1 P.M. to 4 P.M.. Fee.

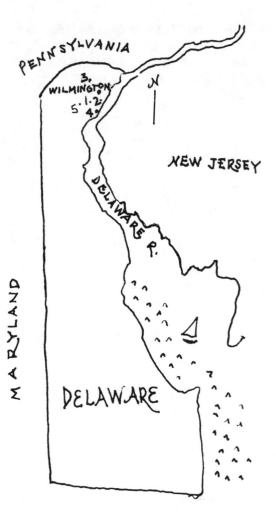

DELAWARE GARDENWALKS

1. Wilmington: Nemours Mansion and Gardens
2. Wilmington: Rockwood Gardens
3. Winterthur: Winterthur

And in Addition . . .
4. New Castle: The George Read II House and Garden
5. Wilmington: Hagley Museum and Library

Delaware

Nemours Mansion and Gardens, Wilmington

Nemours needs little introduction. One of the best known and most often visited country estates in the East, it is also one of the most opulent, with its sumptuous 102-room mansion, formal gardens, and acres of woodlands. Situated in the historical and scenic Brandywine landscape, it is reminiscent of a French chateau.

In fact, Versailles was the inspiration at least for the extraordinary gardens. Extending nearly one-half mile in a sweeping axis from the house to a Temple of Love, the gardens include elegant fountains, pools, urns, statuary, an intricate parterre, colonnades, tree-lined allées, a maze and sunken garden—and vistas at every turn. Everything is on a grand scale, from the 1-acre reflecting pool with its 157 water jets (though not in perpetual motion), to the massive limestone colonnade, to an extravaganza of sculptures against a marble wall, to the 800 feet of flowering borders enclosing one of the gardens.

Nemours (named after an ancestral town in France) was built between 1909 and 1910 by Alfred I. du Pont, though the gardens themselves were not completed until 1932. His goal was to reproduce a version of Versailles, the ultimate in splendor (unlike his du Pont cousins who were creating nearby Longwood and Winterthur on a more modest scale). In addition to the dramatic garden design, he concerned himself with such details as the tree boxes on the terrace, which are like those that held thousands of orange trees at Versailles.

If you stretch your imagination a bit and try to disregard the crowds and modern-day tourist amenities, you will find that coming to Nemours is almost like stepping back into seventeenth-century France. Unfortunately, guided tours of the mansion and gardens are par for the course (and reservations are necessary), limiting your freedom to wander about at will, at your own pace.

INFORMATION

Guided tours (for a minimum of two hours) include the mansion and a bus ride through the gardens (you may also see some of the gardens on foot if you make arrangements with the bus driver). For reservations you can phone or write:

Nemours Mansion and Gardens
P.O. Box 109
Wilmington, Delaware 19899
Telephone: (302) 651-6912

The site is open from May to November, Tuesday through Sunday. Tours are offered at 9 A.M., 11 A.M., 1 P.M., and 3 P.M., on all days except on Sunday, when there is no 9 A.M. tour. There is an entrance fee. No children under 16 are allowed.

DIRECTIONS

From Philadelphia take I-95 south to Exit 8 (Route 202). Go north, turn left at the third light (Route 141), go two more lights, and turn left onto Rockland Road. You will see a long stone wall surrounding the adjacent Alfred I. du Pont Institute. Park at the end of the stone wall. The reception area is located at the parking lot.

Rockwood Gardens, Wilmington

"Gardenesque" is a term that aptly describes this estate's landscape. Surrounding a rather gloomy but impressive midnineteenth-century rural Gothic mansion (with a delectable attached conservatory), these grounds are designed as a pleasurable retreat. Here you'll find many exotic trees from the Orient and around the world, expansive lawns, a walled rose garden, and numerous other country delights. The estate covers a rather rolling terrain and overlooks the Delaware River (though in most places the view is quite overgrown nowadays). You can be guided through the grounds or tour by yourself, map in hand.

The house, built in 1850 by merchant banker Joseph Shipley, is interestingly furnished with all kinds of antiques, and, in keeping with the period design, has many windows looking out over the gardens. Best of all, there is a small but wonderfully sumptuous high-ceilinged conservatory, where rarities and tropical plantings—orange and lemon trees, great ferns, orchids—grow all around you and overhead. The oldest standing greenhouse in the nation, this glass construction has a truly Victorian ambiance.

Outdoors you walk across vast lawns with great trees—we were particularly delighted by the gnarled, curving shapes of the "monkey puzzle" trees that contrast with the tall spires of giant hemlocks and larches. Such design elements are part of the plan in "gardenesque" design. You will encounter a low stone wall all around the gardens; this is called the "ha-ha," so beloved by English novelists. (It is simply a pretty way to keep cattle out of the front yard.)

Also reminiscent of the Victorian English country estate are the pleasure gardens, the walled once-kitchen garden which contains boxwood hedges and little walkways outlining pleasantly over-grown plantings, and a 1911 rose garden featuring rambling roses in white, pink, and mauve in summer. In various other seasons you'll also enjoy Rockwood: the spectacular autumn foliage colors, the pinetum in its winter beauty, and rhododendrons flowering in spring all make this a nice year-round visit.

INFORMATION
Rockwood is located at 610 Shipley Road in Wilmington. It is open Tuesday through Sunday, 11 A.M. to 4 P.M. Tours are offered from 11 A.M. to 3 P.M. Closed on major holidays. Free. Telephone: (302) 761-4340.

DIRECTIONS
From Wilmington take I-95 north to Exit 9 (Marsh Road). Turn right on Marsh Road and right again at first light, onto Washington Street Extension. Make another right at the first light at Shipley Road. Rockwood's driveway is the first on your left.

Winterthur, Winterthur

Winterthur, along with the other du Pont estates that dot the picturesque Brandywine Creek Historic region, is grand and vast, as you might expect. What comes as a surprise—and a welcome one, at that—is the style of its gardens. Naturalistic and free flowing, they are very different from the formal environments traditionally associated with comparable mansions, such as nearby Nemours or Longwood. Set in an idyllic landscape of rolling hills, meadows, ponds, and forests, they are, understandably, among the most popular gardens in the country.

Apparently Henry Francis du Pont, creator of Winterthur's gardens, museum, and library, had two great passions in life: collecting American antiques and gardening. His mansion is now a prestigious museum housing one of the best collections of American decorative arts anywhere; surrounding it are nearly 1,000 acres, including 11 main planted areas that testify to his great love of gardens.

The property, a working farm until 1951, was named after an ancestral site in Switzerland. When first purchased by the family in 1837, it was a 450-acre estate with a 12-room Greek Revival house. By 1925 it had evolved into a much more elaborate complex, including dairy and poultry farms, flower and vegetable gardens, a golf course, sawmill, railroad station—even a post office. But it was Winterthur's fifth owner, Henry du Pont, whose energy and imagination made it what it is today.

From 1926, when he inherited the property, to 1951, when it was opened to the public, he further developed and expanded the farm-land and gardens. Committed to maintaining Winterthur's peaceful parklike ambiance, du Pont engaged an old family friend, landscape architect Marian Coffin, to create naturalistic planted areas that would blend seamlessly with the landscape. As a dedicated and knowledgeable plantsman (he himself had studied horticulture at Harvard), he selected a vast assortment of species from around the world to enhance the natural setting. He was particularly fond of azaleas, rhododendron, dogwood, and quince, whose colors he chose with an artistic eye. With the help of an impressive staff of gardeners, he planned and supervised the blooming sequence of his flowers and shrubs with the utmost precision, so that the season could last as long as possible. To add idyllic charm, du Pont even created four ponds (now home to assorted ducks and geese) from the existing Clenny Run.

The resulting gardens can be viewed by foot, or—for those who would rather not walk up and down the hilly terrain—by tram, a delightful experience in itself. From April through October they unfold like a series of tableaux, with subtle changes in color and fra-grance, from the earliest daffodils and azaleas, to autumn's brilliant shades. Among the offerings are the Azalea Woods, an 8-acre won-derland of rhododendrons, azaleas, ferns, wildflowers, and shrubs beneath towering white oaks and tulip poplars; Magnolia Bend, a spring-fresh combination of pale pink and deep red blossoms; March Bank (dating from 1902, making it the oldest planted area), a glorious hillside of naturalized daffodils, snowdrops, crocus, and glory-of-the-snow; the Quarry Garden (du Pont's last creation), an unusual rock garden made from an abandoned quarry; and the Winter Hazel Area, a proliferation of color that should not be missed in April. Marian Coffin designed three main areas: the Peony Garden and the only two formal gardens at Winterthur, the Sundial Garden (where fragrant plants are arranged in circles around an antique bronze sundial) and the intimate Reflecting Pool, one of our favorite spots. In winter you can enjoy long walks and indoor displays using plant materials.

When du Pont enlarged his mansion in 1929, he wanted an attached garden that would make an inviting transition from house to surrounding landscape. The Reflecting Pool was inspired by Italian Renaissance gardens, with classical and symmetrical proportions and architectural features. Amid the plantings are cherub statues and elegant stone steps leading to a pool (once the family swimming pool) surrounded with potted hydrangeas and asparagus vines. In this tranquil spot you can enjoy the appealing sounds of water jets spouting into the pool.

For all of its bucolic charms, Winterthur is a well-organized site, offering guided tours and lectures; a 30-minute tram ride around the extensive grounds (narrated by a guide); two unusually nice museum and gift shops; a restaurant and picnic areas; a library stocked with books on antiques, art, and history; and other amenities. For those who like to wander about on their own, a map and descriptive brochure are available at the visitors center.

INFORMATION
Winterthur is located on Route 52, 6 miles northwest of Wilmington, Delaware. The museum and gardens are open Monday through Saturday, 9 A.M. to 5 P.M., and Sunday, noon to 5 P.M. Winterthur is open all year, except for Christmas, New Year's Day, and Thanksgiving. The library is open from 8:30 A.M. to 4:30 P.M., Monday through Friday. Entrance fee. General admission includes a tour of the museum galleries (on your own) and a stroll or tram ride in the gardens. Reservations are required only for special tours on decorative arts, gardens and holiday displays. Telephone: (302) 888-4600 or 1 (800) 448-3883.

DIRECTIONS
Winterthur is 30 miles southwest of Philadelphia. Take Route 1 west to Route 52 south to Winterthur.

And in Addition . . .

New Castle: The Read House and Garden
42 The Strand. Telephone: (302) 322-8411.
This is a historic house and garden in a wonderful town for a visit. The gardens are the oldest surviving gardens in the Delaware Valley. They were designed by Robert Buist of Philadelphia in 1846 and installed the next year. The gardens feature a formal parterre with

newly reconstructed gazebos, a specimen garden with exotic trees and shrubs, and a kitchen garden with a pear allée, a grape arbor, and vegetable beds. Open from March 1 through December 31, Tuesday through Saturday, 10 A.M. to 4 P.M., Sunday noon to 4. Open winter on weekends only or by reservation during the week. Closed on holidays. Fee.

Wilmington: Hagley Museum and Library
Route 141. Telephone: (302) 658-2400
This 230 acre site of the first du Pont powder works gives visitors an amazing glimpse into early 19th century industrial and community life with some 60 buildings, as well as justly famous gardens. These elegant, restored flower and vegetable gardens feature French-style flower beds in geometric patterns, borders of dwarf, espaliered fruit trees, a kitchen garden, an intriguing Italianate garden built upon some ruins, and a variety of woodsy trails best visited in spring, when azaleas, dogwood, and rhododendrons are at their best. Fee.

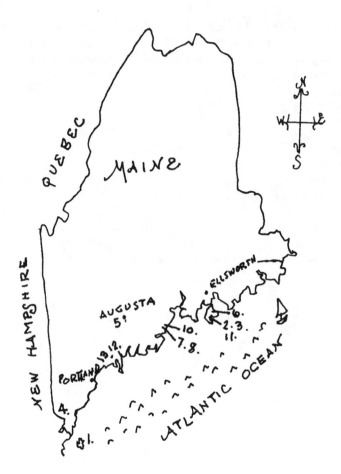

MAINE GARDENWALKS

1. Appledore Island: Celia Thaxter's Garden
2. Northeast Harbor: Asticou Azalea Garden
3. Northeast Harbor: Thuya Lodge Garden
4. South Berwick: Hamilton House Garden

And in Addition . . .

5. Augusta: Blaine House
6. Bar Harbor: Wild Gardens of Acadia
7. Camden: Amphitheater
8. Camden: Merryspring
9. Ellsworth: Woodlawn, the Colonel Black Mansion
10. Rockport: Children's Chapel
11. Seal Harbor: Abby Aldrich Rockefeller Garden
12. Wiscasset: Nickels–Sortwell House
13. Woolwich: Robert P. Tristram Coffin Wild Flower Reservation

MAINE

Celia Thaxter's Garden, Appledore Island

Getting away to an island retreat is an enduring popular fantasy. Among the enticing islands along Maine's rugged coastline that have appealed to garden, nature, and art enthusiasts over the years is Appledore. To visit this off-the-beaten-track pleasure is to relive a fascinating period in the American garden and art scene.

The 95-acre island, the largest of the barren and somewhat bleak Isles of Shoals, located some 9 miles off the coast of Portsmouth, New Hampshire, is the site of a beloved Victorian garden that was immortalized in many paintings and writings. One of the first seaside summer resorts on the East Coast during the mid- to late nineteenth century, Appledore has had an intriguing history. How this garden was created, how it inspired an entire generation of American artists, and what became of it, all add to the lore and appeal of the island.

As early as the sixteenth century, European fishermen found the tiny cluster of islands to be rich fishing grounds and they colonized the islands. A thriving fishing industry, unrivaled in New England, brought wealth to the Isles of Shoals for a brief time. After years of neglect, the islands enjoyed a renaissance when summer tourists rediscovered them in the midnineteenth century. They liked the romantic, rugged, moorlike beauty, windswept landscape, and ocean views they found there. Thomas Laighton, a businessman from Portsmouth, opened the Appledore House Resort in 1848 to immediate success. With him came his family, including his remarkably creative and charismatic daughter, Celia.

The reputation of Celia Thaxter (her married name) as a poet of distinction grew. She attracted the attention of many of the literary and artistic lions of her time, who became her friends and later visited in the summers at Appledore. These luminaries—the list reads like a cultural *Who's Who* of late nineteenth-century America—included James Russell Lowell, John Greenleaf Whittier, Nathaniel Hawthorne, Harriet Beecher Stowe, and Mark Twain and the painters William Morris Hunt and Childe Hassam, to name a few. They were drawn to the island's stark, wild beauty, true, but especially to the intellectually and culturally stimulating atmosphere Celia provided, and to the enchanting flower-filled life-style they could enjoy at the hotel. They were also charmed by the fabled garden she cultivated on a terrace that sloped from her cottage toward the sea. This splendid 50-foot by 15-foot plot of brilliantly colored old-fashioned flowers—poppies, hollyhocks, and larkspur, among many other varieties—contrasted sharply with the stark surroundings of rocks, brush, and sea, a contrast that greatly struck many of these artists.

One artist who was particularly inspired by Celia's garden was the impressionist Childe Hassam, who painted it over and over in its many configurations. He and Celia became fast friends and collaborators. When Celia wrote an account of the joys and frustrations of creating a garden in a physically difficult environment in *An Island Garden*, Hassam illustrated it. He joyously depicted the vitality and sparkle of her garden and other views of the Isles of Shoals in hundreds of oils, watercolors, and pastels over a period of more than 30 years.

Celia Thaxter died in 1894 and, with her, her offshore cultural salon and lovely garden. The hotel and her cottage burned down in 1914, and Appledore was almost forgotten. During World War II the island housed a submarine observation post (a U.S. Army barracks was placed directly over what had been Celia's garden) and, finally, in the 1960s, the Shoals Marine Laboratory, which still exists. In the process of restoring some of the old cottages and building new ones, the laboratory directors had the imagination to reconstruct Celia Thaxter's unique garden, using her book as a guideline.

Today the garden has been restored to include more or less everything Celia grew. It can be enjoyed during the summer months by members of the scientific community, as well as day-trippers. While on Appledore you should also visit the Laighton family cemetery, a lonely, windswept spot located near her garden; it is here that Celia was buried. Day visitors may also ask for permission to tour the classrooms and labs of the Shoals Marine Laboratory and can walk along nature trails to spot gulls, snowy egrets, black-crowned herons, or others of the hundred or so species seen on the island during migrations.

Getting to Appledore requires some planning and funds, but we hope that being on this special site with its melancholy beauty and connections with the past will be inspiring enough to make it worth your effort.

Visitors to Appledore are first taken to nearby Star Island (also a conference center), where there are additional places of interest to see. Nature lovers can walk along the island's rocky coves and cliffs and hope to spot nesting gulls. Be sure to avoid nesting areas during spring and early summer, however; gulls can be quite ferocious and will dive at those who come too close to their nests.

INFORMATION
The ferry for day-trippers (100 visitors per trip, maximum) sails out of Portsmouth, New Hampshire, at 11 A.M., arriving first at Star Island at about noon; from there the Shoals Marine Laboratory launch will transport you for the short trip to Appledore. [To reserve the launch, you must phone ahead, to (603) 862-2994.] The ferry leaves Star Island at 3 P.M. for the trip back to the mainland, so that those going on to Appledore have fewer than three hours to visit. The cost of the ferry is moderate, but we thought admission to the garden was rather expensive.

DIRECTIONS
From Boston to Appledore take I-95 north to Portsmouth exit; continue on to the ferry.

Asticou Azalea Garden, Northeast Harbor, Mount Desert Island

It may seem surprising to find a Japanese-inspired oasis like this one in coastal Maine; it is certainly a treat to visit it. Asticou, which is tucked into a woodsy hillside above the bright cobalt sea below, is a quiet, exotic place, complete with raked Zen garden; ponds, trickling water, and stepping stones; and in early summer, a profusion of blooming azaleas.

Asticou is designed for peaceful contemplation and the enjoyment of native-to-Maine plantings—in an Oriental style. But it is not meant to be precisely a traditional Japanese garden. Instead, the designers have borrowed liberally from that style, using such components as stone, moss, water—and azaleas. Thus you'll find native Maine pines pruned to resemble bonsai, lavender heather familiar to the Maine landscape near a garden with raked white sand, or lichen-covered rocks of granite and mossy mounds that may resemble their Japanese counterparts but also look a bit like the shapes of the islands nearby. It is this odd combination of landscape characteristics of northern New England and Asia that makes Asticou so exotic.

The garden is organized into "rooms," each of which has a different feeling or design. You follow a meandering pale gravel path leading from room to room, occasionally picking your way over stepping stones or a small stone bridge as you cross a trickling brook or approach the lily pond. Many garden rooms are almost enclosed by profuse greenery, so you come upon these different scenes quite by surprise; winding paths through a garden such as this one date back to medieval Japan. Occasionally you'll see typically Japanese stone statuary nestled among shrubbery.

Your route will take you past dozens of different rhododendron and azalea species (best to visit in June when the late spring brings them to their showiest beauty). This is called a "stroll garden," in which your path will lead you by such decorative species as Flame, Pontic, Snow, Roseshell, and Cumberland azaleas—all of which bloom spectacularly in the salty coastal air here. Flowers and shrubs come from several parts of the Orient (Japanese iris, Chinese flowering cherry, and Korean azalea and rhododendron) and from Europe (fothergilla, spring heath, and smokebush), as well as from this rocky, mountainous seacoast of Maine.

You will also come to the raked Zen garden, patterned after that of a fifteenth-century temple in Kyoto; here a large area of ashen white sand is perfectly raked into parallel patterns. This is known as a "dry garden": water and landscape are symbolically represented with raked sand resembling waves and carefully placed rocks suggesting the landscape. (This is the best such dry garden we have seen on our gardenwalks.)

Asticou (which is named for a seventeenth-century Indian chief) was the idea of Charles K. Savage, the same landscape designer who created the gardens at Thuya Lodge nearby. The Asticou area was at that time a swamp of alder thickets and cattails. In 1956, with financial aid from John D. Rockefeller, Jr., Savage began to create a fine garden on the property. He constructed two ponds from the swampland, a running stream, and two rolling lawns. He brought a number of azaleas, rhododendrons, and ornamental trees from "Reef Point," the coastal Maine gardens of his friend Beatrix Farrand, the famous horticulturist. (Reef Point was being dismantled.) With these component parts, granite rocks indigenous to Maine, many additional plantings, and a tranquil Oriental outlook, Asticou gardens were created. Combining both Eastern and Western influences and plantings, they are certainly unique and very lovely. You might wish to combine a visit with Thuya Lodge Gardens just down the road; you will see two very different, very successful approaches to beautiful garden design.

INFORMATION
Asticou is located on the northern edge of Northeast Harbor, with the entrance on Route 198. Telephone: (207) 276-5456. Asticou is open to the public during daylight hours from May 1 through October 31.There is no fee.

DIRECTIONS
Take Routes 3 and 198 to Mount Desert Island. Follow Route 198 to entrance to Asticou just north of the intersection with Route 3.

Thuya Lodge Garden, Northeast Harbor, Mount Desert Island

The pleasures of hiking up a beautiful, rocky, pine-covered (but not too steep) mountain directly above a bright cerulean harbor filled with bobbing sailboats is something many of us travel to Maine to enjoy. We relish the sights and delicious ocean air as we climb, and we look forward to the view at the top. Imagine arriving at the summit to discover a giant and oh-so-elegant formal garden as your reward!

Thuya Lodge and its spectacular garden are at the top of Eliot Mountain, a slight mountain in fact, but high enough to command a wonderful panorama below, and flat enough on top to accommodate a truly magnificent garden. You walk up through the shady woods of spruce and cedar with their alpine plants and lichen-covered boulders on a series of zigzag terraces and handmade stone steps and paths that are never too exhausting, and are always surprising with another scenic overlook (and many benches for resting). These walkways are known as Asticou Terraces and are only about one half mile from Asticou Gardens.

The terraces and path up the mountain and the lodge built of white cedar at the top were the creations of Joseph Henry Curtis, a Boston landscape architect who wanted to build his summer residence high above the harbor and deep in the woods. Curtis summered here from 1880 to 1928, and over the years he created on his 200 acres the amazing system of terraces and the rustic lodge with an orchard behind it. He named the place Thuya Lodge after the "Thuya Occidentalis"—or white cedar.

Curtis arranged to transfer the property in perpetuity for the enjoyment of the public. After his death, the trustee of Thuya Lodge (and a landscape designer himself), named Charles K. Savage, undertook to turn the big flat plain of the orchard into a garden and to put the lodge to use as a fine library of botanical books. It was Savage's idea to create a vast formal garden that would be surrounded by—and contrasted with—the natural Maine landscape of granite rock outcroppings, evergreens, and alpine wildflowers.

Savage was fortunate to have financial help from John D. Rockefeller, Jr., who summered nearby, and botanical help in the form of plantings from the nearby "Reef Point" gardens that belonged to Beatrix Farrand, one of America's most notable garden designers. In fact, Farrand's ideas about landscape design are everywhere in evidence at Thuya Lodge Garden, for she devoted much thought to coastal Maine's particular climate and terrain, and Savage was both a friend and disciple. We can see elements of her taste for the formal and geometric tempered by profuse, English-style plantings. Among the especially notable contributions from Farrand's garden were two Alberta spruce that flank the stone steps of the cross axis.

The task of constructing gardens at the top of a mountain apparently did not daunt Mr. Savage and his cohorts. Thuya Gardens are vast, a masterpiece of coherent design. The entrance is a gate through a cedar stockade fence (to keep the deer out); even the gate is artistic: a carved series of designs from a 1629 gardening book—complete with animal symbols and native American plants.

On entering the gate you are taken by a thrill of surprises: a tremendous garden lies before you. A central north-south axis of grass is bordered with double-sided, English, Gertrude Jekyll–style perennial planting beds in bright, appealing colors and varied textures (all labeled); at one end of the axis is an asymmetrical reflecting pool and at the other a special pavilion for contemplation. On either side of these borders are curving paths leading into still other areas of beauty. A cross-axis divides the planting beds. Flowers are planted in subtly graduating colors, perhaps making the garden seem even longer than it is.

But a formal description does not begin to capture the ambiance of this garden—the areas of quiet shade and brilliant color, the winding paths, and everywhere a delightful use of free-form granite steps and walls and indigenous boulders. And surrounding the cultivated areas is the continued presence of the Maine woods, never very far away. Despite the rigorous design structure, this is a garden that allows natural beauty its full flowering—it feels thoroughly informal.

You can easily spend half a day here exploring the delights of this garden (and perhaps resting up for the downward descent on the many benches and even sofa cushions provided). These gardens are frequently described as the most beautiful gardens in Maine, so allow plenty of time for your visit.

INFORMATION

The entrance to Asticou Terraces for the climb up to the Thuya Lodge Gardens is on Route 3. Parking is on the right; cross the street at the zebra walk to find a small sign indicating "gardens." Thuya Lodge Garden is open from 7 A.M. to 7 P.M., July through September; the lodge is open from 10:00 A.M. to 4:30 P.M., July 1 through Labor Day. Telephone: (207) 276-5130.

DIRECTIONS

Take Route 198 onto Mount Desert Island (in the direction of Northeast Harbor) to intersection with Route 3. Go 1/10th mile south on Route 3 to parking area. From Asticou Gardens (if you wish to combine a visit), you can walk out the back gate of Asticou about 4/10th mile to the entrance.

Hamilton House Garden, South Berwick

We seldom see a formal garden surrounded by the wildest of natural panoramas. But Maine provides that kind of wonderful setting. If you are traveling through southern Maine, this spot is well worth a detour. High on a bluff with a spectacular view of the Piscataqua River and its wetlands and surrounding woods is this stark, white, unadorned 1785 house and its windswept, but curiously formal, garden.

This combination of wilderness and tamed nature in juxtaposition is intriguing. (The owners—The Society for the Preservation of New England Antiquities—must know it, for there are three little chairs set at the top of the hill in the garden for contemplation of the panorama.)

The place has an interesting history. It was built by Colonel John Hamilton, who made his fortune in shipping; but the Embargo of the War of 1812 ruined him, and he sold the 300-acre estate. It was a sheep farm from the 1830s to 1898 when it was sold once again and fell upon hard times. As a great house in a romantic setting, it intrigued Sarah Orne Jewett, the Maine writer who visited it as a child and even set one of her novels there. She persuaded Mrs. Emily Tyson to buy it and restore it to its former grandeur; Mrs. Tyson replanted the gardens in an old-fashioned style and built a pergola and summer house. Her daughter, Mrs. Henry Vaughan, presented it to the public in 1949.

Created at the turn of the century by Mrs. Tyson, the hedged garden is ornamented with terraces and statuary and even a sundial. There are little pathways and steps here and there and occasional big round granite grinding wheels to walk on in each terraced level. Plantings include symmetrical beds with boxwood hedges; many larger bright perennials are charmingly edged with smaller pastels. The garden has a little gate to a shady space farther on. Since you are on top of the hill, there is a view below whichever way you turn.

All of the grounds around Hamilton House, in fact, are beautiful in one way or another. The paths are lined with flowers. And as you walk up to the house and garden from the field below (where you leave your car) there are wildflowers galore (including a profusion of brilliant purple lupine and tiger lilies) all around you. (You will also find Vaughan Woods Memorial State Park adjacent, for picnicking and hiking.) This is a place where your delight in nature—whether untamed or carefully designed—will be gratified, and where you can truly hear the birds sing.

INFORMATION
Hamilton House is open mid-June through mid-September, Tuesday, Thursday, Saturday, and Sunday from 1 P.M. to 5 P.M. (But you can visit the grounds on other days.) Tours of the house are offered. Telephone: (207) 384-5269. Fee.

DIRECTIONS
From I-95 take Route 236 north toward Portland after you cross into Maine from New Hampshire; after junction with Route 91 take first left onto Brattle Street to Vaughan's Lane and follow signs.

And in Addition . . .

Augusta: Blaine House (State Executive Mansion)
State and Capitol streets.
Blaine House, once the home of James Blaine, a presidential candidate in 1884, has a 3-acre garden surrounding it; there are formal plantings and borders of shrubs at this pretty spot.

Bar Harbor: Wild Gardens of Acadia
Sieur de Monts Spring, Acadia National Park. Telephone: (207) 288-3338.
In contrast to the formal gardens elsewhere on Mount Desert Island, these gardens display plants native to the varied terrain of Maine. Founded in the great Acadia National Park in 1961, the Wild Gardens of Acadia now have some 400 native species of flowers, ferns, and fruits. There are ten specific areas of plants indigenous to such habitats as the bog, rocky mountainside, saltwater, meadow, heath, and woodland.

A small stream fed by the Sieur de Monts Spring provides a natural setting for many woodland plants like ostrich ferns, and well-placed granite boulders recreate the rocky habitat for alpine flowers, Bar Harbor juniper, and mountain cranberry. There is even a seaweed filled beach recreation to provide a home for saltwater plants like sea lavender and spreading silver and gold potentilla.

The layout is simple: you follow a winding path (which provides occasional stepping stones), where everything is labeled. For anyone interested in natural plantings and wildlife—of the botanical sort—these are nicely presented and compact gardens, and the wildflower collection is one of the most important in the nation. There is also a museum with educational offerings. Open daily from 8 A.M. to 8 P.M., May through September.

Camden: Amphitheatre
Off Route 1

Behind the library and overlooking the harbor is a charming park: a hillside site with profuse plantings, stone walls, and a fine amphitheater that shows how pretty a public space in the center of a town can be.

Camden: Merryspring
End of Conway Road, off Route 1.

Merryspring is a 66-acre site devoted to indigenous Maine flowers, shrubs, and trees. In addition to nature trails and a 10-acre arboretum, there are 6 acres devoted to flowers: you'll find excellent wildflowers and a woodland garden, as well as cultivated gardens including a lily garden and a rose garden. There are great views too. Open every day year-round, dawn to dusk.

Ellsworth: Woodlawn, The Colonel Black Mansion and Gardens
Route 172 (Surry Road).

This 1902 Georgian mansion and carriage house on a hill has a very pretty restored formal garden behind it. What distinguishes the flower garden (laid out in 1903) is the lilac hedge surrounding it. Cut to about 4 feet, and uniformly pruned, the lilacs make an unusual and sweetly scented border. Best to visit in June when they are in full bloom, but you'll find the gardens lovely all through the season with perennials and other plantings. House and grounds are open June 1 through October 15, from 10 A.M. to 5 P.M. The gardens are free.

Rockport: Children's Chapel
Vesper Hill.

This very simple and touching site high on a hill overlooking the ocean is dedicated to the young. There is a hand-built wooden open-air chapel surrounded by a profuse flower garden and a biblical herb garden, all of it lovely.

Seal Harbor: Abby Aldrich Rockefeller Garden
Off Route 3. Telephone: (207) 276-3330.

These exquisite gardens on a hill above the sea on Mount Desert

Island are open to the public only a few times a year (Thursdays from July through September 5)—by appointment well in advance. Beatrix Farrand collaborated with Mrs. John D. Rockefeller in the 1920s to create this immense garden surrounded by a wall of glazed tiles (from the Imperial Palace in Beijing). Needless to say, you'll find this garden with its Oriental touches amid the Maine woods and rocks unlike any you've ever seen.

Wiscasset: Nickels-Sortwell House
Main Street, at the corner of Federal Street.
In the center of this waterside village is a historic house whose back gardens are now in the process of restoration. But just across the side street, on the site of an old hotel that burned down in 1903, is a lovely garden that Frances Sortwell created in 1912. It is an oasis in the middle of the bustling summer scene.

This deeply sunken garden (its entrance is the short flight of stone steps down that once led to the hotel's front door) has been presented to the town and is kept in flourishing condition—filled with blooming flowers and surrounded by lilacs and shade trees. There are charming parallel brick paths, a bird bath, a table and chair for picnicking or contemplation, both bright sun and brilliant pinks and oranges and purples and deep shade and darkest greens. Visit June through September.

Woolwich: Robert P. Tristram Coffin Wildflower Reservation
Merrimeeting Bay.
One hundred and seventy-five acres of tidal marsh, woods, and fields, much of it home to a great assortment of wildflowers and ferns. Visit in summertime.

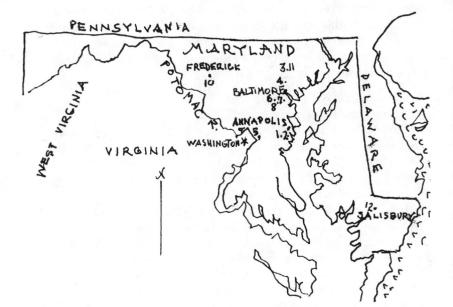

MARYLAND GARDENWALKS

1. Annapolis: William Paca Garden
2. Edgewater: London Town House and Garden
3. Monkton: Ladew Topiary Garden
4. Towson: Hampton National Historic Site
5. Wheaton: Brookside Gardens

And in Addition . . .
6. Baltimore: Cylburn Garden Center
7. Baltimore: Druid Hill Park Conservatory
8. Baltimore: Sherwood Gardens
9. Bethesda: McCrillis Gardens
10. Buckeystown: Lilypons Water Gardens
11. Monkton: Breezewood
12. Salisbury: Salisbury State University Arboretum

MARYLAND

William Paca Garden, Annapolis

The orderly charm of the colonial garden must have been particularly noticeable in the days when America was mostly wilderness. Yet when you visit a historic town like Annapolis, you realize that an elegant and imaginative town garden like that behind the William Paca House was one of many similar "pleasure" gardens on streets of fine homes in colonial cities like Annapolis. Jefferson is said to have commented that Annapolis' "gardens are better than those of Williamsburg." Unfortunately, few are now left, and we are all the more grateful for the careful restoration and upkeep that make the Paca Garden well worth a visit.

This walled garden is surprisingly large (2 acres), considering its center-of-town location. The entire garden is made up of a series of five terraces. Boxwood hedges and brick paths divide one section from another, and the various levels are reached by small sets of steps. Two diagonal pathways intersect the more traditional squares of plantings, each one of which is laid out in a geometric pattern. There are several unusually charming outbuildings, Chinese latticework, a fish-shaped pond, an informal "wilderness area," and a profusion of carefully arranged plantings.

The Georgian mansion that William Paca built from 1763 to 1765 sits proudly on an Annapolis city street. Paca, a rich and prominent lawyer, was a signer of the Declaration of Independence, a senator, and a governor of Maryland. He had the house and garden designed in English Georgian five-part style. (The house is open to visitors interested in the finest colonial decor and antiques.)

After Paca left Annapolis in 1780, the estate was sold or leased many times over the next 180 years. Apparently something of a white elephant, its various tenants used it as a doctor's office and a boarding house; in 1901 it became a hotel. The garden similarly had a long and uncertain history: at various times parts of it became a parking lot, a gas station, and a bus station.

The house was altered extensively by the hotel owners. The original structure became the lobby for the 200-room hotel, and neo-Georgian columns were added to the front of the building. A large part of the gardens became a parking lot for the hotel's bustling business. Carvel Hall, as the old Paca estate was known, became a center of Annapolis' political and social life.

But in 1965 the hotel decided to sell the property to real estate developers for an office and apartment complex. Like so much of our country's past, the Paca house was soon to disappear. (The gardens had already virtually vanished.) The Historic Annapolis Foundation came to the rescue and for $275,000 bought the house, while the state paid for the restoration of most of the original garden.

The ensuing restoration took historians and archeologists years to complete. Using archival drawings and texts, scraps of original material still extant, excavations, and even a portrait of Paca standing in front of his garden, experts reconstructed both the house and garden in its eighteenth-century elegance. The original garden wall (stretching for more than a third of a mile) was still partly standing; the rest was reconstructed. This is truly a success story, for the original estate was well worth recreating.

Your garden walk will begin at the back door of the Paca house. On your left is the rose garden, including nine types of roses grown in Paca's time. Directly across from it you'll find a geometrically arranged seasonal flower bed. Farther to the right is a traditional physic garden of medicinal plants. On the outer edges of both sides of the garden are "necessaries"—quaint privies, now used for storing tools. Herbs, vegetables, and a fruit garden are next as you move away from the house. Traditional eighteenth-century methods are used for pruning. Particularly nice in winter is the holly parterre, to the immediate right of the central pathway and down the first set of steps. Opposite is the formal topiary garden. Plantings in all of these gardens include both native Maryland specimens and rare and unusual plants grown and maintained in the eighteenth-century manner.

Down the next set of stairs you'll find the canal and a Chinese-style bridge leading to the pond (shaped like a giant fish) and the summer house. The water aspects of the garden were both practical and pretty; spring house, canals, pond, and underground passages provided water for house and garden and even a cold bathhouse. Excavations unearthed the original brick foundations for the architectural elements of the gardens, including the summer house, the pavilion, and the bridge. Charles Wilson Peale's portrait of Paca shows the picturesque domed summer house; it was reconstructed accordingly. The Chinese latticework bridge (a design element also found within the house) was popular in eighteenth-century English design books, and here it adds to the graceful charm of trellises and gateways throughout the garden.

At the very rear of the garden you'll find the cold bathhouse (no doubt a pleasant addition in the hot Maryland summer) and the spring house; archeologists found the original conduits for the spring, as well as a basin and floor boards.

The Paca gardens are both practical and aesthetically pleasing—a combination that the best colonial gardens seem to have created effortlessly. It is always hard to believe that despite the dramatic and unsettled times they lived in, early settlers in the colonies cared so much for beauty and design.

INFORMATION
The William Paca House and Gardens are open daily from March through December; in the winter only on Friday, Saturday, and Sunday. Closed on major holidays. You may visit the gardens without visiting the house. There is an admission charge. Telephone: (410) 263-5553.

DIRECTIONS
The William Paca House and Gardens are at 186 Prince George Street, Annapolis. Take Route 50/301 to Route 70 into Annapolis. Follow signs to the historic district. From the State House in the center of the city, take Maryland Avenue which intersects Prince George Street. The Paca House is between Maryland Avenue and East Street. (A good map of the historic district is available at the Visitor's Center.)

London Town House and Garden, Edgewater

London Town is a sturdy brick Georgian (c. 1760) house once called the Publik House. In the colonial days when London Town (not far from Annapolis) was a tobacco exporting center, it was a ferry boatman's house and colonial meeting spot, and then it was used for years as an inn, and, finally as an almshouse. It sits serenely on a bluff overlooking Maryland's South River and a small creek and a stream—almost surrounded, in fact, by water. Its view is very pretty (despite modernish housing just across one vista) and its woodland garden grounds are unusually naturalistic for a colonial era site. In fact, a public building of this sort would probably not have had a pleasure garden at all, so a naturalistic woodland was planned at the site's restoration not long ago. Currently a fashionable spot for weddings, London Town is now a National Historic Landmark with an 8-acre garden.

These 8 acres are on a hillside that runs right down to the water's edge—and all along the curving route to the river (with staircases here and there) are various plantings and benches for enjoying the woodland gardens and the vista beyond. Described as a series of gardens within a garden, they are linked by a pathway. A self-guiding map is available; it takes you from the "The Berms" (where various narcissus, peonies, and perennials are planted near the house) to the Spring Walk (featuring a 30-foot climbing hydrangea), the Azalea Walk, a very charming gazebo with a panoramic view, a winter garden with a viburnum walkway, a camellia walk, and on through holly and wildflowers. Eventually you find yourself at the Dell Pond near the river's edge, where aquatic plants are flourishing. This is not a long walk, but it is hilly and somewhat rustic.

Of added interest are the archeological digs going on at the site; among the many recent "finds" are a series of foundations and thousands of well-preserved artifacts from what was once "Scorton," the eighteenth-century home of Dr. Richard Hill. A surgeon, ship owner, and plantation owner, Hill was also a naturalist, who may have met John Bartram in 1737 (see our description of his garden in Philadelphia on page 236). More than 1,000 items have been found in digging at this site; some are on view here.

INFORMATION

London Town House and Gardens are located at 839 Londontown

Road in Edgewater, Maryland. The house and grounds are open from 10 A.M. to 4 P.M., Tuesday through Saturday, and noon to 4 P.M. on Sunday, year-round except major holidays, but we recommend springtime. Open in the winter by appointment. Tours and educational programs available. Fee. Telephone: (410) 222-1919.

DIRECTIONS
From Route 50/301, which is the route to Annapolis from the Washington area, take Route 665 (exit 22). Take Route 2 south, go over South River Bridge and continue 6/10th mile to light at Mayo Road (Route 253). Make a left turn and follow 8/10th mile to light at Londontown Road. Turn left and go 1 mile to the end.

Ladew Topiary Gardens, Monkton

A fox hunt within the grounds of a formal garden? As unlikely as it may sound, you will indeed find one at Ladew Topiary Gardens in Monkton, Maryland. But, instead of a lively scene of red-coated riders and yelping hounds, you'll find a quiet, green sanctuary. Fortunately for the potential victim, no real fox hunt takes place here—only a giant topiary version of one.

Ladew Gardens were the creation of Harvey Smith Ladew, a prominent and eccentric New York socialite; he moved to the Maryland countryside to pursue his equally great passions for fox hunting and building gardens. The 15 gardens that comprise this 22-acre site were recently restored to their former splendor, some years after his death. Filled with surprises at every turn, they reflect Ladew's wit, whimsy, and peculiar interests.

One of the most delightful spots is, unquestionably, the plant sculpture fox hunt tableau, which includes two horses and riders jumping over a fence following six yew-covered hounds in hot pursuit of a fox. Grassy walks throughout these green acres take you to other topiary delights, interspersed among hedges, behind fountains, and around walkways: a flock of 12 graceful swans "floating" atop a hedge; seahorses, a lyrebird, and a Scottie running toward his bowl and ball; and the somewhat incongruous forms of Winston Churchill's victory sign, a Chinese junk, and a large Buddha.

More conventional gardens representing a variety of styles also grace the elegant premises: a carefully tended wild garden (not such a contradiction of terms within this context), an old-fashioned

Victorian flower garden, a rose garden enclosed in a circular brick wall; a yellow garden, a white garden, a water lily garden, and even a Garden of Eden—with a statue of Adam and Eve surrounded by azaleas and apple trees. A terrace garden features steps flanked by austere-looking topiary obelisks in formal rows. A Temple of Venus (Ladew's "folly," perhaps) overlooks the entire scene from a lofty perch.

The Ladew Gardens are both formal and romantic in tone. Their combination of charm, surprise, and beauty will appeal to young and old alike. (Children will delight in finding and identifying the topiary forms.) An elegant home on the estate is filled with travel memorabilia, artifacts, and photographs reflecting Mr. Ladew's active social life and travels.

INFORMATION
Tours are required to visit the house, although you can wander around on your own in the garden. There is a moderate entrance fee. Telephone: (410) 557-9570.

DIRECTIONS
The Ladew Gardens are located at 3535 Jarrettsville Pike, Monkton, Maryland. From Baltimore take Route 83 to 695; exit 27B (Route 146); cross over the bridge and bear left onto Route 146, the Jarrettsville Pike. Travel 14 miles to Ladew Gardens.

Hampton National Historic Site, Towson

There is something unusually evocative and romantic about this house and garden; it will also be of great interest to garden historians. The elegant (1783–1790) mansion, Hampton Hall, is large and particularly pretty, with its warm, peachy colored exterior and felicitous design topped by a delicate cupola. It is set in a rolling green landscape that has the feel of rural Maryland to it, though it is just beyond the highway. The vast agricultural and industrial plantation, owned by Charles Carnan Ridgely and his descendants until 1948, once comprised 24,000 acres including tobacco farms, iron mine, and foundry. Most of it is gone now, of course, but what remains (67 acres) is gracious and thoroughly surprising. Among the many additional reminders of the past glory of Hampton are the stables, the lovely (reconstructed) orangerie, the smokehouse, and the small family cemetery.

The entire estate combines eighteenth- and nineteenth-century designs in a fascinating way. At first, as you walk around the grounds and behind the house, you see vast lawns and dozens of very very old trees. (There are 200 notable trees.) Some of these died long ago, but, to the credit of the National Park Service, still stand—evoking bygone days in a way that no historically costumed tour guides could do. The layout of the landscape followed the ideas of Andrew Jackson Downing, the preeminent garden designer of the midnineteenth century. Among these great leaning, bending trees are gnarled catalpas (among the most romantic), copper beeches, Norway spruce, a 115-foot-high pecan tree, tulip trees, and the largest Cedar of Lebanon we've ever seen. (It is believed to have been carted in a shoe box from the Middle East.) The serpentine path takes you among the trees, the wisteria arbors, a series of artistically placed ancient marble vases, all the way to the end of this Victorian-style garden.

But—is it the end? When you arrive there you suddenly find you are at the top of a hill. Below you lies the crowning glory of Hampton Hall—the parterre formal gardens. Down grassy ramps— the American eighteenth-century version of England's more proper staircases—are the formal gardens in four neatly arranged terraced rectangles. The gardens were first laid out from 1790 to 1801 and are both surprising and—seen as they are from a distance above—thoroughly decorative. These parterre gardens are among the largest such terraced gardens in Maryland or Virginia. The original idea of the grassy hillside terraces was an optical fantasy—for, viewed from the cupola of the house on the hill, they seem quite flat! The owner had every intention of bringing European-style elegance to Hampton Hall.

Each parterre is different, though all are outlined in boxwood. One features peonies, another roses, a third, spring bulbs. Each is laid out in thoroughly geometric style with its design patterns accented by paths of white pebbles and rows of charming round boxwood plantings. Seen from the hilltop, these gardens are a treat to behold.

A visit here can, of course, include a tour of the mansion as well as the gardens—or you can pick up a very good flyer and walk around the grounds by yourself. Hampton neatly illustrates the changing ideas about gardens through American history; it also is one of the prettiest garden landscapes in Maryland and a delightful place for a picnic.

INFORMATION
Hampton Historic Site is at 535 Hampton Lane in Towson. It is open daily from 9 A.M. to 5 P.M., tours from 9 A.M. to 4 P.M. There is a small tearoom. The site is free to visitors. Telephone: (410) 823-1309.

DIRECTIONS
From the Baltimore Beltway (I-695) north of Baltimore, take Exit 27B and make an immediate hard right turn at the end of the ramp onto Hampton Lane and follow signs.

Brookside Gardens, Wheaton

Just north of Washington in the rolling hills (but busy, built-up suburbs) of Maryland, you'll find the particularly pleasant landscape known as Brookside Gardens. This extensive 50-acre garden lends itself to long walks, good conversation, and all-season recreation. There are both indoor conservatories and formal and informal gardens, a series of ponds with Japanese gardens and tea house, and wonderful stands of trees.

A relatively recent addition to the green spaces of the mid-Atlantic states, Brookside was planned in the 1960s, planted in the 1970s, and is still evolving today. (The gardens are part of the large Wheaton Regional Park system that surrounds it.) While all kinds of programs for educational and recreational use take place at Brookside, the designers have wisely left much of the area free of the overplanning, broken-up spaces, signs, and other intrusions that bedevil so many modern garden parks.

The conservatory is a charming, smallish glass house with permanent tropical displays and five seasonal sections that can be seen at any time of year. This is a particularly good place to visit in the winter, because you have a choice of indoor and outdoor gardens (there is, in fact, a "winter garden" also) to enjoy.

Outdoors, you'll find a gently hilly acreage, with garden areas distributed throughout. You can walk on paths or across the hills themselves. Nearest to the conservatory are formal gardens, including a perennial garden of bulbs and mums (spring through fall), a yew garden, a rock garden, a rose garden graced by a pergola, an educational and thematic garden, a round garden that features plum trees, a fragrance garden with a fountain, and even a gazebo.

More informal areas include a butterfly garden, an aquatic garden that is delightful to behold, a viburnum garden that includes 40 different varieties, and a specialty in spring—the rhododendron and azaleas garden with some 400 varieties of blooms covering about 7 acres of the landscape.

Of particular note is the Japanese "guide" garden. This 9-acre area—at the farthest edge of the park—has sculpted ponds and elegant trees along with a charming bridge and tea house.

Brookside sits within a larger park where you can combine your garden visit with bicycling, horseback riding, ice skating, tennis, and other recreational activities. It is a true oasis in an area filled with bustle, and we recommend it for a family walk.

INFORMATION
Brookside Gardens are open daily, year-round, without fee. Telephone: (301) 949-8231.

DIRECTIONS
Brookside Gardens are located at 1500 Glenallan Avenue in Wheaton, Maryland. From I-495 (Capital Beltway) north of Washington, take the Georgia Avenue exit north for 3.1 miles. Go right on Randolph Road for 2 blocks, then right onto Glenallan Avenue to the entrance to Brookside on your right.

And in Addition . . .

Baltimore: Cylburn Garden Center
4915 Greenspring Avenue. Telephone: (410) 396-0180.
Amid 176 acres belonging to the Maryland Ornithological Society is a Victorian mansion surrounded by greenhouse, formal gardens, and display gardens. Birders will be pleased to know there are wildflower trails through a bird sanctuary—a good vantage point for viewing birds. Open daily, dawn to dusk. (Call to see when the house is open.)

Baltimore: Druid Hill Park Conservatory
McCulloh Street and Gwynns Falls Parkway. Telephone: (410) 396-0180.
This recently restored century-old conservatory is filled with many tropical plants. Watch for special seasonal exhibits, especially at Christmastime. Outside you can walk through a small (1-acre) display

garden with spring, summer and fall blossoms. Open daily, 10 A.M. to 4 P.M.

Baltimore: Sherwood Gardens
Stratford Street. Telephone: 410-366-2572.

This is a 7-acre community-operated garden in a particularly pretty section of Baltimore, where the elegant mansions you see as you drive by all seem to have pretty gardens too. The city block called "Sherwood Gardens" is noted for its tulips, so visit (if you are in the vicinity) at tulip time, or late April into May. The site was once a dried-up lake; in 1927 it was purchased and converted to a public garden by a businessman named John Sherwood. Some 80,000 tulips bloom here, rather surprisingly in single color groups, often in asymmetrical flower beds. There are purple beds, pink beds, red beds—each filled with hundreds of waving tulips. The rest of the fairly flat landscape is grassy with occasional very pretty flowering shrubs and trees—dogwoods, magnolias, and, especially, azaleas. This is primarily a local garden: community organizations also have adopt-a-bed areas, and there is even an annual tulip bulb dig here. (We assume that the 80,000 bulb count is constant, however!) Sherwood Gardens is best visited from mid-April through mid-May for tulip and azalea time, but it is open all year.

Bethesda: McCrillis Gardens
6910 Greentree Road. Telephone: (301) 365-5728.

This garden is unusual in that its informally landscaped 5 acres are designed for shade. The plantings include some 750 varieties of azaleas, including many from Japan. Visit in spring, though open year-round.

Buckeystown: Lilypons Water Gardens
6800 Lilypons Road. Telephone: (301) 874-5133 or 1 (800) 723-7667.

The idea of water gardens is becoming quite popular; here one of the oldest and largest water gardens in the nation provides both display gardens and all the necessaries to start your own. Set in a very flat, very strange network filling 300 acres, Lilypons (yes, named for the great operatic soprano) is comprised of a series of rectangular aquatic gardens. In each pond are either varieties of lilies or other water plants, or types of fish that are happy in water gardens. The ambiance is one of serious purpose, with workers in hip boots fishing out specimens from the ponds and visitors walking gingerly along the clayey raised pathways between aquatic wonders. A trip here is not necessarily the aesthetic experience you may expect from a garden visit, but is interesting nonetheless, and you can watch small component parts of the garden being fished out and sold before your very eyes. Lilypons is open March through October, 9:30 A.M. to 5:30 P.M. every day except major holidays, but we recommend going after May 1. Lilypons is a commercial (and mail-order) establishment.

Monkton: Breezewood
Hess Road. Telephone: (301) 472-9438.
This is an Asian rock garden with an emphasis on Siamese culture; there are pagodas, a pool, and also a museum of Buddhist culture and Southeast Asian art. Open May through October, only on the first Sunday of each month, from 2 P.M. to 6 P.M.

Salisbury: Salisbury State University Arboretum
1101 Camden Avenue. Telephone: (410) 543-6323.
Salisbury State University Arboretum in Maryland's eastern shore is a green oasis of beautiful specimen trees, carefully tended lawns, shrubs and flower beds. The university, set in quiet, suburbanlike surroundings, has in the past several years developed not only into a continually expanding arboretum, but also a sculpture park surrounded with brick walkways, clipped hedges, courtyards, and fountains. Unlike most other campuses, the grounds here are in part maintained by students interested in learning more about botany and horticulture. Here you'll see a wonderful collection of magnolias—some impressively tall—as well as giant hollies, gingkos, oaks, maples, and pines—some quite rare. A central focus is the gracious white-columned, airy pergola, complete with 26 different kinds of vines, hanging baskets, and potted plants.

With a well-designed and informative arboretum map (available at the University's Guerrieri Center), you will discover a butterfly garden, a "secret" courtyard with low, graceful hedges surrounding brightly colored annuals and a central fountain, two greenhouses with tropical plants, a Japanese-style raked garden (now under construction), and luxuriant carpets of creeping junipers and serpentine dwarf boxwoods. You can wander about these landscaped acres on your own, or by guided tour (check at the Guerrieri Center for details). Open daily, year-round.

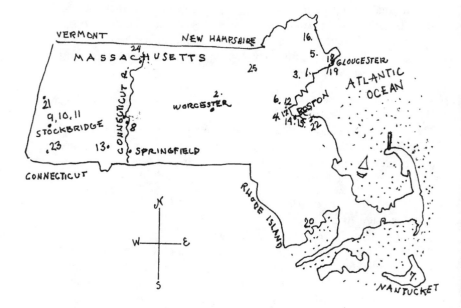

MASSACHUSETTS GARDENWALKS

1. Beverly: The Sedgwick Gardens at Long Hill
2. Boylston: Tower Hill Botanic Garden
3. Danvers: Glen Magna
4. Framingham: Garden in the Woods
5. Ipswich: Castle Hill, The Richard T. Crane, Jr., Memorial Reservation
6. Lincoln: Codman House
7. Nantucket: Cliff Walk
8. Northampton: Smith College
9. Stockbridge: Berkshire Botanical Garden
10. Stockbridge: Chesterwood
11. Stockbridge: Naumkeag
12. Waltham: The Vale, The Lyman Estate
13. Westfield: Stanley Park

And in Addition . . .

14. Boston: Isabella Stewart Gardner Museum
15. Boston Area: Arnold Arboretum
16. Byfield: Newbury Perennial Gardens
17. Cambridge: Longfellow House
18. Gloucester: Beauport, Sleeper McCann House
19. Gloucester: Hammond Castle
20. New Bedford: Heritage Plantation of Sandwich
21. Pittsfield: Hancock Shaker Village
22. Quincy: Adams National Historic Site
23. Sheffield: Butler Sculpture Park
24. Shelburne Falls: Bridge of Flowers
25. Westford: Butterfly Place

MASSACHUSETTS

The Sedgwick Gardens at Long Hill, Beverly

The Sedgwick Gardens at Long Hill, on Boston's picturesque north shore, offer an inviting collection of garden rooms that wind seamlessly in and out of the surrounding woods. These shrub and tree gardens, accented by herbaceous plants, cannot be seen all at once: you discover them gradually, as you walk up and down the hilly site on grassy paths, from one hidden spot to the next, amid flowering trees, shady groves, and terraced lawns. Children should not miss these "hide-and-seek" delights.

Combining formal and informal design elements, the gardens include ornamental features—a circular ironwork pavilion from France at the edge of a croquet lawn, a Chinese gate from Beijing, an assortment of graceful statuary—set on lawns that seem, literally, to be cut out from the woods. Decorative ponds with lilies and lotus flowers and an impressive array of flowering trees (some quite unusual for this northern climate) are complemented by panoramic views of the countryside.

The gardens of this 114-acre estate were originally designed by Mabel Cabot Sedgwick, a horticulturist and enthusiastic writer on gardens. (She and her husband, Ellery Sedgwick, editor of the *Atlantic Monthly* and an author, had purchased the property in 1916 for a summer home.) To existing pasture, wetlands, and woodlands, she added many plantings: mountain laurel, rhododendron, dramatic weeping Japanese cherries, lilacs, roses, azaleas, and colorful spring bulbs. After her death in 1937, the family further embellished the gardens, with a fine collection of tree peonies, Japanese maples, crab apples, and other flowering examples that today make the gardens brightly colored throughout the growing season. With the collaboration of the Arnold Arboretum in Boston, the plant collection has grown over the years to some 400 species, all carefully identified and labeled.

The well-tended grounds include a Hosta Garden, Grey Garden, Tree Peony Garden, Cut Flower Garden, South Lotus Pool, and Horseshoe Garden, all surrounding the 1921 house, a replica of the Isaac Ball House in Charleston, South Carolina. Inside the house you will find elegantly carved doorways and mantels and cornices, which were salvaged from the Charleston mansion. Now this stately house contains a comprehensive library featuring books on horticulture and garden design, as well as the offices of the Trustees of Reservations, which have owned and managed the estate since 1957.

You can explore the gardens on your own or take a guided tour (available by appointment). Long Hill also offers plant sales and a complete horticultural lecture series.

INFORMATION
Sedgwick Gardens are located at 572 Essex Street in Beverly, about 30 miles northeast of downtown Boston. Telephone: (508) 921-1944. The gardens are open daily from 8 A.M. to sunset. Fee. The gardens can be quite buggy in summer, so bring repellent!

DIRECTIONS
From Boston take Route 128 to Exit 18. Turn left on Route 22 (Essex Street) in the direction of Essex and go for one mile, bearing left at the fork. You'll find a brick gatepost and sign indicating the gardens.

Tower Hill Botanic Garden, Boylston

Tower Hill, one of our newest public gardens, is on the site of what was until recently a dairy farm. And what a view those farmers and cows had! Literally at the crest of a good sized hill, this place has wonderful vistas in all directions—and a truly spectacular one of the Wachusett Reservoir and Mt. Wachusett in the distance. We loved standing on the wind-blown terrace of Tower Hill and looking out toward these sites and what seems an otherwise untouched wilderness. In contrast, just behind us was a blooming hilltop garden of great charm and careful design. The site also includes walking trails through 112 acres of field and forest.

The Worcester County Horticultural Society (the third oldest such group in the nation) acquired the property before it could be sold for development. Adjacent to the circa 1740 farmhouse, they built a reception/education center, terraces, walkways and walls, a trellis, a pergola, nice wooden benches, and a variety of well-planned garden areas. Although the whole complex still has a touch of newness, the landscape has been treated with good taste and a minimum of commercialism. The planners tried hard to maintain what was most distinctive about the site, and it is interesting to see a garden just starting the process of becoming mature and venerable.

The major flower gardens lie just beside the old farmhouse. Here in old-fashioned profusion in the Lawn Garden are the perennial beds, a series of circular brick walkways, and an imposing wooden pergola. Because of the newness of the plantings, some of the woody plantings are still in containers. Blooming in the Lawn Garden when we visited were red weigela, peonies, azaleas, rhododendrons, and gorgeous purple iris—all laid out in irregularly shaped beds on the hilltop. The pergola provides a picturesque boundary to the Lawn Garden, as well as framing the view beyond.

A special feature of Tower Hill's design is its Secret Garden. Just beyond the pergola is a lower level, not seen from the garden above. But from the pergola the visitor can look down (or walk down) and enjoy fragrant seasonal flowers.

And farther down the hill is a pretty orchard featuring 119 varieties of apples. The adjacent Wildlife Garden—once a trash dump!—is now being designed to attract birds and bats and, eventually, butterflies. A little screened-in structure has already been built so that bird-watchers can enjoy the site without mosquitoes annoying them. Other plans for the future include a Physic Garden, a Fragrance Garden, and a Shade and Woodland Garden. Clearly those volunteers who are creating Tower Hill can be kept busy here for years!

A visit to Tower Hill is an opportunity to see a landscape taking shape. Most of our country's public gardens are restorations of one or another historic period; Tower Hill is a present-day creation (though not "contemporary" in artistic terms), and it is good to see a new space preserved in such a pretty way.

INFORMATION
Tower Hill is located at 11 French Drive, in Boylston. It is open from
April through December from 10 A.M. to 5 P.M., Tuesdays through
Sundays and holiday Mondays; January through March from 10 A.M.
to 5 P.M., Tuesdays through Fridays. An excellent trail map and garden guide is available at the Center. Closed major holidays. Picnics
are permitted. Telephone: (508) 869-6111. Fee.

DIRECTIONS
From the Massachusetts Turnpike west of Boston take Route 495
North. Take Exit 25 at Route I-290 going west. Exit at Route 24 north,
which is Church Street. Take Church Street toward Boylston to
French Drive (just before the center of Boylston) and turn right.

Glen Magna, Danvers

"Unexpected" or "picaresque" might best describe these elegant and
romantic gardens on 140 acres north of Boston. Both formal and
informal gardens adjoin the stately house called Glen Magna (built
by the Peabody–Endicott families starting in 1814 and continuing
through many generations). There is a surprise wherever you turn
here, for the landscape is like a spread-out collection of garden
rooms, each with its own style and personality. With its great lawns
and avenues of trees, Glen Magna's landscape has a sense of spaciousness that makes the sudden surprises—a statue here, a gate
there, a walled garden, a delicate fountain—particularly pleasing.

Glen Magna is a big white mansion at the end of a long, gracious
drive (first planted with elms in 1816 and now bordered with pin
oaks). Its story and transformation from working farm and hiding
place for cargo during the War of 1812 to elegant summer estate of
various Endicotts and Peabodys, is dotted with interesting historical
tidbits. (Pick up a flyer and guide at the entrance.) We rarely have
the opportunity to learn about (and see) how a major garden
evolved; perhaps the following thumbnail history will give an idea
of why Glen Magna's landscape is so interesting:

In 1814 and 1815 a noted Alsatian gardener named George
Huessler laid out the first Peabody gardens around a large tulip tree
behind the house on the farm. In 1859 the beautiful access road to
the farm was made private and Glen Magna became an "estate." In
the 1890s the architectural landscape firm of Olmsted, Olmsted and

Eliot designed the barn road and circular drive in their customary elegance. In 1896 the Italianate perennial garden was set out—in keeping with the fashion for Italian antiquity. Thirty-four years later it was bordered with walls and columns and pergola of imported marble. In 1898 an English-style shrubbery garden was designed by Joseph Chamberlain (father of Neville and an Endicott husband). In 1901 the most enchanting addition to the landscape was added, when the marvelous eighteenth-century summer house was purchased from a nearby farm. In 1904 the walled rose garden was built behind the summer house. In between, and ever since these major developments, Glen Magna has continued to change. A new garden was being restored as we visited.

This historic overview, however, does not begin to convey the delight of the estate. We walked (with map in hand) through the gardens, marveling at their spaciousness and variety and sheer beauty. We began with the Peabody Gardens, just south of the house. Here peonies (best in June), lilies, hollyhocks, and other perennials bloom in profusion. The 1815 flower bed design was embellished by Charles Eliot in the 1890s, and it looks just as a New England flower garden should! A gazebo with stone steps leads to Lover's Walk, bordered in arbor vitae. The still beauty will transfix you.

The Italianate perennial garden is one of the high points of the estate. The antique Corinthian marble columns and rustic pergola are absolutely covered with wisteria, and the scent of natural perfumes hangs heavy in the air. A fountain sits in the center of this romantic spot. Against the walls are flower beds filled with high blooms of a great variety of textures and colors.

The shrubbery garden (best in spring) has exotic trees and blooms as well as the more familiar dogwood, azaleas and forsythia. Its *pièce de résistance*—and a "don't miss" for children as well as adults—is its stupendous weeping beech, so large that you can walk under its great cascading branches into a dark world within and be totally hidden from the green and sunlit outside world.

Nearby is the Derby summer house (or tea house), an architectural gem created in 1793. It is now a National Historic Landmark. Built for the Derby Farm nearby by a prominent builder and cabinetmaker named Samuel McIntire, this is a confection of design: a two-story Federal-style building complete with delicate columns, festooned window, arched doorways, and two wonderful rooftop statues. (A flyer just about the Summer House is available with the map at the entrance to Glen Magna.) This elegant addition to the gardens over-looks the entire estate and, right below it, the rose garden.

Designed by Herbert Browne in 1904, the garden of roses is orna-mented by a marble-topped brick wall and two fountains, one of which has a shallow pool filled with lilies—a pretty combination with the delicate roses growing around it in a variety of different sized and shaped flower beds.

These are only the high points of a visit; there are also numerous small buildings, columns here and there, Etruscan vases, statues, and walks through the trees.

INFORMATION

Glen Magna, which also has house tours, is at 57 Forest Street, Danvers. It is open from mid-May through mid-October, 10 A.M. to 4 P.M.. Donations are accepted for access to the grounds. Telephone: (508) 774-9165.

DIRECTIONS

From Route 128 north of Boston, take Route 1 north to Danvers. Take the Center Street exit, turning right off exit. After less than a mile you'll see Ingersoll road and a sign for Glen Magna on your left.

Garden in the Woods, Framingham

If a quiet walk in the woods amid wildflowers and native plants sounds appealing, then head for Garden in the Woods, an environ-mentalist's dream. Located on a choice site of high ridges and deep hollows carved out by glaciers, this natural sanctuary is considered one of the premier wildflower gardens in America. Woodland trails wind through a hilly terrain past ponds and rippling streams, high leafy trees and thick stands of pines, masses of rhododendrons, and vistas of wildflowers, shrubs, and ferns.

This 45-acre living museum, owned and operated by the New England Wild Flower Society, contains more than 1,500 varieties of plants, including rare and endangered species. Three miles of well-tended, meandering trails lead to individual gardens specifically designed for each habitat and carefully placed so as to blend with their surroundings. These naturalistic gardens not only feature the woodland, bog, and rock plantings you would expect to find in a woodsy setting, but also, more surprising, meadow and desert varieties. Additional pleasures include a terraced, shaded nursery and natural wooded areas filled with yet more varieties of wildflowers, from late April through fall. As you wind your way along the paths, you can feel fresh breezes rustling through the trees (this is a cool spot even on a hot summer day). The underbrush beneath the trees has been cleared selectively, so that you can enjoy views, say, from a laurel bend to a ridge of evergreens, and the sun filtering through the trees creates a play of light that adds to the ambiance.

Garden in the Woods was developed in the 1930s by Will C. Curtis and Dick Stiles, who were dedicated conservationists. They found this glacier-molded site ideal for creating a garden of wildflowers and rare and diverse species. In 1931 they purchased the 30-acre tract of land and tirelessly set about clearing paths by hand. Garden in the Woods was formally recognized as a botanical garden in the 1940s; in 1965 it was given to the New England Wild Flower Society, which has operated it to promote conservation of temperate North American plants through education, research, and preservation. (An additional 15 acres have since been acquired.)

The Garden is an active place that offers classes, lectures, workshops, guided tours, plant sales, and exhibits. There is a visitor center, a well equipped museum shop, and library, but the atmosphere is surprisingly low key and noninstitutional. It is a popular place for families and ideal for children to explore.

Before venturing forth you will want to pick up a map and self-guided tour available at the visitor center. The network of paths begins at the nursery area, where plants being propagated for the Garden, as well as for research and sales are on view. Although there is a choice of routes—all well maintained—the main one to take is the Curtis Trail, which leads to the specialized gardens. (You will note that all plants are labeled and that hand-crafted wood benches are to be found here and there for a rest or moment of reflection.)

The first group of gardens on this main itinerary includes a woodland garden, which then opens on to a sunny lily pond and rock garden. The contrast of shaded, canopied vegetation followed by a nice feeling of openness is truly inviting.

The next series of gardens—consisting of simulated habitats and including only North American plants—features a laurel bend, tufa rock garden, acid soil rock garden, sunny bog, pitcher plants, pine barrens, western garden, and meadow garden. You might be surprised to discover cactus (in the western garden) or the endangered plants of the New Jersey Pine Barrens thriving in necessarily sandy soil. The tufa rock garden, recognizable for its porous rock and alpine plants, contains an unusually high number of rare species, and the meadow garden is a special delight from early summer through fall, when native grasses and brightly colored wildflowers are at their peak. There is great variety of habitats—perhaps more than you would expect—and you will be tempted to linger at each site, absorbing it all.

The woodland areas come next, with trails looping through so-called second-growth forest (found in middle and southern New England). Many wildflowers also grow here—depending on the season—such as Virginia bluebells, wood phlox, bloodroot, and trout lilies. In late spring the graceful pink lady slippers make their appearance on the hillside of a trail named after them. Along the Hop Brook Trail are ferns, skunk cabbage, and other water-loving plants. With its gurgling brook, this is always a refreshing spot. The last of these woodland trails—Lost Pond Trail—runs through hilly terrain and, when it is fully developed, will display rare or endangered plants of New England.

As you make your way back to the parking lot—perhaps disregarding the occasional precious sign that congratulates you on having completed this hilly walk, for example—you will no doubt feel you have been on a most unusual and special garden walk.

INFORMATION
Garden in the Woods is located at 180 Hemenway Road in Framingham (west of Boston). It is open April 15 through October 31, Tuesday through Sunday, 9 A.M. to 5 P.M. There is an admission fee. Informal guided walks are conducted on Tuesday through Saturday mornings at 10 A.M. for individuals; group tours are arranged by reservation. For all information, telephone (617) 877-7630.

DIRECTIONS
From Boston or points north or south, take Route 128 to Route 20. After 8 miles take Raymond Road (second left after traffic light in South Sudbury) and go 1.3 miles to Hemenway Road, following signs for the Garden.

From points west, take the Massachusetts Turnpike, exit 12, to Route 9 (east). Go for 2.4 miles to Edgell Road exit. At the top of the exit ramp turn onto Edgell Road and go 2.1 miles to traffic lights. Take a right onto Water Street to Hemenway Road (first left).

Castle Hill, The Richard T. Crane Jr. Memorial Reservation, Ipswich

Here at Castle Hill high above the ocean on the coastal North Shore, with spectacular views in every direction, you will find one of those surprising landscapes of eccentricities created by Americans with a desire for grandeur. Original, idiosyncratic estates like this one make garden visiting intriguing; this landscape was apparently created with sheer bravado—as well as a definite taste for European magnificence of the past. We have not seen anything like the alterations to the natural landscape anywhere in our American garden visits.

We are hardly accustomed to "Roman ruins" in Ipswich, Massachusetts, or even to the vast elegance of the grand European landscape design found here overlooking the untamed salt marshes, tidal marshes, and sand dunes. But this very unlikely juxtaposition of wild natural beauty with manicured elegance makes a visit here special. (However, if you are truly interested in flowers, skip this one . . . there aren't very many.)

First—the views: the surroundings include a 4-mile-long barrier beach and tidal estuaries that are in themselves very beautiful. Inlets and serpentine rivulets run through the marshy wetlands, sun gleaming—a veritable delight for the landscape artist (and over the centuries many of them have come to paint these Essex and Ipswich river estuaries). The vistas are breathtaking and can be enjoyed from many different vantage points around the mansion that sits at the top of Castle Hill.

As to the estate itself, it was part of a massive parcel of land, including an island, purchased in 1909 by a Chicago industrialist named Richard T. Crane, Jr. The original Italianate villa he had built was unsatisfactory and was replaced in 1925 by today's large, brick, Stuart-style 59-room mansion designed by David Adler; it is open for tours. (Some 1,400 acres of the land surrounding the house have been bequeathed to the Trustees of Reservations and the remaining 165 acres are part of the estate. The Reservation is open for hiking and birdwatching, and there is swimming at Crane Beach below.)

Mr. Crane had a taste for historical landscape, ranging from Roman to eighteenth-century English. Unfortunately, most of the garden areas have not been restored and, as noted earlier, there are hardly any flowers. Not far from the house are the remains of formal Italian gardens (minus the flowers) designed by the architectural firm of

Olmstead. And across the way you'll find what was once a formal circular rose garden, designed by Arthur Shurcliff in 1913-14; appearing today somewhat like a Roman amphitheater and pavilion, its columns are decaying and overgrown with vines. In fact, Mr. Crane himself couldn't have asked for a more ancient, ruined-looking setting than what now prevails in these evocative, very romantic, unkempt gardens. But the most eye-catching sight here is surely the full half mile mall-like Grand Allée, a very wide, rolling lawn downhill, which has been landscaped to resemble an undulating, unfurling ribbon to the sea. Also designed by Shurcliff, it is a direct translation of the design for the Cypress Allée at the Boboli Gardens in Florence. There are walking paths among the bordering spruce and English statuary. What a dramatic coastal design this is!

INFORMATION
Castle Hill is at Argilla Road in Ipswich. The house is open for tours on Wednesdays and Thursdays from 10 A.M. to 4 P.M., May 1 through October 31, but the grounds and the reservation are open daily year-round. Telephone: (508) 356-4351.

DIRECTIONS
Ipswich is north of Boston. Take Route 1A north (Exit 20A) from Route 128. Follow Route 1A 8 miles to Ipswich. Turn right onto Route 133 East. Go 1.5 miles to Northgate Road and go left on Northgate 5/10th mile to Argilla Road. Go right on Argilla Road 2.3 miles to gate.

Codman House, Lincoln

Codman House combines the charms of a rustic country estate with elegance and style. Located in rural Lincoln, near Boston, the handsome mansion and 16 acres of rolling terrain provide an inviting setting for a quiet walk. As you stroll this genteel world of flower gardens, venerable stone walls, and captivating vistas, you could easily imagine yourself a country squire of another era, looking over the land.

The historic house sits gracefully atop a knoll overlooking a broad landscape of meadows and hills. In the mideighteenth century, when it was originally built, it was a much simpler structure. John Codman, who bought it in the 1790s, embellished and remodeled it extensively, converting it into a Federal-style mansion. The house underwent further transformations during the nineteenth century;

today, it is an elegant, symmetrical building combining Georgian, Federal, Victorian, and colonial-Revival architectural styles. A showplace of eighteenth- and nineteenth-century furniture and decorative arts, it can be visited by guided tour.

The grounds are an appealing mixture of elegance and informality and can be enjoyed freely; there are no fences or gates surrounding the property. Vast fields, complete with horses, form an idyllic background to the plantings and grassy "ha-ha" in front. Magnificent rhododendrons and specimen trees, including a rare magnolia and tall horse chestnuts, surround the house, their leafy canopies providing welcoming shade. Pathways and rolling lawns lead to greenhouses, a carriage house, and the secluded cottage garden. But the single most enchanting thing to see is the Italian garden, across a meadow behind the house.

Dating from the 1860s, this sunken garden was laid out by Ogden Codman, Jr., designer of some of the grand estates in Newport. (He also was known to have collaborated with Edith Wharton in some of her interior designs.) A charming trellis made of stone columns supports a thick arbor with great clumps of grapes; a lily pond with Italianate statuary is surrounded with urns filled with masses of flowers; and beyond the garden are deep woods, silent except for the sounds of birds. This is, indeed, a peaceful oasis to be savored.

INFORMATION
Codman House is located on Codman Road in Lincoln, about 20 miles west of Boston. The gardens are always open and free of charge. The house is open from June through October 15, Wednesday through Sunday, and can be seen only by guided tour. Fee. For information, telephone: (617) 259-8843.

DIRECTIONS
From Boston, take Route 2 west to Route 126 (Concord Road) south. Take a left at Codman Road and look for a small sign to Codman House.

Cliff Walk, Nantucket

Nantucket is an alluring island. Some 30 miles out at sea, it offers long stretches of unspoiled beaches and rugged coastline, softly colored moors, picturesque villages, and the intriguing legacy of a once thriving whaling industry. As inviting are its many private—mostly English-style gardens surrounding seaside villas and guesthouses—and its weathered shingled cottages often literally dripping with climbing roses. In fact, all kinds of flowers seem to proliferate in this surprisingly temperate climate.

You can visit a number of Nantucket's intimate gardens by taking a garden tour, held annually during the summer. Or you can view them while biking or walking along many of the island's cobblestone streets, country lanes, and rustic paths. One of our favorite of these walks is the so-called "Cliff Walk," which combines spectacular ocean panoramas with a row of individual gardens.

Its name notwithstanding, this walk is not physically daunting or demanding; rather, it is a flat, pleasant stroll along masses of wild rose shrubs and grassy walkways. At all times you can enjoy dramatic views of the ocean on one side of the path and charming garden settings on the other. The walk itself takes about an hour, and you can shorten or lengthen it as you wish.

You start in the village of Siasconset (pronounced simply "Sconset"), behind the houses called "Wade Cottages," where a decidedly unobtrusive grassy path "heralds" the walk. (See below for more detailed directions.) The path actually crosses private lawns and gardens attached to their respective houses. (Don't be concerned about invading anyone's privacy, as you are on a public right-of-way.) The path wends its way from one property to the next, alongside old-fashioned flower beds with many colorful varieties, among them hydrangeas, lilies, and roses (which seem to be ubiquitous). Some gardens are enhanced by elegant private hedges surrounding them or forming arched passageways leading to the next property. You will find considerable variety in plantings and garden design; fortunately, however, everything blends in nicely within a basic Nantucket style. On the ocean side of most properties are long expanses of wooden steps connecting the gardens with the sea. They twist and turn somewhat precariously over the cliffs, adding a certain drama to the scene.

Eventually you come to a small sign indicating the end of Cliff Walk. From here you can retrace your steps, or, for a different view, circle back on one of the little streets on the other side of the path.

INFORMATION
The best time to take this walk is during the summer months, when

most flowers—especially the many varieties of roses, both cultivated and wild—are at their peak. However, the site is equally inviting in early fall, when you are likely to have it mostly to yourself.

DIRECTIONS
In the village of Siasconset, find Main Street. Go past the little sea captains' cottages and turn left onto any of the side streets, which will lead you to Sankaty Road. From there, make your way to the Wade Cottages, walk on the right-hand side of the main house to the back, and turn left (east). Here you will find a small path (sometimes difficult to identify because it blends in so well with its surroundings). You have reached Cliff Walk.

Smith College, Northampton

Few college campuses take their gardens and botanical laboratories as seriously as Smith College. We recommend a stroll through this wonderfully inviting campus and its conservatories—as both students and visitors have been doing for over a hundred years. In fact, from its founding, Smith has been known for its spacious campus, replete with greenhouse with tropical plants, outdoor gardens of all kinds, and intensive botanical courses.

In 1872, in its first handbook, the college listed botany and other physical sciences to which "particular attention will be paid." According to the college, serious study of botanical sciences began almost at once, a landscape firm and botanists were hired, and a building erected for the study of botany. "It is the first time in the history of the world," said the president in 1885, "that a building like this has been devoted to the study of science in a female college."

In the 1890s the landscape firm of Frederick Law Olmsted (of Central Park fame) laid out the huge campus, with instructions to make all of it serve as a botanical garden. Each building was to be surrounded with particular species of trees and plants. The first greenhouse was added in 1894 and soon after more greenhouses, laboratories, a "succulent house," a palm house, and potting sheds. Smith College obviously intended its campus to be both beautiful and educational.

In 1894 a collection of exotic plants was begun—including dogwoods from China, weeping cherry trees from Japan, maples from

Manchuria, and numerous other Asian specialties. More recent renovations have included updated conservatories and ever more trees and plantings as the campus expanded. Despite a harsh New England climate, the college has continually replanted and added to its tree collection. Its greenhouses have been put to extensive use, with cool and warm climates, a fern house, and areas for bedding flowers later to be planted throughout the campus.

In fact, a visit to this site may be happily scheduled during one of the two annual flower shows that feature the changing seasons. In spring, dozens of varieties of bulbs—tulips, hyacinths, narcissi, crocuses, and other bulbs—set with primroses and azaleas are featured. These more common American flowers are interspersed with exotic flowers from around the world. In fall, chrysanthemums—both familiar species and rare ones from China—are the centerpiece. Each festival lasts for a week, during which the campus welcomes thousands of visitors.

Your tour of the gardens should include the Lyman Plant House (the major botanical laboratory site), the Rock Garden area (which includes exotic trees from Asia and a "Ben Franklin tree," the Herbaceous Garden Area (where you'll find more than 40 different species depending on the season, including everything from spiderwort to amaryllis, and cabbages to geraniums and sunflowers), and the Arboretum (with some 100 types of trees).

If you wish to see the delights of this campus in an orderly fashion, you should begin your walk at the Lyman Plant House and its entry at the Head House. (You will find it is open every day of the year, and you may pick up a campus map there.) The staff even welcomes your questions.

Your tour of the facilities will take you to the Warm Temperate House (don't miss the grapefruit-sized lemons and the pale violet water hyacinths). Next, the Stove House features goldfish swimming among such unexpected plants as rice, papyrus, and sugar cane. The Cold House comes next; it is filled with potted plants waiting for the spring, such as primroses and azaleas. Show House (between the Head House and the Cold Storage House) is the site of the college's flower shows. Beyond the Cold Storage House is a corridor of changing displays and camellias.

Beyond a series of laboratories you'll find the Temperate House, divided into four temperate geographic regions: Asia, Australia and New Zealand, Africa, and the Americas. Here your interest in exotic flora will be satisfied; specimens range from eucalyptus from New Zealand to American avocados.

From here you'll descend a ramp to the Palm House, a veritable jungle of rare palms and lush tropical plants, banyans and bamboo, cacao and cinchona. The Fern House—one of the oldest greenhouses on campus—is next; it too features plants from Asia as well as New England, including specimens from the East Indies and Tasmania. The Cold Temperate House will be next; you'll recognize it by the fragrant flowering olive tree.

On the south side of the Plant House is the Succulent House, specializing in Old World desert plants on your left, and New World deserts to your right. (The origins of these plants reads like an atlas index: Madagascar, Peru, the Sahara. . . .)

Beyond these buildings you'll come upon the outdoor Rock Garden, where, in season, you'll find an exhaustively wide collection of dozens of plants of international origin—Swiss Edelweiss, African violets from the Pyrenées—we could go on and on. Here, too, is the famous Ben Franklin tree, now almost extinct except in cultivated gardens. The herbaceous garden that you'll come to next is a kind of outdoor laboratory that traces the evolutionary history of flowering plants. There is a pond here too; needless to say, it contains a large assortment of water plants.

You may now continue your walk across the campus to spot the many trees (all identified) and the beautiful layout of Olmsted's design. (We have not mentioned here the many artworks dotting the campus, but they are an added attraction to this outing. Information about them may be found at the college's Art Museum—also well worth a visit.)

There is a winding path—in springtime bordered by blooming trees and shrubs—and numerous trails that will take you to wonderful regions of mountain laurel in season, a giant redwood tree, and many other lovely places. In fact, you may find a stroll through these wilder regions of the campus your favorite part of the outing. But whatever your taste—for identifying the exotic, or merely for soaking up the perfumed and visual pleasures of the natural world—you'll find it here. But do be sure to pick up a map before you set out!

INFORMATION
The campus of Smith College is open at all times to visitors. Call (413) 584-2700 for information.

DIRECTIONS

From New York, take the Hutchinson River Parkway to the Merritt Parkway to the Wilbur Cross (Route 15) to Route 91 north. Exit at Northhampton and follow signs to Smith College.

Berkshire Botanical Garden, Stockbridge

While many of our best gardens are restorations of grand estate landscapes of the past, here we have something entirely different, and every bit as successful. For the Berkshire Botanical Garden is a homemade—and enchanting—setting that is designed, maintained, and enjoyed by local garden enthusiasts. Its ambiance is free and easy, picturesque, unstructured—just the place to spend a Sunday afternoon. And instead of walking sedately through formal garden paths, here you will be tempted to frolic on the great lawn, poke a stick in the woodsy lily pond, lean down to smell the tangy aromas in the hillside herb garden, or wander around the profuse flower gardens (many of which are planted around and atop the great glacial rocks that are strewn across the landscape).

We found this setting idyllic on a hot summer day. Among the 23 separate planting sites are great trees and brilliant orange, yellow, and pink poppies; rock gardens filled with dianthus and phlox; a rose garden; two greenhouses (one solar); and an herbaceous perennial garden. There are also a primrose garden (a lovely idea), an ornamental organic vegetable garden, and 200 types of daylilies. Everything blooms profusely in season, despite the harsh winters and high winds of the western Massachusetts climate. Part of this garden's charm is its rather "ad hoc" layout—on two sides of a fairly busy roadway. But the main portion is a grandly sweeping hillside. And no one tells the visitor where to walk or how to enjoy these gardens. (This is one of the best of all our sites to take small children.)

The Botanical Garden, as it is now called (for years it was the Berkshire Garden Center), was founded by a few likeminded citizens of the Berkshires in 1934. It was designed to be—and still is—very much an educational center, with numerous programs for children and adults, events, volunteer opportunities, flower shows, and group activities—such as how to create herb vinegar. It is still the only garden center of its kind in a large area.

There is a calendar of blooms, as well as a map identifying the location of each (labeled) plant. The gardens are still very much in process with new areas being added and cultivated all the time. (No doubt if you live in the region, your horticultural help would be appreciated!) If abundant bright colored blooms informally set amid a green Berkshire landscape of giant rocks and venerable trees take your fancy, be sure to visit here.

INFORMATION
The Berkshire Botanical Garden is located on Routes 102 and 183 in Stockbridge. Telephone: (413) 298-3926. It is open daily from 10 A.M. to 5 P.M. from May through October. Fee. There are many programs open to the public.

DIRECTIONS
Stockbridge is reached from the Massachusetts Turnpike (I-90) by exiting at Lee (if coming from the east) or at West Stockbridge (from the west). From Lee take Route 102 west through Stockbridge to the intersection with Route 183. From West Stockbridge take Route 102 east. From Route 7 at Great Barrington, go to Stockbridge and turn left on Route 102.

Chesterwood, Stockbridge

The lovely region of Western Massachusetts known as "The Berkshires" is endowed with charming vistas, mountains, rivers, lakes, and little New England villages. The area has long attracted seekers of unspoiled natural beauty, including many artists and writers.

Daniel Chester French, the famed neoclassical sculptor of monumental works, came to establish a summer home, studio and gardens in the shadow of Monument Mountain near Stockbridge. When you visit Chesterwood, his remarkable country estate, you will come away feeling that he could not have chosen a more idyllic spot. He was an artist who really knew how to live.

French became the nation's leading classical sculptor early in this century. At the height of his career, internationally known and able to live in grand style, French decided to create a perfect working and living environment for himself and his family in the country (although he continued to maintain a winter studio in New York).

He and his wife first saw the rustic farm that was to become Chesterwood while on a horse-drawn carriage trip through the Housatonic River Valley in 1896.

Beautifully situated on a rural road, the 150-acre property—now a museum operated by the National Trust for Historic Preservation—would become the Frenches' summer home for the next thirty-three years. It was at Chesterwood—amid the enchantment of romantic gardens, lawns, and woodlands—that French was inspired to create many of his most important works, including the *Lincoln Memorial*, the *Minute Man* for Concord, Massachusetts, and the *Alma Mater* for Columbia University.

Chesterwood itself became a lifelong project for the sculptor. Carefully he fashioned the estate to provide an ideal ambiance for his creative needs, as well as for the many brilliant social gatherings he was fond of hosting for his prominent neighbors and friends. (Edith Wharton came regularly from her nearby estate.) The main house and studio, overlooking majestic Monument Mountain, were designed by his architect friend Henry Bacon; but it was French himself who laid out the gardens and woodland walks.

To him, gardens were like sculptures: a basic design had to be drawn up in order for them to work as art. He planned a central courtyard, an Italianate garden with a graceful fountain, and English flower gardens. Beyond the formal areas he arranged a network of paths leading into and through the hemlock forest, where the walker could enjoy peaceful views. He enjoyed creating aesthetic effects that influenced the quality of daily life. For example, he built a berm (an artificial little hill) abutting the road leading to the house; in that way one could not see the wheels of approaching carriages, which would appear to be "floating" by.

French spent a great deal of time in his gardens, from which he derived much of his inspiration. He regularly studied the effects of light and shadow on sculptures that were destined to be out of doors. He found an ingenious solution to moving these massive works from his studio to the outside. He would put these pieces onto a revolving modeling table set on a short railroad track and roll them out into the sunlight, where he could test them in the natural light. You can still see this unusual contraption when you visit the studio.

French and his wife lived and thrived at Chesterwood with their daughter, Margaret Cresson French, also a sculptor. In 1969 the property was donated to the National Trust and converted into the museum you see today.

When you arrive at Chesterwood you are struck by the beauty of the site: with spectacular mountain views on all sides, it is little wonder that French and his family wanted to be here. The house and landscaping are tasteful and harmonious in every sense; there is nothing pretentious or ostentatious about this estate. As the artist once remarked, "I live here six months of the year—in heaven. The other six months I live, well, in New York." A possibly discordant note (and a recent one) is an ongoing modern sculpture exhibit, which is on view on a rotating basis throughout the grounds (including the woods). The pieces we saw had nothing to do with French, his style, or his era and were in striking contrast to the gracious nineteenth-century setting.

In order to visit the house and studio you must take an organized tour—about 45 minutes of fairly detailed information (more than you might want to hear), including a great deal about the social life of the French family and mores of the time. However, you are free to roam the gardens and woods at will, and can do so at no cost. After you have purchased your tickets for the house and studio, you will probably be directed to the barn to begin the tour. This rustic building, originally part of the working farm that French purchased, has been remodeled into an exhibition gallery. You can wander about and look at the vintage photographs and works by Margaret French Cresson, Augustus Saint-Gaudens, and others.

Aside from the gardens, the studio visit is by far the most satisfying part of the tour. The beautifully designed 22-foot-high structure provided the perfect airy and spacious working environment. It is kept much as it was during French's time, with material, notebooks, tools, and sketches on view. You'll see plaster cast models and preliminary sculptures of some of his most important works, notably his seated Lincoln (of which there are several versions) and his graceful Andromeda. You'll also see the massive 30-foot double doors that were constructed to accommodate French's many large works; they were built when French first made his impressive equestrian statue of George Washington, now located in the Place d'Iena in Paris. In back of the studio is a wide veranda (which he called a "piazza") with wisteria vines and fine views and the rail tracks on which his massive sculptures rolled away. The 30-room colonial revival house (built in 1900) is nearby. Its gracious rooms, wide hallways, and appealing surroundings are what you would expect from a man of French's refined tastes. Surrounding the house are the charming gardens that French carefully planned and so enjoyed. Take a stroll in them and beyond, on the pine-laden woodsy paths in the forest.

INFORMATION

Chesterwood is open May through October 31, from 10 A.M. to 5 P.M. We recommend that you phone first to check on any schedule changes. Telephone: (413) 298-3579. There is a modest entrance fee.

DIRECTIONS

Chesterwood is about 2 miles west of Stockbridge. From Boston take I-90 (the Massachusetts Turnpike), to Exit B3 to Route 22; go about 1 mile to Route 102 to Stockbridge. Take Route 102 west to the junction with Route 183. Turn left onto 183 for 1 mile to a fork in the road. Turn right onto a blacktop road, travel a few yards, and turn left. Continue 1/2 mile to Chesterwood.

Naumkeag, Stockbridge

Naumkeag—the name is Indian for "Haven of Peace"—is a must for those who have a yen for unusual landscape design, in addition to gardens. For here, surrounding a beautiful Victorian manor designed by Stanford White, are fanciful gardens arranged with real panache. Begun in the 1920s, they represent a bold departure from the ornate designs of the time, and today still appear as fresh and original as ever.

Magnificently situated in the Berkshire hills, with vistas over woodlands and mountains, Naumkeag's gardens are full of surprises. Instead of traditional flower beds and borders and paths, the plantings here are set off by a collection of eclectic features—from a painted Chinese pagoda, to brilliantly colored Venetian-like wooden pillars, to serpentine gravel patterns amid rose beds, to the extraordinary "Blue Steps," which alone are worth the trip to the site.

The creative force behind Naumkeag's gardens was Fletcher Steele, a master landscape architect who was a prime mover in the new, modern orientation in garden design just then being introduced. According to Steele, landscape architecture was a fine art, like painting or music—in fact, he saw himself as a landscape sculptor more than anything else. Reacting against the still prevalent nineteenth-century Beaux Arts formalism, he advocated a style that drew its inspirations from the natural landscape, as well as from the artistic movement of the time, abstract modernism. Indeed his gardens at Naumkeag are abstract landscapes created from the reworking of the land. When Miss Mabel Choate inherited Naumkeag in 1926 from her father, Joseph Hodges Choate (a prominent lawyer and diplomat who had built the house in the 1890s as an idyllic summer retreat), she was impatient to redo its Victorian gardens. (Aside from aesthetic considerations, the original flower gardens required more maintenance than she thought appropriate.) She met the already well established Steele in 1926, and a fruitful collaboration between them ensued, lasting through the 1950s. (They were an unlikely pair: she, willful and rooted in her New England ways; he, a sophisticated world traveler.)

After carefully studying the site, Steele concluded that "Neither the client nor her Victorian house, neither Bear Mountain nor the hillside itself wanted a so-called naturalistic affair with a path meandering downhill. A range of terraces in the Italian Garden manner was unthinkable . . . Italian gardens do not fit Victorian wood houses. The only resource was to create an abstract form in the manner of modern sculpture, with swinging curves and slopes which would aim to make their impression directly, without calling on the help of associated ideas, whether in nature or art."

Steele did not completely dismantle the old gardens, for he felt that "the old spirit should be followed . . . the 'feeling' of Victorian elaboration must be continued." True, he moved mounds of earth in places to repeat the curves of the mountain's skyline and enhance the setting, and he created entirely new schemes, but he also rearranged and worked around existing plantings.

Today you can walk up and down and around these wonderful gardens and grassy lawns on your own, using the walking guide available at the entrance, or go on a guided tour of house and garden. On the south side of the mansion is Steele's first creation, the Afternoon Garden, where Miss Choate would take her tea overlooking the mountains. (It seems she repeatedly took Steele to task about the uncomfortable metal chairs he had placed there, but her complaints fell on deaf ears; he considered the chairs pieces of the sculpture to be admired, rather than used.) Screening this theatrical garden are ropes festooned with clematis and Virginia creeper that hang between boldly carved and painted oak posts. A large bronze sculpture of a boy with a heron overlooks four small fountains and a swirling box hedge parterre.

A series of grass terraces with panoramic views leads from one site to the next. You'll see a magnificent ancient great white oak, the largest tree on the estate, on the Oak Lawn below a steep hillside—apparently a favorite picnic site of the Choates; a "Rond Point," enclosed by carefully clipped hedges, where theatrical skits took place; a shady, mossy Linden Walk, inspired by the romantic allées Miss Choate saw in Germany; a tree peony terrace with dozens of these glorious plants featuring giant blossoms in the prettiest warm shades; an arbor vitae walk; and a formal allée of clipped arbor vitae in symmetrical precision, maintained from the original gardens. There is a walled Chinese Garden (Steele's last effort at Naumkeag), including a Chinese-style temple with a brilliant blue tile roof circled by a group of ginko trees, mossy rocks and Buddhas, lions, and other objects collected by Miss Choate in her travels; it is entered through a traditional circular moon gate within a curving brick and stone wall, which is in itself a work of art. Not unexpectedly, there is a rose garden too, but this is hardly your traditional example. View it from a railed terrace above, where its serpentine shapes appear before you like an abstract painting, its delicate arabesques of gravel winding through 16 beds of floribunda roses.

The most innovative feature at Naumkeag, the famous Blue Steps, came about for the most practical of reasons. Because the wooded slope from the Afternoon Garden to Miss Choate's kitchen garden and greenhouses was too steep for her to negotiate with ease, she told Steele "he must make me some steps that would be both convenient and easy . . ." As she later said, "little did I realize what I was in for." The extraordinary design features a descending series of delicate concrete arches, with a double flight of cement steps painted the same blue as the posts in the Afternoon Garden; water descends in a channel through them, trickling down from a water tunnel connecting the fountains of the Afternoon Garden above. Surrounding the steps on each side is a thick stand of white birches, reflecting the same brilliant white as the sweeping painted railing of the steps. To appreciate this truly avant-garde design, you must look up from the terrace below the steps.

Naumkeag, which was bequeathed to the Trustees of Reservations after Miss Choate's death in 1958, remains a tribute to the collaborative efforts of a great landscape designer and a very determined gardener. Try to visit on a weekday, when you are more likely to experience the same peace and quiet Miss Choate did, many years ago.

INFORMATION
Naumkeag is located on Prospect Hill Road in Stockbridge. Telephone: (413) 298-3239. The house and gardens are open daily from Memorial Day weekend through Columbus Day, from 10 A.M. to 5 P.M.. Entrance fee. Tours to the house with an introduction to the gardens are offered, or you can walk through the gardens at will, using the complimentary map.

DIRECTIONS
From Boston, take I-90 (the Massachusetts Turnpike) to Exit B3, to Route 22; go about 1 mile to Route 102 to Stockbridge. From the intersections of Routes 7 and 102 (at the Red Lion Inn) take Pine Street north; bear left on Prospect Hill. You will find Naumkeag's gate about 1/2 mile on the left.

The Vale: The Lyman Estate, Waltham

We often associate with England the very idea of the eighteenth- and early ninteenth-century American country estate with its sweeping expanse of lawns, serpentine paths, and profusion of flower gardens. The Vale, the estate of Theodore Lyman not far from Boston, was designed (and has been restored) in the English naturalistic style. This is a beautiful 30-acre site with a fine house, terrific greenhouses, and a delectable garden, and we found it to be one of the most appealing such places we have seen.

Built in 1793 by Lyman, a wealthy Boston merchant with a taste for horticulture, The Vale was designed to be a self-sufficient country estate for summer use. The fine, very large white manor house was designed by Samuel McIntire and is open to the public (by appointment). The magnificent property (once 450 acres) included rolling farm fields, an ornamental pond, woodlands, a deer park, naturalistic flower gardens, and five greenhouses. (One of the greenhouses here is said to be one of the oldest standing greenhouses in the nation; it was once heated with a Dutch stove.) The property— diminished in size but still beautiful and in the same family's hands—was given to the Society for the Preservation of New England Antiquities in 1952. It is also a National Historic Landmark.

The landscape design of The Vale emphasizes the informal, the pleasingly irregular and free-form patterns of the naturalistic style. Winding paths and nearby woods (celebrating "The American Wilderness") are part of the design. There are few rectangular flower beds here, nor will you find topiary or boxwood hedges emphasizing long, straight lines. Instead the focal point of the flower gardens near the mansion is a wonderful long, high, curving brick wall that provides the backdrop to a spectacular display of flowers. This huge cultivated area for flowers has been restored in a similarly informal way, with what is know as "an English garden"; it is without doubt among the most luscious we have seen.

Here you'll find wisteria vines and roses forming a backdrop on the brick wall, and huge clumps of both flowering shrubs and perennial blooms harmoniously interspersed with one another. There is hardly a bit of space between these plantings, giving the impression of an overgrown—but perfectly kept—garden. Small fruit trees, peonies and iris, glorious shades of lavender and violet are mingled with lamb's ears with their pale gray-green leaves and the delicate pinks and feathery white of flowering shrubs. Two small summer houses complement the wall and its garden; the elegant templelike structure at the end of the wall originally was part of the front entrance of the house.

In keeping with the serpentine design of this flower bed is a display of rhododendrons across the lawn that is allowed to grow into an informal wall of its own. Colors of the flowers range from the deepest rose to bright orange.

A path will take you to the greenhouses. Lyman had a passion for growing exotic plants. He raised pineapples, bananas, and oranges. The Grape House, with its impeccably lineaged vines, includes cuttings from Germany and Hampton Court, England. American horticulturists were wild about camellias, first brought from Asia to the West in 1797. You can visit the Camellia House built in 1820; it is particularly lovely in late winter. One greenhouse is used to provide flowers for the house and for sale. If you like greenhouses with their warm, perfumed profusion of exotic plants, you will certainly like these examples.

A visit to this estate provides a variety of garden experiences; we found it to be quiet and uncrowded (we were there during the week) and thoroughly enjoyable whether you are in the greenhouses, walking across the great lawns or relishing the brilliant colors and shapes of the flowers by the wall.

INFORMATION
The Lyman Estate is at 185 Lyman Street in Waltham. The grounds of the Lyman Estate are open from 9 A.M. to 5 P.M.; the greenhouses are open Monday through Saturday from 9 A.M. to 4 P.M. Tours are available and the house is also open for group tours by appointment. Telephone: (617) 891-1985.

DIRECTIONS
Waltham is north of Boston. From U.S. 20 (which is North Beacon Street and then Main Street) turn on Lyman Street and follow signs to corner of Beaver Street.

Stanley Park, Westfield

Stanley Park is a choice example of what a public park can be with imagination and care: not only is this 275-acre site at the foothills of the Berkshires unusually well designed, but it is impeccably maintained—something of a rarity these days. Its prize gardens, wildlife sanctuary, reflecting ponds, brooks, delicate waterfalls, arboretum, wooded trails, and recreation fields provide a serene environment for walkers, gardeners, nature lovers, and families out for a picnic amid the greenery. The park even serves as a cultural resource in the community, offering summer concerts (including carillon performances from its one-of-a-kind Carillon Tower), arts festivals, and garden workshops. Definitely not your standard park fare.

For us, Stanley Park was particularly inviting as a landscape. Our first impression, as we walked down its shady slopes (the terrain here is mildly hilly), was of being on a movie set, with one picture-perfect scene flowing into the next—and with the sounds of rippling, cascading, and rushing water adding to the bucolic ambiance. One tableau reminded us of a Swiss landscape, complete with hillside, lovely covered bridge, pristine pond, and gliding swans and ducks. Actually a part of the so-called Colonial Pond Area, it became more recognizable as the early American setting it's supposed to represent, once the delightful herb garden and orchard, working mill and waterwheel, old town meeting house, carriage shed, and blacksmith shop all came in view. (Children will be particularly intrigued by the blacksmith shop, which has an operating forge, bellows, and anvil.)

Fortunately, these historic replicas—unlike many we have seen—are tasteful, and not in the least overdone.

A small path alongside a canal leads to the Japanese garden, a particularly graceful interpretation of this style. Here the requisite tea house is surrounded by flowering azaleas and rhododendrons (quite a sight in May and June), arched bridges, stone statuary, and rock gardens with delicate miniature evergreens complete the scene.

You can explore the park's many garden pleasures on your own, as you meander along grassy paths and stone walkways from one to the next: among them, the rhododendron display garden (hundreds of species), herb and perennial display gardens (culinary, medicinal, fragrant varieties), the American Wildflower Society Display Garden (at its most glorious in May and June), and the 5-acre arboretum.

But best of all is the lovely rose garden. Situated alongside the Carillon Tower, it is formally known as the All American Rose Selection, Inc. Public Rose Garden, and has won prestigious awards. You can walk amid the 2,500 rose bushes (at least 50 varieties), taking in, too, the magnificent annual and perennial beds nearby. These are carefully laid out in luscious, colorful patterns and complement the rose garden's delicacy. Both are at their height from June to September.

Stanley Park was the creation of Frank Stanley Beveridge, a forward-thinking entrepreneur and public-spirited individual whose boyhood dream apparently was to build such a public place for everyone's pleasure. Luckily his vision became reality, and in 1949 the park became a charitable corporation to ensure its upkeep for future generations.

We were told that some 250,000 visitors enjoy these vast grounds annually, something that would no doubt please Mr. Beveridge. But while we were there (granted, on a week day), we saw few others and had the place almost to ourselves—which pleased us!

INFORMATION
Stanley Park is at 400 Western Avenue, Westfield, Telephone: (413) 568-9312. The park is open from Mother's Day through Columbus Day weekend, from 8 A.M. to dusk (some of the recreational facilities are open year-round). All facilities and programs are free (except some of the summer concerts). Accessible to disabled people.

DIRECTIONS
Westfield is a few miles south of Springfield. From the Massachusetts Turnpike (I-90) take Exit 3 into Westfield; at the rotary take Court Street west, which becomes Western Avenue. The park is located at the intersection of Kensington (make a left).

And in Addition . . .

Boston: Isabella Stewart Gardner Museum
280 The Fenway. Telephone: (617) 566-1401.
A visit to this venerable museum is a treat for those interested both in fine art and enclosed gardens. The elegant Venetian-style palazzo features an exceptional art collection known the world over. In the center is a truly magnificent courtyard with rare and beautiful plants. This is the exquisite setting for many year-round chamber music concerts and special garden displays. Open Tuesday through Sunday, 11 A.M. to 5 P.M. Fee.

Boston Area: Arnold Arboretum
The Arborway, Jamaica Plain. Telephone: (617) 524-1717.
This important and famous 265-acre arboretum was founded in 1872. Administered by Harvard University, it is a true learning center with plants from all over the world, research greenhouses, and thousands of glorious varieties of trees and shrubs. A walk here, particularly in May and June, is most appealing. There are fine collections of dwarf conifers and bonsai and a delightful Chinese Walk with worldwide plants. Open daily, all day, but check on greenhouse hours.

Byfield: Newbury Perennial Gardens
65 Orchard Street. Telephone: (508) 462-1144
There are 20 display gardens across a large estate here as well as a commercial nursery business. The pretty rolling green terrain was once a "ragged hayfield." The owner has transformed it into a series of elegant gardens focusing on color and texture that fit nicely into the landscape behind his house. There are a variety of lovely (and some very unusual) types of gardens here: a weeping garden; a spectacular shrub border garden that blooms throughout the season and is filled with larger perennials and evergreens; a flame garden featuring yellow, orange, and red blooms near a pond with white

swans; a white garden; an island garden that peaks in June with lupine, peonies, and poppies; a heather garden in delicious shades of gray-greens, yellows, and oranges; hosta and daylily collections; a bog garden; and a newly constructed grotto garden—these are just a few of the interesting sights here.

You will enjoy walking around these thematic plantings, and for any visiting gardener who lives in a fairly cold northern clime like this one in northern Massachusetts, this is a good place to come and see what can be accomplished. (For example, there is a type of azalea that deer do not touch!) You can pick up a map that lets you go around the gardens by yourself, or you can request (in advance) a tour from the welcoming and knowledgeable owner. Fee.

Cambridge: Longfellow House

105 Brattle Street. Telephone: (617) 876-4491

This national historic site, graciously set on one of the most distinguished and beautiful streets in Cambridge, is where Longfellow lived with his family from 1837 until his death in 1882. The elegant house overlooks terraced lawns, brick walkways, large shade trees, lilac bushes, and a delightful enclosed formal garden designed by the poet himself.

You can visit the house and learn about its long history and memorabilia. It was built in 1759 for John Vassall, a young Tory, and later served as George Washington's headquarters. Longfellow first lived here as a lodger, until his future father-in-law gave the house as a wedding gift to the young couple.

The lovely, peaceful grounds can be enjoyed at will or by guided tour. In 1904, Martha Brookes Hutcheson enhanced the original Longfellow garden design with the assistance of the oldest daughter, Alice Longfellow. You enter it through a lattice fence behind the house, walking along winding gravel paths. Colorful arabesque-shaped flower beds of iris, peonies, tulips, and other perennials form decorative patterns within clipped low boxwood hedges. Square corner beds of phlox, marguerites, and heliotrope define the outside edges of the garden. In the center is a decorative sundial. Beyond this charming garden is a wide lawn that features specimen trees. You won't find the famous chestnut tree immortalized by Longfellow's verse—it was cut down long ago (and made into a chair that you can see in the library within) and, in fact, was not precisely here to begin with—but there are other trees that are equally spreading, nonetheless.

The house is open seasonally Wednesday through Sunday from 10:00 A.M. to 4:30 P.M.; there are several tours daily. The gardens are open year-round. There is an admission fee for the house, but no fee for the gardens.

Gloucester: Beauport (Sleeper McCann House)
75 Eastern Point Boulevard. Telephone: (508) 283-0800.
This spectacularly set 40-room house (filled with early American antiques and oddities) can truly be called "waterside." It is situated right on the edge of Gloucester Harbor, overlooking the town, the docks, the boats, and the sea. Beauport was constructed beginning in 1907 (and continuing for 27 years) by a prominent interior designer and collector named Henry Davis Sleeper. (Among his clients were such Hollywood luminaries as Joan Crawford and Frederic March; he also built a house for Henry Francis du Pont, whose Winterthur in Delaware (see page 48) was related in design.) He had a taste for the intimate and cozy rather than the grand and palatial. The style of the house—with dormers, turrets, cozy interiors and colored glass in the windows—was much admired in its day, and a similar intimate taste prevails in the gardens. Surprisingly green for a beachfront setting such as this, the garden's small spaces are also designed as a series of intimate rooms. These "rooms" nestle into each level of a central area created by the different wings of the house and they are divided by little grassy paths and stone steps. Despite the reconstruction effort now under way that will return Beaufort to its early twentieth-century charm, the site is already very pretty in a secret garden style.

Gloucester: Hammond Castle
Hesperus Avenue. Telephone: (508) 283-2080.
Hammond Castle evokes the romance of a distant past, resembling a medieval fortress complete with massive stone towers, drawbridge, and flying buttresses. Spectacularly set atop the rocky cliffs of the Atlantic coastline, it is a vision from a Gothic tale. Its gardens are unlike those of most other 1920s estates. To reach the castle, you descend along a fairly steep slope of stone walls and boulders surrounded with green and colorful plantings. This is not a traditional rock garden of low and delicate alpine plants carefully nestled amid the rockery: here the scene is more dramatic, befitting the site. Waving about in the ocean breezes are tall flowers (mostly perennials) and willowy greens, set between the huge stones. The combi-

nation of sea air, brilliant blossoms, and looming castle with its magnificent ocean views is irresistible.

John Hays Hammond, Jr., a prolific inventor and eccentric, built his home between 1926 and 1929. A music lover (in addition to many other things), he installed in the cavernous Great Hall an extraordinary organ of 8,000 pipes. You can visit the castle today (by guided tour) and marvel at this amazing instrument, along with the many other eclectic furnishings found throughout. But, mainly, walk around these incredible (though not extensive) grounds and enjoy picturesque views through Gothic arches. As you might expect, this is a prime spot for weddings and other functions. Open daily, except during functions (call first). There is an entrance fee to visit the castle, but none for the gardens.

New Bedford: Heritage Plantation of Sandwich
Grove and Pine streets. Telephone: (508) 888-3300.
If rhododendrons appeal to you, visit this 76-acre estate which claims the largest collection of a variety called Dexter Hybrid rhododendrons—some 35,000 strong. In addition you will find many other shrubs and trees that will make a trip here (via jitney bus, if you like) worthwhile. Open daily, 10 A.M. to 5 P.M. Fee.

Pittsfield: Hancock Shaker Village
Junction of Routes 20 and 41 in Pittsfield. Telephone: (413) 443-0188.
This historic eighteenth- and nineteenth-century Shaker community has fine buildings and extensive gardens, including a vast flower garden, herb garden, and vegetable gardens.

Quincy: Adams National Historic Site
135 Adams Street. Telephone: (617) 773-1177.
This 1731 house and garden have been home to generations of the accomplished and illustrious Adams family. The gardens combine traditional flower beds that surround elegant walkways with fine trees and plants, some quite old. You can visit the gardens on your own, but must take a guided tour to see the house. Open mid-April through mid-November. Fee.

Sheffield: Butler Sculpture Park
Shunpike Road. Telephone: (413) 229-8924.
This hilltop sculpture park with panoramic views of the Berkshires

is the home of sculptor Robert Butler. His park contains his contemporary, abstract works. Call for hours.

Shelburne Falls: Bridge of Flowers
Water Street. Telephone: (413) 625-2143.
This one-time arched trolley bridge has been converted into a 400-foot-long flowering walkway, with luxuriant blooms all along the perimeters and even hanging down the sides—a very pretty sight to see.

Westford: Butterfly Place
120 Tyngsboro Road. Telephone: (508) 392-0955.
This is a glass building featuring flowers that attract hundreds of living butterflies—a beautiful experience, and educational, too.

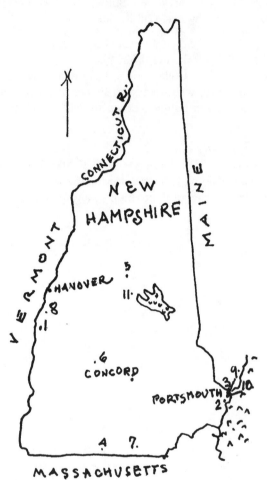

NEW HAMPSHIRE GARDENWALKS

1. Cornish: Aspet, Home and Garden of Augustus Saint-Gaudens
2. North Hampton: Fuller Gardens
3. Portsmouth: Moffatt–Ladd House and Garden

And in Addition . . .
4. Fitzwilliam: Rhododendron State Park

5. Kinsman Notch: Lost River Nature Garden
6. Newbury: The Fells
7. New Ipswich: Barrett House
8. Plainfield: Plainfield Wildflower Sanctuary
9. Portsmouth: Prescott Park
10. Portsmouth: Strawbery Banke
11. Rumney: Mr. Jacquith's Garden

NEW HAMPSHIRE

Aspet: Home and Garden of Augustus Saint-Gaudens, Cornish

If your idea of the nineteenth-century artist living in the depth of a city in a dreadful Bohemian garret needs changing, visit the home and garden of Augustus Saint-Gaudens. Now a National Historic site complete with park rangers and one of the most beautiful landscapes imaginable, Aspet, the artist's summer place and eventual year-round home, is a rarely visited treasure. You may come away thinking that life as one of America's most famous sculptors must have been heavenly.

The National Park Service has made this memorial to Saint-Gaudens an elegant, tasteful, and fascinating place to visit. Though Saint-Gaudens' own experiences there were not so universally glamorous and moneyed as they now appear (including terminal illness and a disastrous studio fire), this estate shows off his art and architecture and garden landscape in a noble fashion. From the distant vistas of fields and mountains, to the charmingly columned and arbored studios, to the delicately set sculptures along garden paths, this is how we would like to imagine an illustrious artist's estate.

The site of Aspet is in rural Cornish, New Hampshire, just beyond the longest covered bridge in the nation. It crosses the Connecticut River from Vermont at Windsor. Nearby, a perfectly kept roadway into the deep woods takes you to Aspet. It was here that the artist discovered an old New England inn set amid a poetic, wild landscape with ravines, waterfall, glorious vistas, and romantic light.

The house and surroundings seemed to us wonderfully remote, like some Shangri-La amid the picturesque New England countryside. The 150-acre property includes the sculptor's home (the original inn), several studios, formal gardens, a deep, wooded ravine, and enough informal garden areas, fields, and lawns to satisfy even a walker without a taste for sculpture. A striking view of nearby Mount Ascutney adds to the vista. Though the art is, of course, the major attraction of Aspet, the gardens are strikingly lovely, creating an aesthetic and inviting surrounding for outdoor sculpture.

Augustus Saint-Gaudens was one of America's premier artists and probably its most beloved nineteenth-century sculptor. His naturalistic approach contrasted with the smooth, controlled surfaces and contours of neoclassical sculpture that had been in vogue. By 1881 he had become an acknowledged leader of American sculptors in an era in which the memorial statue was a necessity in every city square. Other artists joined him in rejecting academicism, which sought to free both painting and sculpture from academic and banal styles of portraiture.

His commemorative statues of famous people (including Abraham Lincoln) were in great demand and are familiar images to us today. But perhaps his best known and most beloved work—beautifully displayed at Aspet—was his venture into a more emotional style: his *Adams Memorial*. This grieving, hooded figure was arguably the most original and haunting sculpture yet achieved by an American.

Saint-Gaudens became a widely respected teacher and leader of other artists. In 1885 after he bought the old staging inn that was to become Aspet, Cornish became the center of an artists' colony that grew up about him. (Legend has it that a friend persuaded him to go to New England in the summertime; he was then at work on an important Lincoln portrait and was told that he would find among the natives of New Hampshire many "Lincoln-shaped" men to use for models.) Aspet became a center both for sculptors and other creative people; Saint-Gaudens' salon attracted poets, novelists, journalists, and actors. Summer visitors and art colony residents were noted in the fields of architecture, landscape, and garden design.

Among them were Charles Platt, who wrote the first treatise in America on Italianate gardens; the illustrator Maxfield Parrish, whose paintings appeared in Edith Wharton's 1904 publication called *Italian Villas and Their Gardens*; architects Stanford White and George Babb; and Saint-Gaudens' own niece, Rose Standish Nichols, a designer of gardens.

It was Babb (an associate of Stanford White) who designed the columned veranda of the house and turned the old hay barn into the delightful Italianate Little Studio. In fact, a classical style reminiscent of ancient Roman villas pervades many of the architectural and garden sites of Aspet: there are colonnades and porticoes, picturesque gates and vine-covered pergolas, as well as formally designed plantings.

Saint-Gaudens took a personal interest in the design of the gardens: he had studied French and Italian landscape design for years and favored a strong architectural layout for the formal gardens. He planted hemlock and pine hedges to enclose each area, creating what might be termed "garden rooms." Within each such area, he laid out terraces and flower beds, geometrically designed paths, central fountains, and statues, of course. There are statues everywhere. Small sculptured heads appear above the boxwood here and there. There are pools, fountains that shoot jets of water through the mouths of fish and turtles (designed by the sculptor), and marble benches for the proper contemplation of it all. (The white bench decorated with figures of Pan playing his pipes is, however, the work of Augustus's brother Louis, also a sculptor of note.) These Italianate gardens are filled with "old-fashioned" perennials and colorful annuals; the overall effect is of a romantic profusion of flowers amid very orderly settings.

Saint-Gaudens also liked games and sports. There is a lawn bowling green in the middle of one garden area, and there are bridle paths, a toboggan run, a swimming hole, and numerous hiking trails on the property. By combining his love of art, sport, formal gardens, and natural scenery, the sculptor sought at Aspet to create a total environment that reflected his view of the best of the American spirit. With its references to classical as well as romantic styles, Saint-Gaudens' Aspet represented a particularly nineteenth-century American vision.

The gardens are on three levels. You may walk around them informally (though the house visit requires a tour). From the upper level (where you exit from the veranda of the house) you take a small flight of brick steps, passing through a trellised pergola, along a path edged with carefully trimmed giant yew spheres.

You arrive at the middle terrace, which contains formal flower beds—outlined in century-old hedges of clipped Eastern white pine. These densely blooming, cottage-style gardens have a particularly bright and tall feeling: hollyhocks, glads, daylilies, snap dragons, bachelor buttons, iris—among other old-fashioned favorites—are gaily massed together. In the center is a delicate statue of Hermes, rising above the waving flowers.

On the lower level, you'll find the Little Studio, a delightful Italianate classical structure whose brilliant white columns are ornamented with clinging vines that contrast with a rose-red wall ("Pompeiian red") and a frieze that copies the Parthenon. (Don't miss seeing the inside of this studio.) Adjoining the Little Studio is one of the most enchanting gardens of all: another garden room bordered by startling white birches and pine hedges. The rectangular area is planted with perennials and divided by pathways, including one that leads to a white painted wooden bench at the end. Its carvings represent the four seasons. Also in this very charming spot is a delicate water garden, with a reflecting pool featuring a classical statue of Pan playing his pipes and small sculpted fish shooting gentle jets of water through their mouths.

On leaving this area, follow the path toward the *Adams Memorial*, in its own garden. Arguably Saint-Gaudens' most stunning work, the shrouded, seated figure was commissioned by Henry Adams on the death of his wife in 1885. Not a portrait, but a striking symbol of mourning, the Adams Memorial brought American sculpture to a new depth of emotion, anticipating expressionism by many years. The statue is surrounded by an enclosing and stately square-cut hedge and elegant plantings.

Through the hedgerow (peopled by small marble heads peeking above the shrubbery) and along the birch-lined pathway, you'll see the bowling green, the carriage barn, and several well-known sculptures (including a portrait bust of Abraham Lincoln and the Shaw Memorial to Massachusetts' black regiment in the Civil War). The sun-dappled garden is surrounded by a white grape arbor.

Across the open lawn you'll find the Gallery, a comparatively modern building housing some of the artist's major sculpture both indoors (a full-length sculpted portrait of Robert Louis Stevenson) and out (another major work, *The Farragut Base*). There is a reflecting pool here and more gardens in a formal, geometrically arranged style.

The estate also includes a dramatic and rather steep descent into a forested ravine. If you choose to take this walk, you will find it exceptionally beautiful, but be sure you are wearing proper shoes for a climb.

The path eventually will bring you to the bottom of the great field where the family burial grounds lie at the foot of a Greek-style columned temple (actually a replica of a stage set). The original temple was erected by the Cornish Colony in 1905 when the Saint-Gaudens family was honored with a dramatic production on the twentieth anniversary of their residence at Aspet.

Certainly one of the most intriguing things about Aspet is the overall design of the landscape, with its winning combination of natural and formal elements. Within the studio and house areas the axial paths and lines of sight are carefully accented with marble paths, groves of trees, and formal hedgerows, while all around it the natural beauty of the New England landscape has been magnificently preserved. This is a site well worth visiting for both garden enthusiasts and art lovers.

INFORMATION

The Saint-Gaudens National Historic Site is open daily from Memorial Day through October 31. The buildings are open from 9:00 A.M. to 4:30 P.M. daily and the grounds from dawn until dusk. There is no admission fee for those under 16 and a modest charge for others. The mailing address is RR 3, Box 73, Cornish, New Hampshire 03745. Telephone: (603) 675-2175.

DIRECTIONS

From Boston take the Massachusetts Turnpike to I-91 north to Exit 8; take Route 131 East and go left onto Route 12A north. Aspet is located just off Route 12A in Cornish, New Hampshire; it is 12 miles north of Claremont, New Hampshire, and 1 1/2 miles north of the covered bridge at Windsor, Vermont.

Fuller Gardens, North Hampton

Just across the street from the Atlantic Ocean in a neighborhood of great summer mansions, you'll find some surprisingly elegant estate gardens that have nothing to do with beach grasses and wild roses. Fuller Gardens were part of the summer estate of Alvan T. Fuller, a governor or Massachusetts, and they were designed in the 1920s by no less a landscape specialist than Arthur Shurtleff, with additions in the 1930s by the Olmsted brothers. These extensive formal gardens—divided into several separate parts—are fine examples of the Colonial Revival style. Though there are a variety of garden attractions here, most people come to see the roses.

The seaside location is apparently ideal for roses, and here you'll find two spectacular rose gardens (as well as a very pretty Japanese garden, profuse perennial beds, and a conservatory of exotic plantings). Some 1,500 rose bushes of all types—grandifloras, floribundas, and hybrid teas—are planted here in a variety of geometric beds; in fact, these are among the best designed rose gardens we have seen anywhere. Rather than the somewhat undistinguished, monolithic rose beds of so many gardens, these have been designed to complement the roses—both in color and texture. (This is, by the way, an official All-America Rose Display Garden for New Hampshire.)

The first of the rose gardens is in an enclosed, squarish garden arranged in geometric patterns with small statues, and fountains to ornament the brilliant blooms. It is charming and intimate and enclosed on one side by a high wooden fence with espaliered apple trees.

The second (behind the Japanese garden) is truly magnificent: in an enormous sunken garden surrounded by very wide, very uniform, waist-high hedges of yew are a series of diamond-shaped rose beds divided by extremely narrow paths. Each bed is filled with a different color and species of rose. Surrounding the hedges are borders of glorious perennials that provide contrast and emphasis. This is an inspired design for the delicate rose!

As you walk around and among the mazelike arrangement of the paths, don't miss the many small decorations that add to the ambiance—the Etruscan urns, the planters at the gates overflowing with pretty blossoms, the little statuary almost behind the flowers.

Between these rose gardens is the Japanese garden, a setting of shade and quiet greenery, with the sound of delicately running water and birds singing. Designed by Shurtleff in 1935, it is a haven of darkness and profuse greenery—interspersed with arched bridges and stepping stones in great contrast to the bright sun-lit rose gardens. This is a Japanese garden without cuteness; it is an oasis of calm and elegance.

There is also a greenhouse with some exotic tropical and desert plantings. In the sheltered lee immediately next to the structure is a series of cold frame beds of perennials that seem to relish the salty air—such as giant yellow sunflowers.

You will find Fuller Gardens very spiffy—not a blade of grass is out of place and little is left to chance. These gardens (carefully labeled) are an unexpected treat in such a windy, cold climate. They are less than an hour from Boston, and well worth the trip.

INFORMATION
Fuller Gardens are located at 10 Willow Avenue in North Hampton. Telephone: (603) 964-5414. Open daily from 10 A.M. to 6 P.M. from early May through mid-October. We recommend visiting in the summer months, though there are thousands of spring bulbs to be enjoyed in May and early June. Fee.

DIRECTIONS
From Boston take I-95 to Exit at Route 101 east; go to Route 1A (at the shoreline). Fuller Gardens are located 200 yards north of the junction.

Moffatt-Ladd House and Garden, Portsmouth

Colonial gardens that have been kept up through the years are among the greatest of rarities—far harder to find than well-maintained colonial houses. Judging by the Moffatt–Ladd House garden, a 1.5-acre pleasure garden behind the house, such gardens were masterpieces of design and charm. We have seldom seen a more felicitous arrangement of terraces, walkways, flowers, shrubbery, trees, and arbors, and even grass steps up and down. This garden shows us what the colonials knew—that the small, well-designed garden can be infinitely more pleasing than the large and formal. Here is a garden to sit in all day!

The Moffatt–Ladd House—a beauty—was built in 1763 with the greatest of elegance. The house took 467 days to complete, by the way, and had its own mast-house and wharf across the street at the Piscataqua River. (A counting office adjoining the house was added in the 1830s.) John Moffatt was a successful sea captain who had the house built as a wedding gift for his son Samuel; it eventually became the home of his granddaughter, Mrs. Alexander Ladd. The property was occupied by the family until 1913, when it was opened to the public and is now preserved by descendants of the Moffatts and Ladds and the Colonial Dames of America. (This is one house tour we recommend, for the architecture, the craftsmanship of the hand-carving, and the fine paintings and furnishings are well worth seeing.)

The garden was laid out behind and to the side of the house in its present design about 150 years ago, following plans and using some plantings that were there before. Alexander Hamilton Ladd, who redid the garden in the midnineteenth century, wrote that some of the plants had been put in by his mother and grandmother; two examples survive from the eighteenth century. You'll see a huge horse chestnut tree planted in 1776 (just after a family member had signed the Declaration of Independence) and an English damask rose planted in 1768.

The garden is perfectly kept, but its neatness is not antiseptic; instead, it is a particularly charming garden in its unusual design. Though there are formal plantings on either side of a 300-foot axis from the house to a wrought iron gate at the end, there are numerous serpentine shapes with winding brick and gravel walkways, surprising trellises including a colonial spiral, and terraces on four levels—the highest reached by rare grass steps cut into the hillside. Other features include a very green lawn separating many small beds planted with the brightest yellow dahlias we have ever seen, as well as feathery cosmos, a trellis of grapes, a great larch tree, a white pergola, beehives, and a new surprise around every bend.

Though not one of the larger gardens included in this book, this is one of our favorites. Here you can see how a smallish, hilly plot, enclosed on all sides and in the middle of a cold-climed, northern city, can be quite magically turned into a place of beauty and repose.

INFORMATION
The Moffatt–Ladd House is at 154 Market Street in Portsmouth. Telephone: (603) 436-8221. It is open daily from June 15 through October 15 from 10 A.M. to 4 P.M.; Sundays from 2 P.M. to 5 P.M.; and by special appointment. Tours are offered, but the garden can be seen on your own. Fee.

DIRECTIONS
Portsmouth is one hour north of Boston on I-95. Take Exit 7 into Portsmouth (Market Street) to #154.

And in Addition . . .

Fitzwilliam: Rhododendron State Park
Off Route 119, 3 miles to town.
This is a 16-acre grove of huge rhododendrons, with hiking trails into the thick surrounding forest. Visit in late spring.

Kinsman Notch: Lost River Nature Garden
Lost River (6 miles west of North Woodstock on Route 112).
Here, amid the glacial caverns and giant potholes and the Gorge at Paradise Falls, you'll find some 300 labeled varieties of native flowering plants, as well as ferns and mosses. Visit between June and September.

Newbury: The Fells, John Hay National Wildlife Refuge
Route 103 A. Telephone: (603) 763-4789
Within this great refuge you'll find a surprising series of fine gardens, as well as the historic (Hay) house, forests, trails, and sweeping green lawns. Of particular interest is the rock garden, one of the best and largest in our entire region. Its peak seasons are June and July and "foliage" in October—like the surrounding mountain scenery. Just as the autumn leaves change color, plants in the garden too turn to brilliant shades of red. There are also a walled woodland garden, and a 100-foot long perennial border at its height in midsummer with pinks and blues and whites. A spectacular collection of lilacs, azaleas, and rhododendrons is best seen in late spring and early summer. Fee.

New Ipswich: Barrett House

79 Main Street. Telephone: (603) 878-2517.

Though more a landscape than a garden of flowers, Barrett House's grounds are a picturesque and evocative place to visit. Here, where "The Europeans" was filmed, are nearly 100 acres of meadowlands and forest with a broad, grassy, terraced walkway through the woods to an idyllic, lacy Gothic Revival gazebo. The imposing house and grounds are open for tours.

Plainfield: Plainfield Wildflower Sanctuary

River Road off Route 12A.

Along the Connecticut River are a slope, field, and riverbank of wildflowers and ferns. This sanctuary is maintained by the New England Wildflower Society. Visit in spring and summer.

Portsmouth: Prescott Park

Marcy Street.

This is without a doubt one of the most beautiful downtown city parks we have seen, not only because of its location right on the water, but because two sisters named Prescott left a legacy of flowers to the city. Every year several extremely large and profusely planted and colorful flower beds are cared for by University of New Hampshire horticultural students. The plantings—while not particularly unusual—are spectacular in their brilliance; there is even a gate of flowers—impatiens—that grow vertically on the fence.

Portsmouth: Strawbery Banke

Marcy Street. Telephone: (603) 433-1100.

This is an entire section of town featuring historic houses, several of which have carefully restored (but not extensive) gardens. If you are visiting Strawbery Banke, note especially the Thomas Baily Aldrich Garden, which was redesigned in about 1907, and is a fine example of Colonial Revival design; the Sherburne House Garden, a vegetable and herb garden based on original archeological research; the Goodwin Mansion Garden, a Victorian and very charming garden created around the Civil War period; and a long perennial walkway through the "Village." Fee.

Rumney: Mr. Jacquith's Garden

Main Street.

Mr. Jacquith has a beautiful garden right on Main Street in this tiny town. Though it's private, he likes visitors and you may leave a small donation to help with its upkeep.

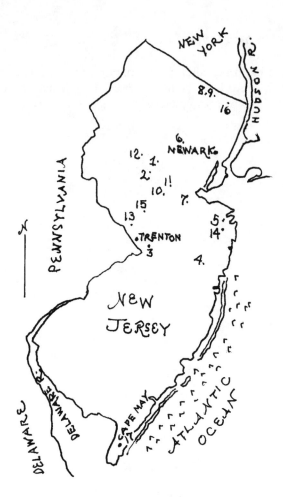

NEW JERSEY GARDENWALKS

1. Bernardsville: Cross Estate Gardens
2. Far Hills: Leonard J. Buck Garden
3. Hamilton Township: Sayen Gardens
4. Lakewood: Georgian Court College
5. Middletown: Deep Cut Park Horticultural Center
6. Morristown: Frelinghuysen Arboretum
7. New Brunswick: Rutgers Gardens
8. Ringwood: Ringwood Manor
9. Ringwood: Skylands Botanical Garden
10. Somerset: Colonial Park
11. Somerville: Doris Duke Gardens

And in Addition . . .

12. Gladstone: Willowwood Arboretum
13. Hamilton: Grounds for Sculpture
14. Lincroft: Lambertus C. Bobbink Memorial Rose Garden
15. Princeton: Prospect Garden
16. Saddle River: Waterford Gardens
17. Swainton: Leaming's Run Garden

NEW JERSEY

Cross Estate Gardens, Bernardsville

This exquisite site is neither large nor especially grand, but its intimate walled gardens are among the loveliest we have seen. Set in a historic area of Morristown's National Historic Park (a famous Revolutionary War site), the gardens are part of an elegant estate that was built as a summer retreat in 1905.

The grounds were laid out by a noted landscape designer named Clarence Fowler, but it was apparently Julia Newbold Cross who was the guiding inspiration for the English-style gardens. Mrs. Cross, who with her husband purchased the house in 1929, was a noted gardener, a member of the Royal Horticultural Society, and a long-time president of the New York Horticultural Society. Now maintained by a group of dedicated volunteers (you might find them working there when you visit—as we did), the gardens have been returned to their original glory after a long period of neglect.

The walled gardens are the centerpiece of a charming landscape that includes a vine-covered pergola, a mountain laurel allée, and a shade garden planted with ferns, shrubs, and perennials. The formal gardens are enclosed by walls and divided by geometric brick paths. The plantings within the garden walls are delightful and ever changing. As in a true English garden, there is a profusion of color and texture and size with flowers set in ornamental beds edged by repeated plantings and embellished with enchanting old-fashioned cast-iron urns and brickwork. Among the plantings you might see when you visit are edgings of white-flowered periwinkle, English ivy, and boxwood, surrounding lemon balm, butterbush, coral bells, potentilla, lamb's ears, and numerous types of daylilies.

This is the kind of garden where you may truly hear birds sing and the sounds of a watercolorist dipping his brush in a glass (there were several blissful painters there on our visit).

INFORMATION
The Cross Estate Gardens property is located on Old Jockey Hollow Road in Bernardsville. It is open daily from dawn to dusk. The best season is spring. Telephone: (908) 543-4030.

DIRECTIONS
From New York, take Route 80 to I-287 south. Turn at Harter Road (Exit A, to your left) to Route 202 southbound. Turn off 202 (also called Mount Kemble Avenue) after .9 mile and right at traffic light onto Tempe Wick Road for 2 miles. Pass the entrance to Jockey Hollow, go left onto Leddell Road at waterfall for 1.1 miles, and turn left again onto long driveway at sign "New Jersey Brigade Area—Cross Estate Gardens."

Leonard J. Buck Garden, Far Hills

Set amid some of New Jersey's prettiest rolling countryside of sprawling farms and thick stone walls is a naturalistic garden that looks as though it has been untouched by human hands.

The Leonard J. Buck Garden, a vast and inviting site deep within a rocky, narrow gorge surrounded by glacial ponds and massive rocky outcroppings, is a delight to explore. And, although it may appear at first to be a wilderness, it is, in fact, a carefully nurtured environment.

This 33-acre garden, now one of the premier rock gardens in the country, was designed in the 1930s with great care by Leonard J. Buck, a wealthy mining engineer. Fascinated by the giant volcanic rock outcroppings on his property, he worked with a landscape architect, Zenon Schreiber, to develop a naturalistic garden using these extraordinary geological formations as the basis for his design. As one of the early ecologists, Buck was interested in the symbiotic relationship among rocks, soil, and plants. His aim was to make his garden look as though it had been created by nature.

Buck and Schreiber set about their task like archeologists and artists. They unearthed some of the rock formations that had been buried beneath loose trap rock and reshaped and sculpted them to add to their visual appeal. Around each outcropping they carefully placed plantings suitable to its particular microclimate and exposure. Always a lover of exotic plants, Buck filled his valley with some rare examples, as well as more familiar varieties. He laid out connecting pathways where wildflowers have since proliferated. He even built a dam.

His imagination and vision, along with the landscape's natural beauty and its continuing evolution have made this a place of enchantment. Rhododendrons, azaleas, ferns, heaths, and heathers grace wooded paths and meadows; ponds and waterfalls add a touch of romance. But the rocky outcroppings with their individual gardens are what make this garden special.

Each of the 13 massive formations has a name (not always labeled, however), such as Big Rock, shaped like a dinosaur, or Horseshoe Rock, so shaped by an ancient waterfall. As you wind your way around the surrounding paths, you'll notice that each rock garden is distinctive from the next. Among the many varieties of plants you might see (depending on the season) are wild columbines, clematis, viburnum, stonecrop, white violets, succulents, mosses, blueberries, ferns, lady's slippers, and wild orchids.

If you're adventuresome and quite fit (the terrain is fairly hilly) and have a particular interest in alpine rock gardens, you won't want to miss this rare place. And if you're not bothered by the occasional noisy intrusion of a nearby highway, you will think you're walking through a remote wilderness.

You can take a guided tour if you are so inclined. However, this is a garden to savor at your own pace, and detailed walking guides and lists of plants in bloom or in fruit are available at the entrance. (The garden is operated by the Somerset County Park Commission, which regularly publishes informative material of geological and botanic interest.) Whether your garden pleasure is scientific or purely aesthetic, we have no hesitation in suggesting you put on your sturdy walking shoes, gather together flyers and plant listings, and head for the New Jersey hills' best rock garden.

INFORMATION
Leonard Buck Garden is at 11 Layton Road in Far Hills. Telephone:

(908) 234-2677. Its hours are 10 A.M. to 4 P.M., Monday through Saturday; 12 noon to 4 P.M., Sunday (winter); 12 noon to 5 P.M., Sunday (summer). A small donation is requested.

DIRECTIONS
From New York City, take the Lincoln Tunnel to the New Jersey Turnpike south to Exit 14; then take Route 78 west toward Morristown, then Route 287 north to Exit 18B, and then Route 202 north to Far Hills. At the train station, turn right just before the tracks onto Liberty Corner/Far Hills Road; go about 1 mile and turn right at Layton Road. The garden is on your left.

Sayen Gardens, Hamilton Township

It is always intriguing to observe an artistic work in progress, be it a painting, a sculpture, or a garden. You note the existing colors, textures, shapes, and general design and wonder what the final outcome will be. Sayen Gardens in semi-rural New Jersey, just east of Trenton, is a garden in progress. Although much of it is now in place, additional parts of this 30-acre site are still being developed.

The property was once the country estate of Frederick Sayen, a rubber industrialist whose passion was botany. From his worldwide travels he brought back many plants, exotic and otherwise, including unusual varieties of azaleas and rhododendrons. He began planning and creating a number of gardens around his English-style mansion, which were not completed during his lifetime. In 1985 Hamilton Township bought the property from the Sayen family and opened it to the public in 1988.

Garden designers have since been following a ten-year plan that more or less corresponds to Frederick Sayen's original idea for the gardens. The once completely flat landscape was contoured (for better drainage), becoming one of gentle hills. Existing overgrown beds and trails had to be reclaimed and new ones were formed.

From the moment you arrive, you are aware that Sayen Gardens is a relatively new site. A pristine brick walk bordered by profuse impatiens marks the graceful entrance. You then reach a striking "contemporary-style" garden situated on an artificially created mound in front of the mansion. Its enormous, carefully—but not formally—placed boulders (excavated when the landscape was contoured) make it too dramatic to be called a rock garden. You can view it as you meander on a rustic woodchip path, up and around groupings of eclectic plantings. The combination of exotic grasses and unusual plants alongside more traditional varieties is attractive and modern. The overall arrangement is also spectacular in terms of colors, shapes, and textures. Unlike traditional botanic gardens, nothing is labeled here; to identify these eye-catching varieties, you can consult one of the gardeners on staff.

A number of paths through pine woods laced with wildflowers lead to other gardens, including some presently under construction. (Be prepared for some muddy spots.) One trail takes you to a pretty Japanese-style garden, where you'll see a pond with traditional arched bridge and gazebo surrounded by tall, willowy grasses. If you visit in springtime, you can enjoy a spectacle of—we are told—80,000 dazzling daffodils in April, and in May masses of azaleas and rhododendrons in brilliant profusion.

Among the gardens still in the planning stage is a fairly large rose garden. Here you can see gardens in the making; if you are planning your own and are looking for some ideas, you will surely find inspiration here.

INFORMATION
Sayen Gardens are located at 155 Hughes Drive in Hamilton Township, New Jersey. The grounds are open daily, year-round. Telephone: (609) 890-3874.

DIRECTIONS
From the New Jersey Turnpike take Exit 7 to Route 33 west. Turn left on Whitehorse Road to the stop sign. Turn right onto Nottingham Way and left at Hamilton Square onto Mercer Street for three blocks. Turn left onto Hughes Drive. The entrance to the gardens is on your left.

Georgian Court College, Lakewood

The very name Georgian Court suggested to us an eighteenth-century setting in an English countryside, with a stately home, arched bridges over gently flowing water, white marble statues, and formal gardens. We were both astonished and delighted to find exactly such a place hidden away in Ocean County, New Jersey, a treasure for garden explorers and art lovers, as well as more than 1,000 college students.

Georgian Court College is a beautifully situated campus that was once a very large private estate. It is enclosed by walls along a wide shady street, and when you enter its palatial gates, you come directly upon a setting of such felicitous proportions and so many neoclassical sculptures that you find it hard to equate it with the general run of the American college campus. Instead of modern kinetic sculpture, you find a fountain statue of Apollo; instead of hard trodden paths from dorm to dorm, you find stone walkways through formal sunken flower beds and a Japanese tea house.

The college (an undergraduate Catholic women's institution, with coed night and graduate divisions) was once the home of George Jay Gould, the financier and railroad magnate. Its 175 acres were purchased in 1896. Gould hired a noted architect, Bruce Price, to design the home in the outskirts of the "winter resort" of Lakewood. The mansion itself (now a college building) was constructed of gray stucco with white terra-cotta brick, marble, and wood. The interior of the original building is elegantly paneled and maintained. There is an indoor marble pool; and outdoors, where the grounds were designed to match the Georgian-era architecture, there is a lagoon and a sunken garden and a magnificent promenade.

Gould's son, Kingdon Gould, sold the estate to the Sisters of Mercy in 1924, and though they transformed it into an educational institution, happily they left its distinctive character intact. In 1985 Georgian Court College was declared a National Historic Landmark.

The estate is situated along the banks of a good-sized lake called Lake Carasaljo in the pines area of south central New Jersey. As you enter the gates you will come first to the Italian or Classical gardens, which harmonize so nicely with the architecture of the original mansion. This elliptical formal garden consists of some 16 flower beds bordered by boxwood. The flower beds are meticulously maintained. A Japanese garden, made in 1925, includes a tea house, wooden bridges, and shrubbery.

As you leave the flower gardens and walk on into the center of the campus, you will find rolling green lawns dotted with pathways and classical marble sculptures. The most notable sculpture is the Apollo fountain designed by John Massey Rhind, a sculptor of public monuments and statues. Its horses plunge dramatically from the serene water, its white marble Apollo heroically in command.

A flight of wide marble steps takes you down to the lake edge and connects the original sunken garden and a lagoon. A promenade in the opposite direction (leading to classroom and library buildings) is flanked on either side by classical sculptures.

INFORMATION
Georgian Court College is open to visitors who wish to walk around the campus. The address is 900 Lakewood Avenue, Lakewood, New Jersey 08701. For information, call (732) 364-2200.

DIRECTIONS
From New York, take the New Jersey Turnpike to the Garden State Parkway, Exit 91. Bear right after the toll plaza and proceed through the first intersection (Burnt Tavern Road) to the next traffic light, at County Line Road, which you take for approximately 5 miles to Route 9. Turn left on Route 9 south and continue to Ninth Street. Turn right on Ninth Street and proceed through the Forest Avenue intersection to Lakewood Avenue. The entrance to the college is to your right.

Deep Cut Park Horticultural Center, Middletown

When visiting gardens, you hardly expect to be involved in a mystery story. It comes as a surprise, then, to learn that Deep Cut Park Horticultural Center in rural Monmouth County is literally a garden with a shady past.

The site was farmland through the nineteenth century. In 1890 it was taken over by the sheriff for nonpayment of taxes, and, after a series of owners, it finally fell into the hands of the infamous Mafia boss Vito Genovese in 1935.

Genovese transformed the old farm and created several gardens. And, true to his reputation as a big spender, he had his Italian stone-masons build extensive walls—including the unusual festoonlike stone wall surrounding the property—a series of ornamental pools, a huge swimming pool, and a replica of Mount Vesuvius, smoke effects and all! He also imported rare plants and trees (among these, the gnarled weeping hemlocks overlooking the terrace gardens).

When, in 1937, Genovese was being investigated by the authorities, his family suddenly left for Europe. It was during their absence that a mysterious fire destroyed the mansion. The incident remains unsolved to this day. After the war (Genovese had spent it in Italy, working with Mussolini), the Mafioso was returned to the United States to stand trial for murder; however, not surprisingly, the key witness against him was poisoned and the case dropped. In 1949 Genovese sold his property to Mary Gladys Cubbage, who eventually sold it to Karl and Marjorie Wihtol, just a few years before Genovese was finally sent to jail on narcotics charges. The Wihtols built the existing house (now the visitor center) and greenhouses and created many of the gardens you see today. In 1977 the county park system took over the property, converting the house into classrooms, a library, gift shop, and offices.

Notwithstanding its turbulent past, Deep Cut is a very pleasant place to visit—and very peaceful, indeed. Named for the narrow stream that forms a deep cut in the landscape, it includes some 53 acres of hillside gardens and greenhouses planned as a living plant catalog for the home gardener.

The gardens are arranged informally, with one flowing naturally into the next, surrounded by nice, hilly views. The first garden you come to, after parking your car, is the Butterfly and Hummingbird Garden. The colorful annuals, perennials, and shrubs you see have been planted to attract these species. A nearby lily pond is graced with a pretty fountain. Next you see formal beds decorated with plants in delicate shades of green and silver. Behind is the Horticultural Center. Here you can pick up a walking guide of the gardens.

Stroll down the path to the hillside gardens. On a summer day you will enjoy the Shade Garden with its canopy of dogwood, tulip, cedar, poplar, and cherry trees. Nearby is the Azalea and Rhododendron Walk; the Rockery (where Genovese's now-huge weeping hemlocks tower over three cascading pools); and a delightful orchard, filled with dwarf fruit and nut trees. If you continue on the walkways you will come to a pretty wisteria-covered pergola, pond, and meadow. It was at this site that Genovese built his lavish pool—now buried. Instead, you will see meadow wildflowers, if you visit in late spring or summer.

The "working environment" sections of Deep Cut come next: a dried flower production field (where annuals and perennials are grown for use in craft classes); demonstration vegetable gardens in raised beds; and a composting site, complete with valuable information for the amateur gardener.

Don't miss the greenhouse, where you can enjoy displays of succulents, orchids, and house plants. (The succulent collection was obtained by Ms. Wihtol using the barter system.) Naturalists on staff are available for information concerning any of the plants you find here or throughout the gardens.

If you love roses, you will want to visit in June or September to see those at Deep Cut, which have received prestigious awards. Early springtime brings forth clumps of daffodils, as well as blooming magnolias, dogwood, and rhododendron. May is tulip month, with thousands bursting forth in brilliant colors. With classes, seminars, plant demonstrations, and displays, you will find plenty to do and see here at any time of the year. You might also wish to combine this visit with a walk in Tatum Park, directly across the street. This large nature preserve includes inviting trails and picnic tables.

INFORMATION
Deep Cut Park Horticultural Center is located at 352 Red Hill Road in Middletown, New Jersey. Hours: June through September, 8 A.M. to 8 P.M.; October through May, 8:00 A.M. to 4:30 P.M. Operated by the Monmouth County Park Commission, the Center offers a reference library, classrooms, and many programs concerning horticulture. For information, call (732) 671-6050. Admission is free.

DIRECTIONS
From the Garden State Parkway in New Jersey take Exit 114. Go east toward Middletown for 1.5 miles to reach the Center (on your right).

Frelinghuysen Arboretum, Morristown

This estate consists of some 127 acres, divided into a variety of botanical garden units. It is a bustling place, filled with activity. A regional center for horticultural programs, including many educational events, it might not be described as a contemplative swatch of natural beauty. But there are nice forest and meadow paths with shrubbery and trees well labeled for education purposes, and some very pretty perennial flower beds. There is a shade garden and a winter garden that contains hollies and such flowers as snowdrops and winter jasmine.

Among the most distinctive aspects of this busy place, however, are its gardens for the disabled and the blind: The Vera Scherer Garden for people with special needs, and the Pikaart Garden, a Braille nature trail. Both are well designed and unusually successful.

The Vera M. Scherer Garden is conceived as a tool to teach the disabled how they can make gardening accessible. For example, raised flower beds are constructed to eliminate bending or stretching and to accommodate gardeners in wheelchairs. (The Frelinghuysen Arboretum includes horticultural therapy programs among its many activities.) This garden is well worth a visit for its ingenious ideas both about accessibility and easy-care flowers and herbs.

Described as a scent, touch, and feel garden, the Pikaart Garden is carefully labeled in Braille. Here gardeners have done a fine job of combining textured and fragrant plants. One interesting feature is a substitute pond—actually a blue (in spring) bugleweed area—which is complete with brass crane statues and a bridge and stream. This fantasy pond is surrounded by plants such as Japanese or candelabra primroses and mountain laurel. Many textured plants include the dwarf horse tail, the heart-leaved begonia, and a variety of ferns.

INFORMATION
Frelinghuysen Arboretum is located at 53 East Hanover Avenue, Morristown, New Jersey. It is open daily except holidays, year-round. Telephone: (973) 326-7600. Free.

DIRECTIONS
From the George Washington Bridge, take Route 80 west to I-287 south. Take Exit 32, turn right at Ridgedale Avenue. Turn right at East Hanover Avenue. Entrance is 1/4th mile on the right.

Rutgers Gardens, New Brunswick

There are all kinds of reasons to visit Rutgers Gardens, but we were particularly taken with its oddest feature: a bamboo forest. If you have ever seen ancient Asian art with its fearsome tigers creeping through a bamboo forest, you will no doubt recognize this mysterious and fascinating type of forest.

Here you'll see hundreds and hundreds of bamboo trees,which grow very close together, tall, thin, and straight against the sky, leaving a carpet of pale leaves beneath them. This is a sight to stay with you. A professor at the university planted only a few of them (he needed some bamboo poles); then nature was allowed free reign, and the result is breathtaking. We walked through the forest on a soft floor of creamy leaves, while the trees made a soaring pattern of vertical and occasionally tipping lines.

Rutgers Gardens are, of course, much more than this. These are teaching and research gardens, specimen gardens, working gardens, community gardens. They are for students and scholars and garden enthusiasts who interest themselves in the many varieties of American holly trees (the most comprehensive collection in the country), in grafting different types of gloriously pink dogwood with one another, in how various plants grow in the shade and sun.

You can walk through 25 or 30 acres of these different gardens and discover both beauty and plant lore. There are greenhouses where the minute work takes place, outdoor paths where you can see all kinds of azaleas, an architect-designed evergreen garden, a series of Stewardia trees with dappled bark from Japan and Korea, and even a brook with waterfalls to create an aquatic plant environment. There is a rare virgin forest here, a large one and a blessing in this overbuilt area of New Jersey. And there are even thematic gardens whose theme is changed each year (fragrances, colors, and species are among recent choices).

We have found few such research gardens in our area, though they are common at the great land grant colleges; Rutgers' was established as one in 1921. (Another is Cornell University in Ithaca.) A visit here is a wonderful way to learn about gardens—and don't miss the walk through the bamboo.

INFORMATION
Rutgers Gardens are located at Ryder's Lane (off Route 1) in New Brunswick. They are open daily from 8:30 A.M. to dusk, May through September, and from 8:30 A.M. to 4:30 P.M. October through April. Fee. Telephone: (732) 932-8451.

DIRECTIONS
From the New Jersey Turnpike, take Exit 9 to Route 1 south (toward New Brunswick). Exit at Ryder's Lane, crossing under the highway to the opposite side of the road. Follow the signs.

Skylands Botanical Garden, Ringwood

Skylands, New Jersey's state botanical garden, is aptly named. To visit this vast site deep in the Ramapo Mountains, you must drive up and up on a winding road—toward the sky.

Finally you reach what appears to be (and once was) a grand—yet surprisingly informal—country estate, complete with elegant Tudor-style buildings, delightful gardens, long allées, and broad vistas. The beautifully designed landscape combines formal and naturalistic areas—separated by a magnificent crab apple walk—broad, panoramic views, and even pieces of sculpture. The ambiance is low-key and friendly. Exploring these spacious grounds (some 125 acres of them) is a most pleasant, even joyful experience, particularly on a bright spring day, when the many blooming plants add their enchantment.

Skylands' origins as a gentleman's working farm are still apparent in its rustic, yet genteel, charms. Francis Lynde Stetson, a prominent, turn-of-the-century New York lawyer, called his property "Skyland Farms." His grounds (which also included the mansion, sweeping lawns, and even a small golf course) were designed by Samuel Parsons, Jr., a protégé of Frederick Law Olmsted.

But it was the estate's next proprietor, Clarence McKenzie Lewis, who was responsible for turning Skylands into a botanical showplace. Lewis, an amateur but dedicated botanist, collected plants from all over the world during the 1920s. With his army of gardeners he planted specimens from Afghanistan, Chile, and New Zealand, as well as his native New Jersey. Although he engaged landscape architects to design the gardens around the house, he had much to say about which plants should go where. Lewis carefully considered the color, texture, form, and even fragrance of each plant, so that it would be part of a harmonious whole.

In the 1960s New Jersey purchased the property, and in March 1984 the 96 acres surrounding the manor house were designated as the state's official botanical garden.

Before setting forth on your walk, you might want to pick up a descriptive guide and map at the visitor's center, where the helpful staff will be glad to give you any additional information. Among Skyland's many offerings are an Annual Garden, Summer Garden, Azalea Garden, Peony Garden, Lilac Garden, Octagonal Garden,

Winter Garden, Magnolia Walk, Crab Apple Vista, Bog Garden, Swan Pond, Wildflower Garden, Heather Garden, a greenhouse collection, and miles of walking to satisfy even the most energetic visitor. The 1920s manor house (made from stone quarried on the estate) can be visited by guided tour only, but you can wander through the broad landscape and individual gardens on your own.

The Winter Garden (which Lewis could enjoy from his library window on even the dreariest wintry day) features a rare collection of some 30 varieties of evergreens. Included are an Atlas cedar, a Jeffrey pine (now grown to giant proportions), an Algerian fir, and an impressive Japanese umbrella pine, which is a main attraction. You can walk around the trees and admire their different shapes, sizes, and shades of green, gray-blue, gray, and even gold.

The nearby formal Terrace Gardens behind the manor house are like individual outdoor galleries. The Octagonal Garden, so named for its central pool and fountain, includes a charming rock garden; the gracious Magnolia Walk, with its fragrant plantings, leads to the Azalea Garden, resplendent with banks of azaleas and rhododendrons on both sides of a reflecting pool. Beyond lie the Summer, Tree Peony, and Lilac gardens. A good place to take a short rest to plot your next route is on a semicircular stone bench at the end of a grouping of hemlocks in the peony garden.

The Crab Apple Vista—an incredible double row of trees that forms the boundary between the gardens near the house and the wilder areas to the east—is undoubtedly Skylands' most enchanting attraction. As you walk on this half-mile stretch, surrounded on each side by over 160 crab apple trees (whose spring blossoms alone are worth the trip), you can enjoy wide views of gardens, meadows, woods, and mountains. At the end of the vista, you'll find the Four Continents statues, opposite the Horsechestnut Collection. Set in a semicircle next to the woods, these timeworn stone forms represent the four continents (minus Australia). Their style is classical with romantic overtones, and they are based on seventeenth-century works.

From here you can wander through the more informal collections to see rhododendron, heather, and different varieties of wildflowers; nearby is Swan Pond, where you are more likely to come upon frogs than anything else.

You'll find there is more to discover and do at Skylands than a day's worth. Also scheduled are special events and classes in horti-culture, nature photography, and nature watercolor painting, all of which will give you the opportunity to experience Skylands from different perspectives.

INFORMATION
Skylands Botanical Garden is located in Ringwood, New Jersey. It is open daily, year-round, from 9 A.M. to dusk. There is an admission fee during summer. Tours are available daily every half hour. For information, call (732) 962-7031, For information on special events or classes, call (732) 962-7525 during the week.

DIRECTIONS
From Manhattan take the George Washington Bridge to Route 4 west to Route 208 north to the end. Stay straight, crossing a bridge; take the first right turn onto Skyline Drive to the end. Turn right on Route 511 and take the second right, Sloatsburg Road. Travel about 4.5 miles to Morris Road, following signs for Skylands Botanical Gardens.

Ringwood Manor, Ringwood

Set amid the hilly terrain of the Ramapo Mountains is a most unusu-al sculpture garden—partly rural retreat and partly European land-scape design, with no less a garden than Versailles as its model. Ringwood Manor is a large, imposing, nineteenth-century mansion surrounded by a magnificent sweep of green lawns, giant trees, stone walls, formal gardens, orchards, lake, and forest. A National Historic Landmark District, it is a place to walk and picnic, as well as to enjoy the art and ambiance of another time.

Ringwood was a center of iron mining and munitions from before the Revolutionary War until the end of World War I. The site had major importance during the Revolution. The Continental Army depended greatly upon Ringwood's iron production under the ownership of Peter Hasenclever and his American Iron Company. In addition, Ringwood was home to Robert Erskine, whom General Washington appointed as his army geographer. Erskine produced some 300 maps for the Continental Army and is buried at

Ringwood. You'll see a charming old stone building or two from this early period.

After the war, the iron industry continued to prosper. In the mid-nineteenth-century Ringwood's mansion was built (1854) and became the country seat of an iron magnate, Cooper Hewitt. Hewitt's fortune was estimated to be the sixth largest in America, and his manor house is suitably grand. (Furnished elegantly and hung with fine art, including Hudson River School paintings, the Manor is open to the public at certain times—see below.)

Descendant Abram Hewitt and his family decided to landscape a portion of the 33,000 acres of Ringwood. The Hewitts laid out their gardens drawing upon classical designs seen during their European travels, particularly those of Versailles and the Villa d'Este. (What Versailles gardeners accomplished with public taxation, Hewitt wished to create on his own—a truly nineteenth-century American aim!) Hewitt and his gardeners set out formal and informal gardens, allées, terraces, and walls—all adorned with sculpture of various origins—some still mysterious. Large areas of pristine landscape were also left in natural state to emphasize the dramatic hilltop views.

In fact, Ringwood gardens are—unlike many more contemporary sculpture parks—home to many incidental marble ornamental sculptures and wrought-iron "confections," rather than primarily settings for art. As in so many European gardens, each sculpture is an integral part of plantings, vistas, and stone-walled enclosures. These intimate spots are intriguing and inviting; each has its own benches and low walls for resting and contemplation.

There are no tags, no labels for identifying the art. Instead, you may simply enjoy the odd stone sphinxes which seem to be some sort of motif (Mrs. Hewitt had several of them copied from the sphinxes at the Louvre), nymphs, and sculptured heads as vaguely "classical" and curiously fitting to their surroundings. A classical statue representing Asia is at one end of the main axis of the formal gardens; her counterpart "Africa" in now gone. (Both reportedly came from the bishop's palace at Avignon.) All around the manor house you'll see wrought-iron works as well, and though these are abstract and ornamental, they seem perfectly appropriate to an iron magnate's home. Among them are a pair of iron lanterns in front of the house that came from the governor's mansion in Albany, New York. There are also three of the four lanterns that once lit the colonial statue of King George in downtown Manhattan's Bowling Green.

A particular oddity is the geometrically divided, stone-walled and terraced hillside above the Manor. (The visitor can stroll everywhere, and children will enjoy walking along the low, flat-topped walls.) One of the most intriguing of these areas is near the mansion, where a grove of straight and evenly spaced trees create an allée in which a series of identical torchieres is laid out. (Their origin was Colonnade Row in New York City.)

Giving the impression of a vast green chessboard, this spot is as eccentric as the giant iron gates which do not seem to lead anywhere in particular at the edge of the crystal lake below the house. (In fact, Hewitt, who purchased them from his Alma Mater, Columbia University, used them to mark the original site of the road used by the Continental Army that went from West Point to Morristown.) In any case, like the art throughout the estate, the gates serve to punctuate and ornament the landscape.

Woods and woodland trails surround the gardens. There are a few picnic tables set with grand vistas in mind. In an outing at Ringwood you can combine nature's wonders with formal gardens, sculpture, and European landscape design.

INFORMATION

The grounds are open year-round, with the gardens particularly inviting in spring and summer. Visitors in parts of December and April can tour the house as well as the grounds. There is a fee for parking in season. For information, call (732) 962-7031 or 7047. (Ringwood Manor is part of Ringwood State Park, which offers swimming, fishing, boating, and hiking in season. Information on facilities and hours can be obtained at the above number.)

The gardens of Skylands (see page 132) are nearby. You may want to combine a visit.

DIRECTIONS

From New York City, take New York State Thruway to junction Route 17 north. Follow signs to Ringwood, approximately 8 miles from intersection. Just after Shepherd Lake sign, turn right at Ringwood Manor State Park.

Colonial Park, Somerset

There are two extraordinary gardens here of major interest—one all roses, the other a fragrance and sensory garden. While they cover only a 1-acre part of a large and spacious county park in Franklin Township, they have a rare quality all their own. Once part of a private estate, the gardens were developed by a horticulturist when they became part of the public park.

The more unusual of the two gardens is the fragrance and sensory garden. Newly designed with Braille plaques and a low handrail, this garden includes especially interesting flowers and plants to smell and touch. Each example has an unusual quality, such as the soft fuzzy lamb's ear, the fragrant lavender plant, and the tasty mint. As you make your way around the garden, you can feel and smell and even taste these odd, fragrant plants and guess what they are, or read the small plaques. There are soft, spongy plants, prickly plants, and aromatic lemony plants. The flat walkway is made to accommodate the handicapped and visually impaired, with flagstone paving and intersecting strips of brick to indicate changes in direction. There are many charming arbored benches for resting. We also recommend this walk for families with children, as it is quite short.

Adjoining the Sensory and Fragrance Garden is the Rose Garden, and what a rose garden it is! Described as "an encyclopedia of roses," the collection includes 4,000 rosebushes (275 varieties) that bloom from early June all the way into fall. One of the sections is called Grandmother's Garden, and contains old hybrid perpetual and hybrid tea roses, while the Dutch Garden is in the style of a formal rose garden in Holland. It is a beautifully designed garden that is constantly in bloom during the long season. Everything is identified. A walk through it on the flagstone paths can be broken with little rests on arbored benches. For the rose fancier, this is a blissful stroll.

If you are of a romantic disposition, you'll find that both gardens have a touch of another time and place about them. We did—on a hot summer day, with the various flowery aromas wafting through the air and the cool shaded benches inviting us to rest for a moment.

INFORMATION
Colonial Park is a vast area, rather overdeveloped, with something for everyone seeking recreation, from paddle boats to a small

forestry nature walk, a nice lilac garden, picnic tables, tennis courts, and a playground, in addition to the gardens described above. There are other walks in the park, of course, including a stroll through the arboretum. Guided tours are also available. The hours are daily from 10 A.M. to 8 P.M., from June to November.

DIRECTIONS

From the George Washington Bridge take Route 80 west onto I-287 south. After passing Bound Brook take country Route 527 (Easton Avenue). Go right on Cedar Grove Lane. Go right again on Weston Road to Elizabeth Avenue. Entrance to park is on your left on Elizabeth Avenue.

From midtown Manhattan take the Lincoln Tunnel to the New Jersey Turnpike to I-287, and follow same directions as above.

Doris Duke Gardens, Somerville

During the cold winter months, no outing is more cheerful than visiting these splendid interconnected hothouses about an hour from New York. The Duke Gardens are part of the estate of Doris Duke, the tobacco heiress, and are one of New Jersey's major attractions (for which well-in-advance reservations are needed). From the moment you drive through the imposing iron gates topped with black eagles, you feel as if you had entered a magical world of free-roaming deer, exotic flowers, and mythical trees. The fact that you are met at the entrance by a van and transported to this fantasy environment adds to the special ambiance.

The conservatories are surrounded by acres of woodsy parkland, with trees planted in formal rows, reminiscent of a European estate. The greenhouses themselves, built in the late nineteenth century for family use, are beautiful. Their ornate glass structure is in an Edwardian conservatory style that is carried into several of the indoor gardens.

The full acre of display gardens was opened to the public in 1964. The Duke family heirs maintains strict control over the management of the estate, and there any many regulations to protect the environment and the valuable plants.

Each of the 11 hothouses has a different theme. You walk from one to the next (in the company of a knowledgeable guide and several other visitors) in about one hour's time. These are total landscape environments that follow the traditions of various countries and eras: there are statuary, rock paths, bridges, and pagodas, as well as a profusion of exotic flowers, shrubs, and trees.

The first stop, the Italian garden, is a wonderful beginning. It includes luxuriant blooms of mimosa, bird-of-paradise, orange and pink bougainvillea, Italian statuary and fountains, gravel paths, and an aura of nineteenth-century romance.

From there you go to the American Colonial garden, more orderly and classical, with well-groomed hedges, baby's tears' ground cover, camellia bushes, huge rounded magnolias, and hanging pink and white petunias. White latticework and brick trimmed paths add to the Colonial flavor.

The next conservatory—the Edwardian garden—is filled with orchids of every size and brilliant color. White, purple, and magenta blossoms are set off by the deep green of rubber plants and palms in the warm, humid surroundings. The orchids are supplied by other greenhouses on the grounds. This is the quintessential garden of turn-of-the-century romantic novels.

The formal French garden is next. Eighteenth-century latticework surrounds this charming formal arrangement of stone paths, niches, ivy-festooned columns, statuary, delicate fountains, and wonderful flowery designs, including a giant *fleur de lis* of brightly colored plants arranged in the style of the gardens of Versailles.

A group of English gardens follows. There is an herb garden, a rockery, a topiary garden, and a marvelous free-style annual garden with wonderful color combinations.

Next, contrasting with this brilliance, is the desert garden with dirt floor and giant cacti reaching up to the glass ceiling. The aura is that of the American Southwest: brown and gray-green tones in knobby, fantastic shapes, giving the visitor the sense of wild, untamed nature.

We then come to the Chinese garden, an oasis of peace and tranquillity. Not as colorful as the European-style flower gardens, it is nonetheless one of the most appealing. Rock formations and goldfish in small ponds, delicate arching stone bridges, mysterious grottos for contemplation, leaning willows, and zigzag walk to ward off evil spirits are among the engaging aspects of this traditional Chinese garden.

The Japanese garden is more stylized, with elegant tea house, tiny running streams, miniature wood bridge, contemplation area with carefully raked soil to represent waves, and the classic gnarled tree forms of Japanese landscape.

An impressive Indo-Persian garden comes next. The most striking feature is its geometric design, from the patterned cutout white walls and long reflecting pool to the crisp designs made by the yellow, orange, and white flowers and citrus trees. Although it represents an Islamic summer palace garden, it seems almost like an illustration to a fairy tale.

The tropical rain forest garden is a mass of jungle plants of many different sizes and shapes of green, with an occasional lady's slipper orchid hidden in the foliage. Spanish moss, banana plants, and huge elephant ears proliferate.

The semitropical garden in the Mediterranean style is the last. Many kinds of purple flowers decorate the edges of the brick paths and terrace, while gloxinias and gardenias in large urns and hanging bougainvillea add brilliant color to the gray-green ferns. Your own garden might seem very pale after this visit!

INFORMATION

This is a walk that we highly recommend for all adults, including the elderly. Although it is not difficult, women are advised to wear flat shoes, as the footing is sometimes awkward over occasional rocky paths. We do not suggest that you bring children, unless they are particularly interested in plants. It is definitely a decorous walk in which everything is rare and special. Cameras are not allowed, nor should you touch anything. There are neither eating or drinking facilities, nor are there picnic grounds.

The gardens are open from October through March, seven afternoons a week, from noon to 4 P.M. On Wednesday and Thursday evenings there are additional tours from 8:30 P.M. to 10:30 P.M. To visit the gardens, you must make advance reservations by calling (201) 722-3700. Call about a week ahead of time. There is an entrance fee. You are not allowed to wander at will, but must accompany a tour (limited to ten people).

DIRECTIONS
From New York, take the George Washington Bridge to Route 80, to I-287 south, to Exit 13 at junction with Route 206 south, to the Somerset Shopping Center. The gardens are located 1.25 miles south of the shopping center, with the entrance on the right. From midtown Manhattan you can take the New Jersey Turnpike to I-287 north.

And in Addition . . .

Gladstone: Willowwood Arboretum
Longview Road. Telephone: (973) 326-7600.
This 130-acre arboretum, named for its extensive collection of willows (over 100 kinds), also features wonderful oaks, maples, ferns, and wildflowers. In spring, cherries, magnolias, and lilacs add their delicate color to the site. Although there are two small formal gardens, including the Cottage Garden with neatly planted vegetables and flowers in rectangular beds, the overall feeling at Willowwood is one of delightful informality and eclecticism. Once a working farm (from the mid-1700s to the early 1900s), the land was later cultivated to grow collections of distinctive plants—a passion of the new proprietors in 1908, the Tubbs brothers. The grounds include the eighteenth-century residence and number of old barns set amid grassy, mowed paths. A small stone bridge in the Japanese style will take you across a pretty stream that runs through much of the land. Among other Oriental touches to note are a Katsura tree, Japanese primrose, and clumps of bamboos. A descriptive trail guide (available at the entrance) will lead you through the arboretum, or you can ramble about at will. Open daily, year-round.

Hamilton: Grounds for Sculpture
18 Fairgrounds Road. Telephone: (609) 586-0616.
Sculpture parks seem to be proliferating, as more people discover the joys of viewing art in natural settings. One of the most striking recent additions to these outdoor museums is Grounds for Sculpture. Situated on 22 acres on the edge of a small lake—once the site of the New Jersey State Fairgrounds—it includes a handsome, airy building for displaying indoor sculpture and the surrounding park (and a soon-to-be-completed additional gallery). The often bold, contemporary outdoor pieces, placed with great care for

visual interaction with their national environment, appear in grassy expanses and courtyards, amid impeccably tended trees, shrubs, and flower beds. The permanent collection is complemented by a varying number of works on temporary display (there are three exhibits each year). A picturesque lotus pond and gazebo (where you can sit, have a snack, and enjoy the view), a graceful iron arbor (a remnant from the past) with climbing wisteria, a pergola, and a colonnade add unusual appeal to this inviting site.

The park, opened in 1992, was the creation of the sculptor J. Seward Johnson, Jr., who as also the driving force behind the adjacent Johnson Atelier, a foundry and art school. In fact, one of the most original works on permanent exhibit is this artist's witty three-dimensional retake on Manet's seminal *Dejeuner sur l'Herbe*. Appropriately called *Dejeuner Déjà Vu*, its lifelike figures sit in secluded splendor on the edge of a small, woodsy pond.

Whether your interests are artistic or botanic—or both—you will enjoy a stroll through Grounds for Sculpture. Open Friday, Saturday, and Sunday from 10 A.M. to 4 P.M., and by appointment, Tuesday through Thursday, 9 A.M. to 4 P.M. Open year-round.

Lincroft: Lambertus C. Bobbink Memorial Rose Garden (Thompson Park)

805 Newman Springs Road. Telephone: (732) 842-4000.

Surrounded by 665 acres of playing fields, tennis courts, a lake, fitness trails, and activity centers, lies the surprisingly intimate Lambertus C. Bobbink Memorial Rose Garden.

This pretty garden was created in the 1970s by Dorothea Bobbink White in memory of her father, the dean of commercial rosarians in America. It is an outdoor art gallery dedicated to the rose, displaying prize-winning varieties that have been evaluated in test gardens around the country. Included are some 1,500 plants, all labeled and documented. An accompanying flyer indicates the latest plant listing—some bear such unlikely names as "Living easy," "Mr. Lincoln," "Brass Band," "Hot 'n' Spicey," and "Voodoo"—along with a complete and systematic description of each. Anyone interested in learning more about roses will find a visit here informative and appealing.

The garden is arranged with artistic flair, enclosed within a relatively small space. Flower beds in unusual zigzag-like shapes contrast with rounded gazebos graced with climbing roses. The abundant rose displays appear in different shapes of red, pink, yellow, and white, creating a vivid and colorful tableau. This is a quiet spot in which to enjoy some of nature's pleasures. Thompson Park— including the rose garden—is open daily from 8 A.M. to dusk. The park offers classes, walks, and demonstrations about plants, as well as many other programs and events.

Princeton: Prospect Garden

Princeton University Campus. Telephone: (609) 258-3455.

This serene flower garden is situated within the Princeton University campus. Aptly named "Prospect" for its views to the east, the property includes a nineteenth-century Florentine-style mansion and gardens. These are circular in design, with beds of perennials and annuals surrounding a central fountain. Around the formal plantings are carefully tended lawns and evergreens. It is easy to see why this romantic spot is often used for wedding parties, as well as traditional outdoor university functions.

In the late 1870s, the once private estate was presented to the university to be used as the residence of its president. (It remained as such until 1968.) Its first occupant, President McCosh, often compared it to the Garden of Eden for its idyllic charms. When Woodrow Wilson became president of the university, he enclosed 5 acres of the then much vaster grounds with an iron fence; this was done to keep unruly undergraduates from trampling the flower beds on their way to class! Mrs. Wilson rearranged much of the garden and planted the evergreens in the background that you still see today.

If you're visiting in the Princeton area, you won't want to miss Prospect Garden, particularly in June, when its roses are in full bloom.

Saddle River: Waterford Gardens

East Allendale Road. Telephone: (201) 327-0721.

The concept of the water garden—with its trickling falls, ponds of blooming lilies, rocks, and reeds—is increasingly popular among home gardeners. Waterford Gardens is a commercial, but very tasteful, enterprise in Bergen County that has display gardens of watery splendor. Here you can walk around a series of brooks and streams, ponds, and falls, and see how a water garden is put together, with a little help from nature. (There is, in fact, a river running through the property.) The company here has vast greenhouses growing all the different types of water plants in a spectacularly humid indoor environment, and it offers a conservatory filled with decorative fish. The oddest things you will find at Waterford Gardens are the almost life-sized topiary animals throughout the Gardens; from a distance you think a small herd of elephants and a llama (or something) are grazing in their watery habitat. Waterford Gardens are open 9 A.M. to 5 P.M. Monday through Saturday, 8 A.M. to 5 P.M. in growing season and 9 A.M. to 4 P.M. on Sunday. Closed on major holidays. Best to visit after May.

Swainton: Leaming's Run Gardens
1845 Route 9 north. Telephone: (609) 465-5871

If you're en route to or from Cape May or other points on the southern shores of New Jersey, you might stop to see Leaming's Run Gardens and Colonial Farm. Self-described as "the largest annual garden in the USA," this 30-acre site features some 25 intimate gardens—reminiscent of old-fashioned flower beds—that are replanted each year. Since a wide variety of blossoms appears throughout the growing season, from early May to October, what you see depends on when you come. (We saw mostly pansies, begonias, and iris when we visited in May.) These gardens are more a celebration of color than anything else, and many are named accordingly (such as the "Blue and White Garden" and the "Orange Garden"). The setting here is woodsy and rustic, including a stream (the original "Leaming's Run") with small, wooden bridges, a reflecting lily pond, and many varieties of ferns. It is not surprising that you experience *déjà vu* on a walk here: a circuitous path winds around like a labyrinth, taking you from one garden vista to the next and back again, so that you see the same spot more than once—but from a different angle. You are asked (through a series of little signs along the path) to admire certain views from designated vantage points, and, from a waterside gazebo, you are challenged to locate five visible gardens (there are garden benches throughout from which to view the surroundings).

At the rustic Colonial Farm (which you eventually reach along the path), you can learn about the origins of Leaming's Run, once a 320-acre plantation operated by whalers (it's hard to imagine that this part of New Jersey was in fact a whaling center during the late seventeenth century!). If you have children in tow, they might enjoy the farm animals living here, especially the chickens and very vocal rooster. You can also follow a map and read about the gardens in a brochure available at the gift shop, oddly enough located near the end of your walk. Birdwatchers take note: Leaming's Run is famous for its hummingbirds (especially in August), so bring along binoculars. Open daily, 9:30 A.M. to 5:00 P.M. from mid-May to mid-October. Admission fee.

NEW YORK CITY GARDENWALKS

1. Bronx: New York Botanical Garden
2. Bronx: Wave Hill
3. Brooklyn: Brooklyn Botanic Garden
4. Manhattan: The Cloisters
5. Manhattan: The Frick Collection
   Gardens

And in Addition . . .

6. Manhattan: Abigail Adams Smith
   Museum Garden
7. Manhattan: Battery Park City
   Esplanade
8. Manhattan: The Central Park
   Conservatory Garden
9. Manhattan: Ford Foundation
   Garden
10. Manhattan: Fort Tryon Park
11. Manhattan: West Side Community
    Garden
12. Queens: The Noguchi Museum
    and Sculpture Garden
13. Queens: Queens Botanical Garden
14. Staten Island: Snug Harbor

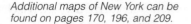
Additional maps of New York can be found on pages 170, 196, and 209.

NEW YORK

NEW YORK CITY

Brooklyn Botanic Garden, Brooklyn

The Brooklyn Botanic Garden at 1000 Washington Avenue is one of those surprises you happen upon in New York. In the midst of busy urban sprawl, around the corner from a dreary stretch of Flatbush Avenue (but very near the lovely Prospect Park), you enter the iron gates of the Brooklyn Botanic Garden. Once there, you find yourself in an enchanting, colorful, and completely intriguing world of planned gardens, elegant walkways, weeping cherry trees, and the many sights and smells of the world's most inviting gardens. The area was reclaimed from a waste dump in 1910. It takes up some 50 acres (but seems actually much larger), and you can walk among them quite randomly, from the Japanese paths along a lake to the former rose gardens, from the Shakespeare Garden to the excellent conservatories. As you will see in the description that follows, there are many pleasures in these 50 acres, particularly if you take this outing in the spring.

Every season highlights a different area or style of garden, but surely April, May, and June are the most colorful times to come, when the ornamental trees, luxuriant roses, and many spring flowers are in bloom. But the rock garden is ablaze with flowers during the entire growing season, and different species of roses bloom through September. A fragrance garden, labeled in Braille for the blind, is another fine section of the gardens; it, too, is open during the spring, summer, and fall.

All of the plants are labeled, and there are more than 12,000 of them. The conservatories and outdoor gardens among them include plants from almost every country in the world. If your taste is for literary references, you can enjoy the Shakespeare Garden, where plantings are related to passages from the Bard's works. If you want to meditate, you might choose to sit along the banks of the Japanese Garden's lovely walkways. If you are a horticultural fan, there is a Local Flora section and many interesting displays of temperate, rain forest, and desert plants.

Sometimes described as "many gardens within a garden" (there are 14 specialty gardens, many linked along a winding stream), the Brooklyn Botanic is one of the nicest places to spend a day in the city. (You can even eat in one of the gardens.) You'll find it a unique blending of intimacy and grandeur that brings to mind the fine gardens of England rather than the wilder acres of the Bronx Botanical Garden or Central Park.

At the two main entrances to the Botanic Garden (on Washington Avenue) you can pick up a very useful map, which will point you in the right direction. A good place to begin your walk is the Herb Garden, near the parking lot. This charming contoured plot contains over 300 carefully labeled herbs that have been used for medicine and cooking since the Middle Ages. Intricate planting patterns in Elizabethan knot shapes form an intriguing design and add a unique element to this garden. From here you can take a lower or upper walkway. The upper path will lead you to the Overlook, bordered by gingko trees and to the grassy terrace known as the Osbourne section, where a promenade of green lawns with stylishly shaped shrubs and freestanding columns await you. The pleasant, leafy lower lane will take you past groupings of peonies, crab apple trees, and wisteria to the Cherry Esplanade. We recommend you see this garden in late April or early May, when the deep pink blossoms of the Kwanzan cherry trees are a breathtaking dreamlike pastel. The trees are arranged in rows alongside tall, Norwegian maples whose dark red-leaves create a wonderful contrast in color.

The adjacent Cranford Rose Garden, with its 900 varieties (over 5,000 strong) is the third largest such garden in the country. In this acre of pure enchantment you can identify the roses and study them carefully or simply enjoy their rare beauty.

On the hillside behind a wooden fence is the Local Flora section, an unusual and less frequented garden. In these 2 secluded acres the nine ecological zones found within a 100-mile radius of the Botanic Garden have been recreated in dioramalike form. Serpentine rock, dry meadow and stream, kettle pond, bog, pine barrens, wet meadow and stream, deciduous woodland, border mound, and limestone ledge habitats are displayed with their corresponding flora and rock formations. This rare outdoor classroom is meant for serious observers and nature lovers (school groups are not invited) who want to spend time carefully examining the 100 or so plant varieties indigenous to this area, such as the many ferns, phlox, grasses, magnolias, pines, rhododendrons, larches, oaks, heather, persimmon trees, mosses, and dogwood found here. If you wish to study the plants further, you can pick up a guide called Local Flora section, available at the bookstore, since the plants in this garden are not labeled.

From the Local Flora section walk down the hill, past the hedge-wheel, a whimsical composition of 18 different hedging plants (boxwood, viburnum, holly, and yew) to the lovely rock garden on your right. Here, rounded glacial boulders define the site that is planted with contour evergreen shrubs, different types of ground cover, and flowering plants that provide a vivid palette of color for much of the year. Along the path are clumps of spring bulbs, honeysuckles, and forsythias. You'll walk past a bed of barberries that contains 20 varieties, from exotic bamboo-like plants to delicate specimens with dainty red and yellow buds. A stream meanders by, flanked by weeping willows, adding to the effect of a romantic English garden.

Eventually you will come to the conservatory complex (called the Steinhardt Conservatory). Here, three new, beautifully designed greenhouses contain a rich collection of tropical, temperate, and desert plants, including some 3,000 pounds of cacti and succulents brought from the Arizona desert. Throughout the year you can enjoy the wonderful flower displays as well as the permanent collection of palms, ferns, and exotic specimens that grace these pavilions. We particularly liked a grotto in the Tropical Pavilion carved

149

out of granite, and filled with ferns and the Aquatic House, containing two pools and various plants according to natural habitat. You can view the deeper pool from two perspectives: at the Aquatic House, where you look down on it, or from windows in the Exhibition Gallery on the lower floor, where these unusual aquatic plants can be examined from an angle people rarely see. One gallery is devoted to bonsai, and you can admire the prized collectors' items (some date from the 1920s) in their many varieties, from the most upright to surprisingly naturalistic styles. The curious and intricate art of dwarfing plants is carefully explained and described. The resulting "tray" gardens are real miniature versions—down to the last detail—of regular pines, bamboos, maples, or elms. While you are within the conservatories, don't miss the Exhibition Gallery in the central lower level. It features horticultural displays and art exhibits relating to plants in an atriumlike space.

Outside the conservatories, next to two reflecting pools, is the elegant Victorian Palm House, once the main conservatory. This lovely old building (now used for special gatherings) adds a dash of turn-of-the-century glamour to the complex. Nearby is the Administration Building, the focus of the many educational and research programs conducted by the Botanic Garden. Workshops, lectures, exhibits, concerts, films, and classes on just about anything relating to plants are held here. In addition, there is an Herbarium (which includes some 250,000 dried plant specimens), a plant and book shop, and a horticultural reference library.

The Magnolia Plaza, just outside, a terrace where over 80 magnolia trees bloom in May, is formally designed with concentric circular and linear paths. The path to your right (as you face the plaza) will take you to the Fragrance Garden, a delightful, intimate spot that is a pleasure to the senses. Here, plants labeled in Braille can also be identified through touching and smelling.

You'll find the Shakespeare Garden off to the east of the pathway. Here the tiny signs not only identify the plants but indicate Shakespeare's references to each flower. This is great fun for those of us who remember our plays and sonnets, and for those who don't, there is a guide available at the bookshop. It also includes a map noting where to find such flowers and featuring apt quotations: "I think the king is but a man, as I am. The violet smells to him as it doth to me" (*Henry V*), "For though the camomile, the more it is trodden on, the faster it grows, yet youth, the more it is wasted, the sooner it wears" (*Henry IV*), and "What's in a name? That which we call a rose by any other name would smell as sweet" (*Romeo and Juliet*). In addition to the many plants of note, the garden itself is laid out in a charming, orderly fashion surrounded by a serpentine wall. An oval brick path, a fountain, and a bench contribute to the impression of an English cottage garden of Shakespeare's times. Be sure to pick up the guide with its many nice illustrations of Elizabethan gardens before you get to this pretty spot, for it will add to your pleasure.

And, finally, you will come to what is arguably the highlight of a visit to the Botanic Garden: the exquisite Japanese Hill and Pond Garden. Designed by Tokeo Shiota in 1914, this prize garden reflects the religious and natural symbolism inherent in Japanese gardens in which various elements are combined to form a harmonious blend of beauty and peace.

INFORMATION
From April through September, the Botanic Garden is open Tuesday through Friday, 8 A.M. to 6 P.M., and weekends and holidays, 10 A.M. to 6 P.M.; from October to March, it is open Tuesday through Friday, 8:00 A.M. to 4:30 P.M., and on weekends and holidays, 10:00 A.M. to 4:30 P.M. Entrance fees are $3.00 for adults. The Conservatory's hours are Tuesday through Friday, 10 A.M. to 4 P.M., and weekends and holidays, 11 A.M. to 4 P.M. For information, call (718) 622-4433.

DIRECTIONS
From Manhattan, take the Manhattan Bridge, whose continuation in Brooklyn is Flatbush Avenue; stay on Flatbush all the way to the Grand Army Plaza at Prospect Park, and take the rotary three-fourths of the way around to Eastern Parkway, which borders the park. The Botanic Garden's entrance is immediately after the Central Library building. There is a large parking area. Fee.

The Cloisters, Manhattan

Among the particularly magical parts of the Cloisters (the Metropolitan Museum's medieval-style museum in northern Manhattan) are the gardens. While the pleasures of visiting the museum's medieval architecture and seeing its exquisite collection of fine art from the Middle Ages may be well known to New York's museumgoers, its gardens are in themselves well worth a special trip. The arcades of five cloisters have been reconstructed with the original stones and integrated into the museum's architecture; four cloisters surround their own unusual gardens. These spots are extraordinarily evocative; in fact, it is hard to believe you have to exit into the twentieth century when you leave.

Though they are small, as gardens go, they are so filled with architectural, sculptural, and botanical interest that you might spend many hours walking round and round, or dreamily sitting on a bench imagining you are in thirteenth-century France, perhaps, or a member of a twelfth-century Cistercian order. Dimly heard medieval music accompanies your walk, and of course, the art treasures of this distant past await you in the stone-walled rooms of the museum.

Two of the cloisters (square-columned walkways that once were parts of monasteries) are enjoyable to visit even out of garden season, for they are in covered areas and are kept flowering throughout the winter. All four of the cloister gardens are at their best in late spring and early summer, of course, when the flowers are blooming, the herbs bright and green, and the espaliers leafy on their trellises. The following thumbnail descriptions should give you an idea of what to expect from each of these (chronologically listed) gardenwalks.

The earliest cloister is Saint-Guilhem le Desert. Formerly part of a French abbey that dates back to a Benedictine order in A.D. 804, Saint-Guilhem Cloister was built in 1206. Its stone pillars are topped by capitals (with decorative carved tops) whose designs are based on the spiny leaf of the acanthus plant. But there are many additional patterns carved on these columns, including a wonderful series of faces, flowers, entwined vines, and elegant foliage. There are small holes drilled into these designs in intricate honeycomb patterns, and no two columns seem the same.

Some of the sculptural decoration can be traced to ancient Roman design (still in evidence in southern France). This cloister surrounds an indoor garden that is planted fully in early spring. When we saw it last in winter, the flowers were potted and neatly arranged. The architectural details occasionally seem to imitate the very shapes of the leaves and flowers.

Almost directly across the central room from the Saint-Guilhem le Desert Cloister is the wonderful Saint Michel de Cuxa Cloister, a beautiful spot both in winter and in spring and summer, when it is ablaze with flowers. This cloister was in a Benedictine abbey first built in 878, though the cloister itself is from the twelfth century. From an area northeast of the Pyrenées, it forms the central part of the framework of the Cloister museum and is appropriately gracious and inviting. Its original function as a communal place for monks to walk, meditate, read, or take part in processionals can be readily imagined. The lovely stone walks surrounded by archways and columns open onto a sunlit garden of individual bedded flowers and plants. Each column is carved with typically medieval gargoyles, two-headed animals, or two-bodied monsters. You will want to spend time examining this garden and its cloisters and, perhaps, sitting on a bench enjoying the ambiance of quiet and beauty.

On the lower level of the museum you'll find the Bonnefont Cloister, a purely outdoor garden walkway. Its origins are in the south of France, near Toulouse. The cloister, with its slender graceful columns in rows of twos, comes from the late thirteenth to the early fourteenth century. Cistercian monks once walked through these cloisters, and the very simple design of the architecture and limited amount of sculptural pattern represent their asceticism. (Decoration was not meant to draw attention away from devotion to duty and God.) Of particular garden interest here is the herb garden, a favorite among New Yorkers. More than 250 species of plants that were grown in the Middle Ages are cultivated in this outdoor space. In the center is a charming little well. The herbs are grown in raised planting beds with fences around them. Among our particular favorites here are the trained espaliers, growing against lattices in the sunlight. Anyone with an interest in gardening will find this cloister irresistible.

Finally, the fourth cloister, also on the lower level, is the Trie Cloister, from a Carmelite building in the Bigorre region of southern France. Reassembled with parts of several other cloisters, this small outdoor garden arcade is of particular interest if you look at the Unicorn Tapestries in the museum. The garden contains samples of the very plants woven into the design of the tapestries some five centuries ago. (Information at the Cloisters will identify them for you.) Part of the charm of this garden is the sight of the red tile roof surrounding it and the fruit trees set among the flowers. This garden, of course, is also cultivated only during growing months.

Though obviously you will get more pleasure out of this medieval garden walk in the growing season, even in wintertime it is nice to wander about the unkempt cloisters outdoors, to see the view of the Hudson, and to contemplate the beauty of the architecture and sculptural designs in the indoor gardens.

Among the many treasures you will want to enjoy in the museum while you are there are the Unicorn Tapestries, the stained glass in the Boppard Room, the wonderful altarpiece by the fifteenth-century painter Robert Campin, and our particular favorites, the medieval wood sculptures. Children, by the way, will enjoy this walk; there are numerous crenellated walls, dark staircases, impressive and picturesque statues that they'll love, and even medieval playing cards on display.

A visit to the Cloisters is perhaps the closest you can get to being in France while in Manhattan. We found the combination of art, history, and flowering plants an irresistible delight.

INFORMATION

Many events of interest are held at the Cloisters; among them are gallery talks on such subjects as medieval imagery, tapestries, gardens of the Middle Ages, and colors in use in medieval France. There are many concerts of medieval music played on early-period instruments. You will also find demonstrations of how medieval art was made, including such techniques as enameling and miniature painting. There is a guide to the gardens in which each plant is labeled and described. For information on all these events, including guided tours, call (212) 923-3700. If you feel the need for additional exercise, you might wish to leave the Cloisters by way of Fort Tryon Park and walk south through this very pleasant park with its terrific views of the Hudson and New Jersey's Palisades. (See page 166)

Obviously, the best time to visit is during the week, when the museum is less crowded (although you might meet groups of schoolchildren). Hours: Tuesday to Sunday, 9:30 A.M. to 5:15 P.M., March to October; Tuesday to Sunday, 9:30 A.M. to 4:45 P.M., November to February. Closed New Year's Day, Thanksgiving, and Christmas. Fee.

DIRECTIONS

Take the West Side Highway (Route 9A, Henry Hudson Parkway) north to first exit after the George Washington Bridge (Dyckman Street). Follow signs. Parking on premises.

The Frick Collection Gardens, Manhattan

Most visitors agree that the Frick Collection is among New York City's most inviting museums. Its exceptional masterworks (by Rembrandt, El Greco, Veronese, Van Dyck, Gainsborough, Turner, Constable, and Fragonard, among many others) are displayed in an unusually appealing, noninstitutional setting, suggesting the grand private estate it once was. The present galleries still seem like living quarters, with elegant furnishings, plantings and freshly cut flowers, and choice artifacts complementing the harmonious decor. And—of special interest to us—are its two delightful gardens: an indoor courtyard and a small outdoor garden framed by one of the neo-classical facades of the building.

The interior court, formerly an open carriage court, was designed by John Russell Pope, who converted the mansion into a museum in the early 1930s. It has a barrel-vaulted glass roof, an elegant central fountain, Ionic coupled columns, and colonnades. Surrounding the pool are bronze sculptures and marble walkways and a wide assortment of tropical plants and flowering shrubs, which are changed frequently throughout the year. On the bleakest of winter days you will be immensely cheered by this exuberant display, as you sit amid the plantings on one of the stone benches.

The outdoor garden, created in the 1970s, was originally meant to be a temporary site until a new gallery could be built in its place; it has since become a permanent—and major asset—to the Frick. Those who are familiar with the work of the well-known British landscape architect Russell Page (see PepsiCo in Purchase, page 187) will be able to identify this as one of his designs. Uncluttered simplicity, serenity, and understated elegance best describe the garden. It adheres to Page's view that "all the good gardens I have ever seen . . . were the result of . . . a simple idea developed as far as it could be . . ." He believed that a city garden in particular ought to exude tranquillity, much like an oasis.

In the tradition of Islamic gardens (which were a source of inspiration for Page), a formal lily pool is at the center of this symmetrically shaped garden, creating the illusion of a larger space. The water level of the pool and its stone edging are virtually flush with the small, rectangular grassy plot surrounding it. A single fountain jet (in typical Page-like restraint) graces the pool, and then is turned on only in winter when there is less plant color to provide interest.

Around the garden are a rectangular path lined with carefully clipped hedges and narrow borders of roses, azaleas, hydrangeas, and lilies. Climbing ivies and wisterias and a few ornamental trees add a sense of verticality to the design, echoed by the tall city buildings in the background. The overall effect of serenity is a welcome respite from the bustle of Manhattan, just beyond the garden gates.

It is not surprising that the Frick is high on the list of most visitors to New York, whether they love art or gardens or both.

INFORMATION
The Frick Collection is located at 1 East 70th Street in Manhattan. Telephone: (212) 288-0700. Hours: 10 A.M. to 6 P.M., Tuesday through Saturday; 1 P.M. to 6 P.M., Sundays (closed Mondays and selected holidays). Note: Children under 10 are not admitted. There is an entrance fee. Concerts, special exhibits, and lectures are held throughout the year. Call for information.

New York Botanical Garden, Bronx

A visit to the New York Botanical Garden in the Bronx, where you are transported to a special world, will lift your spirits at any time of the year. For here, in this wonderful and vast oasis of natural beauty, all sorts of plants and flowers proliferate during much of the year—whether inside the grand Conservatory or throughout the acres of meadows, woodlands, ponds, brooks, hills, and gardens.

The New York Botanical Garden—one of the largest and most important in the country—was the creation of Dr. Nathaniel Lord Britton, a young American botanist. While on his honeymoon in England in 1889, he and his bride visited the Royal Botanic Gardens at Kew outside of London. They were so inspired by what they saw that they were able to convince the Torrey Botanical Club in New York to create a similar public institution for botany and horticulture within the newly formed Bronx Park.

The resulting complex is on a grand scale, encompassing the famous Enid A. Haupt Conservatory, as well as a wide variety of outdoor gardens and buildings housing a library, botanical shop, classrooms, and administrative offices. The Conservatory has been under restoration and has recently reopened.

This elegant Victorian greenhouse, ambitiously patterned after the Palmer House at Kew Gardens (1844) and the Crystal Palace at Hyde

Park in London (1851), has been one of the main attractions of the Botanical Garden since its beginnings. Once the painstaking restoration (including the refurbishing of 17,000 individual panes of glass) is complete, its many galleries, reflecting pools, courtyards, and magnificent plantings and changing displays will again draw thousands of enthusiastic visitors.

Although a portion of the garden's 250 acres are at the present time untended for lack of funds, most visitors find the well-maintained grounds surrounding the Conservatory (some 40 acres) enough to keep them busy. Anyone—from children and casual strollers, to serious gardeners and students of botany—will find something of interest in these gardens.

The Demonstration Gardens outside the Conservatory offer ideas for cultivating home gardens. Among these is a recently renewed fragrance garden, where you can sit and enjoy deliciously scented flowers; a cutting garden, with seasonal plantings; a vegetable garden specializing in late summer and early fall crops; and the Rodney White Country Garden, which features informal, minimum maintenance native plantings (many of which flower well into the autumn) in a rustic setting.

A walk (or inexpensive trolley ride) leads to other specialty gardens. Depending on the season, you'll find peonies (some 58 varieties), daffodils and daylilies, tulips, and chrysanthemums proliferating along bordered pathways. There is a lovely seasonal border that features tulips in spring, annuals in summer, and fall color in autumn; a maze ready made for toddlers and a children's activity center with activities every weekend, spring through fall; a small, elegant herb garden that displays 92 species of European and American varieties; and a fine rock garden, where masses of alpine flowers are interspersed with giant boulders around a picturesque waterfall. There is a native plant garden, with abundant wildflowers growing amid such different environments as forest trees, a limestone outcropping, marshy meadow, and a sandy strip like that of the New Jersey Pine Barrens.

The Peggy Rockefeller Rose Garden is a particular pleasure; its geometric designs are formed by crisscrossing paths amid rose beds containing 2,700 examples of more than 200 varieties. Families with children will take pleasure in the Family Garden, where children can plant, cultivate, and harvest flowers and vegetables within a 1.5-acre plot.

Throughout these varied gardens are avenues of bulb displays, hills of daffodils, circular beds of crocuses, and masses of azaleas and lilacs, flowering crab apples, cherry trees, and magnolias—truly a feast for the eye!

You might also want to explore parts of the forest, which cuts through the middle of the garden. This 40-acre woodland is supposedly the only section remaining of the original forest that once covered all of New York City.

After you have taken in all this natural beauty, you might browse in the Shop-in-the-Garden; in the same building is the impressive library (open to the public for research) with over 190,000 volumes of plant science literature (some dating from the thirteenth century). The library is still considered one of the best of its kind, befitting one of the world's great centers of plant study.

INFORMATION

The New York Botanical Garden is located at 200th Street and Southern Boulevard in the Bronx. It is open year-round (indoor and outdoor seasonal displays make it a pleasure to visit at most any time). Hours: April through October, Tuesday through Sunday, and Monday and holidays, from 10 A.M. to 6 P.M.; November through March, from 10 A.M. to 4 P.M. Library hours: Tuesday through Thursday, noon to 6 P.M.; Friday, noon to 5 P.M.

There are an entrance fee, a parking fee, as well as fees to the Conservatory, and a few of the specialty gardens. Tram tours (tickets for sale on the tram), guided walking tours of the gardens and the forest (information at the Visitor Center), and self-guided family garden tours are available as are combination tickets. Free booklets describing the demonstration gardens can be found on site. There are picnic areas (near Twin Lakes and the Snuff Mill), as well as two cafés and a new restaurant. For general information, call (718) 817-8700; customized group tours, call (718) 817-8687; for garden events, call (718) 817-8777.

DIRECTIONS

From Manhattan take the Bronx River Parkway north, either from the Cross Bronx Expressway (I-95) or from the Triborough Bridge and the Bruckner Expressway (Route 278). Follow signs for Botanical Garden (after the Bronx Zoo). Parking on the premises (fee).

Wave Hill, Bronx

Wave Hill is one of New York City's less known gems. Although familiar to some—particularly gardeners in the know—this rare botanical garden/art environmental center comes as a real surprise to most first-time visitors. Its picturesque setting high above the Hudson River, with remarkable views on all sides, its vast rolling lawns dotted with huge old trees and occasional sculpture, its acres of woodlands, and especially its internationally acclaimed gardens, make this 28-acre park a unique spot. And, as you stroll by its two stately manor houses set amid the plantings, you'll imagine you're enjoying a day at a private estate, miles away from the city.

In fact, in the past Wave Hill was the country home of several prominent New Yorkers. From the time the first of its two houses was built in 1843 by the jurist William Lewis Morris, it was occupied by illustrious people who often entertained members of New York society. As a boy, Teddy Roosevelt spent two summers here with his family, where it is said he learned to appreciate nature. William Makepeace Thackeray visited on occasion, Mark Twain lived here from 1901 to 1903 (and even built a treehouse on the grounds), and Arturo Toscanini occupied the house from 1942 to 1945. Most proprietors of Wave Hill were interested in preserving the incredible natural site from profiteering land developers and in further enhancing it with both formal and naturalistic landscaping.

The financier George Perkins, who moved in during the 1890s, was particularly successful in securing Wave Hill's future. (A conservationist, he also led the movement to preserve the Palisades and organized the Palisades Interstate Park.) He expanded the estate, adding greenhouses, gardens, orchards, pergolas, and terraces. Working with a landscape gardener from Vienna, he created an English landscape–style garden, mingling formal with informal plantings and rare trees and shrubs with more common species. Many of these plantings still remain. In 1960 the Perkins family deeded the estate to New York City to become an environmental center for the enjoyment of everyone.

Today, Wave Hill offers programs in horticulture, environmental education, land management, landscape history, and the visual and performing arts.

But, above all, Wave Hill is a place in which to savor a group of extraordinary formal and wild gardens, both indoor and outdoor. Largely the creation of Marco Polo Stufano, Director of Horticulture since 1967, these gardens plus conservatory greenhouses, and shade borders are surprisingly intimate, in contrast to the grandeur of the surrounding landscape. The plantings have been designed on a small scale, separated by grassy areas and paths; the result is an inviting and personal environment, in keeping with Wave Hill's tradition as a private estate.

The gardens have been conceived as living and changing environments rather than as static historic reproductions. Instead of "going by the book," Stufano has opted for imaginative and not too thought out solutions. The results are artistic displays with unconventional combinations and shapes and unusually vibrant colors. For example, contrary to traditional garden design, brilliant shades of red, orange, and hot pink are sometimes mixed. With color as one of the guiding principles, each of the gardens and conservatories has been planned so that seasonal changes always offer something of visual interest.

The diversity of plants is staggering—some 1,100 classifications of plants and well over 3,000 species. (In the "Wild Garden" an exuberant collection of pure species from all five continents is displayed.)

But Wave Hill is more than an unusual botanic garden with a wide range of species. From the moment you walk through the gates, past the small parking area and onto the meandering brick walkway, you know you're in a very special place—for the landscape has a feeling of space, with breathtaking views and grand vistas. At the same time it has intimacy and charm—unlike most institutional botanic gardens—and an atmosphere of peacefulness and ease. On nice days you sometimes see people sitting in the grass or in comfortable wooden chairs scattered about the lawn, enjoying the view. Others may be sketching, photographing, or wandering among the various gardens.

Directly in front of the entrance is a nineteenth-century Italianate columned pergola, a perfect lookout point to the Hudson River and the Palisades. To the right of the entrance, on the site of the former rose garden, is an enchanting flower garden. Enclosed by a rustic cedar fence, it is reminiscent of early twentieth-century American gardens, with such old-fashioned favorites as peonies, roses, clematis, and hydrangeas. Its 8 symmetrical beds contain vintage plantings, as well as modern perennials, annuals, shrubs, bulbs, and other varieties. The look is carefree and romantic. You will frequently see people examining the flowers with book (or brochure available on site) in hand, admiring the colors and artistic combinations.

Behind the flowers are the conservatory and greenhouses, where you can see tender plants from around the world, as well as exotic palms, cactus and succulents, and tropical plants. These indoor gardens are particularly welcoming in winter.

From here you reach an enclosed herb garden, where you can find a great variety of species (well over 100) that have been used in cooking, healing, ornamentation, or religious observance through the ages. The protected "Dry Garden" comes next, featuring plants from the warmer and dryer regions of the world. Near it are a delightful alpine house and trough gardens with tiny alpine plants and miniature flowers (best seen in late winter and early spring).

Intimate paths along the hillside lead to the Wild Garden, so called because it contains no hybrids. Its inviting nooks are filled with perennials and shrubs of different sizes and shapes arranged in a naturalistic vein. Facing it is one of two trellised pergolas with climbing vines that enclose both the "Aquatic Garden" and the "Monocot Garden." The former is reminiscent of Japanese gardens, with delicate water lilies and ornamental grasses, among other aquatic plants. It is at its best in late summer and through the fall. From the "Monocot Garden" (which displays a single group of plants in its variations) you can see more expanse of lawns and forests, as well as river views. A 10-acre woodland beyond is now being restored with native plants.

Works of an environmental nature are exhibited indoors. They are shown in the Wave Hill House and Glyndor House. The older of these, Wave Hill House, is a handsome nineteenth-century field-stone building with white shutters and a vast terrace overlooking the river. Here you can pick up a map of the area, as well as sundry pieces of literature and brochures relating to exhibits and subjects of horticultural interest. The Wave Hill Gift Shop specializes in garden-related books and gifts for all ages. The Wave Hill Café is open to the public.

INFORMATION

Wave Hill is located at Independence Avenue and West 249th Street in the Riverdale section of the Bronx. It is open Tuesday through Sunday, 9:00 A.M. to 4:30 P.M., 5:30 P.M. in summertime. (The greenhouses are open only from 10 A.M. to 12 noon and 2 P.M. to 4 P.M.) Closed on major holidays. We recommend weekdays, when Wave Hill is free and uncrowded. There are nominal fees Wednesdays through Sundays with the exception of members and children under 6. Admission is free Tuesdays and Saturdays before noon. The park is a joy to visit at any time of the year, even in winter. For information about hours or special events, call (718) 549-3200.

DIRECTIONS

From Manhattan, take the West Side Highway (Route 9A, Henry Hudson Parkway) to Riverdale. After the Henry Hudson Bridge toll booths, take 246th Street exit. Drive on the parallel road north to 252nd Street, where you turn left and go over the highway. Turn left and drive south on the parallel road to 249th Street and turn right. Wave Hill is straight down the hill. Parking on the grounds.

And in Addition . . .

You may be surprised to find several delightful gardens nestled among the bustling streetscapes of New York City. We are not referring here to the glamorous Brooklyn Botanic Garden (see page 147), or to the inimitable New York Botanical Garden in the Bronx (see page 156), or to the city's crowning jewel, its great Central Park, a landscape designed by Frederick Law Olmsted.

We refer, here, to the smallish oases found in the heart of the city—places to rest and contemplate startling aesthetic beauty just around the corner or across the street from the urban cacophony we know as New York. You may wish to spend a lunch hour, or a respite after work, or a weekend afternoon exploring the following special gardens:

Manhattan: Abigail Adams Smith Museum Garden
421 East 61st Street. Telephone: (212) 838-6878.
This charming colonial garden adjoins the fine old house (now a museum open to the public) that once belonged to a daughter of

John Adams. You are welcome to walk around the garden without visiting the museum. Planted in characteristic eighteenth-century way, this quaint garden is a charming example of America's most decorative style. Influenced by the Dutch idea of patterned gardens surrounded by colonial board fences, the flowering area is delightful. We recommend a visit in springtime, when tulips, crocus, and hyacinth interspersed with patterns of brickwork and English ivy make this a bright and charming place to visit. (It is particularly astonishing because it is in the middle of a nondescript block of East Side Manhattan, and invisible from the street.) A brick terrace with old-fashioned benches sits above the flower area. On this level is an herb garden. There are trees and shrubs—many of the flowering varieties, whose best blossoms can be seen in May—including mock orange, viburnum, and flowering quince. Under these trees you'll find a profusion of violets and other bright flowers. But all is orderly in the garden, as recommended by early American (and European) gardeners. This is a well-kept garden, despite the harsh environment of the city. And also a well-kept secret, even among natives of the city. A garden map is available at the desk. Hours: 10 A.M. to 4 P.M., Monday through Friday; 1 P.M. to 5 P.M., Sunday (September through May); and 5:30 P.M. to 8:00 P.M., Tuesdays in June and July. The museum is closed in August. There is a small admission charge to see the house; none for the garden.

Manhattan: Ford Foundation Garden

320 East 43rd Street (entrance to the garden is from 42nd Street, between First and Second avenues).

Also in Manhattan, and surprisingly right in midtown, is the Ford Foundation Building, halfway between First and Second avenues on the north side of 42nd Street. (The official address is 320 East 43rd Street, although the entrance to the garden is from 42nd.) This tasteful, contemporary glass edifice is constructed around one of New York's most fabulous and spacious interior gardens, a 130-foot-high "greenhouse" that can be enjoyed by employees and visitors alike. (The garden is open to the public on weekdays during office hours.) All the interior windows in the building look out onto the spectacular greenery rather than the usual cityscape. The one-third-acre oasis is a lush combination of tall trees, terraced shrubbery, groundcover, and water plants gracing a tranquil pond. Although there are seasonal outbursts of brilliantly colored blossoms, the garden is mostly a subtle study of different intensities and shades of green. One can only wish that more urban corporate centers would create such luxuriant green spaces.

Manhattan: The Conservatory Garden
Fifth Avenue, between 104th and 105th streets.

Nestled into the northeast corner of Central Park is one of the city's most cherished garden spaces, the Conservatory Garden, where you will find yourself in a garden of great elegance and beauty; it was a gift from the Vanderbilt family a century ago. Classically styled with columns, walkways, areas of lawn, flower beds, two fountains, and stairways, this perfectly maintained garden is a delight. You can stroll through its elegant paths, and rest among the vine-colored trellises, admire the changing flower garden. Truly an oasis in the bustle and cement of the city, the Conservatory is a rare, beautifully kept spot.

One of the city's favorite fountains, the Untermyer Fountain with its three dancing maidens, is a centerpiece of the Conservatory Garden to the north. Made some time before 1910, the fountain has three whimsical bronze figures dancing around its single jet of water. It was made by Walter Schott, a German sculptor and portraitist. Its light, airy design is a charming addition to the harmonious spaces and bright colors of the garden. Also in the Conservatory Garden to the south is a memorial to the author of *The Secret Garden* and *Little Lord Fauntleroy*, the Francis Hodgson Burnett Memorial Fountain. The sculpture surrounding the fountain consists of a small boy playing the flute while a young girl holding a seashell listens. A birdbath at her feet spills into a small pool. The fountain was created by Bessie Potter Vonnoh between 1926 and 1937. Hours are daily before dusk.

Manhattan: West Side Community Garden
Between 89th and 90th Streets near Amsterdam Avenue in the heart of the Upper West Side, one of Manhattan's especially "community-aware" neighborhoods, is this intimate and charming green oasis. Here, amid brilliantly colored flowers arranged in circular terraced beds, graceful trellises, shade trees, and small vegetable plots (some tended by local school groups), people of all ages enjoy a quiet respite from the urban scene. To view the gardens up close you can walk on a small path and up wood steps to the different levels of

flower beds. A few random tables and chairs beneath leafy canopies complete the tasteful decor. We only wish that more such inviting spots were scattered about the city!

Manhattan: Battery Park City Esplanade
Battery Park City.
Though not a traditional garden, this riverside landscape was designed by environmental artist Mary Miss. It is an unusual and enchanting way of combining the natural landscape of the Hudson River's dramatic shoreline with urban and people-oriented design. (We recommend a walk through the entire riverside park for a taste of contemporary urban planning, sculpture, and plantings.)

To get to Battery Park in lower Manhattan, cross the Westway highway (either by overhead walkway or by street level at the traffic light) to reach the far side of the World Trade Center complex. Turn south and walk on South End Avenue to Albany Street, where you turn once again west, toward the Hudson River. Battery Park City is a planned community of high-rise apartments and parks that face the Hudson River. The designing of artworks to enhance the site has been a part of the project from the beginning, and works by Mary Miss, Ned Smyth, R. M. Fischer, Richard Artschwager, and Scott Burton (among others) are very much in evidence. The Battery Park City Fine Arts Program has become a sort of test laboratory for the combining of architecture, city planning, gardens, and art at a very spectacular site; it is fascinating to view this contemporary version of an ancient idea.

All the art at Battery Park City was commissioned by the city and was chosen expressly to enhance the new site. One of the most important and successful of these commissions is environmental artist Mary Miss's design for the esplanade at its south end. Her proposal for the shoreline included a lookout, pilings that rise and fall with the river tide, wooden wisteria-covered archways, boardwalks lighted with blue lanterns, and Japanese-style rock gardens. The architect Stanton Eckstut and landscape architect Susan Child helped to execute the artist's design. While the site art is surely a form of gentrification of the natural shoreline (you can see what the banks looked like in a wilder state just over the fence at the edge), it is a major attempt to balance the sophisticated urban setting on the shore with the Hudson's rather wild and somber coastline. From the top of the curving steel staircase, you can enjoy an extraordinary view of the shapes and patterns of Mary Miss's design, as well as of the city, the river, and New Jersey.

Manhattan: Fort Tryon Park

193rd Street and Fort Washington Avenue. Telephone (Department of Parks): (212) 397-3007.

"What the English call a terrace . . . the crescent shaped intermediate space being either a quiet slope of turf, a parterre of flowers, . . . a picturesque rocky declivity treated perhaps as a fernery or alpine garden . . ."—this was the plan described by Frederick Law Olmsted and Calvert Vaux when they proposed turning this spectacular site into a park.

About 19 years after Olmsted and Vaux created New York's "crowning jewel"—Central Park—they suggested this hilly terrain with its glorious Hudson River panorama as a site worth preserving. Their design for the crescent-shaped area in the Inwood section of the city became Fort Tryon Park. This surprising urban oasis is still a beautiful example of park design, with colorful gardens nestled into the highland landscape above the Hudson and affording a magnificent view of the river and the Palisades beyond. Fort Tryon Park has, in fact, been called one of the most beautiful parks in America.

Inwood is a northern, cliffside section of the city, where about two-fifths of the land is parkland, including caves once inhabited by Native Americans. At its northern end you'll find the Cloisters—New York's magnificent medieval museum (with cloister gardens, see page 151). The 62 acres of Fort Tryon Park are landscaped with terraces, rock gardens, paved walks, benches, stone archways, and everywhere—amazing views. This urban design never intrudes on its panoramic setting: miles of Hudson River vistas to the West, and urban landscapes far below to the East. At the southern entrance to the park is a large sloping rock garden; a walk through it will lead to the site of the old Fort Tryon (built in 1777). Much of the park area was part of an estate, purchased by John D. Rockefeller, Jr., and given to the city.

Fort Tryon's gardens are nestled within the terraced hillside. Large flower beds (originally laid out by Olmsted's son) are kept up quite nicely, with dozens of different plantings blooming throughout the growing season. Perennials such as iris and phlox and heather are intermixed with exotic shrubs and flowering trees. The gardens are informal and inviting; instead of appearing to be imposed on the landscape, they fit in with their spectacular surroundings as if they just happened to be there. Which is, of course, what Olmsted surely had in mind.

A visit to Fort Tryon Park can easily be combined with a visit to The Cloisters. Since this is a city park, we recommend that Fort Tryon Park be visited in daylight hours only when it is apt to be filled with strollers.

Queens: Queens Botanical Garden

43-50 Main Street and Dahlia Avenue. Telephone: (718) 886-3800.
Queens Botanical Garden (once a dumping ground) is a pleasant 38-acre park of which about half is dedicated to formal plantings. You'll enjoy the Perkins Memorial Rose Collection (with its more than 4,000 bushes), a rock garden, an herb garden, and a specialized garden for the blind. In spring, flowering cherry trees, crab apples, and thousands of bright tulips add their magic, while in fall you can enjoy a wonderful display of colorful chrysanthemums. Queens Botanical Garden is a small but attractive spot to visit, with flat terrain for easy walking. The garden also sponsors a variety of year-round workshops on such topics as Japanese-style dish gardens and hanging gardens for indoor or outdoor use.

Queens: The Noguchi Museum and Sculpture Garden

32-37 Vernon Boulevard, Long Island City. Telephone: (718) 204-7088.
The Noguchi Museum and Sculpture Garden is about the best disguised art center we've discovered on our wanderings through the city. Set into blocks of old warehouses, it appears to be another nondescript, rectangular building, but on closer inspection you'll see the angles of a contemporary-style building nestling into its triangular city block. Noguchi wanted a home for his works that would be congenial to their style and to his concept of art's relationship to its surroundings. "These are private sculptures," he said, "a dialogue between myself and the primary matter of the universe."

And what you will find at the museum are some 350 works that demonstrate the great Japanese sculptor's spiritual presence, as well as his evolving use of stone and other natural materials. The walled-off sculpture garden brings traditional Asian design to the twentieth century. In these delicate stone works, trickling water fountains, abstract shapes, and patterns catch the light and do indeed give you the sensation of being very far away from both Manhattan and the twentieth century.

Yet Noguchi was, in fact, a quintessentially twentieth-century artist. His search was for abstract realities or what he called "the brilliance of matter" that will turn "stone into the music of the spheres." Everywhere—in the rough stone pillars, the delicate marble pieces, the rounded basalt mounds, the intricate black metal abstractions— you sense the sculptor's preoccupation with pure form and its relationship to the space around it. In this setting of careful calm and contemplation, the word "garden" takes on new meaning. Although this is not art that is "easy" to understand for the layperson, it is nevertheless an experience that will change the way even the most unreceptive observer of contemporary art looks at stone. You will have a new idea of how sculpture can both shape its surroundings and become a part of them. A shuttle bus from Manhattan is available. Fee.

Staten Island: Snug Harbor

Richmond Terrace and Snug Harbor Road. Telephone: (718) 448-2500. This is a delightful "village" of historic buildings and gardens—a true "find" in New York. From its Gothic Revival houses to its conservatory and concert hall and outdoor sculpture, this is a wonderful place for a walk and a cultural outing.

As you enter Snug Harbor you'll first come to the small cottages now used by artists-in-residence. Opposite the cottages are the greenhouse and the particularly charming flower gardens. The landscape of the entire park is Victorian in feeling, and so are the garden areas. Among the high points of this landscape are the trees, including wonderful willows and a superb collection of flower gardens. The Botanical Garden, which moved to the site in 1975, has put in a variety of small gardens: a formal English perennial garden, a butterfly garden (whose plants are specifically nourishing to butterflies), a Victorian rose garden, an herb garden featuring medicinal and culinary plantings, a "white" garden, which experiments with vertical plantings, a bog garden, and—inside the conservatory—the Neil Vanderbilt Orchid Collection. Any garden enthusiast will enjoy the way these small treasures of planting are arranged—each (in its own season, of course) is a treat. A variety of tours, lectures, and demonstrations are available, but you can also enjoy wandering on your own.

Of particular charm near the gardens is the Chinese-style pagoda built by Charles Locke Eastlake of England. This little pavilion is a concert site and an additional Victorian touch to the landscape. At the end of the garden is a dark-green lattice-worked enclosure planted with charming flowers, and you can sit on the white wrought-iron benches and enjoy a summer's day. We found it particularly appealing.

Scattered throughout the lovely grounds of the center are about 20 contemporary sculptures at any one time. Sculptures in stone, metal, and mixed media are widely spaced throughout the green fields. (Pick up a guide to the current show at the visitor's center.) The exhibitions are usually mounted around mid-June and run through the month of October, when most of them are taken down. (A few traditional sculptures remain year-round.) The exhibits of contemporary sculpture are very up to date. A tour of all the sculptures—if you walk at a brisk pace—will take you about one hour. Open daily, 9 A.M. to 5 P.M., year-round; the gardens are best in spring and early summer. Fee.

HUDSON VALLEY

Wethersfield, Amenia

There are many ways in which gardens can be artistic—or appear to be art themselves. Topiary gardens are like parks of living sculpture, while sculpture parks are themselves gardens of art.

At Wethersfield, a country estate near Amenia, New York, you'll find gardens that are at once repositories for sculpture and themselves a kind of spatial work of art. As you walk through the landscaped grounds of Wethersfield you'll have a sense of *trompe l'oeil*—that French style of painting that plays spatial tricks on the unsuspecting (but delighted) viewer.

Wethersfield's gardens are so artful that the eye can be deceived by the long allées and decorative gates, and the geometric shapes of pruned bushes and trees that form the setting for its marble statuary. The gardens within gardens, the sense of perspective, the carefully placed statuary, reminded us of the surreal gardens of Réne Magritte's paintings, where a hat may appear over a hedge in a dreamlike green garden of distant proportions and uncertain boundaries.

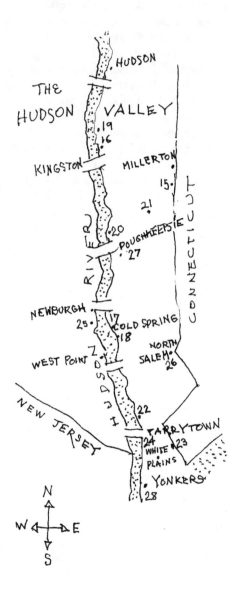

The Hudson Valley

HUDSON

THE HUDSON VALLEY

.19
.16

KINGSTON

MILLERTON
15.

21.

.20
POUGHKEEPSIE
.27

CONNECTICUT

NEWBURGH .
25. .17
COLD SPRING
.18

WEST POINT

NORTH
SALEM.
26

HUDSON RIVER

.22

NEW JERSEY

TARRYTOWN
24 .23
WHITE
PLAINS

. YONKERS.
.28

N
W — E
S

HUDSON VALLEY GARDENWALKS

15. Amenia: Wethersfield
16. Annandale-on-Hudson: Montgomery Place
17. Cold Spring: Stonecrop Gardens
18. Garrison-on-Hudson: Boscobel
19. Germantown: Clermont State Historic Site
20. Hyde Park: Vanderbilt Mansion Gardens
21. Millbrook: Innisfree Garden
22. Pocantico Hills: Kykuit
23. Purchase: The Donald M. Kendall Sculpture Gardens at PepsiCo
24. Tarrytown: Lyndhurst

And in Addition . . .
25. Mountainville: Storm King Art Center
26. North Salem: The Hammond Museum and Japanese Stroll Garden
27. Poughkeepsie: Springside Restoration
28. Yonkers: Untermyer Park

The gardens are the high point of the visit to this country estate (and working farm) that has just opened formally to the public.

Wethersfield was the home of Chauncey Stillman, an investor and philanthropist, who purchased it in 1937. The estate now consists of 1,400 acres. The setting of the house and gardens is magnificent, overlooking a vast panorama of fields and mountains—the Catskills to the west and the Berkshires to the north. The gardens cover more than 10 acres of the estate and provide a marvelous place to walk. There are also woodland paths that you can enjoy at your leisure. Leave yourself plenty of time to see them, and even to walk through the woods to the Palladian arches at the edge of the field. Pick up a map at the upper parking lot, where you leave your car. You'll find the brochures in a basket between two stone lions. The gardens, which you will enter here, are generally neoclassical and French in style. They are simultaneously grand and intimate. You might even see the occasional peacock strolling past. Each garden is separated from the next with hedges or wrought iron gates. Though there are formal flower beds, it is the geometric design of borders and flag-stone paths, reflecting pools, and green walls of hedges that create the special ambiance of this place. There are cones, balls, columns, and boulder-shaped topiary designs, as well as gargoyles and cherubs, temples, animal sculptures and classical figures everywhere, nestling into the greenery and demarcating each individual area.

You'll find a lily pond with sculptured turtles; deer sculptures by John Flannagan; two Pans by Peter Watts, an Englishman; two nymphs and a Hercules of limestone; some charming recumbent sheep, a naiad by the Swedish sculptor Carl Milles gracing a fountain; and a stone stairway leading to a "belvedere" with a stunning view of the landscape.

A Polish artist named Joseph Stachura made many of Wethersfield's sculptures, including the Madonna and other religious works around the grounds. They are representational marble carvings that are graciously placed here and there in shrinelike settings.

All the sculpture is traditional—this is not a venue for the latest in abstract works. Instead, it is a period setting with a strikingly "modern" sense of space. Like an outdoor gallery, the gardens are a form of three-dimensional art, ornamented with sculpture; the emphasis of the landscape design has surely been on form.

But this is not to say that there are not charming flower beds and wonderful trees. There are, in fact, a rose garden, perennial gardens, a cutting garden, and many other distinctive sections. (An army of gardeners works year-round.)

INFORMATION
Wethersfield house, gardens, and carriage house are open Wednesdays, Fridays, and Saturdays, June 1 through September 30. To visit the house or carriage house or garden you must make an advance reservation. The gardens are open noon to 5 P.M. There is a moderate entrance fee. Telephone: (914) 373-8037.

DIRECTIONS
Wethersfield is located in northern Dutchess County, New York. From the Taconic Parkway, take Route 44 north of Millbrook, then take Country Road 86 (Bangall-Amenia Road) and turn right onto Pugsley Hill Road. Follow signs about 1 1/3 miles to the entrance on the left.

In the vicinity are the beautiful gardens of Innisfree (see page 183).

Montgomery Place, Annandale-On-Hudson

Montgomery Place is one of the great Hudson River estates, combining romantic, sweeping landscaped lawns, woodlands, and panoramic views. This 434-acre site includes a nineteenth-century mansion (open for visitors), a few formal gardens, magnificent trees, and a wide variety of walking trails. Though its formal gardens are not yet spectacular (they are in the process of restoration), the overall landscape of ancient trees, wildflowers, and breathtaking views make a long walk here idyllic.

Described in an 1866 guidebook of the fine estates along this portion of the Hudson as "the most perfect in its beauty and arrangements," Montgomery Place was admired for "waterfalls, picturesque bridges, romantic glens, groves, a magnificent park, one of the most beautiful of the ornamental gardens in this country, views of the river and the mountains, unsurpassed . . ."

Built between 1804 and 1805 by a branch of the Livingston family (see their Hudson River estate nearby at Clermont, page 178), Montgomery Place was part of a 160,000-acre family holding. The house, designed in the Federal style, was remodeled in the 1830s to reflect the elegant life-style of the Livingstons of the time.

And it was then that the working orchard and farms and commercial nursery became part of a landscape of "pleasure grounds." The splendid Romantic sweep of the lawns and curving driveways and stone bridges, the plantings of groves of great trees, the variety of settings—these ideas of landscape design were made with the advice of the owners' good friend, Andrew Jackson Downing. He, in fact, described Montgomery Place in his 1859 book as "one of our oldest improved country seats . . . nowhere surpassed in America in point of location, natural beauty, or landscape gardening charms."

The estate stayed in the family's hands throughout the nineteenth century, and the Delafields, descendants of the Livingstons, continued to preserve it. In the 1930s Violetta Delafield, already an amateur botanist and expert horticulturist (with a specialty in mushrooms), created showplace gardens at the estate that flourished until her death in 1949. For nearly 40 years thereafter the gardens declined. Today they are being carefully restored under the direction of Historic Hudson Valley. Using Delafield's writings, oral history, old photographs, and even plant orders, gardeners and landscape historians are attempting to recreate her spectacularly successful gardens. (If you are interested in such detective-cum-horticultural studies, this is the place for you!)

Montgomery Place is very much a tree enthusiast's estate. There are flowering shrubs (lilacs in profusion in May), dogwood, magnolias, massive horse chestnuts, maples, beech, sycamore, and the amazing grove of giant black locust trees that surround the house. The spectacular views range from the nearby Hudson below the bluff—seen from the terrace of the mansion and framed by the locust trees—to spots deep in the woods where the cataracts of the Saw Kill can be enjoyed as they tumble down to the river. A map of the entire estate is available as you enter, so that you can choose your garden or trail or view. Do not come here solely for flower gardens; Montgomery Place is for those garden enthusiasts who think of landscape itself as a form of garden.

INFORMATION
Montgomery Place is located on Annandale Road. (At the entrance don't miss the farmstand of estate-grown apples and berries that helps support the restoration. You can also pick your own fruit in season.) The grounds are open daily except Tuesday, April through October, from 10 A.M. to 5 P.M. (Of course, the shrubs and flowers are most beautiful in springtime as is the foliage in the fall.) During

November, December, and March, the property is open only on weekends; closed January and February, Thanksgiving and Christmas Day. Telephone: (914) 758-5461. Fee.

DIRECTIONS
Montgomery Place is located on the east bank of the Hudson in Annandale. From the Taconic State Parkway take the Pine Plains/Red Hook exit for Route 199. Go west 10 miles on 199 through Red Hook, turn right on Route 9G and left on Annandale Road. Bear left again on River Road to entrance. From the New York State Thruway, cross the Hudson at the Kingston/Rhinecliff Bridge (Exit 19). Turn left onto Route 9G, and follow directions above.

Stonecrop Gardens, Cold Spring

Anyone who likes gardens should find Stonecrop Gardens inspiring. For rock garden enthusiasts, however, this destination is a must. A steep hill off a rural road in Putnam County's rolling countryside leads to this enchanting spot. Here, in an unusually idyllic setting, are some of the most glorious alpine and water gardens anywhere.

The Stonecrop estate enjoys pastoral views over meadows to distant hills. The beautifully designed grounds include a French-style country house with adjoining stable and wood fences, an enclosed garden, potting sheds and greenhouses, ponds and a lake, stone walls, plus the gardens. A woodland garden, pond garden, grass garden, and perennial borders are among the many tasteful plantings. But what gives Stonecrop its special caché are its incredible rock and water gardens and alpine collection.

You'll find a variety of these rock gardens throughout the grounds—from the area next to the house, where the plantings are displayed in tidy beds and in greenhouses, to the magnificent stream and cliff rock gardens beyond. And it's very likely that you won't meet more than a handful of other visitors: you should be able to have the place almost to yourself.

Before embarking on your exploration of Stonecrop, stop at the "office" (located just inside the house) to pay the entrance fee and pick up a map and descriptive guide. You might start with the enclosed garden, accessible from a scenic deck on the side of the house (the panoramic view from here is quite spectacular). Within a high, wooden fence is an English-style garden with square and triangular beds containing vegetables and old-fashioned flowers. You can walk around winding pathways to see espaliers of lindens, dwarf apples and pears, and a romantic grape arbor. (Guarding the scene is a handmade effigy of Gertrude Jekyll, the great English landscape designer, made to look curiously like a scarecrow.)

A path leads to the greenhouses and raised glass-covered troughs for displaying alpines. The carefully labeled exhibits are of museum quality and include every imaginable variety, most shown in the tiniest of pots in neat rows. If you are interested in learning in detail about these plants or care to embellish your own rock garden, this is a perfect opportunity. (You might even compare notes with one of the gardeners, who can often be found working diligently in this area.)

In front of the house you'll see other examples of rock gardens. Many are on raised beds supported by stone or limestone (tufa) walls; especially delightful are miniversions shown on rectangular and round "pedestals."

To reach the most spectacular site of all—the rock ledge and the stream garden that precedes it—walk west from the house. What you see here more dramatically than anywhere else at Stonecrop is the result of an imaginative partnership between nature and human ingenuity. In the 1980s the naturally rocky terrain was enhanced by the addition of yet more rocks—including giant boulders—on the ledge. A network of gently flowing streams and pools was created, emptying into a lake below (with the water recirculating through underground pipes), and thousands of plants—mostly alpines, grasses, dwarf conifers, and Mediterranean species—were carefully placed, for color, texture, and pattern.

The visual effect of the streams gently moving through the delicate plantings, around the rounded rocks, and into the clear pools is magical. But best of all is the fact that you actually walk down the cliff garden, stepping onto rocks that form it. And in so doing, you feel more like a participant than a passive observer looking in from the outside. As with the rest of Stonecrop, everything here is beautifully maintained and the plants all labeled, even the tiniest. You can wend your way on a path of stepping stones at water's edge to a charming wooden pavilion covered with wisteria and bearing a design similar to that of the main house (although in a more Japanese vein); this is a good lookout point from which to enjoy the view.

A network of paths continues around the lake, across a rustic

stone bridge (known as the "Flintstone" bridge), and down the hillside toward the woodland pond. This lower pond is surrounded by
primulas and woodland plants; from it, a path leads through a grove
of bamboo. You can explore it all at will, consulting your map.

Before leaving Stonecrop, be sure to walk on the small path
through the woodland garden: azaleas, rhododendrons, and other
shade-loving plantings have been carefully placed to blend harmoniously with this natural habitat. Nearby is a pond surrounded by
lilies and groupings of an exotic Brazilian species with giant leaves
(apparently the largest herbaceous plant recognized). You would
hardly imagine that this delightful pond was once a swamp: it is
now maintained by artificial streams at each end. This is yet another example of the care, work, and imagination that have made
Stonecrop the rare site it is.

INFORMATION
Stonecrop Gardens are located on Route 301 outside of Cold Spring
(between Route 9 and the Taconic State Parkway). The grounds are
open year-round by appointment only, on Mondays, Wednesdays,
and Fridays, from 10 A.M. to 4 P.M. There is an entrance fee.
Telephone: (914) 265-2000.

DIRECTIONS
From New York City, take the Taconic Parkway and exit at Route
301. Go west for about 3 miles. The driveway for Stonecrop is a
sharp right, directly opposite Dennytown Road (the sign for
Stonecrop is very small and easy to miss).

Boscobel, Garrison-on-Hudson

The garden at Boscobel—an elegant, historic estate high above the
Hudson River—might be described as a garden with a view. What a
lovely garden! And what a view! For those of our readers who are
seeking an exquisite flower garden with a panoramic vista of the
Hudson and its marshes and waterways, this is the spot to see. We
were entranced by the combination of artistic perfection—for such
is the arrangement of Boscobel's dainty gardens—and the wild and
natural patterns of the river below.

Boscobel has a fine house in the Federal style (which you may
visit to see English and American antiques and paintings) set majes-

tically on a wide expanse of sloping lawn. The house was built in 1806 by States Dyckman on a pattern of the great designer Robert Adam. The estate includes a series of gardens nearer the bluff overlooking the river. The grounds—some 30 acres—are varied and well worth walking through. There is a flourishing apple orchard (which actually helps support the restoration), fig trees, fine old white pines, and tubs of oleander lining the walkways. A charming orangerie is filled with fruit-bearing citrus trees and other delicate plants. There is a small pond, wildflowers, and old-fashioned beehives known as skeps. From almost every spot you may glimpse the great river below.

The garden high points for us were the herb, boxwood, rose, and English gardens—all delicate and beautifully planned. Here on a flat portion of the estate are the series of colorful and intimate settings for the planting seasons, such as tulips and daffodils of delicately different shadings in the springtime and roses and petunias throughout the summer. A small fountain is at the center of the formal gardens; edges are bordered in geometric patterns with boxwood and interlocking pathways. Benches are placed for enjoying both plantings and the view below.

Although Boscobel is not unknown to tourists, it is generally not a crowded place—especially during the week. There are some of the trappings of success as at all restorations, but we found the grounds quite unspoiled and, in fact, a place for both aesthetic pleasure and quiet contemplation.

INFORMATION
Boscobel is open daily except Tuesdays from April through December. There is an admission fee for both the house and gardens. Telephone: (914) 265-3638.

DIRECTIONS
Boscobel is located on the east bank of the Hudson River. From New York, take the Henry Hudson Parkway, which becomes the Saw Mill River Parkway, as far as the Bear Mountain Bridge. Do not cross the river, but pick up Route 9D and go north toward Cold Spring. Boscobel's entrance is on your left just past the Garrison town line.

Clermont State Historic Site, Germantown

If you're a romantic, you'll find Clermont as inviting as the most delectable of feasts would be to a gourmet. Walking through these enchanting grounds is a treat to your senses, as you savor its captivating views, gentle river breezes, and delicious garden fragrances.

Everything about this enchanting Hudson River villa breathes romanticism—from its idyllic setting just steps from the river to its venerable old trees and lilac bushes, stone walls, banks of lilies, and sweeping, undulating lawns. You will want to wander at your own pace and follow the grassy pathways that lead to yet more delights.

Clermont has a long history. For over 200 years—and seven consecutive generations—it was the country estate of the Livingstons, a prominent New York family. Originally part of the Manor of Livingston, a 160,000-acre tract granted to Robert Livingston in the late seventeenth century, it was developed by his son, also known as Robert of Clermont. Around 1730 construction of his brick, Georgian-style house was begun; it was named "Clermont," French for "clear mountain," a reference to its views of the Catskill Mountains across the river.

Among its distinguished occupants was yet another Robert Livingston (great grandson of the original owner), who not only administered the first oath of office to George Washington in 1789, but also served in the Continental Congress and helped draw up the Declaration of Independence. During the Revolutionary War, Clermont was burned by the British, no doubt because of the family's support of independence, and Livingston started construction on an elaborate, French-inspired, new mansion (again named Clermont). While in Paris as Jefferson's minister to France, he met Robert Fulton, an inventor fascinated with steam navigation. Together, they built a workable steamboat (popularly called, not surprisingly, the "Clermont"), which made its maiden voyage between New York and Albany in 1807. It was on this occasion that the steamboat first landed at the Clermont dock, where Livingston announced the engagement of his cousin to his great friend and partner, Robert Fulton.

The manor house underwent significant changes over the years; among them, a new French-style roof in the 1870s and a complete remodeling during the 1920s. In 1962 the Livingstons deeded their historic estate to the State of New York, and it was designated a National Historic Landmark in 1973.

For all of its illustrious history, you'll find Clermont surprisingly intimate—and rarely crowded. To reach the estate you drive through a large area of woodlands (the 450-acre Clermont State Historic Park) toward the Hudson. When you arrive, you should pick up a brochure with historic and practical information. The now-white and classically elegant manor house can be visited by guided tour only, but you are free to wander through the garden on your own (although garden tours are also offered) and linger as long as you like.

The exquisite grounds include three main gardens: the sunken spring garden, the walled garden, and the upper garden. As you stand next to the house, looking toward the river, you see below you the sunken spring garden, which includes groupings of magnificent lilac bushes surrounded by vast, rolling lawns, and the picturesque remains of an old stone barn. This romantic image alone is worth a trip to Clermont, particularly in mid to late May. The subtle coloring of the lilacs—ranging from delicate lavender to the deepest purple—are dreamy, as is their incredibly sweet scent. Some winding steps lead to the main garden level, where a vintage stone wall and terra-cotta urns containing flowers grace the side of the house. Surrounding them are manicured, terraced boxwood hedges, a few bird statues, and beautifully maintained lawns.

A flagstone walk will take you to the walled garden, enclosed by a delicate iron gate. Within lies a rock garden created in the 1930s by Alice Delafield Clarkson Livingston. Inspired in part by the Florentine gardens she had admired, it also combines some of the ideas of the noted British landscape designer Gertrude Jekyll.

Through the gate you come to a wilderness garden of iris and lilies. In the center is a pond, a favorite design element of Miss Jekyll's. (The garden carp that once lived here routinely wintered in the house, in the Livingstons' bathtub!)

If you keep walking up the hill you'll come to the upper garden and greenhouse site. Once planted with vegetables, it is now a cutting garden. Here you'll see peonies that date back to the early part of the century.

Plan on spending enough time to explore Clermont and experience it fully. You might even enjoy a picnic (tables are tastefully scattered about on the lawns and under the trees), while admiring the many views. What could be nicer on a bright, sunny day?

INFORMATION
Clermont State Historic Site is located at One Clermont Avenue. The visitor center and historic house are open between April 15 and Labor Day, Wednesday through Saturday, 10 A.M. to 5 P.M., Sunday from 12 noon to 5 P.M. From Labor Day through October 31, Wednesday through Sunday, 12 noon to 5 P.M. Telephone to confirm hours and to check on tours: (518) 537-4240. Note that Clermont offers special events, including the Clermont Croquet Tournament (on those beautiful lawns!), an Old-Fashioned Family Fourth of July, and the Chancellor Livingston's Art Show.

DIRECTIONS
From New York City take the Taconic State Parkway to the Red Hook/Rhinebeck exit onto Route 199 west. Go through the village of Red Hook. Turn right onto Route 9G (north). Drive 6 miles to the entrance sign for Clermont.

Vanderbilt Mansion Gardens, Hyde Park

If you have never visited the Vanderbilt estate in Hyde Park on the banks of the Hudson River you will be astonished by its magnificence. From the 40-room mansion of the Gilded Age, to the vast panoramic sweep of the property and its grand river view, to the ancient and majestic trees—it is a breathtaking place. The beauty of the Hudson River region was an inspiration for landscape designers, as well as painters and writers, and the landscape design of "Hyde Park" (the formal name of the Vanderbilt estate) is spectacular. In 1841 Andrew Jackson Downing said: "Hyde Park is justly celebrated as one of the finest specimens of the Romantic style of landscape gardening in America."

This is one of the premier tourist sites in the nation. High school students studying the railroad monopolies, "great house" enthusiasts, tourists from abroad, and Americana experts are very much in evidence among the gilt and glitter of the house and the well-trod paths of the 240-acre estate.

But you'll find few visitors at the large, extraordinary gardens (which you can see without fee or guide). Placed well away from the house, they are both charming and unexpected—a touch of Italian elegance come upon suddenly from a wooden path. Here you'll find delightful architectural design and open space interspersed with carefully planned flower beds, clinging vines, and statuary. A series of warm-toned brick loggias and arches give this quite vast formal set of gardens an inviting air. Though you may wonder at the gardens being so far from the house, you can only be grateful that their quiet charm has survived the crowds visiting the mansion.

The estate's history includes several previous owners. In 1764 Dr. John Bard inherited the property—through his wife—from the first landowner, Peter Fauconnier. Bard's home was actually across the Albany Post Road (you will still see the sign for Bard's Lane), but he made a path toward the river and the spectacular view.

His son, Dr. Samuel Bard, took possession of the property in 1799 and spent some 25 years there. His house was the first on the magnificent riverside site. He is thought to have planted the giant gingko tree on the south lawn of the mansion.

The next owner (in 1825) was Bard's medical partner, Dr. David Hosack, who was noted for his interest in gardens; he was the founder of the first botanical garden in the United States. Needless to say, when he moved to the property in 1799, he soon engaged a landscape designer. In addition to planting the splendid and exotic trees that you will see throughout the estate, the Belgian designer André Parmentier laid out the sweeping roads, bridges, and lawns in the Romantic, natural style then popular—and still so inviting today. (The trees are so grand and numerous that there is a book devoted entirely to the subject for sale at the estate.)

The Bard/Hosack house burned in 1840. From 1840 to 1895 a family named Langdon owned the property as a summer retreat. They built the first real mansion there and created the formal gardens. The only structures that survive from their time are those near the gardens: the Gardener's Cottage, the Potting Shed, and the Tool House. You will note the High Victorian flavor of those buildings on the edge of the gardens.

It was Frederick Vanderbilt, grandson of Cornelius and son of William Henry Vanderbilt—both the richest men in America—who purchased the estate in 1895. The property was to become a monument to wealth and privilege. The Langdon house was replaced with the palacelike mansion one visits today. (It is open by guided tour.) Vanderbilt also added 64 more acres and several new buildings, including the 16-room Pavilion (where the family lived while the mansion was constructed) and several guest houses for friends.

Vanderbilt, for the most part, however, left alone the magnificent landscape design of his predecessors; the trees and lawns and river viewpoints were already majestic enough to suit his taste for the grand. New bridle paths added to the look and feel of an English country estate. His extensive properties on both sides of the Albany Post Road produced prize-winning flowers, as well as livestock and vegetables.

The formal gardens were of particular interest to Vanderbilt; he had a degree in horticulture from Yale and a lifelong interest in growing flowers and in farming. He asked a series of landscape designers to add terraces to the gardens, a cherry allée, a rose garden, greenhouses, and many small classical statues. Five greenhouses and a staff of 12 gardeners kept the gardens going. The formal gardens we see today are a combination of those from the Langdon and the Vanderbilt eras. Vanderbilt died in 1938, and the property has been a National Historic Site since 1940. During World War II, with funding scarce, the gardens deteriorated and the statues crumbled. Not until 1974 did restoration begin. Reconstruction was undertaken, walls rebuilt, plantings restored. But the gardens are today maintained entirely by contribution and volunteer effort.

You will find the formal gardens to the south of the mansion at the end of a small, winding gravel path that parallels the river bank. The gardens are set in a series of large, flat terraces that descend into a hollow. There are short flights of steps between them. The first impression is of color—the warm terra-cotta tone of the brick walls and loggias, the delicate black wrought-iron curlicues, the brilliant tones of flowers, and green throughout. They are Italianate in style—formal, elegant, and spacious—a style based itself on Greek and Roman plans. A particularly appealing aspect of these gardens is that the tier arrangement allows a view of all parts of the gardens from above.

The highest terrace, adjacent to the Gardener's Cottage, has a charming gazebo with a wishing well constructed of the same warm red brick and wood. Just below it is the first tier of the garden. Here there are two long lines of square red brick columns ornamented with delicate ironwork. The rows of columns are imitated by an allée of cherry trees and contrasted with oddly patterned flower beds. (Some 8,000 annuals and 4,000 perennials bloom in these spacious and elegant tiers.)

Just below is the second terrace, featuring statuary and pediments and a delightful pool garden surrounded by geometrically patterned flower beds. Iris, peonies, daisies, and poppies were in bloom when we visited. A grapevine-covered pergola with classical statue forms the boundary of this tier, and gray-green ferns decorate the borders. Each tier has inviting benches for visitors; you will feel far from our familiar civilization here.

The lowest level contains the rose garden, dating to 1910. Planted with 1,000 rose bushes in differently shaped beds, this tier has a fountain and Italianate loggia that are enchanting. You can get a particularly nice overview of this level from the tier above. These gardens are only formal in design; they seem surprisingly warm and inviting.

Visiting the Vanderbilt estate can provide every sort of garden experience in one visit: you will delight in the majestic views and sweeping grounds and splendid trees, and you will find the Italianate formal gardens as special as any we have seen in our region.

INFORMATION
The grounds are open every day without charge. Guided tours of the gardens are available during summer months. The mansion is open (with fee) for tours April through November. Call for hours. Telephone: (914) 229-9115.

DIRECTIONS
The Vanderbilt estate is located about 80 miles north of New York City on the east bank of the Hudson River. From the Taconic State Parkway take Route 55 West onto Route 9 North for 6 miles. The entrance is on your left. (From the west bank of the Hudson, take the bridge at Kingston to Route 9.)

Innisfree Gardens, Millbrook

The artistic gardens of Innisfree, near Millbrook, New York, are well worth a foray into the countryside. Created in the 1920s to reflect the philosophy and aesthetic of Chinese gardens, they bring you to a very different world from that of most gardens in our region. Experiencing Innisfree means taking an inspiring journey and exploring nature through ancient Chinese artistic tradition. In fact, a walk here is akin to finding a series of Chinese landscape paintings that are real and three dimensional and then strolling right into them.

Walter Beck, a painter, and his wife, Marion, spent 25 years creating these vast gardens. Their inspiration came primarily from the eighth-century Chinese scrolls of the poet/painter Wang Wei, where scenes in nature are unfolded gradually. The basic design idea of Innisfree is the "cup garden"—a Chinese tradition dating back hundreds of years. The Chinese would set apart an object by "framing" it in such a way that it would be distinct and apart from its surroundings. According to Lester Collins, the landscape architect who has been in charge of Innisfree for many years, "You build a picture of nature; you control the floor and the walls, and you bring the sky down." Walking through Innisfree is analogous to walking through an art gallery from one picture to the next—from a meadow to a rock covered with moss, to a lotus pool—in each case concentrating on the element before you. As in the case of a work of art, each destination has been created carefully to affect the viewer's senses in a certain way. Nature has been tamed completely, and even though the terrain at Innisfree may look wild and free, nothing has been left to chance. The land has been cleared, and waterfalls, streams, and pools have been created. "In their gardens," says Collins, "the Chinese express life and death and everything together—the pain and the wonder." The two main elements of Chinese gardens—mountains and rocks (yang) and water (yin)—are very important in this garden and provide the necessary counterpoint of life. Yin is passive, dark, and moist; yang is active, bright, and aggressive. According to the Chinese, a harmonious arrangement of mountains and water can give the viewer a spiritual experience of universal harmony. Water and rocks of all sizes and shapes are everywhere set amid soft foliage, shrubs, and trees. Flowers are not an important element in Chinese gardens, but here you will find delicate clematis growing on an arbor, primroses, forget-me-nots, water iris, and hydrangeas.

Innisfree is a garden for all seasons, since it emphasizes the architecture of its basic elements in harmony with one another. (Note, however, that it is open only from May 1 through October.) You can enjoy it under any weather conditions, as a great garden "is good aesthetically and has nothing to do with climate," according to Collins. In fact, on one of our visits we experienced torrential rains. But the downpours only echoed the usual sounds of the nearby streams and waterfalls, and the soft colors of the foliage were rendered the more vivid by the rain.

Before setting out on your walk you can pick up a map near the parking lot. A network of paths will take you around the lake (from where you'll see a tantalizing little island of pines that can be explored) and up and down gently sloping hills. Chinese gardens are supposed to be miniatures of nature's way; here, too, you will walk past small evocations of mountains, streams, and forests, experiencing each sensation as a traveler might in the open countryside, or as a viewer who encounters an unfolding Chinese handscroll landscape painting. You'll come across a mist fountain, a rock garden waterfall, a curious "Fu Dog" stone statue, a hillside cave, a brick terrace (where you can rest and take in the view), fantastic rocks in the shapes of turtles and dragons, bird and bat houses, water sculptures, and hemlock woods. Don't fail to look about you at distant views as well.

INFORMATION
Innisfree is open May through October, Saturday and Sunday, 11 A.M. to 5 P.M., Wednesday through Friday, 10 A.M. to 4 P.M. Telephone: (914) 677-8000.

DIRECTIONS
From New York City, take the Henry Hudson Parkway to the Saw Mill River Parkway to the Taconic State Parkway; exit at Poughkeepsie/Millbrook (Route 44) and go east on 44. Look for Tyrrel Road on your right. The entrance to Innisfree is from Tyrrel Road.

Kykuit, Pocantico Hills

When we first heard early in 1994 that Kykuit, the Westchester estate of the Rockefeller family, was going to open to the public for guided tours, we were as intrigued as everyone else. Aside from a natural curiosity to see one of the private homes of this mythic American family, we were particularly anxious to view firsthand the extraordinary art collection we had all heard about. Judging from the large number of tourists who have since visited (despite the fairly hefty entrance fee and two-hour tour that must be booked in advance), the interest in this extraordinary site continues. And with good reason.

Kykuit (the name means "lookout" in Dutch) is a grand early-twentieth-century American villa magnificently situated with sweeping views of the Hudson River. It includes the imposing (although not ostentatious) mansion complete with its impressive art collection and antiques and, of greatest interest to us, the spectacular gardens filled with first-rate sculpture.

On the tour you are told (in mostly anecdotal fashion and perhaps greater detail than necessary) about the genesis of the estate—surprisingly modest in its earliest version—and its evolution with succeeding generations of Rockefellers, about the life-style of the family and its impact on the configuration of the house, and about the provenance of the many artworks and objects. As we savored the gardens, we felt special admiration for the landscape architect, William Welles Bosworth, a personal friend of John D. Rockefeller, Jr., who designed them in the first place.

Bosworth's gardens are considered among the finest examples in American landscape design. He placed two formal gardens—now containing the wonderful sculpture collection—on each side of the house, so they could be enjoyed both from inside and outside and could command the most formidable Hudson River views: one, a rectangular enclosed garden including a stone walk, manicured lawn, and clipped hedges; the other, an elegant rose garden. Bosworth also designed a Japanese garden (unfortunately not open to the public) and discreet spaces for golf and tennis; and throughout the gardens he added an eclectic but harmonious mix of classical motifs—terraces, pergolas, pools, fountains, classical temples, and grottos.

Subsequent planting schemes (some under the watchful eye of Abby Rockefeller, a dedicated gardener in her own right) have enriched the gardens: a brook garden, particularly enchanting in spring with its blooming dogwood and azaleas, and additional ornamental plantings on sleek green slopes and elegant terraces.

But the most impressive addition to these spaces has been the superb collection of modern sculpture, acquired and placed by Nelson Rockefeller. After having given away much of his art to major museums, he left some 70 important and large outdoor sculptures here. As you wander around the lovely terraces and gardens, you can enjoy the works of such twentieth-century masters as Brancusi, Giacometti, Nadelman, Matisse, Lachaise, Moore, Calder, and Maillol. They have been carefully placed to enhance each piece, as well as the surrounding ornamental gardens, lawns, or walls.

Most of the sculptures have been left exactly where Rockefeller placed them, even in such unlikely places as the golf course. The majority are situated in the formal gardens next to the house. In the enclosed garden surrounded by linden trees, you can see Elie Nadelman's *Two Circus Women* (another version can be found at the New York State Theater at Lincoln Center), Gaston Lachaise's *Elevation*, and Aristide Maillol's *Chained Action: Torso of the Monument to Louis-Auguste Blanqui*, to name only a few. Some works have been dramatically placed to accentuate their relationship to the stunning panorama: for instance, David Smith's *The Banquet* on the villa's west porch against a scenic backdrop of the Palisades, Henry Moore's *Knife Edge Two Piece* against surrounding rolling hills, and Alexander Calder's *Large Spiny*, overlooking the Hudson.

You will probably wish for more time to linger in these glorious sculpture gardens that combine the best in contemporary art and landscape design.

INFORMATION
Kykuit is located in Pocantico Hills, Westchester, New York. To make a reservation, you must call the Historic Hudson Valley at (914) 631-9491. You can also take a boat trip to Kykuit from Manhattan and New Jersey. For information, call (800) 53-FERRY.

DIRECTIONS
To reach the Kykuit visitor center at Philipsburg Manor in Tarrytown (from where you will be taken by minivan to Kykuit), take the New York Thruway (I-87) to Exit 9, and go 2 miles north on Route 9, following signs for Philipsburg Manor. Or take the Hutchinson River Parkway and follow signs to the Thruway.

The Donald M. Kendall Sculpture Gardens at PepsiCo, Purchase

We have no hesitation in inviting you to take this outing; it is truly one of our favorites both with and without children in tow. You may wonder how PepsiCo—so well known for its mainstream popular culture advertising—would find itself in a book about gardens. But you are in for a wonderful surprise. While there are many public gardens and corporate art collections in America, few are available to the public to enjoy with the scale, variety, and quality of the Donald M. Kendall Sculpture Gardens at PepsiCo.

A walking tour of these 112 acres (more a landscape than a garden in the traditional sense) will introduce you to some major works of sculpture, as well as to a shining example of how a corporation can enhance its surroundings with beautiful grounds. The former CEO of the company, Donald M. Kendall, conceived the idea and was active in having the gardens designed and in collecting the sculpture to provide "an environment that encourages creativity and reflects essential qualities of corporate success."

In 1970 the massive PepsiCo office building designed by Edward Durell Stone was opened on this former polo field. The building (which is closed to the public) is made up of seven square blocks that form three courtyard gardens around a central fountain. The architect's son laid out the surrounding acreage of rolling green terrain; there are fields, pathways, a lake, distinctive trees, flower gardens, fountains—and everywhere you look—sculpture.

The gardens themselves were planned by the internationally known landscape designer Russell Page and Stone; they continue to be developed today by François Goffinet. Pieces of art are carefully placed in relation to their surroundings, so that each knoll or valley provides a gentle setting for its work of art. There are both formal gardens—where smaller pieces of sculpture are bordered by clipped hedges and precisely groomed plantings—and vast fields—where monumental examples of contemporary sculpture stand starkly against the horizon. There is a lake and well tended woodland. And then there is the newest addition to the gardens: a spectacular iris garden. The park is so carefully designed and maintained that even the parking lots are concealed by plantings, and an army of gardeners seems always to be at work.

To begin your walk, leave your car in one of the hidden parking lots (to which discreet signs direct you). No appointment is necessary, but check the hours listed below. You will seldom find this vast place crowded. After parking, go to the Visitor Center, pick up a numbered map, and enter the "Golden Path"—a nice, winding walkway designed by Russell Page. It meanders through the entire acreage. (You may wander on your own if you prefer or stay on the path and follow the map, which identifies works of art and garden areas.)

As you come to the first fork in the path, go to your right onto the Golden Path, along a woodsy area dotted with daffodils and other spring flowers, and later with pink and white azaleas; in summer, European foxgloves are sprinkled among the red maples. The first sculpture, just to the left of the path, is Alexander Calder's *Hats Off*, a giant work in orange-red metal, unmistakably Calder's. It is set against a backdrop of white fir and Colorado blue spruce, bringing its brilliant color vividly to life.

Also to the left of the path is Jean Dubuffet's painted black and white abstract work, *Kiosque Evide*. And a little farther along, also to your left, is a work by Arnaldo Pomodoro called *Grande Disco*, a variation on the form of a globe eaten away by some mysterious forces.

Leave the path and walk left toward the building entrance to see a work by David Smith. This piece, called *Cube Totem Seven and Six*, is set just in front of the trellis to the giant headquarters building, amid a charming grove of plane trees. On the terrace above you'll find works by two twentieth-century Italian masters. First, you'll see Marino Marini's charming signature piece, *Horse and Rider*. Also on the terrace are two Alberto Giacometti statues: *Standing Woman I* and *II*, their tall thin figures sharply defined against the building's wall.

Back on the Golden Path is Auguste Rodin's *Eve*, perhaps the most traditional work on this walk, charmingly set among holly trees and shrubbery. Nearby, to the right, is an interesting work by Max Ernst, *Capricorn*. Don't miss this surrealistic group of figures with animal parts suggesting fish, a cow, and birds.

One of today's leading sculptors is represented next; in a kind of garden area to your left, you'll find Kenneth Snelson's *Mozart II*. This is a giant aluminum construction of geometric shapes and wires, a most contemporary tribute to Mozart. The backdrop for this sculpture is a pair of ornamental banks of pink Japanese rhododendron, crimson barberry, and spirea, among other delicately toned shrubs.

Go back to the path and turn left at *Mozart II*, near the building's walls. Here is a spectacular view of sweeping lawn and great trees. You'll also see George Segal's *Three People on Four Benches*, a characteristically superrealistic work that may remind you of PepsiCo's workers relaxing during their lunch hour break. Nearby is Claes Oldenburg's *Giant Trowel II*, one of the most memorable sights at PepsiCo (and one that garden lovers can easily relate to). In fact, it is so startling against its background of pine and dogwood trees that you blink to see if the giant spade is really there, digging into the green earth.

Moving farther along the path you'll next see George Rickey's

Double L Eccentric Gyratory II, a typical Rickey work made up of stainless steel windmill-like blades that shift gently in the breeze. From here you can see a graceful stand of 13 different types of white birches coming from all around the world and planted in patterns. In contrast are blue grape hyacinths, in spring, and golden conifers.

On the edge of the cultivated lawn area, and in front of a wooded section, you'll come to Tony Smith's abstract *Duck* and Richard Erdman's *Passage*. Nearby you'll find the newest and most glorious of PepsiCo's garden innovations. In a woodsy setting criss-crossed by streams and small bridges is the new Iris Garden. Here, more than 100 species of this glamorous flower have been imported from Japan and planted in undulating patterns among the trees. This is a sight not to be missed in late May.

Walk toward the building past the Oak Grove. Across the road you'll find the dwarf tea crab apples blooming in glorious pink during April. You will next pass the Franklin tree, one of the world's rarest specimens, discovered in 1765 by John Bartram (see Historic Bartram's Garden in Philadelphia, page 236). This unusual tree is at its peak in August, when it appears in full white bloom. The Ornamental Grass Garden is next, a fascinating composition of different textures and colors.

You will now wish to see the courtyard garden, charmingly landscaped collections of plants and art. These are in the center of the building complex. Most artworks are representative of the earlier schools of contemporary sculpture, including two Henry Moores, two Henri Laurens, and an Aristide Maillol. There is also a Seymour Lipton work and a David Wynne, *Girl with a Dolphin*, in the center of a fountain. Of particular note are the wonderful heavy figures of Laurens, *Le Matin* and *Les Ondines*. At the center of one of these sunken gardens you'll see an unusual Japanese star magnolia. And don't miss the pool, where you may walk on stone slabs through a watery environment that heightens your appreciation for the art so beautifully placed.

Exit the courtyard and go left, proceeding up a slight incline. On the terrace is *Personnage*, a 1970 work by the "old" master Joan Miro above the lily pond. This delightful garden spot, designed by Russell Page, has a perennial flower border and water lily pool. Here also is a charming gazebo inspired by the eighteenth-century English landscape design of Humphrey Repton—a perfect place for a quick rest. A series of rectangular pools connected with stone slabs and grassy areas, this site is characterized by flowers and shrubs planted in pleasingly asymmetrical patterns. The overall effect is one of tranquillity. Brightly colored gold fish swim among the lilies. Above is a hillside filled with rosebushes and flowering shrubs and Japanese cherry trees.

Next you'll come to one of the most memorable and defining works in the sculpture park: Arnaldo Pomodoro's *Triad*, a dramatic group of three modern, but ancient-looking, columns set starkly against the grassy landscape.

As you walk across the vast lawn you'll come across several major sculptures and the entrance to the Azalea Garden. These brilliantly colored shrubs are at their best in May and June. Nearby are rare trees, including a lacebark pine from northern China and a European hornbeam.

The well-known British sculptor Barbara Hepworth is represented here, with a typical work, *Meridien*. Here also are the works of two noted sculptors who have defined contemporary sculpture in our time, in very different ways: Isamu Noguchi and Louise Nevelson. Noguchi's work, *Energy Void*, is a characteristically formalistic work framed with gray-green weeping hemlocks. Nevelson's *Celebration II* is a dark collection of geometric metal forms set in soft ground cover amid a stand of copper beech trees that reflect the color of the sculpture.

You have now reached the lake, bordered by graceful willows. In your walk around it, you'll see several of the major works in the collection. First is Robert Davidson's three giant totems that will remind you of Northwest Coast Native American carvings. This work, appropriately called *Totems*, stands out by its audacity, bright colors, and dramatic design. Another contemporary work, Asmundur Sveinsson's *Through the Sound Barrier*, is also next to the circular path around the lake. And at the intersection of the lake path and your original entrance to the grounds is one of the most beloved sculptures (particularly by children), David Wynne's realistic *Grizzly Bear*. The last work on the grounds is Henry Moore's *Double Oval*, which sits on the edge of the lake as a splendid monument to contemporary art.

Those of you who are interested in more detail concerning the rare plantings, including trees from all over the world, will find a list of these available at the Visitor Center.

The PepsiCo Gardens are an unparalleled example of how in the twentieth century a grand property can combine vast landscape, formal gardens, and informal plantings with fine art.

INFORMATION
The Donald M. Kendall Sculpture Gardens at PepsiCo's headquarters are on Anderson Hill Road in Purchase, New York. Telephone: (914) 253-3000. The Sculpture Gardens are open from 10 A.M. to dusk, seven days a week, year-round. There is no entrance fee.

DIRECTIONS
From New York City, take the Hutchinson River Parkway north to Exit 28 (Lincoln Avenue). Follow sign indicating SUNY/Purchase (which is directly across the street from PepsiCo). After exit go left on Lincoln Avenue to its end. Turn right onto Anderson Hill Road; entrance is on the right.

Lyndhurst, Tarrytown

The words "grand" and "spacious" immediately come to mind in describing Lyndhurst. As you enter the gates of this 67-acre Hudson River villa, you drive through a parklike landscape dominated by broad lawns with giant specimen trees. Finally, you reach the mansion, considered to be one of America's finest Gothic Revival houses. Looming dramatically on the horizon, as in a romantic novel, it commands sweeping views of the river. Around it are majestic copper beeches, lindens, sycamores, chestnuts, and maples.

It comes as quite a surprise to discover, in the midst of this imposing setting, an unusually intimate and charming rose garden. Rose fanciers will find it irresistible and alone worth the trip to Lyndhurst, especially on a bright day in June. The garden is situated in a grassy spot, away from the house and near the intriguing remains of a once very grand conservatory. Circular in design, it is built around arched trellises surrounding a graceful Victorian gazebo. In the midst are shrubs and vines of roses in all shades of red, pink, yellow, and white. Some are arranged in fanciful garlands. The roses are deliciously fragrant—and profuse. Indeed, there are more than 100 varieties, some over a century old. The rose garden was, in fact, created during the Victorian era, some 50 years after the house.

Lyndhurst, originally known as "Knoll," was built in the late 1830s for William Pauling, a former New York City mayor. It was the first of a series of picturesque Hudson Valley estates designed by Alexander Jackson Davis. Each of its subsequent owners added his own imprint, especially railroad tycoon Jay Gould, its most famous occupant.

Gould purchased Lyndhurst as a summer home in 1880. In addition to changing the house and gardens to suit his own taste, he decided to rebuild the greenhouse that had been destroyed by fire. He commissioned John William Walter, a designer of ecclesiastical architecture, to create an imposing Gothic-style conservatory in keeping with the aura of the mansion. Once the largest in the country, today it appears as a glassless and quite ghostly structure, awaiting further renovation.

It was Gould's daughter, Helen, who created the rose garden. (She took charge of the property after her father's death in 1892.) A source of joy to the Gould family and friends for years, it was unfortunately abandoned during World War II. But soon after Lyndhurst was bequeathed to the National Trust for Historic Preservation in 1961, the garden was fully restored to its former splendor. Today it is impeccably maintained by the Garden Club of nearby Irvington. No stray leaf or rose petal is to be found anywhere!

In addition to the rose garden, you won't want to miss the Victorian fern garden near the entrance gate, also maintained through volunteer efforts; the Rose Cottage, a children's playhouse; and the Carriage House (its café features weekend lunches during the summer). If you are interested in learning more about the life of a bygone era in American history, you can take one of the regular guided tours of the mansion.

INFORMATION
Lyndhurst is located at 635 South Broadway, about one-half mile south of the Tappan Zee Bridge, in the Village of Tarrytown. It is open May through October, Tuesday through Sunday from 10 A.M. to 5 P.M.; November through April on weekends only. Entrance fee. For information, call (914) 631-4481.

DIRECTIONS
From New York City, take the Henry Hudson Parkway north to Route 9 to Tarrytown; Lyndhurst will be on your left. From locations west of the Hudson River, cross the Tappan Zee Bridge and take the first exit (Route 9) and go south for about 1/2 mile, following the signs for Lyndhurst.

And in Addition . . .

Mountainville: Storm King Art Center

Off Route 32. Telephone: (914) 534-3115 or 534-3190.

This is a major art site (more than a garden site), but it should not be omitted from any list of important outdoor places where nature and art interact. Storm King is a must-see 112-acre landscape of rolling hills and spectacular contemporary sculpture; the startling contrast between blossoming trees and towering modern art is unmatched anywhere we know of. There are semiformal gardens near the central building (set with David Smith sculptures) and rolling green hills dotted with flowering trees and shrubs amid the art. Open daily except Tuesday from April 1 to November 30. There are free walking tours at 2 P.M. Fee.

North Salem: The Hammond Museum and Japanese Stroll Garden

Deveau Road. Telephone: (914) 669-5033.

This intimate Japanese garden is situated at the very end of a rural road in the northeast corner of Westchester. Befitting the Asian garden as oasis for contemplation, it is about as silent and peaceful a place as you could find—except for the welcoming sounds of songbirds, crickets, even frogs. A small gravel path dotted with stepping stones winds around a lotus pond, past groves of specimen trees and shrubs and tiny individual gardens. With trail guide in hand (available at the entrance), you can identify katsura trees, bamboos, and Japanese varieties of flowering quince, larch, locust, cedar, and smoketree, among many others. Carefully placed rocks—some in the vertical position associated with Asian gardens—and stone statues of religious significance are scattered here and there, on a small island in the pond, by a flowering shrub, next to raked gravel gardens or the gently cascading miniature waterfall. You'll find garden benches along the way from which to contemplate it all.

Especially recommended in late May and early June, for blooming azaleas, iris, and cherry trees, or in October, for vibrant fall foliage. A little outdoor café beneath a grove of plane trees serves a pleasant lunch during the summer months (call for reservations). The garden is open from May through October, Wednesday through Saturday, 12 noon to 4 P.M. Fee.

Poughkeepsie: Springside Restoration
Academy Street. Telephone: (914) 454-2060.
Springside, a hilly, woodsy site once designated as an "ornamental farm" by Andrew Jackson Downing, is being restored by a hopeful, industrious group of volunteers. You may enjoy taking an authentic and detailed plan of its original state describing Downing's "landscape of the picturesque" in hand and walking through the still overgrown grounds. Open daily, or by tour.

Yonkers: Untermyer Park
U.S. 9 at intersection of Odell.
This intriguing park was once part of an elegant estate whose 113 acres were designed in a neoclassical tradition by William Welles Bosworth. Beautifully set high above the Hudson River, there are graceful plantings and classical antiquities galore, including a small temple, a grotto, Ionic columns, a Roman mosaic pool, and numerous ancient sculptures set among the flower beds, fine Japanese maples, and spectacular massive oaks. Open daily, year-round.

LONG ISLAND

Longhouse Foundation Gardens, East Hampton

Like many gardens in history, those at the Longhouse Foundation in the eastern end of Long Island skillfully use the elements of surprise and illusion. But, rather than employing traditional *trompe l'oeil* or playful water works that suddenly assault the unsuspecting passerby, the surprise and illusion in this quintessentially contemporary environment come from an unexpected boldness of juxtapositions and combinations.

The Longhouse Foundation, creation of a noted textile designer named Jack Lenor Larsen, includes 16 acres of grounds with a remarkable glass and stone house inspired by a seventh-century Shinto shrine in Japan. Larsen, long fascinated by exotic icons from other cultures around the world (especially Asian, it would seem), has incorporated many of these elements not only in his craft, but also in the design of other objects and places—including this site.

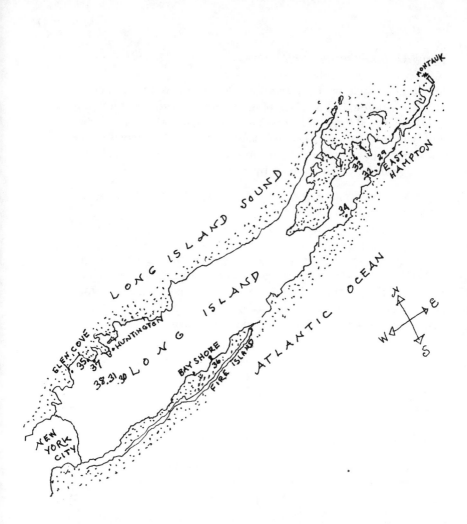

LONG ISLAND GARDENWALKS

29. East Hampton: Longhouse
    Foundation Gardens
30. Old Westbury: Old Westbury
    Gardens
31. Roslyn: Nassau County Museum of
    Art Sculpture Gardens
32. Sagaponack: Madoo, the Garden
    of Robert Dash
33. Sag Harbor: The Garden of April
    Gornik

34. Southampton: David and Helga
    Dawn Rose Garden

And in Addition . . .
35. Mill Neck: John P. Humes
    Japanese Stroll Garden
36. Oakdale: Bayard Cutting
    Arboretum
37. Oyster Bay: Planting Fields
    Arboretum
38. Roslyn Harbor: Cedarmere, the
    William Cullen Bryant Estate

However, there is nothing traditional about the house or its surrounding gardens.

Longhouse was built in the early 1990s as a showcase for contemporary life-style. In both house and garden the emphasis seems to be on design for its own sake as an experimental art form rather than as a complement to the surrounding natural environment. (The experiment is ongoing, since the garden, at least, is still evolving.) The imposing architecture of the house, with its overhanging roofs and stark, geometric forms, sits high on raised piers. Underneath is a huge outdoor living space leading to a patio. On one side, facing a rectangular reflecting pond, are crossed boards atop high cement pillars, appearing to be futuristic windmills. Within the house are 18 spaces individually conceived and designed by Larsen to display primitive and folk arts and crafts, as well as twentieth-century furniture.

The Asian theme of the house extends to a moonviewing bridge that connects to the gardens. Larsen has treated the outdoor spaces with the dramatic flair of a theatrical designer, obviously considering the relationship between artifice and nature. Near the house is a surprising group of man-made sand dunes topped with beach grasses. Apparently, during the excavation of the house and pond, huge amounts of soil were piled up high. Larsen's imaginative way of concealing this inevitable eyesore was to have sand brought in by the truckload from nearby beaches. The sand covered the soil, and the fake (but very decorative) dunes were born.

Throughout the gardens Larsen has left his unmistakably strong design imprint. He has contoured the otherwise flat landscape, fashioning artificial levels, berms, and pathways. The gardens are astonishing in their boldness of colors and materials. An extraordinary red garden includes an allée of cedar trunks painted a brilliant orange-red (much like the ceremonial "torii" gates of Japan), surrounded with masses of red azaleas, Japanese maples, and flowering plums. At the end of the walkway is an imposing Japanese stoneware pot. (In fact, the gardens are an outdoor gallery for displaying arts and crafts, as well as plants.)

Amid the grasses, bamboos, heathers, and seasonal plantings, you will find examples of contemporary sculpture, as well as pottery and other artifacts. Some of the works are part of Longhouse's permanent collection, while others are on temporary display. Among the artists represented are Grace Knowlton, Jesus Bautista Moroles, Constantin

Nivola, Toshiko Takaezu, Alfonso Ossorio, John McQueen, and Mary Frank.

The grounds include manicured woodlands with grassy trails, meadows, walled gardens, an impressive conifer collection, a laburnum walk, and two 1,000--foot-long hemlock hedges. There is a "white garden" with checkerboard plantings of boxwood and ilex alternating with white blossoms, a charming heather garden next to a long lap pool, and a sunken rose garden. (Roses are also paired with clematis, climbing onto long steel arches along a pathway.) In spring, Longhouse has spectacular displays of daffodils along its winding paths. In fact, Larsen has planted some 100,000 daffodils in 220 different varieties. Continually experimenting with new hybrids, he is now concentrating on miniature varieties.

You will find walking through this unusual landscape (where garden equipment and machinery testify to its ongoing development) a rare experience, unlike any other in this otherwise flat stretch of Long Island. Both house and garden reflect Larsen's talent for creating new patterns and textures and his continuing interest in generating public understanding of contemporary art and design. Longhouse is open to the public on a limited basis for the time being, although plans are being made for more exposure. The various facilities include an outdoor acoustical amphitheater and indoor auditorium.

INFORMATION
The Longhouse Foundation is located at 133 Hands Creek Road in East Hampton. The gardens and house are now open to the public from 2 P.M. to 5 P.M. on Wednesdays during June, July, and August, as well as on occasional summer weekends. An audio tour is provided. For information, call (516) 329-3568. Fee.

DIRECTIONS
From New York City, take the Long Island Expressway to William Floyd Parkway south to Route 27 east to East Hampton. From the center of town make a left onto New Town Lane, continuing straight, past the high school; turn right onto Stephen Hands Path; make two sharp rights onto Cedar Street. Hands Creek Road is 8/10th mile north of Cedar Street.

Old Westbury Gardens, Old Westbury

The magnificent black iron gates and the grand allée beyond introduce you immediately to the glamorous ambiance of Old Westbury Gardens. Here is the splendor of the magnificent European-style formal gardens of the past, their harmonious elegance graced with outdoor sculpture. This is a great estate on the grand scale, bringing to mind hazy romantic scenes involving Edwardian images and moonlit nights. In fact, the gardens are used frequently for movie sets and picturebook weddings, as well as by historians of landscape architecture of the past.

Just a stone's throw from the ultimate contemporary highway landscape, this site is all the more intriguing in its contrast with Long Island sprawl. The estate, built in 1906 by John S. Phipps, a financier and sportsman, is not the only grand house in Old Westbury, where many of the rich and fashionable built their homes at the turn of the century. (Nearby are the William C. Whitney Racing Stables, for example.)

Mr. Phipps hired the London architect George Crawley to construct a Stuart-style "country" mansion, to please his English wife. Westbury House was built atop a hill; its symmetrical elegance is set off by a master plan of landscape design. In fact, the estate is a rare example of landscape and architectural planning that went hand in hand; the complementary designs of the house and its surroundings are worth noting and are of great interest to modern designers.

The interior of the house is elegant and formal. It is open to the public and will appeal to those who enjoy seeing how such country retreats were designed and furnished—from fluted Corinthian columns and French windows to polished antique tables and ormolu clocks. You will also find paintings by John Singer Sargent, George Morland, Joshua Reynolds, and Sir Henry Raeburn.

But of particular interest and delight to us were the gardens, which—even without the many sculptures—are a work of art in themselves. Designed by both Crawley and a French landscape architect named Jacques Greber, the master plan called for a formal geometric arrangement of grand allées, softened by English "romantic" or picturesque gardens. The combination, based clearly on the layouts of the grounds of English stately homes, is an unqualified success.

Among its charms are a lake walk—yes, of course, there is a lake—leading to a "Temple of Love," a boxwood garden, a garden with flowers of all the colors of the rainbow, a "ghost walk" of dark hemlock trees, and a walled garden where you can easily imagine— or enjoy—the most romantic of trysts. There are numerous rare and magnificent trees and plantings, including many from the Orient. Almost 300 species of trees flourish at Old Westbury Gardens. Depending on the timing of your visit, you may see profusions of rhododendrons, lilacs, roses, and too many other of nature's most beautiful flowers to list here.

Sprinkled liberally throughout these enchanting areas are neo-classical sculptures and columns and various other artworks that add to the ambiance of European elegance. Ceres is sheltered in a pergola of wisteria, while a terra-cotta Diana the huntress graces a curving colonnade within the boxwood garden. There are ornamental cherub fountains in pools of lotus and lilies; a pair of bronze peacock statues with topiary tails; an elaborate shell mosaic in the style of Italian grotto decoration of the seventeenth century; a sundial topped with rampant lions; groups of nymphs and satyrs on the roofline of the house; a pair of lead eagles and stone vases on pediments, surrounded by lilacs; and a sculpture of the quasi-mythical athlete Milo of Cortona wrestling a tree stump from the earth.

INFORMATION
Old Westbury Gardens are open from 10 A.M. to 5 P.M. daily except Tuesdays, May through December. Fee. We suggest weekdays when gardens are not crowded. Pick up a guidebook and pamphlet at the mansion. Telephone: (516) 333-0048.

DIRECTIONS
Old Westbury Gardens are located at 710 Old Westbury Road. From New York City, take the Midtown Tunnel to the Long Island Expressway to Exit 39S (Glen Cove Road). Continue east on the service road of the expressway 1.2 miles to Old Westbury Road, the first road on the right. Continue 1/4th mile to the garden entrance on your left. (Also reachable by Long Island Railroad to Westbury from Pennsylvania Station in New York and by taxi from the Westbury station.)

Nassau County Museum of Art Sculpture Gardens, Roslyn Harbor

This surprising treasure in the suburban sprawl of Long Island is a delight both to garden enthusiasts and art lovers. Here you'll find spacious and charmingly landscaped grounds providing a setting for a distinguished collection of twentieth-century sculpture, as well as a formal garden complete with gazebo. In addition, the museum's outdoor display includes a fine garden devoted entirely to the sculpture of Aristide Maillol.

The museum (well worth a visit in its own right) occupies the former Henry Clay Frick mansion. Frick bought the property from the noted poet and preservationist William Cullen Bryant. (See page 208 for another nearby Bryant site.) It was Frances Dixon Frick, his son's wife, who, with distinguished landscape architect Marian Cruger Coffin, laid out the gardens. Their inspired design has lasted very well and is kept in pristine condition today. (It is now owned by Nassau County.)

The 145-acre estate is atop a hill and is spacious and inviting for walkers. There are numerous fine trees, including a pinetum of hundreds of conifers from throughout the world. The woodsy walking paths and rolling fields are set with sculpture by such noted artists as Reuben Nakian, Fernando Botero, Marino Marini, Roy Lichtenstein, and Mark di Suvero. (A printed guide to the sculpture is available at the museum desk.) To one side of the building you'll find the sloping, evocative Maillol garden.

The formal garden is different both in style and sensibility, though it too contains contemporary sculpture set amid the natural beauty. While the sculpture park is rambling and the works of art almost incidental to their settings, the formal garden is a throwback to earlier aesthetic taste. (These contrasts add to the enjoyment of the outing.)

Bordered by low boxwood hedges that accent the geometric walkways, the formal garden is divided into specific areas. Each path leads to another sculptural setting. There are a fountain and two odd figures called *King and Queen* by Spanish artist Xavier Corbero set amid the flowers, and statues by Chaim Gross and Jose deCreeft beautifully placed within the arrangement of the flower beds. A lacy dark-green gazebo lies near the rose gardens and an ever-changing display of seasonal plantings.

This is an outing that might particularly interest families with children, for it offers an opportunity to introduce both artistic and natural interests in a most enjoyable way.

INFORMATION
The Nassau County Art Museum and Gardens are open Tuesday through Sunday, 11 A.M. to 5 P.M., year-round. For full garden pleasure, we recommend visiting in spring or early summer. Tours are available by appointment. Fee for museum entry only. Telephone: (516) 484–9338.

DIRECTIONS
Long Island Expressway to Exit 39N (Glen Cove Road north). Go approximately 2 miles to Northern Boulevard (Route 25A), and turn left. At the second light, turn right into entrance.

Madoo (The Robert Dash Garden), Sagaponack

Madoo is the quintessential artist's garden. It is a vibrant collection of colors and shapes, compositions and patterns. Robert Dash, an abstract expressionist painter who developed as a landscape realist and then returned to his abstractionist roots, has created a garden that reflects his artistic interests and spontaneity in some 40 intersecting and interrelated garden parts. Unlike many designers of great gardens, he believes in the irregular. The overall abundance and ever-changing whimsy of Madoo makes this an "original"—unlike any garden we have visited.

Madoo (which means "my dove" in Scottish dialect) is a garden without the usual rules. Plants are mixed together with an eye for design and color; pieces of decor, such as painted vases, a jauntily posed straw hat, or sudden bits of brightly colored furniture are deliberately placed like bits of still life. Blueberries and roses share one area. Another is surrounded with high boxwood hedges that enclose a channel for rainwater; nearby is a sod bench like that seen in medieval woodcuts. There is an arched Chinese bridge, a laburnum walk, and abundant privet pruned to resemble dancers. Each section of the garden can be seen as a fanciful outdoor room with its own decor and visual logic. But these separate "rooms" of the garden share boundaries with one another, and from certain vantage points, the viewer can see many sections as part of a whole.

Set on almost two acres of windswept land on Long Island's south shore, Madoo is directly next door to a working farm. The contrast between the neighboring long, straight rows of crops and Dash's wildly irregular plantings adds to the visual delight.

When the artist first bought the property in 1966, it contained only some eighteenth-century sheds and a 1740 barn. Since then, he has moved structures and built two studios and two houses; some of the buildings form a low compound creating a sheltered courtyard for part of the garden. Even the brown weather-beaten, shingled buildings become part of the riot of color; the woodwork is presently painted violet and chartreuse, apparently to complement the current colors in the garden.

Begun in 1967, Madoo has evolved over the years into a whimsical and luxurious fantasyland. For the past few years it has been open one day a week in season as a "conservancy," but the artist's creative personality (and amiable presence on visiting days) make a visit here a far cry from touring the usual impersonal (and formal) conservancy garden.

When you arrive (and pay the rather steep price, which does help to keep the garden going), you are given a map of Madoo. It designates the 40 connecting garden areas and tells you how to get from one to the next—there are some playful walkways, steps, and bridges if you follow the plan carefully. (One such construction is described as "a stairway to absolutely nowhere.") The map's accompanying description gives some idea of the scope of the artist's range of horticultural interests—from mazes, bird-welcoming plants, a high Renaissance "view-sweeper", and several notable sculptures including a late Matisse, to a fifth-century quincunx bed like that mentioned by Cyrus the Great. There is even a hermit's hut ready for occupancy.

Many of the plantings were chosen to withstand the heavy gales of this seaside site. Among the numerous flowers to be seen are some three dozen varieties of primula, rugosa, ship's rose and several other exotic rose species, Silver Moon clematis, and yellow lilies and verbascum. Exotic trees and shrubs include wonderful gingko trees, sculpturally pruned lilac and false cypress, weeping English oak, taiga birch, native pawpaw, and pollarded willows twisted in the wind. Three small ponds support a variety of grasses and border plants, as well as frogs and fish. The main ponds are connected by a meandering rill with its own waterfalls.

But all is not neatly arranged or described. There is an overall feeling of playful disorder and jungly overgrowth in parts of the property that make a visit here a bit like touring a funhouse in garden form. One section even has mirrors. And the artist's constantly evolving designs make it certain that every visit here will be different from the one before.

INFORMATION
Madoo is open only on Saturdays, May through September, from 1 P.M. to 5 P.M. Children under 6 are not permitted, but we recommend the garden for older children. There is a fee. Telephone: (516) 537-8200.

DIRECTIONS
Madoo is located at 618 Sagg Main Street in Sagaponack not far from Easthampton on Long Island. From New York City, take the Long Island Expressway (495) to Exit 70 to Route 27 East (Montauk Highway). One mile east of the Bridgehampton Village Monument turn right at traffic light onto Sagg Main Street. Go 1.3 miles, to #618; entrance is on the right.

The Garden of April Gornik, Sag Harbor

From the moment you step into the magical garden of contemporary painter April Gornik, you know you are seeing nature through the eyes of an artist. Located just outside the quaint village of Sag Harbor, on the eastern shores of Long Island, this 2-acre site combines colors, shapes, and textures with the visual sense and imagination of a painter.

In its charm and informality, the garden is in the English style, with colorful perennials arranged in beds and borders. The luxuriant flowers seem to spill forth in carefree abandon, although they have been placed and tended with great care. Flowering vines, shrubs, and towering hemlocks surround a mowed lawn. Graceful trellises support climbing roses, their delicate scent perfuming the air. A small pond with stone steps—to accommodate turtles occasionally visiting—sits near a privet hedge.

In front of the garden is the nineteenth-century frame house, where Ms. Gornik lives with her husband, painter Eric Fischl; in back is Mr. Fischl's studio, its stone and wood facade almost hidden by masses of blossoms. It is difficult to believe that this peaceful spot—where you are more likely to hear the songs of birds than the intrusive sounds of contemporary life—is only a few miles from the bustling "Hamptons."

To visit the garden you must telephone April Gornik for an appointment. You will find her to be an enthusiastic and engaging guide, eager to relate her garden experiences and ideas. Surprisingly, her garden is fairly new, having been created only in the past few years.

When Ms. Gornik moved here in the 1980s, she visited other gardens in the area in order to learn about the types of plants that would thrive in the region. Her experimentation, adventuresome spirit, and artist's touch have paid off: the result is a wonderful variety of plants and color combinations. Colors change with the growing season. In June there is a predominance of pale lavenders, pinks, creamy whites, and soft blues; hotter shades—deep scarlets and golds—take over in high summer and early fall.

Having discovered that daylilies proliferate in this climate, Ms. Gornik has collected an astonishing variety—some 100, including hybrids. You will find these mixed in with many other plants, such as iris, coral bells, and Scotch broom.

Perhaps most enchanting of all in this artist's garden are its many roses, in shades of pink, red, and cream. Throughout the summer they continue to bloom, gracing flower beds and arched trellises, adding their unmistakable touch of romance to the ambiance.

INFORMATION
You can arrange to see the garden by telephoning April Gornik, whose number is listed in the Sag Harbor directory. She will give you directions. Note that the garden can be visited from May through September only.

David and Helga Dawn Rose Garden, Southampton

This is a private, prize-winning rose garden so glorious that you may wish to drive all the way out to the south shore of Long Island just to see it. (In fact, you may easily combine a visit here with several neighboring gardens listed next.) Here, in sight of a tidal creek and tongues of blue water of Shinnecock Bay and the nearby Atlantic Ocean, is a spacious green garden that is lavishly and expertly garlanded with roses—more roses of more different colors, sizes, and species than you probably ever knew existed.

There are roses climbing on trees, growing on a pergola, decorating the house, clinging to looping chain garlands on the edges of the garden, growing in clumps and beds and edgings—roses every-where. Their colors vary from the palest of pinks and creams to the most brilliant crimson and peach and luminous white. Their sizes range from the tiniest and most enchanting to the largest and most lavish full-blown blooms. Hybrids and prize-winning examples of varieties from Sweden, England, and Germany are intermingled with more familiar American species. A fragrance garden for Helga Dawn is in front of the house, while there are also some species with no fragrance at all.

David Dawn began his rose garden on the island about 20 years ago. He became increasingly interested in roses and traveled wide-ly to collect new varieties. The result is one of the most successful private gardens we have come across.

Mr. Dawn is a genial and interesting host, and may take you around the garden in his golf cart, identifying any and all roses for you. Visitors are most welcome. While we were there, photogra-phers from a magazine were taking pictures of the pergola, so cov-ered with blooming roses that a walk through it was like passing through a tunnel of heady crimson and white and golden blossoms. We were told that the garden is fully in bloom from June through September, with one variety of rose replacing another when its sea-son is past. If you like gardens with only one type of flower imagi-natively and lavishly designed, don't miss this enchanting spot.

INFORMATION
David and Helga Dawn live in Southampton, and may be tele-phoned for an appointment to visit in the summer. You will find them informal and hospitable to visitors. Telephone: (516) 283-2834.

DIRECTIONS
Southampton is on the south shore of Long Island. From New York City, take the Long Island Expressway (495) to the William Floyd Parkway south to Route 27 East (the Montauk Highway). Take Route 27A into Southampton, and the Dawns will direct you from there.

And in Addition . . .

Mill Neck: John P. Humes Japanese Stroll Garden
Dogwood Lane. Telephone: (516) 676-4486.
This is a contemplative 4-acre Zen garden including stones, plants

(especially many stands of bamboo), a tea house, and carefully designed spaces for contemplation. Open Saturday and Sunday 11:30 A.M. to 4:30 P.M., April through October 1. Tours, explanations, and Japanese tea ceremonies available. Fee.

Oakdale: Bayard Cutting Arboretum

Route 27A (Montauk Highway. Telephone (516) 581-1002.

The Bayard Cutting Arboretum is one of the nicest landscaped places to take a walk on all of Long Island. Its plans were drawn up by the landscape architectural firm of Frederick Law Olmsted, beginning in 1887. This elegant former estate of some 690 acres has everything: wonderful waterside paths overlooking a picturesque inlet with many white swans and geese, marsh gardens, azalea and rhododendron gardens, sweeping lawns, small flower beds, and the most stupendous weeping beech tree we have ever seen. (If you love tremendous trees, this spot should not be missed; there are many other fine old specimen trees, and the collection is considered the best on Long Island.) The grassy and woodsy acres of the arboretum surround a grand old 1880s mansion, the home of the Cutting family, who surely knew how to live! Although there are a few formal planted areas in this arboretum, this is more a landscape than a garden. But it is a landscape for all seasons, even in winter, when it is especially beautiful. Numerous classes and events are held here, and Heckscher State Park is next door. The Arboretum is open year-round. Fee.

Oyster Bay: Planting Fields Arboretum

Planting Fields Road. Telephone: (516) 922-9201.

This splendid and vast arboretum, designed by the noted Olmsted brothers in the early part of this century, is a horticultural showplace not to be missed. Its elegant grounds (once the private estate of the Coe family) include majestic beech, linden, oaks, and magnolia, as well as unusual shrubs imported from Europe and Asia. Among its many offerings, you'll find a "Synoptic Garden" with plantings alphabetically arranged by botanical name.

A visit to the arboretum's two magnificent conservatories will lift anyone's spirits on even the bleakest of wintry days. The first, the recently renovated Camellia Greenhouse, contains an outstanding collection under glass. Camellias in delicate shades of red and pink are set among a delightful array of lilies. While these flowers are at their peak in February, the main greenhouse features brilliant seasonal displays year-round. Its poinsettias in December are almost

legendary. Other plantings include orchids, delphiniums, bromeli-
ads, and Spanish moss. An ivy-covered arch graces a corner, adding
a graceful Victorian touch. The greenhouses are open daily, 10 A.M.
to 4 P.M.; the grounds are open daily, 9 A.M. to 5 P.M.

Roslyn Harbor: Cedarmere, The William Cullen Bryant Estate
225 Bryant Avenue. Telephone: (516) 571-8130.
This estate of the romantic poet, journalist, and antislavery crusader
William Cullen Bryant (1794–1878) suggests a nature poet's sensibil-
ities. Now listed on the National Register of Historic Places and just
being renovated, the lovely 7-acre estate overlooking the water
includes a large house, a boathouse, a duck house, a watermill (built
by Bryant to provide his own power), great trees romantically
reflected in the pond, a charming bridge, ducks, and newly restored
flower gardens. Bryant was an avid horticulturist; the restoration is
in accordance with his own notes and photographs. As of this writing the scenery retains an overgrown and pleasingly romantic aura;
it is to be hoped that the restoration does not neaten up the place
too much. Open Saturdays from 10:00 A.M. to 4:45 P.M. and Sundays
from 1:00 P.M. to 4:45 P.M.; by appointment during the week from
April through September. Tours available.

UPSTATE NEW YORK

Martin Lee Berlinger's Clove Valley Gardens, High Falls

This private garden is set in deep country, the Shawangunk
Mountains in Ulster County. But the steep, wooded hillsides and
startling rock formations are surprisingly close to civilization, so a
visit here is within easy reach of urbanites seeking a serene and
unusual garden site.

In fact, serenity is precisely what Mr. Berlinger's gardens are
about. There are half a dozen different gardens here: they are primarily Asian in conception and design, and each garden "room"
offers a contemplative setting visible from the various windows of
his house. He combines an obvious delight in the natural landscape

UPSTATE NEW YORK GARDENWALKS

39. High Falls: Martin Lee Berlinger's
    Clove Valley Gardens
40. Saratoga Springs: Petrified Sea
    Gardens

And in Addition . . .

41. Ashford Hollow: Griffis Sculpture
    Park
42. Buffalo: Buffalo and Erie County
    Botanical Garden
43. Canandaigua: Sonnenberg
    Gardens

44. Clinton: Root Glen
45. Elizabethtown: Colonial Garden
46. Esperance: George Landis
    Arboretum
47. Ithaca: Cornell Plantations
48. New Paltz: Mohonk Mountain
    House Gardens
49. Rochester: George Eastman
    House
50. Rochester: Highland Park
51. Syracuse: Mills Memorial Rose
    Garden

that surrounds his property with a deep response to the mystical meanings of Oriental gardens. Each of the settings, with their careful designs of delicate, symbolic plantings, raked stones, and running water, opens out through a wooden gate to the magnificent landscape beyond.

Mr. Berlinger, an enthusiastic and knowledgeable guide, is a professional landscape designer who spends half of his time in Asia. With his Thai wife he has created an ambiance—both indoors and out—that is a surprising mixture of East and West. His interest in Thai and Japanese design is evident throughout his large, rambling house (which he hospitably offers to show too) and most of his gardens. This is a private site—neither large nor particularly showy—that truly invites visitors. As the owner is continually working on new plans, this could undoubtedly be termed a "growing" garden.

In each garden room a different design has taken shape, but in all of them there is an attempt to capture something calming and orderly. These gardens are not dramatic statements; they are complete, small-scaled environments that suggest tranquillity. You'll see the tall, exotic grasses (which deer do not care to eat); the asymmetrically shaped, stone-edged goldfish pond below the newly built pagoda (decorated with teak carvings recently carried back from Thailand); the delicate gates handmade from fallen trees and broom straws; the small statues of Asian deities hidden among the decorative shrubbery; and many stone benches for contemplative enjoyment. One garden, reachable through sliding doors from the bedroom, contains two stone islands, one symbolizing a tortoise, another a crane—representing wisdom and long life—floating in a sea of gravel. Each planting and positioning of stones has symbolic meaning; for example, the carefully pruned cedar tree suggests clouds, while the raked gravel represents waves.

But you need not understand the symbolic references to appreciate the design and atmosphere here. "I try to really change a space—its life, its feeling—because that will also change our lives as participants in that garden. Each garden creates different thought patterns, and each has its own effect on you," says Berlinger.

The Asian gardens are only part of the pleasure of visiting here. You will also see an English-style garden of great charm, filled with bulbs and perennials—and particularly in springtime—a profusion of color. Delicate pale green lamb's ears nestle next to brilliant yellow coreopsis, while red bee balm and scarlet crosomia Lucifer are set off by the white Casablanca lilies and pale veronica. The English garden, though, also has a Thai touch: a statue of an Asian flute player perched amid the flowers.

And at the edge of the cultivated gardens there is a pathway into the adjacent wooded area with its striking stony cliffs, which Berlinger has cleared of brush but left otherwise undisturbed in its natural glory. His 7 acres abut a great forest preserve, with hiking trails throughout. A visit to this garden and its surroundings will suggest many new ideas to the amateur gardener—among them how to combine an appreciation for the natural wonders of a rural setting with carefully cultivated gardens of one's own.

INFORMATION
Martin Lee Berlinger can be telephoned for an appointment at (914) 687-7895.

DIRECTIONS
High Falls is ten minutes from New Paltz, New York, at Exit 18 on the New York State Thruway (I-87). Mr. Berlinger will provide directions to Clove Valley Gardens.

Saratoga Springs, Petrified Sea Gardens

While we've described many historic gardens, how about one that predates recorded history—one that is 500 million years old? The Petrified Sea Gardens will capture the imagination of anyone interested in geology, fossils, Native American culture, and—surprisingly—growing plants.

Here, in a beautiful woodsy spot, you'll discover for yourself the huge and mysterious rock formations covered with fossilized "cabbages" that were once at the bottom of the Cambrian Sea. It is a rare and evocative—even cosmic—experience to walk on what was, during the Ice Age, an ocean reef; to see the great cracks which seem to descend to the inside of the earth; and to touch with your fingers the fossil designs of growing things of an era beyond our imagining.

Surrounding these great slabs of stone are some more modern areas: a few landscaped paths and a charming rock garden (of course!), a pond with goldfish and lilies, and great trees. Though declared a national Landmark by the United States Government, the Sea Gardens are very rustic: there are handmade signs with bits of information and a little museum and fossil shop, all run on a shoe-string by the family who owns the land (and many volunteers). Open since 1993, the place has a nice lack of commercialism. There are no guides; you make your way with a little map and can stay as long as you like examining this curious spot. We know of no other garden in the East in which the modern plantings are so much less important than the rocks on which they grow!

Five hundred million years ago, this area was at the edge of the Cambrian Sea: tides created great reefs, which were later polished by the glaciers into the smooth stone you see today. This fossilized reef is called a stromatolite reef because fossil remains of single-cell blue-green algae (known as sea cabbages) and trilobite (sea bugs) cover the surface. The great crevices and small holes in the reef were the result of melting glaciers—some a mile thick—that wore down the rockface. (The spot was found in 1923 when a wandering cow fell and became stuck in such a crevice. Its rescue caused the fossilized reef to be discovered in modern times.)

When you take the walk (on delicious red pine needle paths) as outlined by the map, you come first to a limestone grotto described as a place "where the earth can be seen to have slipped." Nearby along this forested path is the first section of the reef—truly an amazing sight. (Though the area is quite flat, wear "sensible" shoes. And watch out for the many cracks and holes created a mere 12,000 to 15,000 years ago.) Note the different sorts of crevices, holes, and scratch marks—described on the map.

Having traversed two great sections of the sea garden, you will come to what are known as glacial erratics: odd rocks and boulders carried along by glaciers and deposited here and there. To give you an idea of the glacier's force, one of the three groups here weighs an estimated 200 tons.

We are not the first people to feel the cosmic force of these nat-ural surroundings. This area is at the end of the Mohawk Trail. The Iroquois Indians who inhabited it thought of its glacial erratics in spiritual terms. Called "Indian Stones," they were oriented to the sun at the solstice (perhaps including an altar) and had great significance for tribes in the area. There is also a circular "Medicine Wheel" and a stone labyrinth. Also of importance to the Iroquois here was the great white pine, now 300 years old. Because it has five limbs reach-ing upward like a hand, it was called a Witness Tree; the Indians considered a vow made beneath it sacrosanct.

There are other, more familiar features at the Sea Gardens too: the rock garden—of a more contemporary nature—is very pretty, and there is a lily pond complete with a small Buddha. You'll also find dinosaur footprints here, and a small museum of fossils. Bring the children! This is one garden in which they'll be thoroughly interested, and you too will find it intriguing to note that Mother Nature had her own unusually patterned "gardens" so long ago!

INFORMATION
The Petrified Sea Gardens are at 42 Petrified Sea Gardens Road in Saratoga Springs. They offer tours and educational events as well as self-guiding maps. Telephone: (518) 584-7102. The Gardens are open every day from May through October. Small fee.

DIRECTIONS
Saratoga Springs is located north of Albany. Take Exit 13 of the New York Thruway (I-87) and Route 9 north to Saratoga Springs; in town it becomes Broadway. At the intersection with Route 29 downtown, make a left and go west three miles to Petrified Sea Gardens Road; follow signs.

And in Addition . . .

Ashford Hollow: Griffis Sculpture Park
6902 Mill Valley Road (Ashford Hollow is south of Buffalo). Telephone: (716) 257-9344.
This is a vast sculpture park comprising about 400 acres of grassy hills, deep ravines, woodland, and open meadows—all set with a wide variety of contemporary sculpture. Open daily, April 1 to November 1. Tours by appointment.

Buffalo: Buffalo and Erie County Botanical Garden
South Park Avenue and McKinley Parkway. Telephone: (716) 828-1040.
Twelve greenhouses provide more than 2 acres of gardens under glass here—a special pleasure in winter in this harsh climate, and there are outdoor gardens too. Open daily 9 A.M. to 4 P.M. Free.

Canandaigua: Sonnenberg Gardens
Gibson Street (Route 21). Telephone: (716) 394-4922.
These turn-of-the-century gardens were designed by Ernest W.

Bowditch of Boston. The Smithsonian called the Sonnenberg "one of the most magnificent late Victorian gardens ever created in America." The splendid estate includes conservatories, a rose garden, an Italian Garden, lawns, ponds, and a belvedere. Later additions are a Moonlight Garden, Rock Garden, and a Pansy Garden, a Japanese garden with a tea house, and aviaries and a deer park. The Conservatory, built in 1903, contains an outstanding collection of tropical and desert plants. Open mid-May to mid-October. Fee.

Clinton: Root Glen
107 College Hill Road. Telephone for guided tours only: (315) 859-7193.
This large wooded garden was created on lovely rolling terrain 150 years ago by Oren and Nancy Root. It features over 50 species of trees and flowering shrubs, as well as peonies, iris, lilies, heathers, primulas, azaleas, daffodils, and raised beds of alpine plants. Visit in spring and early summer for best blooms. Open daily dawn to dusk.

Elizabethtown: Colonial Garden
Route 9. Telephone: (518) 873-6466.
A well-loved, miniature garden adjoining the Adirondack Center Museum recreates features of Britain's Hampton Court and Williamsburg's restored colonial gardens. This delightful retreat in a picturesque mountain setting has many colonial features: patterned brick and gravel walks, raised flower beds, a sun dial, a 1776 cistern with dolphin fountain, iron benches, and a summer house surrounded by a traditional white picket fence. Flowers common to the eighteenth century include delphinium, heliotrope, phlox, dwarf cockscomb, columbine, foxglove and cineraria; they bloom inside a border of cedar hedge. The garden is at its most beautiful in July and August, but its careful design makes it interesting even under a blanket of snow. A dense woodland adjoins the garden and is filled with wildflowers in season. Open daily from mid-May to October. Fee.

Esperance: George Landis Arboretum
Lape Road (Route 20); Esperance is west of Schenectady. Telephone: (518) 875-6935.
A 97-acre public garden, this Schoharie Valley arboretum is an ideal setting for long nature walks. Gardens feature 30 acres of formal plantings, a 20-acre woodland (where you'll see a white oak reportedly 500 years old), and numerous seasonal displays and programs

concerning flowers, trees, birds, and other natural history topics. Open year-round, but for flower gardens visit from April 1 to November 15.

Ithaca: Cornell Plantations
100 Judd Falls Road. Telephone: (607) 255-3020.

On these 1,500 acres there are all kinds of gardens including a synoptic shrub garden, wildflower gardens, peony, herb, and azalea collections, and for those of you with a taste for something entirely different, a well-known Poisonous Plants Garden. An arboretum designed by Olmsted protégé Nelson Wells and a conservatory of tropical and desert plants can also be seen here. Open daily, dawn to dusk. Tours available.

New Paltz: Mohonk Mountain House Gardens
Route 299 west. Telephone: (914) 255-1000.

This gigantic nineteenth-century resort hotel known as the Mohonk Mountain House is set in 7,500 acres of magnificent Catskill mountain scenery—including a lovely lake—whose beauty dwarfs any man-made flower beds or other additions to the natural panorama.

While there are very pleasant formal gardens, as well as a fern trail and a wildflower trail here, you should not pay the very stiff entrance price just to see these decorations to the sloping green that surrounds the back sides of the bustling resort. But if you wish to enjoy (and pay for) the many highly organized recreational facilities (including canoeing, paddleboating, golf, horseback riding, and miles of hiking trails) or the view from the vast veranda overlooking the bright blue lake below—or a copious meal here—then note the gardens while you're here. (And plan to call in advance for a reservation.)

We think you'll find the Victorian structures and the mammoth stone outcroppings that dominate the landscape of as much interest as the pretty rows of flowers (all labeled) and the hand-hewn wisteria arbors set amid the neatly cultivated lawns. (A particular pleasure to children is a treehouse with a ladder almost completely obscured by vines.) There is a greenhouse that supplies the changing flowers seasonally, many gazebos, and several nice resting benches within these orderly beds, but not too much in the way of innovative design or exotic plantings. Nature's own extravagant beauties here are hard to compete with. Nevertheless, there is a formal rose garden, an herb garden, a show garden that dates back to early days at Mohonk, a rockery and pool garden, and wildflowers and fern trails.

Guidebooks to the arrangement of the gardens and the trails (including a "find-it-yourself" trail) are available at the gift shop within the main building.

The Mohonk Mountain House resort is open year-round. To secure the least expensive access to the hotel and grounds, call ahead for a breakfast reservation, which affords you entrance to all the resort's facilities and grounds, including horse-drawn carriage rides to a spectacular mountaintop vista, for the day.

A similarly glorious setting is also nearby for free (or a nominal fee in summertime) at Lake Minnewaska, a park a few miles down the road. Here is a deep deep blue lake surrounded by huge cliffs of white stone that rivals any scenery we've come across. There was once a similar resort inn here too, but no more. You can hike around the glacial lake or into the woods; there are numerous other free trails for hiking all along Route 299.

Rochester: George Eastman House
900 East Avenue. Telephone: (716) 271-3361.

George Eastman, the father of popular photography, hired noted landscape architect Alling S. DeForest to create gardens all around the fine home—now a museum—on this 12.5-acre estate. Today four beautiful flower gardens have been restored to their original elegance following Eastman's own photographs and the original plans. Among the pleasures here are a rock garden with 39 varieties of perennials in scalloped-shaped beds, a grape arbor, a pergola, a sunken oval lily pond, seventeenth-century Venetian wellheads, a garden house, and over 90 varieties of perennials (labeled). There are many shrubs and vines and great trees. Open Tuesday through Saturday, 10:00 A.M. to 4:30 P.M., and Sunday, 1:00 P.M. to 4:30 P.M.; every day, May through September. Fee. Tours are available.

Rochester: Highland Park
180 Reservoir Avenue.

This is considered to be the finest lilac collection in the world—there are some 500 varieties here! For best viewing come in late spring. And there are also roses and a great conservatory collection of some 40,000 plants on these exquisite grounds designed by

Frederick Law Olmsted. Grounds open daily until 11 P.M.; conservatory daily from 9 A.M. to 5 P.M.

Syracuse: Mills Memorial Rose Garden
Thoren Park.
You'll find over 10,000 roses, and lots of other perennials, blooming here in season. You can even visit this garden at night; it is illuminated! Open daily; come in June and July to see roses at their best.

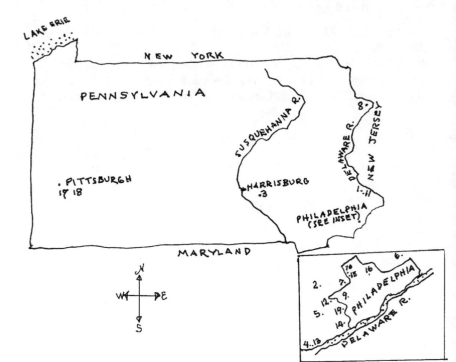

PENNSYLVANIA GARDENWALKS

1. Pipersville: Cedaridge Farm
2. Gladwyne: The Henry Foundation for Botanical Research
3. Hershey: Hershey Gardens
4. Kennett Square: Longwood Gardens
5. Malvern: Joanna Reed's Garden (Longview Farm)
6. Meadowbrook: Meadowbrook Farm
7. Merion Station: Barnes Foundation Arboretum
8. Milford: Grey Towers
9. Philadelphia: Historic Bartram's Garden
10. Philadelphia: Morris Arboretum
11. Washington's Crossing: Bowman's Hill State Wildflower Preserve
12. Wayne: Chanticleer

And in Addition . . .
13. Chadds Ford: Brandywine Conservancy
14. Media: Tyler Arboretum
15. Philadelphia: Fairmont Park Horticultural Center
16. Philadelphia: Wyck
17. Pittsburgh: Pittsburgh Civic Garden Center
18. Pittsburgh: Phipps Conservatory
19. Villa Nova: Appleford

PENNSYLVANIA

Cedaridge Farm, Pipersville

The relationship between art and gardens has surely been a long and mutually satisfactory one. Throughout history we find both artists using nature's beauty as their inspiration and garden designers making nature into art. In this collection of visits you will find gardens that are closely identified with well-known art, whether as the subject of a famous painting or as the recreation of a landscape from a distant time or place.

No garden we have seen has made such a conscious (and successful) effort at reproducing an entire era of gardens—and paintings of them—as Derek Fell's Cedaridge Farm. Fell is a photographer and writer with a specialty in gardens and their history. His great interest is the French Impressionist and Post-Impressionist landscape. Using reproductions of some of the most famous paintings ever made by such artists as Monet and Van Gogh, he has created living versions of their subjects. At Cedaridge Farm you'll see bright-colored iris under a red arched Japanese-style bridge, just as Monet pictured, and perennial flower border around vegetable garden, just as painted by Pissaro. There are fields of flowers as pictured by Van Gogh, a leaf tunnel as described by Cézanne, and a jungle garden that captures Rousseau's oversized foliage.

A visit here is, in fact, a very odd experience. For the pure appreciator of pretty and well-designed gardens, it is a large, lovely, and ever-changing landscape. For the art lover who is familiar with the painting on which each garden tableau is based, it is beautiful, but somewhat unnerving. It is a bit like a visit to a famous portrait gallery in which each painted face has come to life.

This is a case of art imitating (and designing) nature and nature, in turn, being used to imitate art. We must remember that the Impressionists planted their own gardens with paintings of them in mind. Monet, for example, chose and planted the flowers in his garden at Giverny because he liked their color harmonies, and he actually scattered seeds for tiny white flowers such as baby's breath across the landscape in order to include such delicate touches in his work. Cézanne is known to have cut leaf tunnels through the flowering shrubs in his garden at Aix-en-Provence, giving it a sculptural outlook amid carefully harmonized greens. Renoir, another of Fell's inspirations, created a garden of wildflowers under the olive trees at his home near Nice, relishing the naturalistic look for his paintings. (By the way, all these artists' gardens in France are open to visitors.)

Using the Impressionists' choice of plantings, color, and design, Fell has chosen to recreate a number of these sites. The flyer and map that you receive when you enter the property takes you from garden to garden; there is a pleasantly informal atmosphere on this self-guided walk, and nothing is commercialized or numbered on signs. You can see color reproductions of the paintings in the small house that is used as a gallery and headquarters for visitors. You may look first at the paintings and then see the gardens or, as we did, reverse the process. In any case, the verisimilitude is astounding, and we think you will relish following the map whether you are there merely to enjoy the pretty settings or are an Impressionist painting enthusiast.

You begin your trip through an Impressionist meadow of wildflowers and a rose arbor, which in turn will take you to a swamp garden. Next you will find your first garden inspired by a specific artist: Cézanne's Leaf Tunnel. This appealing spot is a study in light and shade, by means of close plantings of bright-green Japanese hakone grass and sassafras, scarlet maples, and black walnut trees.

From here you will traverse lily ponds and a stream garden, visit a Victorian-style conservatory, and enjoy a profusion of flowers in an old-fashioned cottage garden. Soon you will come to Van Gogh's

Cutting Garden, a brilliant recreation of a scene the artist painted in Provence.

A gate designed and painted by Caillebotte (for a Paris garden) is nearby. A moon garden—one of our favorites—features a collection of flowers that are all white or pink so that they will reflect the light of a summer moon. From here you'll find a perennial-bordered, walled vegetable garden based on Pissaro's unusual design: it includes both plants arranged for color and shape and a familiar wooden wheelbarrow and several watering cans artfully displayed. Nearby is a tableau featuring a rope swing like that was painted by Renoir.

Le Douanier Rousseau's giant-leaved plants grow in a junglelike setting at the bottom of a sloping hillside. There, oversized plants include the umbrella plant, Joe Pye weed, plume poppy, and sunflowers. (This is a particularly exotic recreation since the artist's own paintings were imaginary rather than interpretations of the landscape. You might find yourself searching for a monkey or a lion amid the foliage.)

The Monet Bridge, with its delightful red arch, is surrounded by, and contrasts with, brilliant purple iris; it truly makes you feel you have wandered into Giverny by mistake. From here you come upon Van Gogh's Woodland Garden, a grove of birch trees that forms a setting like that in his painting *Two Figures in a Landscape*. A visit to a moss garden and a ramble through the woods bring you back to the visitor's center.

These are only a few highlights of Cedaridge Farm. The garden is apparently still being developed; perhaps when you visit there will be additional settings bringing to mind the shimmering colors and flickering light of the French Impressionists and the shapes and forms that inspired the artists who followed them.

INFORMATION
Cedaridge Farm is open from late April through the end of October by appointment. Telephone: (215) 766-0699, weekdays.

DIRECTIONS
Pipersville is reached by the New Jersey Turnpike to Route 202 toward Lambertville, New Jersey. You will be given specific direction when you telephone for an appointment.

The Henry Foundation for Botanical Research, Gladwyne

While most of the rock gardens we have visited consisted of small, delicate plantings set amid gentle, rocky slopes, the Henry Foundation Gardens are something different. Here the rocks are giant boulders, dramatically punctuating the rolling hills. These striking outcroppings are massive hunks of Baltimore gneiss, and they give this garden a design all its own.

If you (and definitely your children) like climbing around midst rocks and flowers in a free-form environment, this is certainly a place for you to spend some time. The Henry Foundation Gardens have used nature's amazing forms—including the unusually lovely, spacious terrain—to create a distinctive garden.

Finding this public garden is not easy. Even nearby neighbors did not know of its existence. Set deep in the countryside of Philadelphia's Main Line, it takes some winding roads and a final dirt and gravel one to come to the entrance. But like the proverbial Shangri-La, once you enter through the rustic gate (with a nearly illegible sign), you are in an unusually enchanting—if eccentric—spot. From the original mansion of the Henry family with its door wide open to the public, to the outbuildings that remind you of rural France, to the unbroken expanse of meadow and rock gardens, the Henry Foundation surprises with its charm.

The gardens date to the 1920s, when Mary Gibson Henry, a field botanist, began laying them out around the family home. She searched the American continent for more than 40 years for plants that could survive in this rough and rocky terrain. By growing many such unusual specimens at her Pennsylvania estate, Mrs. Henry found that she had created a true research garden. The Foundation for Botanical Research—now 40 acres—was created in 1948 to continue her work with rare and endemic plants. Her daughter, Josephine de N. Henry, is also a plant expert who has gone on with the task of assembling and nurturing rare species for the past 28 years. You may still find her cataloging or talking with visitors in the open house.

The diversity of the landscape—from fields to steep slopes to rocky outgrowths to woodlands—has provided microclimates for plants with a great geographical range of origins. The plantings include warm-climate specimens from Texas and Florida and cold-climate examples from as far north as British Columbia and Nova

Scotia. You'll find—depending upon the season—liliums and amaryllis in spring and amazingly colorful blooming Amaryllidaceae in the winter. There are many flowering shrubs, rhododendrons, styrax, trillium, and bee balm to be seen.

The rock garden is spectacular, due both to the natural shape of the boulders on the hillside and to the plantings of gentians, yuccas, and silver bells, among many other flowering plants. It is an energetic climb up to the boulders, but there is a great view once you get there.

Though there are occasional identifying labels, this is not a uniformly tagged garden. There seems to be little organization—in the sense of a scientific, botanical center—but the planners' delight in color and design is evident throughout this unusual and comparatively unknown garden.

INFORMATION
The Henry Foundation for Botanical Research is open year-round on weekdays from 10 A.M. to 4 P.M.. You might wish to time your visit not only by which season's flowers you enjoy, but by when you might like to do a rather hilly and rough walk. We do not recommend this walk unless you are both energetic and good at climbing (unless you just wish to view the garden's delights from the driveway that runs through the middle to the estate). Telephone: (215) 525-2037.

DIRECTIONS
From the Pennsylvania Turnpike (I-276) take exit at Interstate 76 (Valley Forge). Go south on 76. Take the Gladwyne Exit (29) and turn left. Turn right on Route 23 and go for 2 miles. [From Route 476 (Philadelphia) take Exit 6A to Route 23 East.] Route 23 is also called Conshohocken State Road. You'll find Henry Lane, a right-hand turn. After a short distance on Henry Lane, the road seems to end with a small park, but turn left and you'll see a private driveway and a small sign for the Foundation.

Hershey Gardens, Hershey

Hershey Gardens are uncommonly pretty. Despite a surrounding atmosphere of nearby amusement park, noted Hershey chocolate factory, tours, and hotels, these gardens are an oasis of pleasing landscape, brightly colored flower beds, very green mowed lawns, and amazing trees. The trees, in fact, almost outshine the famous rose gardens. Not that the rose gardens are not magnificent. They are, and so are all the other flower beds and special landscape designs.

This is, however, as much a landscape as a flower garden, with nice brick pathways through a rolling terrain, beautifully punctuated with gardens of all types and massive (labeled) trees. There are a pond and a fountain, brightly decorative annual and perennial beds, occasional statues and commemorative pieces, scattered benches and gazebos, and an extensive Japanese garden complete with boulders and stream. A walk here can take as long as you have to spend, for each of these 23 acres has something of botanical interest. It is rather hilly; wear your walking shoes.

The Hershey Gardens were developed over a 59-year period (beginning in 1937) from a 3-acre plot of roses into a 23-acre botanical garden and arboretum. Though originally planned at Milton S. Hershey's request (for a "nice garden of roses" to complement the community he had constructed for his workers), the years have seen a tremendous increase in area and sophisticated plantings. In its original planting, 12,000 roses in 112 varieties were set out. The garden was an immediate success, drawing visitors from far beyond the town itself. By 1941, 17 more acres of unused farmland were added, and the garden was soon displaying—in addition to its roses—annuals, flowering bulbs, and the beginnings of its specimen tree collection—now so extraordinary. In the 1960s and 1970s dwarf and weeping conifers and flowering shrubs and many other beautiful trees were added. Today, under the operation of the Milton S. Hershey Foundation, the gardens are kept elegantly, and their flower displays ever changing and brilliant in color.

We particularly appreciated the unpretentious, low-key, civilized atmosphere here: there were few signs—though occasional labels, few guards—though helpful people at the desk—and a nice self-guiding map. Because of the many mowed lawns, a walk here is a bit like walking across a golf course with flowers.

Of major interest to most viewers is the rose garden, a sampler of dozens of species (all labeled) and planned to bloom throughout the growing season. Though rose gardens tend to be rather formal, these include old-fashioned gardens of "roses grandmother used to grow," as well as the original terraced Hershey Rose Garden. Colors range from the palest pink to salmon, lavender, and deepest crimson. Mermaid roses of pale yellow border the small lake, where swans and water birds and goldfish live. There are trellises of climbing roses, the orange Tropicana rose, and a planting of the M. S. Hershey Rose, floribunda, grandiflora, tea roses, and miniatures. During the summer months (and often through October) some 30,000 roses bloom!

Your walk through the gardens will take you to a variety of other planted areas nestled among the specimen trees. You will see a rock garden, an ornamental grass garden, a plant doctor's trial garden, and in spring, some 600 brilliant azaleas and rhododendrons. The special display gardens change with the seasons. In spring 30,000 tulips bloom, as well as thousands of daffodils, hyacinths, and other bulbs. There are some 5,000 chrysanthemums in fall. These display gardens are laid out in patterns—a windmill design of tulips, for example, or geometric rows of similar color that resemble giant flags of flowers spread across the grounds.

All across the landscape are great trees, including varieties of gingkos ("nature's living fossils"), three California redwoods, incense cedars, bluish Atlantic cedars, a golden chain tree, and the extraordinary sinuous shapes of dwarf evergreens. There are maples and a giant weeping beech tree, poplars, elms, and dozens of other trees. As you stroll from garden to garden here, these magnificent trees provide not only shade and interest, but a sense of wonder and permanence.

INFORMATION
The Hershey Gardens are on Hotel Road in Hershey. Telephone: (717) 534-3492. There is a moderate fee for seeing the gardens on your own, and there are also daily tours. Open from mid-May through October. There is a yearly "bloom schedule" available.

DIRECTIONS
Hershey Gardens are located 90 miles west of Philadelphia. From Highways 76, 78, 81, and 83, take Route 422 to Hershey. Follow signs to the Hotel and the Gardens.

Longwood Gardens, Kennett Square

The Longwood Gardens hardly need an introduction. Among the finest of their kind in the East, they are a major tourist attraction year-round. And with good reason. The meticulously tended flower beds, topiaries, sunken gardens, grand allées, water gardens, and conservatories are a delight to all, young and not so young alike. There are some 350 acres to explore, including an arboretum with ancient trees, a Victorian grotto, meadows of wildflowers, and forest lands. Walking through these beautiful grounds is a joyful experience; it is also easy and pleasant, as the terrain is flat and many paths paved. You can join a guided tour (Longwood is well organized in that respect) or pick up a walking guide at the visitors' area and launch out on your own adventure. You will find you can easily lose the crowds in this extensive area, as you wander through the many individual gardens (18 in all), walk around the idyllic lake (complete with Grecian temple), or enjoy a picnic in the pastoral parkland.

Visitors are particularly drawn to the wonderful conservatories and the water gardens with their exceptional spectacles. Indeed, water gardens were the passion of Pierre S. du Pont, founder of Longwood and dedicated gardener in his own right. He had admired the exquisite water gardens in Europe and tried to duplicate them here, adding touches of whimsy and elements of surprise that continue to fascinate today's visitors.

A collection of fountains, canals, pools, basins, and moats graces the landscape, and the soft and appealing sounds of moving water are often heard. The Main Fountain Garden—a hugh 5-acre sunken area with rows of carefully trimmed maples surrounding the waterways—features special water events: water pours from the mouths of carved mythical creatures during five-minute intervals; 200 water jets shoot off water in fanlike shapes and arcs three times daily during the summer; and on summer evenings extravaganzas of fountains, lights, and music are held, much in the tradition of the French "son et lumière" shows (some say these are even more spectacular). At the Open Air Theatre a curtain of water completes the decor and water displays occur regularly during and after dance performances.

Unlike the water gardens, the conservatories—seven in all—of 4 acres can be enjoyed at any time during the year, especially in winter, when their bright blossoms are most appreciated. The glass gardens include an orangerie (a charming 1920s crystal palace), the East Conservatory (where children can amuse themselves wandering in an ivy maze designed especially for them), and five interconnecting conservatories, including the Azalea-Camellia, Rose, Desert, and Palm greenhouses.

There is an orchid house with changing displays, a Silver Garden, Cascade Garden, a collection of insect-eating plants, bunches of brilliant flowers hanging from baskets, topiary forms in large tubs, artistically arranged vegetable displays, and neat rows of nectarine trees. In spring you can enjoy the Flower Garden Walk with masses of lilacs, roses, tulips, iris, and peonies bordering each side of the brick path; the Rose Arbor; the Hillside Garden with its azaleas and bluebells; and the peony and wisteria gardens. The Topiary Garden, with 60 yews trimmed in curious geometric shapes, is always a popular spot.

The main house on the estate—surprisingly modest, considering it belonged to one of the country's wealthiest families—can also be visited. There are many special events at Longwood Gardens, in addition to the water displays, and you might wish to coordinate your visit accordingly: a November indoor and outdoor Chrysanthemum Festival; Christmas displays of poinsettias; indoor spring flower shows; band concerts, organ and choral recitals, and ballet performances; special programs for children; and classes in horticulture and gardening for adults. There are even firework displays on special occasions during the summer.

The Longwood Gardens are indeed a year-round celebration of nature's joys.

INFORMATION
The Gardens are open daily, April through October, 9 A.M. to 6 P.M.; November through March, 9 A.M. to 5 P.M. There is an entrance fee. Conservatories and shops are open daily, 10 A.M. to 5 P.M. (later, when there are special events). The du Pont House is open daily, April through December from 11 A.M. to 3 P.M.

Facilities include a restaurant, cafeteria, and gift shop. Gardens, conservatories, and shops are all wheelchair accessible. For information on special events, call (610) 388-1000.

DIRECTIONS
From New York City, take the Lincoln Tunnel to New Jersey Turnpike south to Exit 2, Route 322 west, across Commodore Barry Bridge into Pennsylvania. Continue on Route 322 west (it becomes I-95) for about a mile, following signs for West Chester. At intersection with Route 1 turn left and take Route 1 south for about 8 miles. Follow the signs for the Longwood Gardens.

Joanna Reed's Garden (Longview Farm), Malvern

Joanna Reed's Garden is not just a garden, in the sense of a carefully designed and planted area, or the formal section of a larger estate. Instead, this is a garden environment—so beautifully and naturally a part of its surroundings that even the house and outbuildings of her old farm seem to be part of it. A visit here will make you want to go home and rethink your own ideas of gardens, of natural landscape, or of how plantings can enhance every outdoor corner of your home. For Joanna Reed, with what seems to be sleight-of-hand, has created a charmingly personal approach to landscape arrangement and space, color harmonies, sizes and shapes, variety of plantings—all the many elements of appealing and informal garden design.

The site of her wonderful garden is a 37-acre farm with a circa 1804 farmhouse (part of it dates to the midnineteenth-century) that perches charmingly over a sloping hill. Just across the wagon track from it is a great old barn, and other outbuildings, including an ancient corn crib and another house too. Everything looks old and natural in the best sense: unspoiled, rustic, picturesque. Joanna Reed started gardening here in the 1940s, and for some 50 years her garden has aged gracefully along with the buildings; here too, nothing looks new or recently planted (though, of course, annuals are put in each season). There are plantings everywhere: wisteria vines over the porch, an espaliered apple tree against the barn, and fields filled with daisies and coreopsis. The land is pleasantly uneven; there are many corners and steps and paths and stone walls and odd spaces before the farm gives way to meadows, woods, and typically lovely Pennsylvania scenery. (Unfortunately, there is also a roar of highway that now comes too near to this bucolic scene.)

Though she began with growing vegetables during World War II, it was flower gardening that captured Joanna Reed's imagination. She studied with Elizabeth Farley and at the Barnes Arboretum in nearby Merion, and little by little transformed Longview Farm. Plantings and seeds came from as far away as the Royal Horticultural Society in England and as near as local neighbors. Some specimens were found in walks through local woods. Her knowledge of gardening is deep and in demand. She still lectures, still gardens daily. Some 2,000 people come here yearly, informally or on tours. She may greet you as you visit, answer your questions, perhaps guide you through the property. Her welcoming manner is thoroughly in keeping with the atmosphere created by the garden itself.

Longview Farm is what she describes as "a country garden." Much of it is carefully (but unobtrusively) organized within a series of geometric patterns created by fieldstone walls. (She built them herself.) These many different stone walls create the intimate spaces for flowers—a profusion of them. One is a rock garden, another a delightfully laid-out herb garden in which subtle tones of green are balanced and edged by brick borders. (The herb garden is just below her second-story porch; perhaps she will let you view it from above, where its artistic design is particularly clear.)

Another charming spot lies next to the barn-red old barn, where bright tulips, daffodils, anemones, and other spring blooms contrast in color with the faded wood wall behind them. There is a pond, generously covered with water lilies, a well surrounded by flowers, an area of all-lavender flowers. And yet nothing seems arbitrary or arranged. Her unusual mix of wild and nursery flowers adds to the naturalness of the gardens and the woods beyond; flowering trees and shrubs (including pink crab apple, golden pepperbush, and azaleas, dogwood, and euonymous in different shades of pink) are just as carefully placed and cultivated as the flower beds.

From early spring through the fall, each growing period sees one bloom replace another in an unending series of color and design. Even in winter snows, the garden is alive with color (Christmas roses, winter berries, etc.). This is the gardener to ask if you want to know how to plant and maintain a year-round display in your own garden.

It is Joanna Reed's accomplishment that you can't imagine her garden having been "designed" at all, though of course the most picturesque country garden is a masterpiece of unobtrusive planning. This is not art imposed upon landscape, but nestling within it.

MICHAEL BOWELL'S GARDEN

Just down the road is a very different sort of place—here, in Rousseaulike jungly profusion, is Michael Bowell's place. Not precisely a garden—if designed plantings deserve that term—it is, nonetheless, a collection of potted, or planted, or green-housed, or indigenous, flowers and shrubs. Much of it is waiting to be distributed to other gardens by Mr. Bowell's landscape design business, or to display gardens like the annual Orchid Show in Philadelphia. You may enjoy the rampant disorder of this garden—

or these sets of vibrant growing things—as they riotously bloom among one another: huge leafed plants interspersed with pots of petunias and pansies, delicate orchids under glass, giant exotic grasses, climbing vines.

INFORMATION
Joanna Reed's Garden is open April through October or by appointment. Fee for groups only. Otherwise, no appointment is needed. Telephone: (610) 827-1268. Michael Bowell's Garden can be seen by appointment.

DIRECTIONS
From the Pennsylvania Turnpike (Route 276) take Exit 24 south. Take Route 202 about 9 miles (toward West Chester). Exit at Route 401, heading west, through two traffic lights, and at the top of a steep hill, turn right onto Valley Hill Road. (Though there is no sign here, there is one a block into it.) Take a left fork 1/8th mile at the stop sign. Longview Farm is down the hill on your left; park in the field across the road. Michael Bowell's garden is on the right, just over the little bridge beyond Longview Farm.

Meadowbrook Farm, Meadowbrook

As you wind your way along the quietly elegant tree-lined streets of Philadelphia's "Main Line," you pass fieldstone houses set amid venerable old trees, generous lawns, and old-fashioned flower gardens. On one such street you might spot a discreet sign for Meadowbrook Farm, which could easily be overlooked by the casual passerby. This site includes a commercial—but unusually tasteful—greenhouse and, of particular interest to us, the exquisite gardens of the owner's private estate. These are a must on any gardener's itinerary.

Meadowbrook Farm is the ongoing life work of horticulturist J. Liddon Pennock, who has been designing, creating, and tending its remarkable gardens for almost 60 years. A descendant of a long and illustrious line of florists who first came to Philadelphia in the seventeenth century, he clearly was born with a green thumb. And an artistic eye.

Mr. Pennock's splendid 30-acre property includes meadows and woods, the greenhouse and many colorful plantings around it, and his adjoining house with formal gardens.

The gardens occupy about 1 acre surrounding the elegant vintage stone structure. Combining intimacy with picturesque views, they are arranged in graceful sequence: one flows to the next, connected by brick walkways, allées, stone stairways, and terraces. Each is an individual room with focal points—among them, an intriguing rotating fountain making graceful figure eights, a classical gazebo graced with Corinthian columns, and a pond with bright and lively goldfish. Water—in pools, ponds, and fountains—is a prevailing motif, true to the traditions of classic gardens. But, as Mr. Pennock is quick to point out, these are not "water" gardens.

Most striking in the overall design is the combination of colors, shapes, and geometric patterns you'll find. These visual effects are formed by hedges in arabesques and rectangles, topiaries in varying types and sizes, and the always abundant flowers—jasmine, hibiscus, primroses, pansies, oleander. Complementing the plantings are graceful urns, small gray statues of animals and mythological themes, and well-placed benches from which to enjoy it all. Every inch of the gardens has been carefully planned, leaving not one bare, untended, spot. They could have been designed by an interior decorator!

Gardens being the living, evolving, entities they are, it is not surprising that Mr. Pennock and his staff are still creating and adding new, equally enchanting ones, extending from existing sites.

The greenhouse, from which many of the plants in the private gardens are routinely taken, is also worth a visit. This group of appealing conservatories is especially welcoming on cold, wintry days. Here you will find well-arranged displays of many different plants—some quite unusual. Outside you can wander around at will and enjoy more displays—extensive beds of annuals and perennials (hundreds of varieties), shrubs, and wonderful old trees.

Although the greenhouses are always open to the public, the private gardens are accessible on a limited basis—by reservation to small groups and only two days a year. But don't be put off: try to make an appointment for your own private visit (well worth the effort) by phoning Mr. Pennock, who is sympathetic to fellow horticulture enthusiasts. And, chances are, Mr. Pennock himself, with or without his assistant, will take you around and show you the gardens and the parts of the house leading to them. On our last visit, this most engaging host regaled us with stories about his garden—a memorable experience.

INFORMATION
Meadowbrook Farm is located at 1633 Washington Lane in Meadowbrook, Pennsylvania (about 15 miles north of downtown Philadelphia). Telephone: (215) 887-5900. The commercial greenhouse is open Monday through Saturday, year-round. The private gardens are open only by guided tour to groups by appointment, in May and October. (Check exact schedule.) Or call and speak to Mr. Pennock directly, for your own private visit.

DIRECTIONS
From New York City, take the New Jersey Turnpike to the Pennsylvania Turnpike south. Take Exit 27 (Willowgrove) and go south on Route 611; turn left on Route 63 and go about 2 1/2 miles. Go right on Washington Lane for 1/2 mile. Meadowbrook Farm will be on your left.

Barnes Foundation Arboretum, Merion Station

The Barnes Foundation Arboretum is distinctive for its connection to the internationally renowned museum bearing the same name. The Barnes Collection, one of the richest—not to mention eclectic and eccentric—private art collections anywhere, has long been an object of fascination. It consists of hundreds of paintings by some of the greatest masters, as well as thousands of valuable artifacts and *objets d'art*. (The works are displayed in a decidedly unorthodox fashion: crowded, sometimes four or five deep, they are mixed together without apparent consideration for style and period. Their donor stipulated that they always remain as originally arranged.) The fact that access to the collection has been—and continues to be—fairly limited has made it all the more intriguing to the outside world.

The arboretum and the art gallery are parts of what was once the estate of Dr. Albert C. Barnes. This Philadelphian chemist, physician, and art connoisseur became a millionaire at age 35 from his invention of popular medicines. In the early 1900s he began to purchase paintings by many contemporary artists who were yet to be widely recognized—particularly Renoir, Cézanne, Matisse, and Picasso. He also collected old masters and pieces of African art. The Barnes Foundation was established in 1922 to hold his remarkable collection and provide free art instruction to deserving students. The 12-acre grounds (now the arboretum) surrounding the house were planted with diverse species and varieties of flowering plants to complement the art appreciation classes offered. To this day both the art gallery and arboretum are meant to further the educational and aesthetic benefits gained from studying art, trees, and flowers. Visitors view them together. (They are open at the same times and the admission fee includes both.)

While for most people the art gallery can be an overwhelming experience, the arboretum provides a pleasing and welcoming respite. Here, amid groves of lilacs (more than 250 varieties), rows of formal flower plantings, and many rare and mature tree specimens, you can contemplate nature's beauties—or the art you have just seen inside. Among the arboretum's many offerings are a recently restored formal rose garden with trellises and central fountain; an enclosed garden with stone walkways; a green-iron domed trellis graced with cascading wisteria; a woodland; and Mrs. Barnes' original greenhouse, where herbaceous plants are grown from seed. Most of the plantings are carefully labeled (but you must know your botanic terms in Latin).

INFORMATION
The Barnes Foundation Arboretum is located at 300 N. Latch's Lane in Merion Station. Telephone: (610) 664-8207. The arboretum and gallery are open at the same times: Thursday from 12:30 P.M. to 5:00 P.M. and Friday, Saturday, and Sunday, 9:30 A.M. to 5:00 P.M. Get there early and be prepared for lines. Admission fee.

DIRECTIONS
From New York area, take the New Jersey Turnpike to the Pennsylvania Turnpike (Exit 6) to Route 476 south to I-76. From the City Avenue exit, follow Route 1 South to Old Lancaster Road. Turn right and go for about 2/10th mile to North Latch's Lane. Turn left. You'll find the Barnes Foundation about 1/10th mile down the road, on the left.

Grey Towers, Milford

Few gardens that we have seen have such an elaborate—or eccentric—architectural design as those that surround the medieval-style castle called Grey Towers. Here, in a rural, off-the-beaten track area of eastern Pennsylvania, you'll find this castle and its 100 acres of grounds beautifully situated on a wooded hill beyond the small town of Milford (40 minutes from the much traveled Route 80). Like the mansion, the complex garden structures, walls, patios, and pergolas and the many outbuildings are all made of native bluestone, a picturesque and evocative material. The design of the entire estate creates a romantic sense of faraway times and places.

Grey Towers was constructed in 1886 by the Pinchot family, long residents of the area. The first Pinchot emigrated from France in 1816 (his charming house in Milford in now the Community House and public library). James Pinchot was a prosperous manufacturer; his son, Gifford, was a noted environmentalist, appointed by President Teddy Roosevelt to head the U.S. Forest Service. Gifford Pinchot became governor of Pennsylvania in 1927 and lived at Grey Towers until his death in 1946. The site was designated a National Historic Landmark (with President Kennedy in attendance) in 1963. Pinchot's lifelong interest in conservation continues at Grey Towers today, where environmentalists still use the estate for conferences.

And what an estate it is! The 41-room mansion with its three great stone towers is, in itself, a cross between French medieval design (and furnishings) and affluent nineteenth-century taste. Its architect, Richard Morris Hunt (who designed the Metropolitan Museum, among other grand buildings), created an American castle curiously set just outside a modest village. (The house is open for public tours in summertime.)

Around the castle are many small buildings and garden areas. These constructions have such intriguing names as "The Finger Bowl," "The Baitbox," and "The Letter Box," as well as the more familiar moat, ice house, and pergola. Pinchot's ideas for the grounds were the result of extensive travels—apparently both to foreign countries and into the past of his imagination.

Immediately beyond the dining room's French doors, for example, is "The Finger Bowl," a raised pool surrounded by a mosaic terrace and tanks for aquatic plants. The "bowl" (a unique type of water table) was created after the Pinchots returned from the South Sea Islands. Here the family occasionally dined by candle light, sitting round its edges and eating from Polynesian serving bowls that floated in the water.

Steps lead from this terrace to another enclosed stone-walled area (once the family's swimming pool) and now beautifully landscaped with wisteria vines and garden areas. The surroundings of the mansion include a complex set of gardens on different terraced levels—all of them created by the use of bluestone paths and walls and steps, as well as ancient-seeming pergolas and trellises. Many of the surrounding terraces contain gargoyles: turkeys and eagles, among other beasts, appear in small niches and atop marble columns. And numerous statuary decorate the place, including a bust of the Marquis de Lafayette in a niche on the second story of the house. There are vined gazebos, a rock garden, a lily pond, benches, fountains, and mosaics. There are a reflecting pool and an amphitheater (used by the family for theatricals and campaign gatherings). At the far end of the reflecting pool is "The Bait Box," built as a playhouse. Various millstones taken from local grain mills also adorn the gardens. In among these many man-made divisions and artistic ornaments are luxuriant flowers and other plantings. These are gardens in which very little of the design seems left to chance or to Mother Nature's own instincts.

All of these sites offer splendid views of the fields and wooded hillsides stretching into the distance. The trees—including a noted sugar maple planted by General Sherman a century ago—are notable. And the vast wooded sections, including a spectacular and mysterious hemlock forest are—of course—administered by the U.S. Forest Service. This is an inviting place for a walk.

A visit to Grey Towers might suggest a central question about gardens: Can the design created by architectural elements be overwhelming? Or are flowers and other plantings at their most beautiful when organized by stone structures rather than the boxwood hedges or groves of shrubbery favored by so many landscapists? Grey Towers is perhaps the most architecturally designed garden we have seen and, as such, is well worth a visit to this out-of-the-way spot.

INFORMATION
Grey Towers is open from 9 A.M. to 5 P.M. except weekends. Call for specific dates. Telephone: (717) 296-9630.

DIRECTIONS
Grey Towers is in Milford. From Route 80, take Route 206 north to its end where it crosses the Delaware River. Milford is just over the bridge. Go through traffic light. Continue for 1 mile until road forks. Bear left, and follow signs. Grey Towers is on the left.

Historic Bartram's Garden, Philadelphia

While many restored colonial gardens show us the orderly and useful aspects of early American gardening, John Bartram's extraordinary, less than orderly historic garden takes us on a flight of fancy. Located on the banks of the Schuylkill River on the outskirts of the city of Philadelphia, Bartram's Garden is a botanist's and historian's delight, as well as a pleasure to look at and wander through.

Here on a 27-acre hillside, just behind the 1730 house, are hundreds of tree and plant specimens that Bartram brought to the site more than 200 years ago—and that are still flourishing. The visitor here gets a special sense of American history because the garden has been tended continuously and Bartram's design—and in fact many of the plants and trees themselves—kept intact. And unlike many colonial gardens, this pleasantly disordered place gives some sense of the excitement of settlers in a new world.

John Bartram was a Philadelphia Quaker who lived from 1699 to 1777. A farmer and botanist, he began the first thorough collection of native plants in this country. His garden was begun in 1728 and increasingly became a passion, as he collected plants, seeds, and specimens of nature's bounty on the American continent. The adventurous botanist traveled all over the eastern half of the continent (as far as the Ohio River to the West and Appalachian Georgia and Florida to the South), carrying specimens back to Philadelphia in an airtight ox bladder. With his son, William, who continued the collection well into the nineteenth century, he established a commercial nursery, supplying seeds and plantings by mail to such other great gardens as Mount Vernon and Monticello. In addition to his own discoveries, Bartram received specimens from all over the colonies, the West Indies, and botanists worldwide. His carefully cataloged (and pictured) collection formed the first botanical garden in the country, including an astonishing 4,000 species.

The Bartrams also introduced some 200 varieties of American plants to Europe. Internationally known and admired, the father and son presented in England such subsequent staples of their world as mountain laurel and sugar maple. In the autumns Bartram put together for shipment abroad "five guinea boxes" of the seeds of plants discovered on his travels.

When you visit the garden you will see—just behind the house— his "common flower garden," his medicinal, vegetable, and herb gardens. But of particular interest is the fascinating collection of 82 different types of shrubs and trees about 400 yards down the gentle hill toward the river. Here you'll find giant oaks (known as Bartram oaks), and the famous Franklin tree from Florida, now extinct in the wild. There are ginkgo trees, prickly ash (whose bark was known for its toothache remedy), indigo bush, witch hazel, and bald cypress, interspersed with mountain laurel, cucumber magnolia (brought from the shores of Lake Ontario), and the Fraser magnolia (from the Smoky Mountains). You'll see a pawpaw tree (of which legend has Bartram sending the fruit and flowers back to England in a bottle of rum) and in springtime masses of flowering dogwood, azalea, and wisteria. At the very bottom of the hill you'll come upon some old rocks and an evocative landing spot on the river.

Despite the occasionally weedy aspects of this garden—no doubt historically accurate—you'll relish the sense of history and the mental image of the colonial Quakers arriving home from the American wilderness to plant ever more specimens of flowers and trees in their Philadelphia garden. (If you find Bartram's garden of interest, do not miss the collection of William's delicate and meticulous watercolors of plants or his interesting description of traveling and plant collecting published in 1791. Information on these historic items and even tours recreating the Bartrams' journeys is available at the headquarters of Bartram's Garden.)

INFORMATION
John Bartram's Historic Garden is open year-round dawn to dusk, free. Tours may be scheduled 9 A.M. to 5 P.M. daily. The house is also open to visitors; call for hours and fee. Picnics are allowed and lunches can be ordered in advance. There are numerous educational and horticultural events. The grounds are hilly and have occasional rough footing. Telephone: (215) 729-5281.

DIRECTIONS
John Bartram's Garden is located at 54th Street and Lindbergh Boulevard in Philadelphia. From the New Jersey Turnpike take Exit 4 south of Philadelphia to I-295 to Route 76 West. After crossing the Walt Whitman Bridge, exit going west on Passyhunk Avenue. Turn north on Lindbergh Boulevard; the entrance is on your right at the corner of 54th Street. From I-95 in Philadelphia, take Island Avenue/291 West, turning right on Lindbergh Boulevard. Continue about 3 miles to entrance on your right at 54th Street.

Morris Arboretum, Philadelphia

Morris Arboretum of the University of Pennsylvania is located well outside the city in a greenbelt. This is a lovely Victorian-style park, filled with both flowers and sculpture. Though the plantings and pathways are quintessentially Victorian and some of the loveliest we have seen, the sculpture in anything but old-fashioned. In fact, you might consider most of it totally unrelated to its surroundings.

The Morris Arboretum is at the site of a great house called Compton, which once belonged to a prominent Quaker brother and sister named John and Lydia Morris. Though the house is now gone, the 166 acres of landscaped grounds remain, and are kept in the most beautiful condition. This is a rather long walk if you want to see everything—and you should.

Originally designed by Charles Miller (an American of Anglophile tastes), the park is a marvel of charming paths, flowering shrubs, fountains, and clustered garden areas. There is a Temple of Love on a Swan Pond. There are numerous great trees—including twelve redwoods bordering a stream—a grove of cedars, the most magnificent flowering cherry tree we have ever seen, and many rare trees from the Orient. (You can pick up material on the arboretum—including a map and information on what's blooming—when you enter.)

There are also many flower beds in the English style, as well as an indoor fernery with more than 500 types of tropical ferns. The rock garden, azalea meadow, and holly slope are all worth seeing. In June don't miss the rose garden bordered by a wisteria allée. We could go on and on about the flowers and trees, but you will discover for yourself the natural beauties of Morris Arboretum. Be sure to plan your visit according to the season you most enjoy.

The artworks are somewhat dwarfed by the beauties of the landscape. The Butcher Sculpture Garden contains predominantly contemporary art of which there are about a dozen permanently installed sculptures. Several Cotswold sheep made of two-dimensional Cor-Ten steel by Charles Layland are "grazing" at the base of Magnolia Slope. A giant bronze and steel sculpture by Linda Cunningham evokes the garden idea; its name is *Germination*.

At one end of the garden is a group of modern works by Scott Sherk based upon classical Greek mythology (but without classical visual connotations). Thomas Sternal has made two wood sculptures from felled trees from the arboretum's own grounds: one is called *Table*, the other, *Altarpiece.*

The Morris collection also features several more traditional pieces, including a *Mercury at Rest* (a copy of an antique sculpture excavated at Herculaneum) and some portrait sculptures of the Morrises themselves. Children will enjoy the Lorraine Vail whimsical animal character, a 5-foot bullfrog.

The sculpture is widely separated by glorious patches of nature, which may give some viewers a sense of the art as a secondary source of decoration (as in Edwardian times). In fact, this type of massive contemporary art does not readily lend itself to such cultivated surroundings—except for young Mercury seated on a stone. Nonetheless, you shouldn't miss the experience of modern sculpture amid the blossoms.

INFORMATION
The Morris Arboretum is at 100 Northwestern Avenue, Philadelphia. Telephone: (215) 247-5777. It is open daily 10 A.M. to 4 P.M. (Open weekends until 5 P.M. April through October.) Handicapped accessible.

DIRECTIONS
Take Pennsylvania Turnpike to Norristown/Plymouth Meeting exit. Follow signs for Germantown Pike East; go 4 miles to Northwestern Avenue. Left on Northwestern about one-quarter mile.

Bowman's Hill State Wildflower Preserve, Washington's Crossing

As you walk along the woodsy trails and gentle creek in this lovely spot you'll feel you are miles from the bustle of the highway and civilization. The preserve has managed to include in its 100 acres quite a variety of habitats—forest, meadows, ponds, bogs, an arboretum, and preserves for shrubs and flowers. An azalea trail leads to a path of bluebells, a marsh walk brings you to marigolds and holly areas, you pass the charming dam on the Pidcock Creek and come to the evergreen area. The list is extensive, and the walk—quite hilly—is always interesting. You can choose your own paths—up and down and around about—with the help of a map and a variety of printed guides that are available near the parking area. We found it quite uninhabited in midsummer, but spring with its profusion of wildflowers is apt to be busier. Still, there is enough room for many walkers, and the trails are woodsy enough to absorb a fair number of people. The more energetic can hike to the famous Bowman's Hill Tower at the top of a surprisingly high hill in the preserve (or drive there) and complete their visit to this historic and lovely place.

Established to preserve Pennsylvania's native plants, Bowman's Hill opened in 1934. It is made up of 26 trails, including a trail for the handicapped (wheelchair accessible) and a famous arboretum called Penn's Woods, which has more than 450 different trees and shrubs. The general atmosphere of Bowman's Hill Preserve is relaxed. It is rather like wandering through a large private nineteenth-century estate. There are few signs telling you what to do or not to do, and the fences and steps are made of natural materials that seem to have fallen in place by accident. The signs identifying the various walks and plants are almost hidden by foliage and are never obtrusive, so you don't feel as if you are in a preserve but in a series of natural habitats.

Pick up a guide to the various walks and a tree and flower guide to the preserve at the headquarters where you leave your car. You might want to take your own identifying books, too. Insect repellent, sturdy shoes, and a picnic are all recommended.

This walk, particularly if you climb to the lookout tower, can be rigorous. But if you want more gentle trails, the preserve has those as well. We recommend this outing for anyone who enjoys wildflowers, woods, and hiking. It is ideal, too, for children, who can roam freely.

When you drive to Bowman's Hill Preserve, you will pass a picnic ground and public facilities near the entrance. Keep going and leave your car at the lot behind the headquarters. You can choose which of 26 trails you wish to take, but most run into one another and you can't go wrong whichever you take. If you go down hill from the car park, you will come to the creek, which you can follow along its winding path. If you continue along the roadway (not accessible to cars) to its end, you will come to a rugged climb to Bowman's Tower. If you go back in the direction of the entrance you can walk through the arboretum. All the trails should be seen, and the total walk is not beyond most walkers' endurance.

Among the 9 acres of woods are familiar sugar maples, pitch pines, and American lindens, as well as the more rare chinquapin chestnut, cucumber magnolia, pawpaw, and black haw.

Bowman's Hill Tower stands on a hill 380 feet above sea level—one of the highest points along the Delaware River. The hill has long served as a landmark, and before Washington's crossing of the Delaware it was used as a lookout and signal station. The present tower commands a view of 14 miles of the Delaware River Valley, including the very spot that Washington crossed. The tower can be visited and climbed (every day but Tuesday). There is a small admission fee.

The hike up to the tower takes you through some rather dense underbrush, but your effort is well rewarded at the top. If you prefer, you can get back in your car and drive out of the preserve, go back onto Route 32, turning to the right as you exit, and you will soon come to a sign to the tower. A winding drive brings you to a parking area at its base.

One of the most unusual and educational parts of this park is devoted to plants with medicinal uses, both real and legendary. This medicinal trail is a special walk for herb fanciers and those who are interested in natural curing or Indian herb uses. Native Americans often used herbal medicines, and modern science has frequently verified their effectiveness. Some have even been synthetically reproduced. Many plants are still used in pharmacology, but others are of no proven value—their curative properties are nothing more than old wives' tales. The medicinal trail includes some of each kind, with a descriptive flyer that tells you what you're seeing and what it's good for—or what legends say it's good for.

The trail, which is about 620 feet long, is slow going if you stop to examine each plant. While you are warned not to taste anything yourself—some of the plants are extremely poisonous—you are encouraged to go slowly and study each plant's story as you go.

The trail begins with mountain laurel, the juices of which the Indians supposedly drank to commit suicide (but by 1800 a tincture made from its leaves was being used to treat several diseases). Next comes mayapple and bloodroot, a source of morphine that Indians chewed to cure a sore throat. Other plants include white oak, spicebush, wild ginger, alumroot, fairywand, and witch hazel. Among the old wives' varieties is ginseng, which Europeans thought restored youth (and which has been used for centuries as a cure-all in China). The list is a fairly long one, and a walk among these plants is extremely interesting.

This outing, due to the dangerous nature of many of the plants, is not recommended for small children, particularly if you read the more disturbing legends aloud.

There are a tree identification trail, wildflower trails, and several kinds of nature walks in this preserve. During the year the preserve offers guided mushroom walks, bird walks, native plant and fern identification walks, as well as other wild plant walks.

INFORMATION
The preserve is open year-round except for major holidays. Of course, wildflowers are best in spring and early summer, but there is something to be seen in any season.

DIRECTIONS
Take the New Jersey Turnpike to Exit 9. Take Route 1 south toward Trenton. Pick up I-95 (I-295) south after Princeton (at Bakersville) and take the highway to the exit at Yardley. Turn back to Route 32. Bowman's Hill Preserve is several miles northwest on Route 32.

Chanticleer, Wayne

The appealing landscape of Philadelphia's Main Line is just right as a setting for natural-looking gardens. Many of the elegant houses are surrounded by gently rolling hills, deep green lawns, ponds, and stately trees—a perfect foil for all sorts of individual flower beds and garden design. Main Line estates like Chanticleer have room enough to spare; the flower gardens here are only part of an overall planned landscape.

Chanticleer was just recently opened to the public, and is under continuing garden renovation. It still retains the feeling of a private domain, from its discreet entrance and its elegant lawns, to the huge mansion with its walled gardens. Nonetheless, it is a pleasantly accessible place where you are allowed to wander as you wish, without a tour. The 30 acres of Chanticleer are enticing to explore, for they are often surprising in their plantings and design and are of both botanical and artistic interest.

When the Rosengarten family built the stately house in 1913, they chose the fashionable landscape designer Thomas Sears. (He also created the gardens at Appleford—see page 247 in the Villa Nova write up—and many other private estates on the Main Line.) Sears decided to design formal gardens very near to the house, so that one could step directly into them from indoors.

Thus, there is a courtyard garden that is unusually intimate. It has intriguing plantings, including a rubber tree. And, by terracing the hillside just outside the library door on the east side of the house, Sears created the "pleasure garden" (are any flower gardens not for pleasure?)—a high Victorian concept that is beautifully adapted to this setting. It has a large slate terrace, formal walkways, stone walls, elegant plantings. Surrounded by a hemlock hedge, the formal gardens include rose beds that are underplanted with rare specimens and herbaceous borders. Viburnum, dogwood, and other flowering trees make this a particularly pretty place in late spring.

This garden also has a view of uncommon beauty. Looking out over the expanse of sloping meadow, you can see the trellises of the brilliantly colored summer perennial garden far below, as well as a small pond and venerable trees. Walk down through the meadow (there is an agreeable absence of signs telling you where you may and may not go). In season you'll find wildflowers and native prairie plants throughout the meadow; this area is to complement the more formal sections of the estate. In April you may look back toward the house for an especially pretty sight, some 50,000 daffodils in bloom.

Just beyond the meadow you'll find the newly created "Asian Woods." Plantings—trees, shrubs, perennials, and vines native to Japan, China, and Korea—are interspersed with the great sycamores and maples. This will be a shade garden in which woodland plants—many rare in this part of the world—can be seen. You are encouraged to wander off the path.

From here you will come to the pond and stream, bordered with flowering herbs and ornamental grasses. On a still day the plantings are wonderfully reflected in the water. The path leads farther into a woodsy area of evergreens and tall Oriental spruce; May and June are the best times to enjoy this part of the garden.

Farther along this path is the orchard, recently planted with 40 blooming trees, including decorative flowering crab apples of various colors. And nearby are the English-style cutting garden, the flourishing vegetable gardens, and the summer perennial garden. The brilliant collection of flowers grows in wild profusion (especially recommended in July and August). Both the flower gardens and the vegetable garden are visual delights: each area shows how an eye for design can change the look of a garden—a wonderful espaliered border in diamond patterns edges one flower garden, while the green of the vegetable garden is dotted with giant brick-red, terra-cotta urns.

A visit here can be educational as well as aesthetic; an identification list of the many rare and exotic plantings is available on the grounds. Chanticleer can be described as a botanical garden in a country estate setting.

INFORMATION
Chanticleer is open Wednesday through Saturday, 10:00 A.M. to 3:30 P.M., April through October. Suggested donation. Telephone: (610) 687-4163.

DIRECTIONS
Chanticleer is located at 786 Church Road in Wayne, on Philadelphia's Main Line. From Route 276 (the Pennsylvania Turnpike) take Route 476 south. Exit at Route 30 and head west. In the downtown of Wayne, go left on Radnor Road to Conestoga Road and turn right. Turn right again onto Church Road.

And in Addition . . .

Chadds Ford: Brandywine Conservancy
Route 1 (southwest of Philadelphia). Telephone: (610) 388-2700.
Noted for its conservancy of wildflowers, this museum features the Wyeth family's artworks and a preserve (unfortunately next to a busy highway) that includes 5 acres and a 1-mile nature trail with wildflower displays. Pick up a map and listing at the museum desk. Grounds are free; there is a fee for the museum. Open daily, year-round.

Media: Tyler Arboretum
515 Painter Road. Telephone: (610) 566-5431.
This extensive (650-acre) and inviting arboretum, one of the oldest and largest in the Northeast, is an ideal place for a long walk. You can enjoy miles and miles of beautiful, carefully marked paths and trails where you will see impressive collections of shrubs and trees (some quite ancient and imposing) in the most natural of settings. A vast pinetum features spruces, pines, hemlocks, firs, and larches;

groupings of flowering cherry, crab apple, holly, lilac, and magnolia brighten the ambiance; specialty gardens surrounding a pretty stone granary include fragrant, butterfly, and bird gardens. Perhaps best of all are the historic so-called "Painter trees," some 20 specimens well over 100 years old. They are named after Jacob and Minshall Painter, two brothers who began the arboretum in 1825. Setting aside some of their land, they went about planting over 1,000 trees and shrubs in a most systematic fashion.

Among the arboretum's many offerings today are classes, lectures, workshops, and other special events you might want to investigate. But we think the best way to enjoy these lovely grounds is to set out on a bright spring day, walking guide in hand (available at the visitors' center) and soak up the atmosphere. Open daily, 8 A.M. to dusk. There is a small entrance fee.

Philadelphia: Fairmont Park Horticultural Center
Horticulture Drive near Belmont Avenue. Telephone: (215) 878-5097.

This is the largest city park system in the nation (and in the world), and its 8,000 acres include 23 acres of fine garden displays, both indoors and out, many of seasonal interest. Of particular note is the Japanese House and Garden, an authentic Monoyama-style reconstruction (sixteenth and seventeenth century), complete with golden carp pond, arched bridge, bamboo grove, and native and Asian plantings. There is also a series of demonstration gardens, including Penn State's Accessible Garden, created by visually impaired volunteers; it has raised beds, Braille signs, and other innovations for the disabled and features ornamental and medicinal herbs and many unusual flowers. There are numerous events in the greenhouse complex and outdoor areas. The horticulture areas are open May to August, 11 A.M. to 4 P.M., Tuesday through Sunday; September and October, weekends only and by appointment. Fee.

Philadelphia: Wyck
6026 Germantown Avenue. Telephone: (215) 848-1690.

Wyck is certainly one of Philadelphia's best kept secrets. This historic colonial house and garden, in the heart of the once elegant Germantown (now, unfortunately, a bit shabby) is not generally known. The home of nine generations of a prominent Quaker family named Wistar, it even predated Independence Hall. Its collection of eighteenth- and nineteenth-century furniture, paintings (including family portraits by Rembrandt Peale), ceramics, china, and other objects accumulated over 300 years are a testament to its long history.

Wyck's enclosed grounds are intimate and delightfully old fashioned. Outbuildings typical of traditional country properties—carriage, smoke, and ice houses—are set amid flower beds and grassy expanses. But best of all is the rose garden. Its many (at least 35, we are told) varieties of old roses are still arranged according to the original early nineteenth-century design. This gracious garden includes circular walkways, a fountain, and gazebo.

To visit the house you must take a tour, but the garden can be seen either by guided tour or on your own. (In the latter case you must call first to notify the staff, since there is a watchdog on the premises!) Tours on architecture, decorative arts, garden history, and Quaker history are offered.

Phone ahead for information. Wyck is open for tours April 1 through December 15 on Tuesdays, Thursdays, and Saturdays from 1 P.M. to 4 P.M., or by appointment year-round.

Pittsburgh: Pittsburgh Civic Garden Center

Mellon Park, 1059 Shady Avenue. Telephone: (412) 441-4442.

Mellon Park is a pretty, spacious, 13-acre city park in which a series of gardens have been created on the former grounds of a Mellon family estate. Though the house is now gone, the gardens have been maintained since the 1930s, and there are some very nice antique-feeling touches here and there—stone steps and an occasional boulder or small statue, a sunken knot garden, a Shakespeare garden, an alpine garden, and even a model planting bed. This is a nice place for a walk among the shrubbery in spring or the deep green, leafy trees on a hot summer day. Open every day, dawn to dusk. (And bring your dog; he'll have a lot of company.)

Pittsburgh: Phipps Conservatory

One Schenley Park. Telephone: (412) 622-6914.

This Victorian gem on a hill is the largest glass-housed conservatory in the nation. Each of the 13 display rooms has a different type of plantings: among them are a palm court with marble statuary; a garden of topiary animals, bonsai, and desert plants; and orchid collections. There are changing exhibits as well. Open Tuesday through Sunday year-round; closed on some holidays. Fee.

Villa Nova: Appleford
770 Mt. Moro Road. Telephone: (610) 527-4280

This is a 22-acre preserved estate with a pretty antique stone Pennsylvania farmhouse, duck ponds with waterfall, nice walks, venerable trees, and two small formal gardens that have a certain charm all their own. Created by the landscape designer Thomas Sears, Appleford's overall look is of natural hilly fields and a woodsy stream. But the high point for some garden enthusiasts is a very low boxwood maze that will delight many little children (even if they can see over the tops of the complex design), as well as older visitors tagging along through its twists and turns. The formal rose garden is walled, decorated with statuary, and pleasingly intimate. The property is delectable in spring, with daffodils, rhododendrons, and lilacs in profusion. Open daily year-round (but choose the flowering seasons). Tours of the house by appointment.

RHODE ISLAND GARDENWALKS

1. Bristol: Blithewold Gardens and Arboretum
2. Kingston Area: Kinney Azalea Garden and Nearby Pleasures
3. Newport: Hammersmith Farm and the Gardens of the Great Mansions
4. Portsmouth: Green Animals
5. Providence: Shakespeare's Head and the Stephen Hopkins' Garden

And in Addition . . .
6. Westerly: Wilcox Park
7. Wickford: Smith's Castle

RHODE ISLAND

Blithewold Gardens and Arboretum, Bristol

Blithewold means "happy woodlands" in Middle English, and a happy spot this is! The 33-acre estate combines delightful gardens, woodlands, and sweeping lawns idyllically set at water's edge. Walking through these carefully landscaped grounds—enjoying the old-fashioned flower beds, rose arbor, rock and water gardens, enchanting bosquet, and picturesque views overlooking Bristol Harbor and Narragansett Bay—is a joyful experience. The ambiance is both gracious and informal, befitting a stylish country house of a bygone era.

In 1894 Augustus Van Wickle, a coal magnate from Pennsylvania, bought Blithewold as a mooring site for the new steam yacht he had just acquired as a surprise gift for his wife. The mansion, surrounded by its romantic waterfront property, became their summer home. To embellish the grounds he hired John De Wolfe, a Brooklyn-based landscape architect. After Van Wickle died suddenly in a hunting accident, De Wolfe continued his work under the guidance of Van Wickle's wife, Bessie. He planted many exotic trees and shrubs that were just being introduced to America from China and Japan. The gardens were nurtured and tended by Marjorie Lyon, the Van Wickles' daughter, until her death at age 93. (Her will stipulated that funds were to be spent first and foremost on the grounds, and only then on the house.)

Today Blithewold is maintained by the Heritage Trust of Rhode Island. The existing seventeenth-century, English-style mansion was built in 1907, after the original house burned down; it can be visited by guided tour. Inside you'll find the many eclectic objects and furnishings Bessie Van Wickle collected on her world travels over the years—from Tiffany lamps and Chinese vases to a mantel from Queen Victoria's nephew's house. But it is in the inviting gardens that you will want to linger most—and at your own pace.

There are seven gardens in all, connected by informal gravel paths and grassy walkways and broad lawns dotted with stone benches: the rose garden, north garden, water and rock gardens, the enclosed garden, cutting and vegetable gardens, and the bosquet. You will find those areas unusually artistic in their color schemes and design. Before setting forth, pick up a walking guide of the grounds (available at the entrance booth); it also indicates the rare plants and trees not to be missed—such as the Japanese tree lilacs and a 90-year-old giant sequoia, apparently the largest of its kind in the east.

Your first stop is the enclosed rose garden, reached through an arched passageway. Though quite small, it contains several varieties tastefully arranged. Just beyond it is the stone and stucco mansion framed by a graceful circular entrance.

The north garden, next to the house (and easily visible from its windows, porches, and brick terrace) is a formal, though intimate, garden. It consists of perennials—mostly blue and yellow—set around a small pool and fountain.

Next is the bosquet and airy forest of lush rhododendrons, ferns, carpets of myrtle, and other woodsy delights. In spring its many thousand daffodils add even more enchantment to these "happy woodlands."

A prettily shaded path meanders along, eventually reaching the water and rock gardens. Their picturesque waterside setting makes them especially enticing. Adjacent to one another, they are both inspired by the Japanese style. In the water garden a weeping willow hangs over two tiny ponds with a connecting arched stone bridge. Wildflowers and grasses surround the garden. The rock garden, literally on the edge of Bristol Harbor, contains many carefully labeled plants artistically set among stones and rocks. Some of the plants are Asian specimens, such as the Japanese anemone. This garden is almost always colorful, with flowering plants blooming from spring through the fall.

At this point you can choose to follow a shoreline path (which will eventually wind around back to the mansion) or continue on your garden tour. The panoramic view overlooking the harbor is irresistible, and you will want to pause and perhaps even put your feet in the water.

The cutting and vegetable gardens are rustic and multicolored. There are beds of poppies, lavender, marigolds, phlox, and other offerings. You are likely to find an army of dedicated volunteers busy at work, picking and weeding. On your right is a wonderfully thick bamboo grove that you can walk through. The bamboo plants, in the softest shade of yellow, move gracefully with the sea breezes.

The last garden to visit is the enclosed garden, an oasislike, peaceful spot. Surrounded by hemlocks, rhododendrons, and other evergreens, it features many specimen trees of different sizes and shapes, including the previously mentioned giant sequoia. Many of Blithewold's visitors are horticulturists—amateur or otherwise—and this specimen garden is of great interest to them.

Blithewold is not often crowded; when we last visited on a brilliant, late summer day during the week, we had the place almost to ourselves. There are special events during the year (see below), and picnicking, bird watching, photography, painting, and drawing are permitted on the grounds.

INFORMATION
Blithewold is located at 101 Ferry Road in Bristol. The grounds are open all year from 10 A.M. to 5 P.M.; the mansion is open April through October, 10 A.M. to 4 P.M. There is an admission fee. Special events include a Valentine's Day Concert, spring bulb display (April), plant sale (May), concerts by the bay in summer, Christmas celebrations, and horticultural and historical programs. Telephone: (401) 253-2707.

DIRECTIONS
From Boston, take Route 24 to Mt. Hope exit; cross the Mt. Hope Bridge, bear left onto Ferry Road (Route 114). Blithewold is 1/8th mile on the left.

From Providence, take Exit 7 off Route 195 east and Route 114 south through Barrington, Warren, and Bristol to Blithewold.

The Kinney Azalea Gardens and Nearby Pleasures, Kingston Area

An unexpected and gorgeous surprise in this rocky New England coastal area, these azalea gardens are spectacular in season. And it's a nice long season too—there are so many varieties planted here that the blossoms in this chilly climate near the oceans last from mid-May through the first week of July.

Azaleas here are planted over a large woodsy area. There are grassy paths and wonderful rough stone walls (one of our favorite features of the Rhode Island landscape), but the overall feeling is of walking through a natural woodland that just happens to have over 500 varieties of the flowering shrubs. Among the varieties—in every color you can think of, except blue—are many rare species including Geisha azaleas and one hybrid variety that produces both pink and white blossoms simultaneously. Many are glorious in color: deep rose or peach, palest lavender, dark orange. The deciduous varieties in yellow and orange bloom into July. And the azaleas are mixed in with many other woodland pleasures: huge umbrella pines, rhododendrons, pink dogwood, flourishing licothowe that climbs over the walls, and numerous forest flowers including trillium, jack-in-the-pulpit, and periwinkles.

The Kinneys are a longtime botanical family. Mr. Kinney, Sr., who started the gardens, was a professor of botany at the university nearby, with a specialty in rhododendrons. His son and wife and daughter (and numerous students through the years) have turned this into one of the loveliest New England gardens we have seen.

A map is available at the Kinneys' house. This is, by the way, a perfect garden to visit with children, for the rather labyrinthine paths (with some small statuary—pixies, for example—hidden here and there) will make it a treat for the younger set. This is not a place where you cannot touch or step. There were many children there scampering through the woodsy paths when we visited. And if you come on a Saturday in mid-May you might be in time for a longtime tradition at the garden's height here: Azalea tea!

INFORMATION

The Kinney Azalea Gardens are at 2391 Kingstown Road in Kingston. Visit in May, June, or early July for best viewing, but open all summer.

DIRECTIONS
From I-95 take Route 138 East. Pass the University of Rhode Island
and turn south on Route 108. Continue on Route 108; you'll find the
gardens on your left outside of Kingston. (Also on Route 110, by the
way, in late May and early June you'll find a display of white-blos-
somed mountain laurel growing profusely all along the road.)

THE GARDEN AT THEATER BY THE SEA, MATUNUCK
Not far away are two other unusual gardens, depending on the season. One of the nicest summertime gardens is at the oceanfront theater by the sea at nearby Matunuck Beach. Here, bordering the nice
New England–style shingled summer stock theater complex is a rare
garden. Dozens of exotic and spectacular plants grow here in profusion in the salt air. These are exceptionally well-maintained flower
beds cared for by people who really know their gardens. There is a
vast pergola/trellis arrangement and a series of walkways in a rectangular design, and every bit of it is covered or surrounded with
plantings of the most exotic nature. If you attend a matinee—or just
stop by—you'll see this garden in daylight, and evening perfor-
mance will find you viewing these luxurious plants by mysterious
night light. Visit in July or August to see this garden at its best.

DIRECTIONS
From Route 110 go to its end at Route 1. Go east on Route 1 to
Matunuck Beach Road, and head toward the beach. Just before its
end, you'll see signs for the Theater.

DING HAO GARDEN, PERRYVILLE (SOUTH KINGSTON)
In late summer, also off Route 110, visit Ding Hao, a very unusual
garden. Though it has all sorts of plantings on a couple of rocky,
rustic hillsides, this place specializes in chrysanthemums. Dozens of
varieties start blooming in August and continue through autumn—a
sight to see (and to purchase if you wish). These hillside gardens are
very diverse too, and a good place to explore a very informal and
delightful style of planting in a rocky, hilly, New England landscape.
Nothing is artificial looking here; plants and trees and rocks and garden shed and tools and you-name-it share this picturesque space.

DIRECTIONS
Ding Hao is located at 2105 Old Post Road at the corner of

Ministerial Road (Route 110). It is in the part of South Kingston called Perryville. It is also just off of Route 110.

Hammersmith Farm and the Gardens of the Great Mansions, Newport

Newport, Rhode Island, has a unique place in American history and architecture. On this coastal peninsula, just on the edge of an eighteenth-century fishing and sailing village, some of the greatest mansions of our late nineteenth century were fashioned after French chateaux and mythical castles. The architecture and gardens of Versailles with their stately elegance and incredible opulence were, of course, a major inspiration. In fact, two Newport estates were based on Versailles: Rosecliff was a copy of the Grand Trianon at Versailles, while Marble House imitated the Petit Trianon. The tourist can still visit eight of these palaces of the Belle Epoque (some were actually called "summer cottages"!) that are as grandiose and lavish as royal residences. They line Bellevue Avenue like great sailing ships behind regal gates and walls.

When these—and many other—grand homes were built by the giants of industry, most of them had elegant gardens to match. Their landscaping and flower gardens were palatial, often patterned on the formal French designs of earlier centuries. But the seaside setting and violent winds and storms of the coastal region made it very difficult to maintain such gardens. Hurricanes over the years uprooted rare trees, and flower gardens needed constant care and replenishment. Today, though you can visit eight Newport mansions and walk around their extensive grounds, only four have gardens of outstanding interest. (If, however, you enjoy seeing fully these relics of the Gilded Age with or without gardens, a ticket for sale by the Preservation Society, available at any of the great houses, allows you to tour the houses and gardens of all seven of them, except Hammersmith Farm, which requires its own ticket.)

The most elaborate of the extant Newport Gardens is at Hammersmith Farm, the home of Jacqueline Bouvier Kennedy's stepfather, Hugh Auchincloss. This large, shingled, turreted, rather odd-looking mansion is perched over the sea (Narragansett Bay) on the opposite side of the peninsula from the great houses of Bellevue Avenue. The Kennedy wedding reception took place here; the gala event dominates every aspect of a visit to the estate except the gardens. Hammersmith Farm has become a tourist attraction, now run by an organization called Camelot Gardens. (You can, however, get a ticket here to see only the grounds.) Please be sure to call before you come, for the future of this property is uncertain.

When Hammersmith Farm was built (in 1887) on a hill with sloping meadows down to the sea, Frederick Law Olmsted was engaged to design the 97-acre landscape. The Olmsted design specified formal gardens, allées of trees, a lily pool, fountains, sculpture, arched walls and pergolas, and sunken garden beds. The formal garden areas were to be divided by winding paths and more naturalistic areas; Olmsted—as always—wanted his design to conform with the natural beauties of the land rather than to impose upon it.

Over the years the gardens fell into disrepair. After World War II the Olmsted firm was asked to redesign the gardens in a simpler style. Gardens became lawns and sculpture was stored. (We see the original gardens in photographs and paintings in the mansion.) Today, in many parts of the estate the remnants of the original landscape combined with great empty spaces—lawns and fields—where once elaborate gardens bloomed. This juxtaposition of elegant stonework and sunken gardens with emptiness is certainly very odd. But enough of the original Olmsted design remains to make this an intriguing outing, rather like viewing parts of stage sets that had been designed for a variety of different dramas.

Begin your tour of the gardens by walking to the north of the house. You will follow along Olmsted's allée of Japanese cedar trees toward the formal gardens. This path will take you to a stone arch, also from the original plan, and to two shorter allées of silver linden trees. Here, in a strikingly empty space, was the huge lily pond, now filled in. Among the several formal flower beds in this section are sets of connected stone arches that nowadays eerily seem to lead nowhere. The sunken beds, however, are filled with colorful plantings and well-kept shrubbery. Opposite, in the woods, other stone arches remain—today covered by overgrown vines. Also in this formal area are a sunken rock garden and an old-fashioned fountain— both remnants of a charming nineteenth-century–style garden. There is a deeply shaded walkway that leads through another stone arch as you head back to the house.

Nearer the house—on the south side, and in view of the blue sea below—is the terraced English flower garden. This recently renovated and luxuriant garden surrounded by stone walls and espaliered pear trees is charming and bright throughout the season. One of the only remaining statues from the Olmsted period is placed at this spot. (Here you may rest on a garden bench under a grape arbor and look out over the expanse of lawn and bay.)

Not far away is an enormous cutting garden of some 100 varieties; its informality is a nice contrast with the formal gardens to the north. You may also enjoy walking through the well-kept lawns and paths of the estate down to the dock. (The waterfront landscape was used in filming *The Great Gatsby*.)

On the other side of the peninsula you'll find several gardens of the great houses that are worth a visit. Marble House (1892), designed by Richard Morris Hunt for William Kissam Vanderbilt, was, as we have said, patterned after Versailles' Petite Trianon. Its grounds contain a large, surprising, and brilliantly painted Chinese pagoda set in a carefully designed landscape.

At Rosecliff (1902), designed by Stanford White, you'll find elegant rose gardens in season. The house design included protected terraces on both sides; it is here that the roses grow despite the ocean winds. There are dozens of varieties including climbing roses along the wall of the mansion. The setting of these five formal beds is spectacular, with ocean waves easily visible beyond the lawn. Graceful statues by Augustus Saint-Gaudens adorn the gardens. By the way, the best time to see this garden is July to mid-September.

But our favorite Bellevue Avenue gardens are those of The Elms (1901), a glamorous and somewhat overgrown setting thoroughly reminiscent of eighteenth-century French chateau gardens. The Elms, designed by Horace Trumbauer, was a copy of the 1750 Chateau d'Asnieres outside Paris, and the gardens capture the ambiance and grace of the period. Around the mansion there are numerous rhododendrons, bronze and marble statues, and evergreen shrubbery clipped in topiary shapes. A wisteria balustrade is brilliantly purple in springtime. Great trees, including giant weeping beeches, dot the lawn (but no elms remain). There is a beautiful pathway from the side of the mansion leading to the formal gardens: a mixture of statuary and marble gazebos, busts of mythical figures, and pergolas, fountains, vines, and a formal sunken garden edged in boxwood. The overall impression is delightfully romantic. Since the gardens of The Elms are slightly more sheltered from the ocean's winds, they seem to have survived better over the years.

Before leaving Newport we recommend the Cliff Walk, which wends its way along the ocean edge of many of these estates. From here you will have a view not only of the dramatic sea but of some of the mansions and their gardens as well.

INFORMATION
Hammersmith Farm is open for guided tours or visiting grounds only, daily from April through mid-November. Fee. Please telephone before visiting. Telephone: (401) 846-7346. Newport Preservation Society Mansions (including those described above) are open daily year-round, but to see the gardens, we recommend spring, summer, and early fall. The Preservation Society also schedules special holiday events. Fee. (A comprehensive ticket for all mansions and grounds is available, as are individual house and combination tickets.) Telephone: (401) 847-1000.

DIRECTIONS
To reach Newport from New York, take I-95 north to Exit 3 in Rhode Island to Route 138 east across the Jamestown Bridge and across Newport Bridge. For Hammersmith Farm, once in Newport follow signs to Ocean Drive and Fort Adams State Park. Hammersmith is just beyond the park. Bellevue Avenue is reached by continuing on Ocean Avenue until it intersects with Bellevue.

Green Animals, Portsmouth

If you like animal sculptures prettily set along garden paths—and wish to see some whimsical examples that are neither stone nor steel—make a visit to this topiary garden where growing trees and bushes are trimmed into myriad shapes, both abstract and realistic. Green Animals is a small estate whose gardens are filled with members of the animal kingdom, including a giraffe, a giant camel, a bear, a swan, an elephant, a rooster, even a unicorn, all made of greenery. Set into a formal garden of flowers and hedges and geometric pathways, these cavorting animals are a particular delight to children.

Green Animals, not far from Newport, overlooks Narragansett Bay. It is the oldest topiary garden in the country. The 7-acre estate includes a summer house with original furnishings from its nineteenth-century past and a toy collection, but it is particularly the topiary garden that draws visitors.

Green Animals garden was the idea of a family named Brayton

who were enchanted by the topiary gardens they has seen in the Azores. They and their gardeners, Joseph Carreiro (a native of the Azores) and his son-in-law, George Medonca, designed the gardens, beginning their work around 1893. Green Animals' sculptures, made from yew and privet, are both realistic and fanciful. The garden includes about 100 pieces of topiary art, including geometric shapes, arches, and ornamental designs, and some 21 animals and birds. Other specialties of the garden are 35 seasonally planted flower beds in the most perfect condition. There are peach trees and fig trees and grape arbors and various other horticultural pleasures.

In pleasant weather children can sit on tiny animal-shaped rocking chairs out among the topiary fantasies. Green Animals is included in a combination ticket with several of the mansions of Newport or can be visited separately (at what we thought was an unfortunately rather steep price. If you would enjoy visiting Newport's great houses with their elegant period furnishings and art, however, the combination ticket is worth the cost.

INFORMATION
Green Animals is on Cory's Lane in Portsmouth. It is open daily from 10 A.M. to 5 P.M. from May through November. There is a fee. Telephone: (401) 847-6543.

DIRECTIONS
From Providence take I-95 at the Wyoming exit and Route 138 each to Newport. At junction of R.I. 138 and Route 114, take 114 and continue for about 7 miles north to Cory's Lane. Entrance is on the left.

Shakespeare's Head and the Stephen Hopkins House, Providence

These two small but elegant eighteenth-century gardens are within walking distance of one another. Seeing the two gardens on the same outing is both enjoyable and instructive: they provide a glimpse of "living" history in a notable and charming part of Providence. In this hilly section of the city, fine eighteenth-century homes of brick and clapboard sit almost immediately next to one another along the narrow streets. (Many of these houses in this historic district bear the names and dates of the original owners.) Tucked into the little spaces between and behind them are their gardens—wonderful examples of what can be accomplished in small urban spaces.

Colonial gardeners knew precisely how to combine practicality with beauty. Within parterres and geometrically designed planting beds, these jewel-sized gardens contain both herbs and flowers, amid brick walls and boxwood hedges. The restorers of these two gardens were both highly successful in creating a sense of eighteenth-century order and charm: in one case they were able to draw on existing walls and terraces, and in the other on a plan by a descendant of Stephen Hopkins.

The Stephen Hopkins House, built in 1743, is on Benefit Street— a delightful colonial roadway on the hill—at the corner of Hopkins. Stephen Hopkins was a governor of colonial Rhode Island, a chief justice of the superior court, an energetic supporter of colonial rights, and a signer of the Declaration of Independence. His house is open to the public.

About 40 years ago a restoration of the garden was begun by the Dirt Gardeners Club of Providence. They used a design for the garden that was made by Alden Hopkins, a direct descendant of the original owner. He is said to have based his design on gardens at Williamsburg. The gates and entrance to the house are immediately on the street; you enter the garden by descending five steps. A high wall surrounds the property. The parterre garden has geometric beds outlined by low brick walls. In the center is a sun dial around which is engraved a quotation by Stephen Hopkins: "A garden that might comfort yield." Despite its small size, the garden does just that.

Not far away, on steep Meeting Street, is the garden of Shakespeare's Head. This rather more elaborate colonial garden is also tiny, but its ingenious use of terraces makes it seem larger. It is part of the property of a historic and interesting house. Built in 1772, the house was the home of the publisher of Providence's first newspaper. The sign at the establishment bore a wood carving of Shakespeare's head as a symbol of literacy—hence the name. In the 1930s the dilapidated building was purchased by the Shakespeare's Head Association, restored, and eventually designated a National Historic Landmark.

The garden restoration was begun in 1939 following a plan (based on the excavation of the remains of walls and cobbled areas) by landscape architect James D. Graham. Though there were no plans extant, Graham's idea was to restore the gardens on their three parterre levels, using eighteenth-century historical English-style garden plans and retaining the brickwork from the past. The house is on a steeply sloping street, and the gardens are terraced to conform with the hillside.

The house is at the lowest level of the gardens. Here also is the largest garden. This parterre garden—entered by means of a gate on the south side of the house—contains boxwood hedges that outline geometric flower beds. Each has a quince tree in the outer corner. In the center is the sundial. To the north of this level is a low stone wall with steps at either end leading to the middle terrace. Here is a promenade level bordered by crab apple trees on one side and peonies on the other. (Spring is the recommended time for a visit here.) There is also an herb garden on this level. The third level, edged by a retaining wall, includes hedges and ivies and other perennials. The entire garden is delightfully full—nowhere is there an impression of emptiness. In fact, the felicitous combinations of plantings and walkways, walls and steps, flowers and trees in such an intimate space makes this a fine example of what can be accomplished in the middle of a city—whether in the eighteenth or twentieth century.

INFORMATION
Hopkins House is located at the corner of Benefit and Hopkins Streets. Shakespeare's Head is at 21 Meeting Street. Both gardens are open daily, year-round. There is no fee for either of them. Telephone (Shakespeare's Head): (401) 831-7440.

DIRECTIONS
The historic district of Providence is located just off Interstate 95. Take the City Hall exit in downtown Providence to South Main Street and the Brown University historic district. Benefit Street runs parallel to Main; Meeting Street crosses Benefit Street.

And in Addition . . .

Westerly: Wilcox Park
Grove Avenue.
This public park is located behind the public library in the historic center of this oceanside town. A pleasant 18-acre expanse of flowers, shrubs, statues, fountains, and a duck pond, the quiet oasis was

designed by Frederick Law Olmsted in the late nineteenth-century. It is the perfect spot for a leisurely walk. You will find young mothers with children, workers on their lunch break, and other strollers enjoying the many shaded pathways.

After your walk, visit the Romanesque-style library—which has a public art gallery with changing exhibits—or take a stroll on Westerly's main street, lined with Gothic-style and Greek Revival houses.

Wickford: Smith's Castle

Route 1 (opposite the State Police barracks).

The setting of this historic house and garden is spectacular—a sweep of lawn right on a serene and unspoiled ocean inlet with rocks and water fowl. The small 1678 colonial house—hardly a castle—where Roger Williams preached to the Indians is adjoined by a charming eighteenth-century garden. This prize-winning recreation of a period garden was made using only plants from listings of the time, including globe amaranth, herbs, rose of Damascus, and gas plant dittany—all precisely set amid the boxwood borders of the colonial era. While in the neighborhood, be sure to visit the village of Wickford—a picturesque and historic spot. Smith's Castle is open daily except Thursdays year-round; Sundays only in the afternoon. Fee.

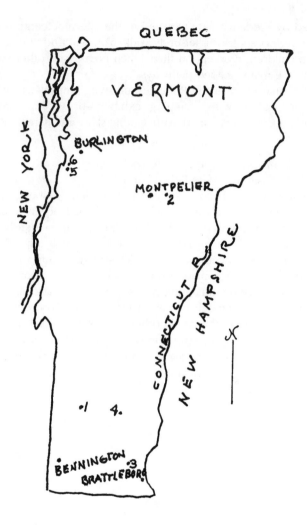

VERMONT GARDENWALKS

1. Manchester: Hildene
2. Plainfield: Great Woods Gardens at Goddard College
3. South Newfane: Olallie Daylily Gardens

And in Addition . . .

4. Andover: Vermont Perennial Gardens
5. Charlotte: The Vermont Wildflower Farm
6. Shelburne: Shelburne Museum Gardens

VERMONT

Hildene, Manchester

Picture an elegant, formal, plateau garden—brilliant with peonies—set dramatically between two Vermont mountain ranges with forested ravines and distant views all around. This unlikely—and very beautiful—setting is what you will find in a spring or summer visit to Hildene. Surrounding this formal garden are a variety of lovely landscape features laid out by the ubiquitous and always admirable firm of Olmsted and Company of New York: a great lawn, a hawthorne allée, walkways, woodland garden, and a pond. This is a great place at any time of year for a walk or even a cross-country ski outing.

The mansion with its spacious grounds in a pristine Vermont village was the summer home of Robert Todd Lincoln, son of the president. Various Lincoln descendants, including the president's granddaughter, Jessie, lived in the fine Georgian Revival house until 1975. Having spent many years in England (her father was ambassador) and greatly admiring the gardens there, Jessie came back to Vermont around the turn of the century with an ambitious garden plan.

She laid out the formal garden design in 1907 on the plateau set so grandly between the Taconic and Green mountain ranges with the winding Battenkill River Valley below. She apparently relished the contrast between the natural beauty of the surroundings and the formal organization of her garden. The great vistas in all directions—and all shades of green—accent the precision planting of the gardens in a most unusual way. We have rarely visited a garden placed so spectacularly within a naturally glorious setting.

Formal beds like these, however, take constant tending, and for over 40 years Jessie's garden was left in a chaotic, uncared-for state. By 1990 privet hedges had grown to 20 feet high, and the neat brick paths that intersect the gardens were covered inches deep with soil and grass. The hawthorne allée extending south from the house had filled in with vegetation. In the past few years, however, the gardens have been restored magnificently—some 75-year-old peonies and fine old lilacs were even found still blooming—and today the garden you see is as close to perfection as constant gardening will make it.

This is a truly restored garden, for everything planted in it is a historically turn-of-the-century kind of flower, and the original paths and flower bed shapes are exactly as they once were. (Anyone interested in before-and-after garden restoration can inquire at the entrance desk; there are several articles describing in detail how such a historical reconstruction took place.)

The flower bed design so lovingly recreated (and kept in order by dozens of volunteers) consists of a series of privet-edged squares and arcs, each with grassy centers and paths, resembling a maze. Each of the 16 interconnecting beds was planted in a different color: 4 yellow, 4 pink, 4 white, and 4 blue. Each bed was surrounded with a (now severely trimmed) hedge. The overall effect was to resemble a vast stained glass window; at the peak was the rose garden.

The plan has been ingeniously worked out: each color is kept consistently abloom by a calendar of different flowers. The blue bed, for instance, contains lupin, delphinium, Siberian iris (spectacular), Veronica, phlox, lythrum, and blue-fringed daisies. (And that's just the list for June and July.)

We could tell you a great deal more about how this very precise garden idea is implemented. But perhaps it is best to advise visitors to see for themselves the lovely overall atmosphere of this most pleasing formality midst a glorious mountain setting.

INFORMATION
The entrance to Hildene is on Route 7A in Manchester. Telephone: (802) 362-1788. There are daily tours of house and estate mid-May through October, and you can wander around the grounds from 9:30 A.M. Fee.

DIRECTIONS
Manchester is located on Route 7A. Either take (scenic) Route 7A North from Bennington to about 7 miles beyond Arlington (entrance on your right), or take the Highway (Route 7) to Manchester Center exit and take Routes 11 and 30, turning left (south) at intersection with Route 7A. Go 2 miles to Hildene entrance on your left, 1/2 mile past the Equinox Hotel.

Great Woods Gardens at Goddard College, Plainfield

Tucked into the lovely Vermont greenery here on a bucolic college campus is a very special garden. At the moment it is more architecture than plantings—or perhaps it is just more overgrown than most formal gardens. But that is part of its beauty. The structures of garden design are all very much intact, and as the current renovations continue, no doubt it will become quite a showplace. But as of our writing, this is much in the nature of a secret garden—a place with ineffable charm.

The Great Woods Gardens were laid out in 1925 by the well-known and always artistic designer Arthur Shurcliff. Willard Martin was the owner of the estate that became Goddard College in 1938. His gardens were as much architectural statements as flower beds, and fortunately the stonework has remained remarkably intact, even as the gardens were quite abandoned. Although a renovation (by a student) took place in 1973, and was aided briefly by the college, it is only recently that real, serious restoration has begun.

These are gardens on several levels, each outlined with spectacular stonework. Mixed Vermont granite and slate have been elegantly crafted to create walls, fountains, summer houses, arches, pergolas—and all the architectural splendor that converts a garden from just being flower beds into a work of art. At the north end of the upper garden there is a deep circular pool with a canal that runs from a fountain. There are balustrades and small delicacies of carving. Stone steps lead down to the next level, where, surprisingly, five ram's heads high on a stone wall spurt water from above into another pool. From here, more steps lead to a formal (once elegant) rose garden, in which a still perfectly serpentine pattern of boxwood separates the rose bushes. This walled garden is delightful, though unkempt, and its setting—on a perfect axis with the upper garden—is jewel-like: it nestles into the landscape like an heirloom lying in a velvet box.

The pergolas and a small stone tea house are also part of the three-tiered design here. (Note the small carved stone animals on each corner of the slate roof.) Each level has other repeated motifs as well—arched doorways, for example. All of this structural material makes the plantings—there are already several very pretty restored flower beds—seem unusually lovely. Come visit in the springtime, or in rose season, and sit on the curved stone bench in the upper garden. Here you can look down on the lower levels and capture the special pleasures of this small but quite wonderful garden.

INFORMATION
Goddard College is open year-round to visitors. The garden is near the tennis court—just beyond the parking lot.

DIRECTIONS
Plainfield is northeast of Montpelier. Take I-89 to Montpelier (Exit 8). Take Route 2, about 8 miles, toward Plainfield (east). The entrance to Goddard is on your left.

Olallie Daylily Gardens, South Newfane

This is a garden literally in a meadow—one of those lovely green Vermont meadows surrounded by mountains and brooks. The owners took their flat 6-acre meadow and turned it into a patchwork quilt of flowering lilies, and Siberian iris, and other brilliant perennials. They sell these flowers (by catalog and on the spot), but the atmosphere is not at all commercial. In fact, as you wander freely along the grassy paths in this field of flowers, you have a sense of stepping into and through a Van Gogh painting of a flower farm.

Owned by the Darrow family, Olallie means "place where berries are found" in a West Coast Indian language. The flower farm has horticultural history. Its founder Dr. George Darrow—who began growing lilies in Maryland—was a horticulturist and plant geneticist for the U.S. Department of Agriculture. He started breeding daylilies for his own interest with astonishing success: some 59 varieties are now registered with the Olallie prefix. About 15 years ago his son transplanted many of the lilies to the family farm here in Vermont, and this thriving flower farm was opened to gardeners and other visitors.

You are probably familiar with the bright orange Tiger Lily so common on New England's roadways. But here they say you'll find some 800 varieties! Daylilies come in a great array of species, colors, sizes, and blooming times. They range from large shrubs that fill the back of a flower bed to the most delicate miniatures. Here you are introduced to many hybrids and species (some of which they will dig up before your eyes and hand over to you to your surprise and delight). You will discover that you can have a daylily garden that blooms continuously from June until the first frost—or even longer if you live in a warmer clime than frosty Vermont. (As you might guess, plants that bloom so profusely in Vermont's harsh climate are very hardy—like Vermonters themselves.)

Daylilies come in delicious colors, described, for example, as "clear melon," "spidery red wine purple with near black eye and chartreuse throat," or "peach opalescent sheen." This display is truly an artist's pleasure. In addition to the flower farm, there is an old-fashioned perennial garden and a rock garden, and if you visit in August, you can pick luscious high-bush blueberries. Needless to say, anyone with an interest in growing daylilies will be welcomed and advised here, but you need not be a prospective lily grower to enjoy this garden walk.

INFORMATION
Olallie is located on Marlboro Branch Road in South Newfane. It is open from May 4 to September 4, 9 A.M. to 5 P.M. Closed on Tuesdays and occasional other days, so call to be sure. Telephone: (802) 348-6614.

DIRECTIONS
Take I-91 North to the Brattleboro exit; then follow signs to Route 30 north. Take the turn-off for West Dummerston about 7 miles north. South Newfane is the next town after West Dummerston; follow signs. At the crossroads in center of South Newfane, take Marlboro Branch Road (you'll see a sign indicating the Marlboro direction), and you'll find Olallie after about a mile on your left.

And in Addition . . .

Andover: Vermont Perennial Gardens
Dorman Road. Telephone: (802) 875-2604.
This is a partly private, partly commercial garden, but wholly lovely, particularly its rock gardened hillside deep in the Vermont woods. The color and stillness here are very special. Visit in summer.

Charlotte: The Vermont Wildflower Farm
Route 7. Telephone: (802) 425-3500.
This is a woodsy 6 acres of fields and forest, where the largest wildflower seed center in the East displays all the many different wildflowers that grow in this northern clime. Careful labeling and pleasant paths are nice for the kids too.

Shelburne: Shelburne Museum Garden
Route 7. Telephone: (802) 985-3346.
The gardens here are only a small part of the very large complex of Americana on display. The vast property does include a large lilac collection of some 90 varieties, roses, a medicinal herb garden, and

a pretty perennial garden called the Bostwick Garden. It is a circular, walled, flower garden found between the lighthouse (a real one moved to this meadowy location) and one of the antique houses of the some 40 sites here. Open year-round; call for hours, fees, and tour information.

VIRGINIA GARDENWALKS

1. Alexandria: River Farm
2. Arrington: Oak Ridge Estate
3. Charlottesville: Monticello
4. Charlottesville: Pavilion Gardens, University of Virginia
5. Mount Vernon: Mount Vernon
6. Richmond: Agecroft Hall
7. Richmond: Virginia House
8. Williamsburg: Williamsburg's Colonial Gardens

And in Addition . . .

9. Fredericksburg: Kenmore
10. Lorton: Gunston Hall Plantation
11. Norfolk: Norfolk Botanical Gardens
12. Richmond: Bryan Park Azalea Garden
13. Richmond: Lewis Ginter Botanical Garden at Bloemendaal
14. Richmond: Maymont
15. Stratford: Stratford Hall Plantation

VIRGINIA

River Farm, Alexandria

George Washington purchased this farm above the Potomac River (and just minutes away from Mount Vernon), in 1760. Though he never lived on the farm, he planted wheat, rye, and corn there, and is thought to have planted the walnut trees in the meadow. Now the headquarters for the American Horticultural Society, it naturally has extensive and very pretty gardens.

The site of River Farm is at the top of a hill overlooking the Potomac and its curious meandering shores. There is a large elegant house and a series of garden areas, including various types of gardens—as befits a horticultural society. In fact, you'll find here many types of garden settings, ranging from an "America's Front Yard Garden," a "Children's Garden," a "Wildlife Garden," and even that English necessity, a "ha-ha wall," to the more traditional rose garden and perennial plantings. Many are trial gardens run by the society; the dahlia beds are one of seven such trial sites in the nation, and there are over 100 types of daylilies in another spot. Some of the garden features go quite far back in history: the boxwood hedges, for example, were planted in Lincoln's time.

Each of the display gardens is extensive and very luxuriant in season, and obviously well worth visiting, for these gardeners are definitely experts. The herb garden, for instance, was designed by a specialist from the United States Botanic Garden. It has herbs for aromatherapy, flavor, habitat, and health, surrounded by various unusual trees, like the silver weeping peach.

Spring shrubs are well represented here. The dogwood collection is filled with rare species, as is the azalea garden (which is maintained by the Azalea Society of America). Both gardens are particularly dazzling in April and May.

The frontyard garden is planted with flowers and ground covers indigenous to North America, while the wildlife garden has a small pond at its center and is home not only to aquatic plants but to turtles and lizards as well. Great trees including a ginko and Kentucky coffee trees, and the largest Osage orange tree in Virginia (second largest in the United States) can be seen nearby.

The children's garden is a particular pleasure, and we recommend it—there is a bat cave, an alphabet garden, and even a garden that displays all the ingredients found on the average pizza! Kids will love this spot.

For the traditionalist, the flower-filled spaces behind the house are very lovely. Under a series of brick arches, and surrounded by brick walls, these beds include All-American selections (labeled) of every kind of bloom beloved by home gardeners. You can walk from garden to garden, all of which are kept constantly blooming with a variety of seasonal plantings.

While River Farm's gardens are the specialty of real horticulturists, the property has little overall architectural or landscape design in the grand manner of so many planned estates. It was, after all, a working farm for centuries, including a stint as a dairy farm. But each of the series of gardens is a pleasure on its own, and the views and walks are surely inducement enough for a visit. Or a beautiful wedding.

INFORMATION
River Farm is located at 7931 East Boulevard Drive in Alexandria. It is open Monday through Friday, 8:30 A.M. to 5:00 P.M. from May 1 through October 30 and some weekends year-round. Telephone: (703) 768-5700 or (800) 777-7931.

DIRECTIONS
In Alexandria take Washington Street, which becomes the George

Washington Parkway, toward Mt. Vernon. Go 1.5 miles. Proceed under the overpass and make a left turn onto East Boulevard Drive, where a sign indicates the American Horticultural Society at River Farm.

Oak Ridge Estate, Arrington

We approached Oak Ridge on a narrow drive through what seemed miles of picturesque rural scenery—and in fact, a lot of it belongs to this amazing estate: some 4,800 acres. When we finally reached the fine white mansion and gardens, we were struck by the overwhelming sense of the past. Everything about Oak Ridge is old, and a lot of it somewhat decayed—in the nicest sense. A reconstruction is taking place here, and we can only hope that the current owners retain the evocative air of faded elegance and eccentricity.

If your idea of a plantation estate is a spiffy reconstruction complete with costumed ladies, this is not the place for you. On the other hand, if you respond to a decidedly Southern ambiance with a grand old mansion set in a lovely green landscape with great oak trees (one some 350 years old), winding paths, the haunting, grass-filled skeleton of a conservatory, and ancient statues amid overgrown gardens, this is certainly the place to come. The sweeping panorama of Oak Ridge is a taste of the Deep South in rural Virginia, only a short drive from sophisticated Charlottesville. And unlike most Southern open-to-the-public plantations, its major period of elegance came well after the antebellum period.

The original estate dates to the eighteenth century, when two British merchants lost their stake in it during the Revolutionary War. The mansion was constructed in 1802—influenced by Thomas Jefferson's designs—by Robert Rives, a tobacco planter. Its owners through the Civil War included his unmarried daughter, who successfully ran the plantation herself, and a number of notable Virginians, including a Confederate congressman.

After a period of neglect at the end of the nineteenth century, Thomas Fortune Ryan took possession. Oak Ridge's glory days began in 1901. Ryan, a Virginian who was a poor orphan as a child, became one of the nation's richest men (the richest of all in the South), and Oak Ridge was to become his showplace—his very own, personal city.

Like the Vanderbilts in New York, Ryan traveled about on his own train car; one of the delights of this visit is seeing his private station and the track and siding and gilded railroad gate that bisect this vast property. Don't fail to walk down through the sloping grounds to this piece of Americana!

The station was just one of many parts of Ryan's Oak Ridge enterprise, which was the largest privately owned plantation in the South. The agricultural part produced tobacco and then apples. There was an ice house, a generating plant, a reservoir, a race track, a telephone company, a golf course, a chapel, a school, the telegraph and railroad office—all in addition to the mansion and the gardens. Some of this massive enterprise is still to be seen, like the lovely stone water tower or the decayed greenhouse, but many of the other structures are long vanished, for not long ago the estate was again abandoned and in a state of neglect.

Nowadays, the house—to which Ryan added a third story and two wings—is in elegant shape and its first floor is open for tours. And the grounds, which you can walk about yourself, are exceptionally attractive.

Ryan employed some 300 people at Oak Ridge, among them a legion of gardeners, lawn keepers, beekeepers, and an estate florist to provide arrangements for the house. Gardens were apparently very important to him. He had the once-elegant Italianate formal gardens installed and a large rose garden (not yet restored) put in. The great conservatory, modeled after the famous domed greenhouse at the Crystal Palace in England, was built near the house. Today you can see the structure in its evocative ruined state. (Seeing grass and vines growing inside old buildings is surely one of the most appealing ways of sensing the passage of time.)

Behind the mansion the formal gardens are terraced and are outlined in boxwood. There are a number of statues and ornaments and an old well cover adorning the gardens and accenting the geometric patterns of the plantings. Some of the statues are purported to be from the Renaissance. At the edge of the terraces, near the steps at the back of the formal gardens, is an artistic waterfall designed by Mrs. Ryan and called "Crabtree Falls Cascade." These are very pretty gardens, and will be prettier still as renovation continues and the roses are replanted.

Oak Ridge shows us several historical eras all at once. (Perhaps the clearest evocation of the different historical periods here can be seen at the grave sites: the oldest graves are in a simple, pretty, iron-fenced area under the great oaks; Ryan's grave is a great mausoleum.) The current life at Oak Ridge includes historical, landscape, and botanical tours; Civil War reenactments; and the hosting of a local Hunt Club. Plans are afoot for the reconstruction of various buildings and garden areas (and, worryingly, for a restaurant and tourist center). But a visit today is a pleasantly untouristy affair, and we recommend it highly.

INFORMATION
Oak Ridge is at 2300 Oak Ridge Road in Arrington, midway between Charlottesville and Lynchburg. It is open for house tours and self-guided grounds tours by appointment, and in summer Tuesday through Thursday from 10 A.M. to 3 P.M. Fee. Telephone: (804) 263-8676.

DIRECTIONS
From Charlottesville take Route 29 south for about 35 miles and exit left at Route 653 (Oak Ridge Road), just beyond Lovingston. Go 2.4 miles to driveway entrance and follow signs.

Monticello, Charlottesville

Every inch of this beautiful place built and landscaped by Thomas Jefferson is so deeply connected with history and significance that it's hard to separate and describe just the gardens. In fact, if your only interest is flower gardens per se, you'll have to block out a fascinating collection of extraneous material on your tour—for each corner of Monticello has something to capture your attention. Monticello is one of the nation's most worthy and delightful historic estates, the physical representation of Jefferson's genius. He was a gardener par excellence, as well as an architect and statesman, and here at Monticello you'll find many of his ideas about gardens and nature and economy that were put into practice in the early nineteenth century (all elegantly restored today).

Jefferson was a man with a vision—indeed many visions—but in particular, a view of the ultimate Virginia environment for work and recreation. His notes, correspondence, and drawings have guided the Garden Club of Virginia and the Thomas Jefferson Memorial Foundation to reconstruct this landscape accurately. Thus, any visitor with an interest in Jefferson as well as beautiful gardens will find this a fascinating and rewarding visit.

Monticello is set in the scenic rolling hills of western Virginia, not far from the Skyline National Park. The vistas are magnificent, and Monticello sits on a high hill with a panoramic view. The tour you will take comprises the entire site—it includes the beautiful red brick and white-columned mansion, the excavations, the slave quarters, gazebos, and old log cabin and the many other structures that made up this self-contained estate. There is a lovely graveyard enclosed by an iron fence, and there are many sorts of outdoor and indoor inventions, all revealing Jefferson's wide and varied pursuits.

Monticello's gardens were an abiding interest in the years that Jefferson lived there. And throughout his old age he delighted in them. "No occupation," he wrote, "is so delightful to me as the culture of the earth, and no culture comparable to that of the garden. . . . But though an old man, I am but a young gardener."

This magnificent 2000-acre mountain-top site includes a "grove" or ornamental forest and many varieties of flowering trees, as well as two orchards, a vineyard, and fruit, vegetable, herb, and flower gardens, some with spectacular seasonal plantings. The flower gardens themselves are at the four corners of the house; here 20 oval-shaped beds with a winding gravel walk through them are especially pretty in spring and early summer. The serpentine walk and surrounding lawn are bordered with flowers, and everything is labeled. Among the great varieties of blooms here are not just the familiar spring bulbs, but such rarities as a Jeffersonia diphylla (named, of course, for the master) and a Columbian lily (a discovery of Lewis and Clark).

Among the interesting sights are a 1,000-foot-long terraced vegetable garden, which features delightful patterns and climbing varieties, including some of the 20 types of peas Jefferson grew—peas were apparently Jefferson's favorite vegetable. He grew over 250 types of vegetables and herbs here. This garden, which is divided into 27 growing beds, has a stone wall with a reconstructed pavilion where Jefferson sat to read among the vegetables. (There is a research facility now at Monticello that studies propagation and historic plants; you can purchase historic seeds too.)

To appreciate fully the grand plan of Monticello's gardens requires understanding Jefferson's goals and preoccupations. Material available at the site explains, demonstrates, and details everything, and there are knowledgeable tour guides, too. But you can also walk around and enjoy this elegant and historic site with only a minimum of historic knowledge (and perhaps this barest of thumbnail descriptions).

INFORMATION
Monticello is located a few minutes from downtown Charlottesville. It is open daily year-round, but spring and summer are recommended. Hours are 8 A.M. to 5 P.M. in growing season, 9:00 A.M. to 4:30 P.M. in winter. The gardens near the house are easily seen on a tour of the estate; tours devoted primarily to the garden (including the more distant landscape) are given on Saturday mornings. A large visitor's center has all kinds of information, including material specifically about the gardens. Fee. Telephone: (804) 984-9822.

DIRECTIONS
From Charlottesville, take I-64 to Route 20. (Here you'll find the Visitor's Center.) Take Route 53 for 1.6 miles to a left side entrance.

Pavilion Gardens, University of Virginia, Charlottesville

Thomas Jefferson's campus at the university here is a graceful, green wonder; its beautifully aged brick walls and white pillars harmonize completely with the landscape. In addition to the architectural delights set amid the lovely landscape with its grand, imposing trees are the pavilion gardens that the master statesman, architect, and gardener included in his plan. Though Jefferson did not himself lay out each of these ten gardens, his original design included the serpentine garden walls and the concept of the individual gardens in conjunction with the groves of academe. The pavilions are behind each of the old brick houses; their object was to provide a place for contemplation and study for members of the "academical village."

The visitor to the campus can take a formal tour or pick up a brochure describing each pavilion garden, walking unescorted from one to the next, through little white doors here and there that connect the gardens. The high walls provide a privacy that makes each entrance to a garden a new experience. The gardens are divided into two sections, matching the two facing rows of arcades that border the great lawn and the Rotunda. Behind these original buildings you'll find the East Pavilion Gardens and the West Pavilion Gardens. There are ten pavilion gardens. Each is different; those on the west side (gardens I, III, V, VII, and IX) are predominantly flat, while the east gardens (II, IV, VI, VIII, and X) are hilly and terraced. The overall sense of the gardens is of Jefferson's time, and a variety of experts (and the Garden Club of Virginia) have managed to recreate Jefferson's eighteenth-century era in both the geometric design and plantings. But each garden is differently laid out within those constraints and has its own ambiance.

If you begin your walk on the west side with Pavilion Garden I, you'll find a geometrically patterned garden with a serpentine walk reflecting the curving walls and small oval flower beds with plantings typical of the eighteenth century. A center stone was an attempt by Jefferson to carve capitols for the Rotunda from local stone. This garden is abloom in spring. Pavilion Garden III next door has raised oval flower beds and unusually pretty trees, among them a silverbell and a goldenrain. Next door in Garden V are two of Jefferson's favorite apple trees, set in the center of a series of squares with parterres and gravel walks. This garden is divided into upper and lower sections; the higher part includes a formal boxwood garden and lovely crape myrtle trees. Pavilion Garden VII is characterized by benches along curving, serpentine walks bordered by roses. It now is part of the Faculty Club. Finally, on the west side is Garden IX, also with a two-part design. The lower garden is cool and shady, with large trees and pomegranate shrubs, while the upper section features a four-part formal arrangement of viburnum, peonies, and lilacs.

On the east side of the great lawn is Pavilion Garden II, which is divided into three sections; you'll see great trees here, including an umbrella magnolia and a pecan tree, as well as a grape arbor and many fruit trees. Next door in Garden IV there is a combination of formality in a boxwood garden and informal flower beds in natural settings. Garden VI is one of the best known; here the Merton Spire (given by Oxford University to honor Jefferson) is in the center of a naturalistic rhododendron and laurel garden. Garden VIII is a summer garden, with profusely blooming shrubs and an "aerial hedge" of goldenrain trees such as Jefferson saw in England. The final garden in this row is Pavilion Garden X, one of the largest. Its design is actually based on the Monticello gardens, with an oval lawn flanked by two smaller ovals (called elephant ears) and a romantic setting of benches amid Kentucky coffee trees.

These are only thumbnail descriptions of a series of delightfully individual gardens. In addition to this very special collection of gardens—which demonstrate the many ways historic design and natural ingredients can be combined in small areas—do not fail to walk around the entire landscape of the university's original campus. You'll seldom see a prettier one.

INFORMATION
The Pavilion Gardens at the University of Virginia are open year-round, but are at their best from mid-April. There are additional gardens at various sites on campus; for full details pick up a flyer at the Information Center. Telephone the Rotunda at (804) 924-7969.

DIRECTIONS
The University is located in Charlottesville; take Route 29 south and follow signs for University information.

Mount Vernon, Mount Vernon

Mount Vernon, the legendary home of George Washington, is a serenely green and spacious eighteenth-century plantation overlooking the Potomac. This picturesque site has an elegant aura of history, with its imposing, columned mansion, period exhibits, and scrupulously restored colonial gardens (largely based on Washington's diaries and letters). Not surprisingly, it draws over a million visitors a year, from school children to foreign visitors, history buffs, and—yes—garden lovers. Here you can get a taste of the gracious plantation life of the time and catch a glimpse of the private world of Washington as gentleman farmer and assiduous botanist. But because the grounds are so vast—including some 500 landscaped acres within an extensive property easily four times that size—the crowds are not necessarily intrusive, and a self-guided garden walk here, amid flowers and fruit trees and herbs and boxwood, is highly recommended.

Today the grounds include the stately mansion (after visiting the rooms, be sure to stand on its columned portico for a spectacular view over the wide lawn and river beyond); a large bowling green, with gardens on either side; a collection of restored buildings (plantation workshops, the kitchen, carriage house and slave quarters); and a monument and museum (housing Washington memorabilia). The tomb where George and Martha Washington remain buried (despite repeated efforts on the part of Congress to move them to the Capitol) is down the hill toward the boat landing.

George Washington's legacy as a gifted gardener and horticulturist—and even designer—lives on at this homesite. Largely responsible for its preservation (in as strict accordance with Washington's original plans as possible) has been the Mount Vernon Ladies' Association. The oldest preservation society in the country, it purchased the badly neglected property in 1858, refurbishing it and maintaining it to this day. Apparently Mount Vernon is now quite like it was at Washington's death in 1799.

After Washington acquired the property in 1761 (it had been in the family for some time, and he had actually lived here before), he set about enlarging the house and grounds and embellishing the landscape. While serving as commander-in-chief of the Continental Army and, later, as president, he obviously could not tend personally to much of the work at hand, but nevertheless kept weekly contact with his plantation manager, sending him precise instructions. Whenever possible, though, he himself transplanted flowering shrubs and trees from the surrounding woods and planted unusual botanic specimens (many of which he brought back from his travels). A 1781 letter to a French officer (whom he had invited to Mount

Vernon) shows his particular love for trees: "I repeat to you the assurance of my friendship and of the pleasure I should feel in seeing you in the shade of those trees which my hands have planted, and which by their rapid growth at once indicated a knowledge of my declining years and their disposition to spread their mantles over me before I go hence to return no more. For this, their gratitude, I shall nurture them while I may."

Between 1783 and 1785, when he actually stayed put at Mount Vernon, Washington saw personally to the property. He laid out the bowling green, flanked on either side by specimen trees (some of which still exist), serpentine walks, and symmetrical gardens. (In keeping with the ideas of balance and perspective embodied in eighteenth-century garden design, the bowling green is aligned with both river and mansion.)

On one side of the expansive green is the large "Upper Garden," a formal composition of flowers, blooming shrubs and trees, and boxwood. Uncharacteristically, Washington's diaries and letters do not specify the exact flowers used; thus, recent restorations have included only plantings typical of the eighteenth century, such as heliotrope and foxglove, pansies, bloodroot, larkspur, and Canterbury bells, set in alternating patterns with vegetables. Espaliered fruit trees against brick walls and boxwood hedges, both favorites of Washington's, are also found here. (Some of the boxwood was actually rooted by Washington himself and has been carefully nurtured ever since.) A dwarf box parterre features a *fleur de lis* pattern, a popular design in many eighteenth-century French gardens.

The "Lower Garden," entered through a boxwood arch from the south side of the bowling green, is a less formal kitchen garden. Here, on two terraced levels surrounded by brick walls, are herb-bordered geometric vegetable beds (featuring more than 30 varieties) and yet more espaliered trees—figs, apples, pears, peaches, and, of course, cherries. The aroma from the deliciously scented herbs and fruits can be quite heady. During the 1930s and 1940s, the kitchen garden was entirely renovated (with the help of landscape designers and the Arnold Arboretum in Boston) and a picturesque beehouse added, based on early reproductions.

A third (almost completely restored) garden area is the Botanical Garden, next to the Upper Garden. This spot was used for experimenting on imported seeds and plants, and several varieties were grown for later transplant. Those interested in botany will find it particularly intriguing.

INFORMATION
Mount Vernon is in the town of Mount Vernon, just south of Washington, D.C. and Alexandria. Telephone: (703) 780-2000. The site is open from 9 A.M. to 5 P.M. daily, March through October, and from 9 A.M. to 4 P.M. daily, November through February. Entrance fee (except on Washington's birthday holiday). There are no formal guided tours, but interpretive guides are stationed in the house and gardens to answer questions.

DIRECTIONS
From Alexandria, follow George Washington Parkway south for about 8 miles. Mount Vernon is clearly indicated.

Agecroft Hall, Richmond

This house and garden truly seem to carry the visitor back in time—not just to colonial propriety or to the nineteenth-century "gardenesque"—but to Tudor and Stuart times in an England transposed to Virginia. Every stone of the elegant house, Agecroft Hall, was rescued from wrecking in Lancashire, England, and brought to this pretty setting by a Virginia businessman named T. C. Richards. It was reconstructed here on a picturesque riverfront of Richmond in 1928. The large, half-timbered Tudor-style mansion is a fabulous house, and, of course, it is properly outfitted and furnished in the appropriate style. You can tour it, enjoying the four-century-old ambiance of aged oak and ancient decor and imagining yourself in merrie old England in Tudor times.

The 23-acre gardens, at the house level and on a sloping hillside down to the James River, were designed to maintain the Tudor atmosphere, and are no doubt much as the originals might have looked when strolled through in the seventeenth century by an Englishman and his lady. There are picture-perfect grounds, green hillside lawns, elms and magnolias, and, best of all, a set of semiformal gardens and walkways that are both charming and curious. These "pleasure" gardens are especially inviting in springtime; each garden "room" is outlined in boxwood hedge and accented with small statuary and seasonal flowers.

You begin in an almost fully enclosed courtyard, which is equipped with seventeenth-century tools used for farming and other Tudor chores. Here you begin to feel you are going back in time as the great house and walls shut out the twentieth century behind you.

Walking through the courtyard doorway to the first of the pleasure garden rooms, you come to a fragrance garden—the nearest to the house, so that its sweet odors presumably would waft through the open leaded windows. Among the many (identified) flowers here whose scent and very names are intriguing are the pheasant's eye narcissus, the heliotrope, and the gillyflower.

Next is the sunken garden with a raised pond—a replica of one at Hampton Court, and truly a pleasure garden both in design and color. Lilies and iris are planted here and there, giving a sense of perfect harmony in this enclosed garden room.

A particularly intriguing walkway comes next. Here 50-year-old crape myrtle trees with their gnarled and graceful branches edge the path; their pale beige bark color is matched by the tan walkway, and in summer they bloom profusely. Tudor-style shelters from the sun add charm to this odd and pleasing connecting link to the next section, the knot garden.

A traditional part of early gardens, the knot garden is a formal, enclosed garden in which patterns are created by the plantings themselves. This is without a doubt one of the best we've visited: there are four sections, including a vegetable garden in which radishes, lettuce, and cabbage plants criss-cross through the bed, and another where various herbs form the patterns. Colored stone and crimson barberry create color contrast. What an amusing way to grow food!

The next garden is named for John Tradescant, the English botanist who first came to Virginia in 1637 to collect American plant specimens. This garden is, naturally, filled with rare and exotic plants once collected by Tradescant and his son. Here too the garden is divided into quadrangles, and its lovely walls are home to espaliered pear trees.

The herb garden borders the Tradescant garden: some 85 types of herbs used for medicine or cooking grow here. There is also a still house where herbs were dried and several beehives woven of rye, bulrush, and cattails against one wall. This is a garden where you can almost imagine yourself puttering about in the seventeenth century, a recipe book of herbs and honey in hand.

These six garden rooms comprise the formal part of Agecroft Hall's grounds, but there is also a cutting garden and a serpentine path through a sloping landscape dotted with flowers, ferns, and woodland, which takes the stroller finally to the riverbank.

A visit to Agecroft Hall suggests an era when gardening was both for pleasure and purpose, when even the most useful growing was done with an eye for beauty. We can easily recommend a visit here (perhaps in a felicitous combination with Virginia House next door).

INFORMATION
Agecroft Hall is located at 4305 Sulgrave Road in Richmond. It is open year-round, Tuesday through Saturday, from 10 A.M. to 4 P.M., Sunday from 12:30 P.M. to 5:00 P.M. There is a fee, which includes a house tour; garden tours are self-guided. Telephone: (804) 353-4241.

DIRECTIONS
From I-95 into Richmond, exit on I-195 (southwest), and then turn right onto Cary Street, which is also Route 147. Make a quick left at the light onto Canterbury Road, which will merge with Sulgrave Road. The entrance will be on your left.

Virginia House, Richmond

This garden fairly takes your breath away. Not just because of the heady aroma of thousands of blooms, among them a glorious rose garden, but because it is so aesthetically lovely. Virginia House, a big, rather gloomy mansion reconstructed stone by stone in 1925 from its English incarnation as a twelfth-century priory called St. Sepulchre, is virtually surrounded by gardens of contrastingly bright, light, colorful flowers. These are divided into garden rooms, called "pleasances," mostly walled, and one more delightful than the next.

Those who wish to can tour the house, which has an extraordinary collection of treasures acquired by the owner, diplomat Alexander Weddell, during his career with the U.S. government. You'll find objects and furniture from everywhere—Tibet to Africa—and every era—ancient Greek to American Renaissance. These are dark, powerful rooms with heavy hangings and stained glass windows and heraldic arms emblazoned.

But when you venture out of doors, everything is pale lavenders and pink, rose and jasmine. We were truly enchanted by the variety and design here; the creators of these gardens (landscape architect Charles Gillette, known for his designs in the "picturesque" style, and Virginia Weddell) had a real eye for color, proportion, and line, as well as an interest in rare plants and exotic trees. More modern additions retain a similar style. Gillette is sometimes called "the Interpreter of Southern Gardens," and in fact, he created one here that is quintessentially Southern in its old-world charm. Take your time; anyone who ever planned a garden will appreciate the sleight-of-hand demonstrated here.

This great estate, fashioned during the "country-place movement" that saw Americans recreating glamorous European-style estates, covers 9 acres. The land slopes sharply down to the James River. There are great trees—weeping willows, Cedars of Lebanon, and flowering magnolias. The hilly terrain has been terraced to create the many garden areas near the top and to encompass meadow and bog areas and wonderful water vistas (don't miss the view from the terrace).

Your tour of the garden (on your own with a map in hand or with a guide) begins at the terrace behind the house. From this terrace, you'll have an expansive view of the estate and the water beyond, and you'll get a feeling for the overall design. The alignment of a distant pergola, a canal, pools, and sundial with garden walls and planting demonstrates the strong east-west axis (in contrast with the north-south axis of the staircase to the house and the downhill path). This carefully planned arrangement suggests the European stylistic origins of Virginia House's landscape.

The first garden we visit is the water garden. This enchanting spot is fashioned after one designed by Gertrude Jekyll and Edwin Luytens in Berkshire, England. The use of water—running in an east-to-west canal—is one of the most appealing of any water garden we've seen. Instead of the ubiquitous floating lilies in stagnant ponds of so many water gardens, this one includes a rectangular court enclosed by boxwood and a low brick wall; within the water are clumps of Japanese iris, sagittaria, and pink and white lotus flowers—all blooming successively. The effect is breathtaking, for the combination of geometric design, small statues, and free-form plantings is both graceful and poetic—seemingly cut off from the world.

And speaking of walls, each "pleasance" has its own wall surrounding it, and no two are the same. Varied designs are built into them, and they are here and there dotted by statuary, small fountains, a sundial, and antique vases. These walls, like the fine frames on great paintings, add rather than detract from the composition within.

The next two gardens are devoted to a perennial bed featuring a mixture of blooming shrubs, perennial flowers, and clinging vines and a four seasons bed. The last includes little statues of the seasons, and here—in spring—the unusual combination of waving tulips in a sea of forget-me-nots is original and thoroughly delightful. This is a Victorian-style garden in the best sense.

As you continue your walk, each additional area has its own mood. The azalea and laurel beds surrounding a fifteenth-century stone birdbath are spectacular in late spring. (Here also is a pets' graveyard.) The rose garden, including several espaliered varieties, is enclosed in special walls with openwork to allow the air to circulate. The tea garden is grassy and bordered with flowers of all types (see a month-by-month listing available when you enter). Each of these areas has its own color scheme and its own design and ornament.

Below these more formal garden rooms are the wildflower meadow and the bog garden, where some 125 species of plant grow in wetlands (poetically set beneath a weeping willow). Beyond is a woodland walk, and then the riverbank.

While we can't begin to describe the many types of plantings in these gardens, we can tell you that this is certainly one of the outstanding gardens in our book. Don't miss it!

INFORMATION
Virginia House is at 4301 Sulgrave Road (next door to Agecroft Hall) in Richmond. The grounds are open from 10 A.M. to 4 P.M., Tuesday through Sunday. Choose spring or fall for best viewing. There are educational programs. Fee. Telephone: (804) 353-4251.

DIRECTIONS
From I-95 exit in Richmond onto Cary Street (Route 147), heading west. Make an almost immediate left onto Canterbury Road. This merges with Sulgrave Road. The entrance to Virginia House is next door to Agecroft Hall.

Colonial Gardens, Williamsburg

Colonial Williamsburg is the most famous living restoration of eighteenth-century Virginia. Though you may know of it for its careful recreation of colonial life, landscape architects and horticulturists prize it as well for its fine gardens. Like the well-maintained houses and streets of its 175 acres, the 90 acres of greens and gardens of Williamsburg are historically restored—delightfully so. The numerous gardens range from intimate, neat, colonial-style flower beds behind the townhouses to the elegant grounds of the Governor's Palace. For anyone with an interest in eighteenth-century garden design—and an appreciation for Virginia's glorious flowering season—Williamsburg is an enthusiast's pleasure. There are no fewer than 90 residential gardens, of which 25 are open to the public daily, with the others visitable by appointment or tour.

The English-style colonial garden had a small, formal layout on the 1/2-acre lots assigned by the laws of colonial settlement. In contrast to the frightening wilderness surrounding their colonial towns, the settlers favored carefully planned, rigorously neat gardens. These small plots typically featured bright flower beds that were part of the overall architecture of the colonial property, including the dependencies—the wellhouse, privies, workshop, dairy, smoke house, stable, and beehives, and all the other service areas. Vegetable gardens and fruit trees complete the design. Here you will see the espaliered and dwarf fruit trees that look so charming—but that also saved space by growing against the fences.

The garden sections typically included bright flower beds, outlined by English boxwood hedges in geometric patterns. The use of evergreen mixed with other plants provided both variety and contrast. Topiary circles and squares to ornament the hedges can be found in some gardens, while one can even see an adventurous hen-shaped topiary (in the Bryan Garden across from the Bruton Parish Church); you'll also see dwarf and tree boxwood here. One of the best of these geometric gardens is the formal boxwood design at Wythe House.

Typically, the flowers in these town gardens included such English favorites as larkspur, hollyhocks, traditional roses, phlox, foxglove, and the colonial specialty—tulips. (One of the best tulip gardens is at the Ludwell–Paradise House.) But these familiar

English plants were also interspersed with native American plants: dogwood, coreopsis, black-eyed Susans, and redbud.

Great trees provided shade in a steamy summer climate. Don't miss the tremendous variety of trees here; many are as old as the colony. Some were introduced from abroad: the horse chestnut arrived in 1736, the paper mulberry from the Orient in the mideighteenth century (see the Carters–Sanders House), and the beautiful crape myrtle with its pale bark and fantastic forms from China in 1747. Flowering shrubs—both native to America and imported—are everywhere; the Ludwell–Paradise House is noted for its summer-blooming shrubs.

The grounds of the Governor's Palace, in contrast to these more modest gardens, show us the elegance of the Dutch–English traditional style introduced by William and Mary. The landscape gardens here are said to have matched the elegance of the great European estates of the time (to the displeasure of some democratically minded colonists). Designed in 1713 for Alexander Spotswood, this landscape will make you imagine you are at a Great House in England. Here you'll see a holly maze (bring the kids!), evergreen parterres, a peached hornbeam allée, espaliered fruit trees, and the spectacular formal garden of 16 boxwood diamonds accented with topiary cones at each corner. This picturesque setting is ornamented with urns and benches, as well as spots of color: scilla, periwinkle, daffodils, hyacinth in spring. Beyond are a series of fields and vegetable gardens, a wooded area for deer, and numerous compartmentalized gardens for herbs, vegetables, a fish pond, and "Falling Gardens." It is a wonderful place to explore. (Pick up a map at the Visitor's Center.)

Williamsburg has come under fire for being too perfect in its reconstruction. While undoubtedly every garden in its colonial era was not as impeccable as it now looks, the reconstructions have been historically accurate and so give us the chance to study the way it might have been and to enjoy its perfection now. We don't have many opportunities in this country to see the colonial period's gardens laid out before us so appealingly.

A pleasant anachronism at Williamsburg, by the way, is the formal contemporary garden called the Lila Acheson Wallace Garden at the southwest corner of the historic area. Opened in 1986, it has an oblong reflecting pool with perennial borders, statuary, holly in containers, and a lovely pergola.

The best way to see Williamsburg's many garden sites is to identify in advance (from material given out at the Visitor's Center) those that have specialty gardens, in addition to the Governor's Palace—which you will not want to miss. (If you only have time for a few, choose those mentioned above.)

INFORMATION
Colonial Williamsburg is a full village restored for tourists. It is open year-round and is very crowded in tourist season, so try to visit on weekdays, early in the day. By calling (804) 229-1000, you can order a trip planning kit; you can also buy an Official Guide, which includes a map. You can take tours or wander by yourself. An entrance fee entitles you to visit almost all of the grounds, but the Governor's Palace charges an extra fee.

DIRECTIONS
Williamsburg is just off I-64 between Richmond and Norfolk. Take Exit 238 and follow signs to the Visitor's Center.

And in Addition . . .

Fredericksburg: Kenmore
1200 Washington Avenue. Telephone (540) 373-3381.
This early American home and garden belonged to George Washington's sister Betty and her husband Colonel Fielding Lewis, for whom it was built in the 1770s. The gardens, recreated in the 18th century manner, are nice examples of colonial elegance; they feature boxwood, formal walkways, a cutting garden, and a Wilderness Walk. Open March through December; weekends only in January and February. Closed on major holidays.

Lorton: Gunston Hall Plantation
Route 242. Telephone: (703) 550-9220.
Surrounding the historic home of George Mason, one of the authors of the U.S. Constitution and the Bill of Rights, you'll find gardens with the original nineteenth-century plantings. These lovely gardens with a view of the Potomac River feature a 12-foot high allée of English boxwood and formal boxwood parterres and dome-shaped holly bushes. An authentic colonial knot garden can be found behind the elegant Georgian mansion.

Norfolk: Norfolk Botanical Gardens
Airport Road. Telephone: (804) 853-6972.
Noted especially for its thousands of azaleas and Azalea Festival in April, these 175 acres of gardens also display 20,000 tulips, 7,000 roses, and a specialty collection of orchids. There are oleander and crape myrtle trees and special gardens including a Japanese garden, a colonial garden, and a fragrance garden for the blind. Open every day from dawn to dusk.

Richmond: Bryan Park Azalea Garden
Hermitage Road and Bellevue Avenue. Telephone (804) 780-5712.
Fifty thousand plants on 20 acres, with a specialty of 600 white dogwood and great azaleas are the attractions here. Visit in springtime. Open daily.

Richmond: Lewis Ginter Botanical Garden at Bloemendaal
1800 Lakeside Avenue. Telephone: (804) 262-9887.
This large botanical garden surrounding a lake features a giant perennial garden—one of the largest in the East, in fact. It boasts 12,000 plants that cover 3 of its 90 acres! There are all sorts of other garden areas including a Japanese tea house garden, a children's garden, narcissus and daylily collections, and 850 types of daffodils. Grounds are open year-round, 9:30 A.M. to 4:30 P.M. every day. Fee.

Richmond: Maymont
1700 Hampton Street. Telephone: (804) 358-7166.
If you have a taste for Italianate gardens with their romantic, wisteria-draped, columned pergolas and statuary and even an adjacent waterfall, don't miss Maymont. There are also a series of other types of gardens on these 100 acres, including an English courtyard garden and a daylily collection. If you especially like the heady aroma and delicate blooms of wisteria, as well as a profusion of blossoming shrubs and flowers, visit in spring; but summer and fall are also beautiful here. Open from April 1 through October 31, 10 A.M. to 7 P.M.; from November 1 to March 31, 10 A.M. to 5 P.M.

Stratford: Stratford Hall Plantation
Off Route 214. Telephone: (804) 493-8038.
Here at the historic Lee Plantation, with its fabulous setting on the Potomac, you'll find two formal gardens (one on either side of the mansion) with 3,200 boxwoods surrounding elegant plantings and—best of all for the kids—a maze. The house and grounds are open and are extensive places to visit, year-round. Open every day except Christmas from 9:00 A.M. to 4:30 P.M. Fee.

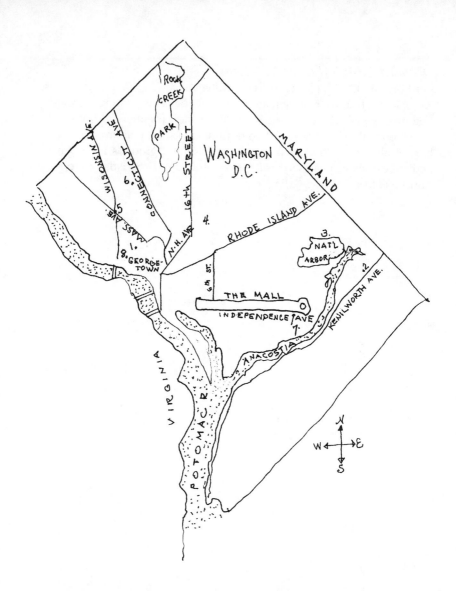

WASHINGTON D.C. GARDENWALKS

1. Dumbarton Oaks Gardens in Georgetown
2. Kenilworth Aquatic Gardens
3. United States National Arboretum

And in Addition . . .

4. Franciscan Monastery Gardens
5. Gardens of the Washington National Cathedral
6. Hillwood Museum
7. United States Botanic Garden
8. Old Stone House Garden in Georgetown

WASHINGTON, D.C.

Dumbarton Oaks Gardens, Georgetown

In 1921, Robert and Mildred Bliss commissioned the noted landscape gardener Beatrix Jones Farrand to create gardens for their newly purchased mansion, and a masterpiece of American garden design was conceived. The inspired Farrand–Bliss collaboration, based on a mutual admiration of European garden tradition, resulted in the Dumbarton Oaks Gardens. Representing a delightful blend of English, French, and Italian styles within an American landscape, the gardens combine classicism with naturalism in a unique and contemporary—and nonderivative—manner.

The well-traveled and cultivated Farrand had learned her craft through trips to Europe and intense training at Boston's Arnold Arboretum under Charles Sprague Sargent. But her inspirations came in large part from her aunt, the novelist Edith Wharton—herself a garden enthusiast and author of the widely regarded *Italian Villas and Gardens*—and the illustrious English landscape gardener Gertrude Jekyll. From Wharton, a key figure in the revival of Italianate gardens in America, she acquired her love of classical gardens; from Jekyll came the emphasis on horticulture over architecture and the idea of garden "rooms"—a recurring twentieth-century theme.

Farrand, who believed that the success of professional garden design required a close working relationship with the client, found an ideal partner in Mildred Bliss, an imaginative gardener in her own right. (Mrs. Bliss was also a talented designer and, among other things, created some of the ironwork motifs found throughout the grounds.) Together, Farrand and Bliss sought a balance between the traditions of formal European gardens (to which Mrs. Bliss was partial) and the natural landscape, a challenging 50-acre property with steeply sloping terrain. Their goals were that plants be chosen for beauty and interest for year-round visual pleasure (there is a high proportion of evergreens and ground covers); that the design take advantage of the dramatic site with terracing, flights of steps, and vantage points from which to enjoy garden vistas and the landscape beyond; and that architectural features—pergolas, paths, walls, statues, urns, fountains, pools—be included. (Mrs. Bliss had quite a collection of European garden ornaments which she was anxious to display.) The gardens were also to provide living spaces—enclosed areas for recreation. (In addition to a swimming pool and tennis court, there is a small amphitheater, in the tradition of seventeenth- and eighteenth-century European gardens.)

Farrand ingeniously devised a scheme of successive formal—and naturalistic—terraces and enclosures that would allow for distinctive garden segments, each with different design characteristics, planting styles and architectural ornaments—and degrees of formality. The gardens flow from one to the next in a seamless transition, from very formal, next to the house, to informal, down below. And, though they evoke the Renaissance gardens so admired by Mrs. Bliss—with two main axes extending at right angles from the house, symmetrical fountains, elegant stairways and ornamentation, and broad vistas—they also represent the garden as horticultural delight, focusing on plant colors, shapes, and patterns in the English tradition. Farrand was detail oriented; she carefully planned such elements as patterns of mosaics and stone paths, grass-covered brick steps, shapes of garden beds (some are rectangular, other romantically arabesque)— even garden furniture, some of which she designed herself. Because of her primary interest in horticulture, she kept track—in meticulous detail—of each and every planting throughout the grounds. (In "The Plant Book" for Dumbarton Oaks she tells it all.)

The 10-acre gardens were completed between 1921 and 1941, with a few additions later on. In 1940, the Blisses donated 16 acres (including the mansion and gardens) to Harvard University to create the Dumbarton Oaks Research Library and Collection. (The remaining 27 acres became a park operated by the National Park Service.)

In 1944 Dumbarton Oaks was the site for internationally attended meetings that formulated the basic principles of the United Nations. Today both the gardens and the museum (a treasure in itself, with noted Byzantine, Pre-Columbian, and European art collections and rare books), are open to the public.

At the garden entrance you will be given a carefully prepared and descriptive self-guiding walking tour, which identifies 18 stops of particular interest. You will want to discover and savor each garden room, walkway, and vista at your own pace, lingering at the remarkable views and marveling at the cascades of tumbling forsythia, the romantic wisteria arbors, the graceful courtyards and formal rows of trees and winding steps, the glorious plantings—more than we can describe here.

Some highlights: the Orangerie, a winter garden featuring a climbing fig from the nineteenth century and clusters of potted plants; the Green Garden, affording magnificent views of formal gardens just below; the Beech Terrace, the setting of one of the grandest American beeches we have ever seen, its roots covered with flowering bulbs; the Urn Terrace, with its beautiful curved pebble mosaic designs; the Rose Garden, a favorite of the Blisses, with its 1,000 plants in geometric beds; the Fountain Terrace, its enchanting classical cupid fountains and grassy lawn bordered with colorful bulbs and perennials; Melisande's Allée and Lover's Lane pool, site of the Roman-style amphitheater; the glorious English-style Herbaceous Border and vegetable garden, a feast of color combinations in true Jekyllian tradition; the Ellipse, a group of formally clipped ironwood trees (squared off in the French manner) around a small pool with iris; and the magnificent Pebble Garden, an enclosed parterre featuring pebble mosaics in intricate designs and shapes similar to the raised beds of ground cover next to them. The North Vista, a succession of four graceful grass terraces, connected with very gradual brick and grass steps, leads back to the mansion. On your walk you will have gone up and down the contoured slope, on carefully designed (and beautifully kept) pathways of stone, brick, and grass.

At the end of her long career, Beatrix Farrand stated that Dumbarton Oaks was outstanding among her many gardens, "the best and most deeply felt of a 50-year career." You will come away feeling that you have experienced a rare aesthetic and horticultural treat.

INFORMATION
Dumbarton Oaks is located at 1703 32nd Street, N.W., in the heart of Georgetown. Telephone: (202) 339-6400. The grounds are open from April through October, 2 P.M. to 6 P.M. daily (except Monday), and from November through March, 2 P.M. to 5 P.M.. The museum (entered around the corner from the garden entrance) is open 2 P.M. to 5 P.M. daily, except Monday; closed for major holidays. Entrance fee.

DIRECTIONS
In Washington, D.C., make your way to Wisconsin Avenue in Georgetown; if you are coming from M Street in the center of Washington, turn right onto Wisconsin, and again right on R Street. The garden entrance is on the corner of R and 31st Streets. If you are arriving in Washington from the north, take Wisconsin Avenue and turn left on R Street, following the directions above.

Kenilworth Aquatic Gardens

Peacefully set amid 44 acres of tidal marsh of the Anacostia River, but just a stone's throw from urban bustle, these 12-acre gardens provide a wonderfully naturalistic ambiance in which to view aquatic plants. Maintained by the U.S. Department of the Interior, the specialty gardens feature dozens of ponds filled to capacity with water lilies and lotuses (especially spectacular in June, July and August) as well as cattails, iris, water primrose, and hyacinths. Grassy (and sometimes muddy) paths circle the ponds, where you might also see turtles, snakes, frogs, migratory waterfowl, and other birds. With walking guide in hand (available at the entrance), you can identify each site.

This national park was once the private waterside garden of Civil War veteran, Walter Shaw, who decided to plant water lilies to remind him of his native Maine. From a few specimens the gardens grew and grew, as his daughter Helen traveled around the world in search of more exotic varieties. Helen became proprietor in 1921; she continued to oversee the gardens until her death in 1957. When the property was threatened by a dredging plan along the river, it was sold to the government for preservation. In the last decades the Kenilworth Aquatic Gardens have been dedicated to the propagation of water plants—both native and exotic—and to the preservation of the last natural tidal marsh in Washington.

When you see these dazzling blossoms, you will find it hard to believe that it all began when three seeds from an ancient lake bed were brought here and germinated!

INFORMATION:
Kenilworth Aquatic Gardens are located at 1900 Anacostia Drive, SE. Telephone: (202) 426-6905. The Gardens are open from 8 A.M. to 4 P.M. year-round. Water blossoms are best seen in mornings; the best times of year to visit are in July (for lotus blossoms) and August (for tropical water lilies). Tours are available. Free.

DIRECTIONS:
From the Capital Beltway (I-495) take I-95 toward the city. Take I-295 (Kenilworth Avenue), turn right and follow the signs to the gardens.

United States National Arboretum

The United States National Arboretum is much more than a collection of trees. Here, amid 444 acres of rolling parkland, are magnificent specialty gardens, many of which are among the best of their kind in the country. The mission of this vast facility—the only federally funded arboretum in the United States—is "to conduct research, provide education, conserve and display trees, shrubs, and other plants to enhance the environment." It includes some 37 sites that can be visited (preferably traveling from one to the next by car, given the distances), all carefully labeled and identified. You will drive (or walk, if you choose) in a landscape of remarkable trees, ponds, and vistas, seeing important collections of Asian plantings (including dazzling bonsai displays), dwarf conifers, azaleas, hollies, crabtrees, wildflowers, woodland plants, and some spectacular formal gardens.

This is an enormous place; before you start out, pick up a map (at the administration center and information/gift shop) numbered according to their suggested route. The administration center itself contains a huge herbarium with more than 600,000 pressed varieties from all over the world. Surrounding the glass and concrete building are elegant rectangular pools with fountains and statues and brightly colored Japanese carp (some 300 strong!) and aquatic plants—lotus, water lilies, bog plants—some floating, others standing upright. A small sign points to the National Bonsai and Penjing

Collections and National Herb Garden, without doubt among the most remarkable displays in the Arboretum.

The bonsai compound contains the largest and most complete bonsai collection in North America. Here, amid shaded stone and gravel walkways, moon gates, and enchanting little interior gardens—our favorite was the Japanese stroll garden with its carefully placed stones, gently trickling water, and delicate plantings—are the fine exhibits, housed in various pavilions and greenhouses. The bonsai on display in the airy Japanese pavilion include some 53 that were presented as a bicentennial gift to the American people. These rare and precious treasures, representing one of Japan's most revered art forms, can reach a venerable old age—one is apparently already more than 360 years old! The colors and textures of these great trees in miniature vary—some feathery and light, others dense and somber.

The Chinese pavilion displays its Penjing collection, which features plants that have been dwarfed using a different technique from the bonsai; here, too, are Chinese artifacts, such as large watering jars and stone lanterns, as well as the craggy symbolic rocks and tiny arched bridges and stone paths traditionally found in Chinese gardens.

Directly across the street from the bonsai collection is the wonderful 2.5-acre National Herb Garden, the largest designed herb garden in the world. You enter through a walkway of fragrant boxwood; once inside you will want to linger in this carefully ordered world of clipped hedges, graceful trellises, fountains, and plantings in intricate patterns. Beyond is a grand panorama reminiscent of an English romantic landscape, with a broad expanse of meadow framing a group of great columns soaring in the distance. Known as the National Capitol Columns, these can also be seen up close (check your map). The columns, originally part of the east central portico of the U.S. Capitol, were salvaged and stored when the building was renovated after the Civil War; in the 1980s they were placed in the Arboretum under the personal supervision of the noted landscape designer Russell Page, who added a fountain, water stair, and reflecting pool to enhance them.

The Herb Garden is made up of three separate gardens: the Knot Garden, Historic Rose Garden, and the oval specialty gardens. The elegant Knot Garden is a formal arrangement of dwarf evergreens in interlocking designs surrounding a circular brick terrace and fountain; on each side are arbors covered with clematis and grapevines. The Rose Garden contains specimens of historic interest, many quite rare and of ancient origins; they come from various parts of the world and are all identified. This garden is a paradise for rose fanciers!

The tiny specialty gardens are all thematic and herbal. Contained within a 1-acre grassy oval, they include a garden dedicated to plants listed by the ancient Greeks; a dye garden planted with specimens used in the dyeing of fabric; an early American garden in the colonial tradition; an American Indian garden with herbs used by Native Americans for beverages and medicines and crafts; a medicinal garden; a culinary garden; a wildbird garden; an industrial garden containing plants of economic value, such as rubber, rice, flax, and hops; a fragrance garden; an Oriental garden; and a beverage garden.

There are many other garden sites to enjoy in the Arboretum, perhaps too many for one visit. If you have limited time, we especially recommend Fern Valley and the Gotelli Dwarf and Slow-Growing Conifer Collection.

The first is a naturalistic wonder in a valley of deep woods, tall evergreens, century-old beeches, oaks, and tulips, a gentle stream, and meadow garden. From the meandering, hilly path you see thousands of native plants: ferns, wild ginger, and flowering shrubs, among others. The habitat is largely maintained by an enthusiastic group of volunteers (in fact, throughout the Arboretum we saw a number of volunteers working alongside the staff). Fern Valley is a lovely place for a quiet walk.

The Gotelli Dwarf and Slow-Growing Conifer Collection is a rare experience, considered one of the finest such gardens in the world. It began when Gotelli, a building contractor whose hobby was conifers, donated his impressive international collection of some 1,500 specimens. Magnificent varieties of fir, cedar, juniper, pine, hemlock, spruce, and other specimens are set on 5 hillside acres with views of downtown Washington in the distance. Here is a fascinating assortment of plants in different shapes, textures, and sizes set in well tended, rounded gravel beds, separated by grassy pathways. Surrounding them are ornamental grasses and bulbs, all carefully identified.

There is something of interest year-round at the Arboretum, and this is one place you will doubtless want to return to, whether to study plants and their environment, find inspiration for a specific garden you are contemplating, or simply to enjoy the beauty of the gardens.

INFORMATION
The United States National Arboretum is located at 3501 New York Avenue, in the northeast section of Washington D.C. Telephone: (202) 245-2726. It is open daily, year-round except Christmas, from 8 A.M. to 5 P.M. on weekdays and 10 A.M. to 5 P.M. on weekends (check hours of the bonsai collection). Free.

DIRECTIONS
Take New York Avenue from the center of the city northeast to Blandensburg Road and follow signs.

And in Addition...

Franciscan Monastery Gardens
1400 Quincy Street, N.E. Telephone: (202) 526-6800.
In a secluded hilltop setting within some 45 wooded acres, these serene gardens embellish the impressive and grand Franciscan Monastery. The 15 acres of well-tended gardens are in two parts: next to the church and cloister are formal flower gardens, and below, amid a naturalistic setting native shrubs, flowers, trees, and boulders are evocative recreations of famous religious shrines from the Holy Land.

The commanding yellow brick main church, Rosary Portico, and cloister—all with graceful, rounded arches in an architectural style reminiscent of the Spanish Colonial—date from 1899, but it was not until 1920 that the landscaped gardens were open to the public. Beautiful rose parterres (including some 2,000 plants) ornament the cloister, along with perennial borders, a small Asian garden near the chapel, and a collection of religious statues (including St. Francis, of course!) framed by geraniums and other blossoms. From these enclosed formal gardens you take a somewhat steep, shaded path that winds around to the quiet valley below. Along the way, in the cool of the deep woods, you'll find the Stations of the Cross enhanced by tall evergreens, magnolias, ferns, ivy, and masses of azaleas and rhododendron. (In spring profusions of blooming bulbs and dogwood add a touch of color.) The path leads to faithful replicas of such spiritual sites as the Grotto of Lourdes, the Grotto of

Gethsemane, and the Tomb of Mary, with imposing rock formations and trickling fountains adding to their mysterious ambiance. From a pretty little brick shrine to St. Anne at the bottom of the hill you can enjoy a panorama of meadows with weeping willows, cedars, and magnolias—hardly what you would expect within an urban setting. You will find a visit to these gardens a peaceful and reflective experience. Hourly tours (from 9 A.M. to 4 P.M. daily) of the church and catacombs are available; you can walk through the gardens on your own. The grounds are open 8 A.M. to dusk, year-round.

Gardens of the Washington National Cathedral
Massachusetts and Wisconsin Avenues, N.W. Telephone: (202) 537-6200.

Any visitor to the nation's capital won't want to miss the imposing National Cathedral—a true Washington landmark—and its famous, historic gardens. Consistent with the fourteenth-century-style Gothic cathedral (started in the early 1900s and not completed until 1990), the gardens—designed under the guidance of none less than Frederick Law Olmsted, Jr., and Beatrix Jones Farrand, among others—were to contain "plants of historical interest, plants of the Bible and Christian legends, and native plants." The formal and informal enclosed gardens are a living museum of biblical and medieval European gardening history.

Before embarking on your gardenwalk, pick up the excellent, descriptive self-guided tour available at the Herb Cottage (also a visitor center). You will be surprised to discover how much more complex these intimate gardens actually are than you might think at first glance. Combining unusual architectural features, such as authentic medieval archways, bas reliefs, gates, sculpture with perennial borders, herbaceous plantings in intricate patterns, a rose garden, and flowering shrubs and trees of particular significance (such as cedars and figs), they are a study in symbolism. Among the most evocative is the Bishop's Garden, a medieval garden made up of several tiny parts; it was created by Olmsted for the bishop's private use. You'll find a Yew Walk (symbolizing immortality), a lower perennial border, a "Hortulus" (small geometric raised beds planted with herbs used in Charlemagne's time), a rose garden (with fragrant floribundas), an herb bed of aromatic and culinary varieties, an old English sundial, a small pool in the shape of a primitive cross, and a stone wall with fifteenth-century bas reliefs and martyrs and saints. Each of these areas invites careful scrutiny. You walk from one garden "room" to the next, along small brick pathways edged with boxwood, its delicate scent permeating the air.

Other garden sites to visit include the Herb Cottage Garden, the woodland pathway bordered with native wildflowers, and the Cloister Garden, featuring a dramatic contemporary bronze fountain. To the west of the cathedral, next to the West Portal Court entrance, is a grove of stately trees, lawns, plantings, walkways, and benches in a parklike setting typical of Olmsted's landscapes. Throughout the grounds are dogwood, hollies, camellias, azaleas, and other flowering shrubs. There is a greenhouse specializing in herbs, shade perennials, cacti, and seasonal annuals; many plants are for sale.

Before leaving, be sure to see the interior of the majestic cathedral. Built of Indiana limestone, it is the sixth largest Gothic construction in the world. Guided tours are offered, but you can also wander about on your own. The gardens are open daylight hours, year-round; the Herb Cottage is open 9:30 A.M. to 5:00 P.M. Monday through Saturday and 10 A.M. to 5 P.M. on Sunday.

Hillwood Museum

4155 Linnean Avenue, N.W.Telephone: (202) 686-8500.

This beautifully landscaped site surrounded by deep woods features the elegant mansion and grounds of the noted heiress Marjorie Merriweather Post. The Georgian-style house (1920s), which contains Mrs. Post's impressive collection of eighteenth- and nineteenth-century French and Russian fine and decorative arts, became a public museum in 1977, shortly after her death. One glance at the mansion and meticulously groomed gardens—both formal and informal—will tell you that Mrs. Post knew how to live. Among the garden pleasures are an elegant and formal French parterre with a central pool and fountains; an enchanting rose garden (designed in consultation with landscape architect Perry Wheeler, who also contributed to the White House Rose Garden); a Japanese garden with stream, rocks, pools, and picturesque arched bridges; and a 1930s greenhouse with an important orchid collection. More naturalistic and native plantings include azaleas, rhododendron, dogwood, boxwood, and clusters of trees—some very tall and stately. You can walk around the grounds on your own, though reservations are required for the two-hour house tour. Open Tuesday through Saturday, 11 A.M. to 3 P.M. (closed in February).

United States Botanic Garden

245 First Street SW. Telephone: (202) 225-8333.
The United States Botanic Garden describes itself as a "living museum." It is, in fact, surrounded by the capital's world-famous museums up and down the Mall. But it hardly seems like a museum when you visit it, because you are surrounded by living things; riotous color, delicate shapes, exotic blooms.

The present conservatory—rather charmingly old-fashioned—was built in 1933 and is now undergoing renovation. When last we visited there was an extraordinary exhibition of orchids, as well as a Desert Garden, and splendid fossils. The updated conservatory promises brand new displays. In addition, there are outdoor plantings across Independence Avenue from the Conservatory in Frederic Auguste Bartholdi Park. Named for the famous sculptor, whose historic foundation is the centerpiece, the park features seasonal displays. Bartholdi Park is open daily year-round; since the conservatory is undergoing renovation, please call before visiting. Free.

Old Stone House Garden in Georgetown

3051 M Street N.W. (between 30th and 31st streets) Telephone: (202) 426-6851
Behind this charming 1764 fieldstone house, Washington's only surviving pre-Revolutionary building, is a very pretty, old-fashioned garden. The terraced property is graced with fruit trees, perennial flower beds in great masses, wild roses, curving lawns, and brick stone paths. You can visit the garden (which is partly visible from the road) and the house, featuring colonial furnishings and artifacts, on your own; costumed guides are on hand to answer questions. Open Wednesday-Sunday, 8-4:30.

garden. The terraced property is graced with fruit trees, perennial flower beds in great masses, wild roses, curving lawns, and brick stone paths. You can visit the garden (which is partly visible from the road) and the house, featuring colonial furnishings and artifacts, on your own; costumed guides are on hand to answer questions. Open Wednesday-Sunday, 8-4:30.

RECOMMENDED GARDENS IN OTHER STATES THROUGHOUT THE COUNTRY*

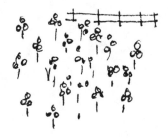

*This is a selected listing and is not all-inclusive.

ALABAMA

Birmingham: Birmingham Botanical Gardens
2612 Lane Park Road. Telephone: (205) 879-1227.
This 67.5-acre park boasts the largest conservatory in the Southeast. In addition you'll find a Japanese Garden, Touch and See Trail, Fern Glade, and a fine assortment of roses, daylilies, iris, and wildflowers. Open daily, sunrise to sunset.

Birmingham: Birmingham Museum of Art Gardens
Oscar Wells Memorial Building, 2000 8th Avenue North. Telephone: (205) 254-2565.
This city oasis offers a sculptured fountain, reflecting pool, and many flowering plants and fruit trees, all set amid large oak trees. Open daily (except Mondays): Tuesdays, Wednesdays, Fridays, and Saturdays from 10 A.M. to 5 P.M.; Thursdays from 10 A.M. to 9 P.M.; and Sundays from 2 P.M.to 6 P.M.

Gadsden: Noccalula Falls Park
1500 Noccalula Road. Telephone: (205) 543-7412.
These lovely 65 acres include a spectacular waterfall, thousands of azaleas, giant evergreens, a picturesque covered bridge, flower beds, and a fine botanical garden. Open daily 8 A.M. to sunset. Fee.

Theodore: Bellingrath Gardens
County Route 59. Telephone: (205) 973-2217.
These 65 acres of formal estate gardens have spectacular displays of camellias, azaleas, roses, and other native and exotic plants that are planted to bloom in each month of the year. There is also a mansion filled with rare porcelains and antiques. Open daily, year-round. Fee.

Wetumpka: Jasmine Hill Gardens
Jasmine Hill Road. Telephone: (205) 263-1440.
This 17-acre garden is a setting for classical Greek and Roman statuary, including an exact copy of the ruins of the Temple of Hera in Olympia. There are pools and an amphitheater set amid cherry trees, azaleas, and long-leaf pine. Each sculpture is a focal point in its own setting, such as the goddess head that is reflected in the rectangular lily pond or the avenues of flowering cherries that frame mythical lions. Open March to November, Tuesdays through Saturdays, 9 A.M. to 5 P.M. Fee.

ARIZONA

Phoenix: Desert Botanical Garden

6400 East McDowell Road. Telephone: (602) 947-2800.
More than 1,500 cacti and 10,000 other plants from deserts and arid regions all over the world are featured here in a natural desert setting. Blooming season is late March through May. Open daily, year-round. Fee.

Tucson Area: San Xavier Del Bac Mission

Mission Road, 9 miles southwest of Tucson. Telephone: (602) 294-2628.
This walled mission garden is known as the "White Dove of the Desert." It features native desert plants including mesquite and cholla, as well as figs, pomegranates, almonds, and fragrant herbs. Open year-round. Fee.

ARKANSAS

Little Rock Area: Daffodils on Wye Mountain

Route 113, north of SR 10, at the west end of Lake Maumelle.
Daffodils are the springtime specialty of this hillside garden—16 acres of them. Visit in early spring.

CALIFORNIA

Fresno: Forestiere Underground Gardens

5021 W. Shaw Avenue. Telephone: (209) 271-0734.
This is one of the more unusual garden complexes in the country. A Sicilian immigrant named Baldasare Forestiere came to California at the turn of the century and created a lush Mediterranean setting around his home. During a period of over 40 years he built sunken gardens, patios, grottos, and stone archways, all linked by paths and filled with an assortment of trees, shrubs and flowers. These 5 acres are well worth a visit. Open late December to November. Fee.

La Canada: Descanso Gardens

1418 Descanso Drive (Los Angeles). Telephone: (213) 790-5571.
These picturesque gardens, whose name means "where I rest," provide a peaceful and color-laden oasis within the still growing Los

Angeles area. Many individual gardens featuring camellias, azaleas, rhododendrons, cactus, and eucalyptus grace its paths, but the grand displays in the famous "History of the Rose Garden" draw the most attention. In this superb garden the history of the rose is traced, from the pre-Christian era to the present. And don't miss the Japanese Garden with its tranquil pool and elegant plantings; on most days tea is served under the Japanese lanterns of its tea house. Open year-round except holidays. Fee.

Malibu: J. Paul Getty Museum and Gardens
17985 Pacific Coast Highway. Telephone: (213) 454-6541.
Inspired by the ancient Roman Villa dei Papiri in Herculaneum, the building and grounds of this important museum are the result of archeological research. The four classical gardens include statuary, mosaics, a tranquillity garden, pomegranate trees, and terraced olive groves. Advance parking reservations are required. Open Tuesday through Saturday.

Montecito: Lotusland
Sycamore Canyon Road (between Ashley and Cold Springs). Telephone: (805) 969-9990.
This bizarre, primeval landscape of overgrown and profuse rare tropical plants was the creation of an eccentric would-be opera singer who turned to gardening when all else failed. Ganna Walska (her story is as weird as the garden itself) bought Lotusland—an isolated, sun-baked spot—in 1941, and after both her sixth marriage and operatic aspirations ended, dedicated herself to making it into the truly off-beat prehistoric-looking plant collection it is. Creeping and crawling succulents of all sorts—euphorbias, golden barrel cacti, Peruvian apples, cycads—and other exotics were planted in great masses and unlikely configurations on what had been a sparse landscape. This grand opus took some 43 years (Mme. Walska died in 1984 at age 97), and the results are pure horticultural folly. If you have a taste for the unusual, you won't want to miss this site!

Lotusland is open to the public from mid-February to mid-November. Reservations are necessary.

Monterey: Casa Amesti
By appointment only. Write to the Monterey History of Art Association, Monterey, California 93940.
Formal Italian-style gardens within high adobe walls were elegantly

laid out by Frances Elkins, well-known interior designer, and her architect brother, David Adler, in about 1918. The nineteenth-century house is also open for visitors.

Oakland: El Cerrito
944 Arlington Avenue, north of Berkeley.
Here is an unusual and intriguing set of gardens: each is designed in the patterns of Persian rugs and American patchwork quilts. These displays are the work of an Indian horticulturist who sketches the patterns of rugs and quilts and then designs and plants the gardens. Open daily, including Christmas, when he designs a Nativity scene in flowers.

Oroville: Chinese Memorial Temple
1500 Broderick Street (North Central Region). Telephone: (916) 533-1496.
This Chinese courtyard garden features plants of Chinese origin in a tranquil environment. Open January 15 through November. Fee.

San Diego: Balboa Park
Laurel Street and Sixth Avenue.
These gardens were the site of an international exposition in 1915. The 1,800 acres feature Spanish-Moorish plantings to match the buildings and formal gardens that date to 1868, including English, rose, and desert gardens, as well as a botanical garden that houses 500 species of tropical and subtropical plants and ferns. Open all year, closed Fridays.

San Francisco: Strybing Arboretum
9th Avenue and Lincoln Way (Golden Gate Park). Telephone: (415) 661-1316.
This wonderful arboretum features collections from around the world, as well as sections devoted to native plantings. In addition, you'll find a Japanese tea garden, along with a delightful Victorian conservatory of tropical plants. Open daily.

San Marino: Huntington Botanical Gardens
1151 Oxford Street (near Pasadena). Telephone: (818) 449-3901.
This is truly a magnificent series of gardens, mansion, art gallery, and library. You will want to spend a great deal of time exploring its various parts. The gardens consist of plantings and settings from all over the world. Arguably the most famous desert gardens in the

nation, the Huntington boasts magnificent cacti and other desert plants, but there are also a notable Japanese garden, a Shakespeare garden, formal gardens with statuary, and virtually every other type of garden you can imagine. Open year-round except October and except Mondays and holidays. Fee.

San Simeon: Hearst San Simeon State Historical Monument
Off Highway 1, San Simeon. Telephone: (805) 927-4621.
This grand Moorish-style castle with extensive gardens was created by publishing tycoon William Randolph Hearst in the late 1920s. Of the 85 acres that make up the estate, 5 are formal gardens with terraces, pools, fountains, flowering plants, a rose garden, and many specimen trees. Guided tours only; reservations recommended. Open daily. Fee.

Santa Barbara: Santa Barbara Botanic Garden
1212 Mission Canyon Road. Telephone: (805) 682-4726.
Here in a splendid mountain setting are 70 acres and 5 miles of trails for hiking, as well as a site called the Old Mission Dam dating to 1806. The garden areas feature a variety of California's native habitats and vegetation, including desert plants and meadow flowers, chaparral plants, ferns, redwoods, and other indigenous trees. Open daily.

Saratoga: Villa Montalvo Arboretum
15400 Montalvo Road (near San Jose). Telephone: (408) 867-3421.
This 175-acre landscaped setting includes formal gardens, walking trails and fountains. The villa houses a center for fine arts. Open year-round, Tuesdays through Sundays.

Woodside: Filoli Gardens
Canada Road (San Francisco area). Telephone: (415) 366-4640 or 364-2880.
Any garden enthusiast visiting the San Francisco area won't want to miss Filoli Gardens. Located 30 miles south of the city, on the eastern slopes of the Coast Range, the elegant estate includes a historic mansion and 16 acres of formal gardens, picturesquely framed by the extensive wild areas beyond.

The gardens are in the Italian and French style, with parterres, terraces, pools, and lawns. There is a series of garden "rooms"—a rose garden, sunken garden, walled garden, cutting garden, and a magnificent knot garden with interwoven plantings in shades of lavender and plum. A grand yew allée with espaliered apple and pear trees leads to the "High Place," a semicircle of columns decorated with wisteria. This idyllic spot affords fine views of the gardens, house, and fields below.

Filoli was built in the early part of the century for Mr. and Mrs. William Bowers Bourn II, prominent San Franciscans. Their landscape architect, Bruce Porter, designed the gardens to complement the natural site. He oversaw the transplanting of more than 200 Irish yews from the Bourns' summer estate. The gardens were further developed by the Roth family, who bought the property in 1937. The rich variety of camellias, rhododendrons, magnolias, and roses were planted by Mrs. Roth, a horticulturist in her own right. (The formal gardens have been named in her honor.)

Reservations are recommended for house and garden tours, although some tickets are available at the site. You can also purchase tickets to visit the gardens on your own. Filoli Gardens are open Tuesday through Saturday, 10 A.M. to 1 P.M.; closed mid-November to mid-February. Fee.

COLORADO

Colorado Springs: Garden of the Gods Park
30th Street and Gateway Road.
For something different, try this spectacular park (donated by a railroad magnate), with its magnificent red sandstone formations and array of wildflowers.

Colorado Springs: Horticulture Art Society Garden
980 North Glen Avenue. Telephone: (719) 475-0250.
If you're curious about what grows best in the semiarid Colorado climate, visit (preferably in summer or early fall) this demonstration garden featuring trees, shrubs, flowers, and vegetables. Included, too, is a fragrance garden for the blind. Open daily, from sunrise to sunset.

Denver: Denver Botanic Garden
909 York Street. Telephone: (303) 575-2547.
This botanic garden is actually two—and at two separate sites: 50 acres are in Denver and 150 more on Mount Goliath, 50 miles away.

Featured displays in Denver include a water garden, herb garden, and conservatories of native and tropical plants and cacti; on the mountain are displays of alpine plants. Call for hours.

Denver: Harper Memorial Garden
University of Denver, University Park Campus.
This lovely park, with its flowers, trees, shrubs, ponds, and waterfalls, serves the university community and others seeking a pleasing natural environment. Open daily.

Pueblo: Mineral Palace Park
19th and Santa Fe.
Here are formal gardens, including a surprisingly large rose garden surrounded by annual beds, two greenhouses, an English rock garden, and even a small arboretum. Open daily, year-round.

FLORIDA

Coral Gables: Fairchild Tropical Garden
10901 Old Cutler Road. Telephone: (305) 667-1651.
A major tropical garden, this 83-acre botanical garden is noted for its palm collection and tropical flowering trees. Open year-round except Christmas. Fee.

Cypress Gardens: Florida Cypress Gardens
SR 540 (2 miles southwest of Winter Haven). Telephone: (813) 324-2111.
Among the most famous nature sites in the country (and among the most commercial, too) are these spectacular gardens boasting one of the world's most comprehensive displays of tropical and subtropical plants growing naturally. In addition to the well-known water ski show on Lake Eloise, guided tours in canals, and assorted live entertainment, you can enjoy a delightful rose garden, an aviary, and many educational exhibits—not to mention lots of "people watching." Open daily, sunrise to sunset. Fee.

Delray Beach: Morikami Park
4000 Morikami Park Road. Telephone: (305) 499-0631.
For a change of pace from Florida's tropical gardens, you will enjoy this Japanese museum and its gardens. Here you can learn about aspects of Japanese culture through permanent and changing

exhibits, including, of course, a bonsai collection. There are a 1-mile self-guided nature trail and picnic sites. Open daily 10 A.M. to 5 P.M., except Mondays and holidays.

Fort Myers: Edison Winter Home and Botanical Gardens

2350 McGregor Boulevard. Telephone: (813) 334-3614.

This historic riverfront estate—where Thomas A. Edison spent many a winter—includes his house, now a museum filled with memorabilia and inventions, as well as a 14-acre botanical garden. Here you can walk amid an impressive array of trees—many planted by the inventor himself—and see what is claimed to be the largest banyan tree in the country. Open Monday through Saturday, 9 A.M. to 4 P.M.; Sunday, 12:30 P.M. to 4:30 P.M. Fee.

Harbor Island: Inland Waterway Side of Juniper Island

A true island garden, this picturesque spot is reached by a Japanese bridge and features South Florida plants. Open daily, year-round.

Homestead: Coral Castle

28655 South Dixie Highway. Telephone: (305) 248-6344.

This fascinating sculpture/architecture site, situated within a walled compound, conjures up visions of an ancient Druid realm. Immense gates (one weighing 9 tons!) reminiscent of Stonehenge open into a world created in the 1920s entirely by Edward Leedskalnin, a Latvian emigré. Built as a reclusive home for himself and a longed-for bride, it includes a two-story tower and curious outdoor garden rooms, all chiseled from coral rock. The rooms contain handmade stone furniture—beds, tables, love seats, a couch, and bathtub—as well as bold sculptures shaped like obelisks, moons, and stars.

The fiercely independent and eccentric Leedskalnin conceived of this 10-acre site as his castle. Wishing to be self-sufficient of the outside world, he planted vegetables and fruit trees, flowering vines, shrubs, and flowers. These gardens, interspersed among the sculptures, feature species native to South Florida, as well as subtropical exotics.

Surprisingly, Leedskalnin welcomed occasional visitors to his private world. A bell is still located next to the front gate, instructing you to ring twice—no more, no less—as it did during his lifetime. Coral Castle is open daily, from 9 A.M. to 6 P.M.

Jacksonville: Cummer Gallery of Art
829 Riverside Drive. Telephone: (904) 356-6857.
Surrounding this fine museum (featuring ancient to twentieth-century art) are formal gardens replicating the Villa Gambreraia garden in Italy. These 2.5 acres are picturesquely set on the banks of the St. John's River. Open daily (except Monday).

Lake Wales: Bok Tower Gardens
U.S. 27A north. Telephone: (813) 676-1408.
Surrounding an impressive 53-bell carillon tower located at Florida's highest point is a naturalistic landscape designed by the eminent Frederick Law Olmsted, Jr. Included are collections of azaleas, camellias, live oaks, and magnolias. Open daily, 8:00 A.M. to 5:30 P.M. Fee only for cars.

Miami: Fairchild Tropical Garden
Old Cutler Road. Telephone: (305) 667-1651.
For tropical plant fanciers this vast garden is not be missed. The largest tropical botanic garden in the continental United States, it includes many varieties of palms, orchids, ferns, and cycads.

Miami Area: Villa Vizcaya Museum and Gardens
3251 South Miami Avenue. Telephone: (305) 579-2708.
The spectacular gardens of this palatial mansion are fan-shaped, based on Italian Renaissance designs with historical French influences. Among the many elements are grottos, fountains, sculpture, water displays, parterres, and numerous glorious other features. Open daily, year-round, except Christmas. Fee.

Orlando: Harry P. Leu Gardens
1730 North Forest Avenue. Telephone: (305) 894-6021.
If you need a respite from the nearby Disney hoopla, visit these 47 lakeside acres. Included in the gardens are unusual plants from all parts of the world, a conservatory, and a rich collection of orchids. Fee.

Ormond Beach: Ormond War Memorial Art Galleries and Gardens
78 East Granada Avenue. Telephone: (407) 246-2620.
This 4-acre garden surrounding a contemporary art gallery has a

nice collection of flowering trees, azaleas, magnolia, and daylilies. Streams with tropical water plants and feathery native bamboos also grace the grounds. Open daily in the afternoons except Wednesdays, closed during September.

Palm Beach: Royal Palm Way

Royal Palm Way. Telephone: (305) 655-7226.
This tropical garden is noted for its Chinese Courtyard Garden, which is decorated with ancient Chinese sculptures. The site houses a library and art gallery as well. Open year-round.

Palm Beach Area: Cluett Memorial Garden

Church of Bethesda-by-the-Sea, South County Road and Baron Avenue. Telephone: (305) 655-4554.
To reach this surprisingly large formal tropical garden you must go through a 1925 Gothic church. Privately maintained, it features the exotic plantings familiar in this part of the state.

St. Petersburg: Florida's Sunken Gardens

1825 Fourth Street North. Telephone: (813) 896-3186.
Any exotic plant aficionado won't want to miss the many tropical plants found here, which include 50,000 flowers set in each year and a rare collection of orchids—more than 1000 examples. Also included is an aviary with tropical birds and a jungle section devoted to other animals. Open daily, from 9 A.M. to sunset. Fee.

Sarasota: Marie Selby Botanical Garden

800 South Palm Avenue. Telephone: (813) 366-5730.
In this luxuriant garden you'll find a variety of plants from the tropical rain forest, including ferns and orchids. Open year-round except Christmas.

Sarasota: Sarasota Jungle Gardens

3701 Bayshore Road. Telephone: (813) 855-5305.
To reach these formal gardens you walk on winding brick trails through an untamed landscape. Once there you can enjoy thousands of different plants—and birds (both wild and tame). Birdwatchers won't be disappointed! Open daily 9 A.M. to 5 P.M. Fee.

Tallahassee: Maclay State Gardens

3540 Thomasville Road. Telephone: (904) 487-4115.
Luxuriant camellias and azaleas (among the finest collections in the

South) proliferate in these 308 acres of flowering shrubs and beds. Once a private estate, the gardens include nature trails. Open daily, January to April, from 8 A.M. to sunset. Fee.

Tampa: Busch Gardens, The Dark Continent
3000 Busch Boulevard. Telephone: (813) 977-6606.
If you like bustling environments with things to do, see, and buy, then don't miss these famous gardens. Included in the 300-acre park are the requisite flowers, tropical trees, and shrubs, as well as a good-sized zoo, bird and dolphin shows, skyride, monorail, and brewery tour. Open daily year-round. Fee.

Winter Haven: Slocum Water Gardens
1101 Cypress Gardens Road. Telephone: (813) 293-7151.
This delightful water garden includes ponds of water lilies, fountains, goldfish, and aquatic plants. Open year-round; closed Sundays and holidays.

GEORGIA

Adairsville: Barnsley Gardens
597 Barnsley Gardens Road. Telephone: (404) 773-7480.
These beguiling gardens in the rolling northwest Georgia mountains combine the romantic ruins of an Italianate villa with 30 acres of landscaped grounds and flower gardens.

Once the much vaster country estate of Godfrey Barnsley, an Englishman who came to Georgia in the nineteenth century to seek his fortune in cotton, it has had a long and rich history, one even tinged with tragedy. (It was the scene of a family murder in the 1930s). In 1841, Barnsley built this quite extravagant estate—which he called Woodlands—for his wife, Julia, and their growing family. An avid amateur botanist and gardener, it seems he based his landscape designs on the published manuals of Andrew Jackson Downing, the most renowned landscape architect of the time. With its many exotic plants from around the world, as well as native rhododendrons and azaleas (literally hundreds), Woodlands was a real showplace. So much so, in fact, that, during the Civil War, General McPherson and his troups were careful not to damage it.

Unfortunately, during the late nineteenth century, the property suffered from lack of care; on top of everything else, a vicious tornado left the manor house without a roof in 1906. The sad deterioration of Woodlands was reversed in the 1970s, when Prince Hubertus Fugger of Germany bought the estate. It has since undergone extensive restoration. The romantic ruins of the main house have been reclaimed from a jungle of wisteria vines and preserved, as have other historic structures on the property, and the once-fabled gardens are being brought back to life.

The haunted looking brick mansion is now the picturesque setting for a semioutdoor art gallery and museum documenting the intriguing—sometimes ghoulish—history of the site. (You can still see the bloody spot where the murder was committed.) You will want to walk around its arched passageways and explore it, as well as the surrounding gardens, fields, and woods.

Among Barnsley Garden's many attractions are a boxwood parterre with Renaissance-style fountain, a rose garden, broad lawns with herbaceous borders, rock and bog gardens and a fernery, a group of ponds surrounded by ornamental grasses and other plantings, a wildflower meadow; and a rhododendron hill. You are free to walk around on your own or take a specialized guided tour conducted by a horticulturist or historian. Open February through mid-December, Tuesday to Saturday, 10 A.M. to 6 P.M. and Sunday, noon to 6 P.M. Fee.

Athens: University of Georgia Botanical Garden

2450 South Milledge Avenue. Telephone: (404) 542-1244.
Located on 293 acres of woods, plains, and bluffs are horticultural display gardens and ecological habitats for scientific study. Check for educational programs of interest to gardeners. Open daily, from sunrise to sunset.

Atlanta: Atlanta Botanical Garden

1345 Piedmont Avenue. Telephone: (404) 876-5859.
A lavender wisteria vine covering a wood trellis graces the entrance of this delightful 30-acre urban oasis. Within lies a world of spectacular flowering trees and blossoms, from pink and white dogwood, to cherries, azalea, and crab apples. In spring you'll enjoy fine collections of tulips, hyacinths, pansies, iris, and many wildflowers. A rose garden adds elegance and charm, and is the setting for many weddings.

At one end of the garden is the imposing glass conservatory, one of its main attractions. Here you can wander through a desert environment with its many succulents to a veritable tropical jungle, complete with exotic plants and even parrots. Open Tuesday to Sunday, 9 A.M. to 7 P.M., April through October; 9 A.M. to 6 P.M., November through March.

Buena Vista: St. Eom's Land of Pasaquan
Seven miles north of Buena Vista on County Road 78, between Routes 41 and 137. Telephone: (912) 649-9444.
Situated on 4 acres in Marion County is The Land of Pasaquan, an intriguing and unlikely garden of temples, pagodas, totems, and undulating walls and plantings. The curious forms are decorated in brightly painted bas reliefs and friezes depicting haunting faces, body parts, flowers, astronomical signs, and religious and sexual motifs. This psychedelic world was created by Eddie Owens Martin, a cultist. Over the years, "St. EOM," as he called himself, had a series of visions which resulted in this work.

He began to transform his mother's traditional house and garden into an extraordinary environment. With the help of locals he constructed the sculpturelike structures, including the many curving walls of various heights that separate areas of the garden. A trip to Mexico in the late 1960s inspired him to paint everything in brilliant colors. His fascination with mythology, Hindu religion, sexuality, and the cosmos is evident in the recurring images you see throughout—stars, planets, prisms of light, Hindu deities, representations of the lost world of Atlantis, and symbols of fertility. After his death, St. EOM's private sanctuary was left to the Marion County Historical Society. The site is open on Saturday from 10 A.M. to 6 P.M.; Sunday, 1 P.M. to 5 P.M.; and on weekdays by appointment.

Columbus Area: Callaway Gardens
Pine Mountain. Telephone: (800) 241-0910.
These vast grounds include 2,500 acres of public gardens, as well as walking trails, lakes, and woodlands. Horticulture enthusiasts will enjoy the 700 varieties of azaleas that grace this extensive park, in addition to the 5 acres of greenhouses with year-round displays. Open year-round. Fee.

Columbus Area (Fort Valley): Massee Lane Camellia Gardens
State Road 49. Telephone: (912) 967-2358.
One of the finest collections of camellias in the country is found

here, the national headquarters of the American Camellia Society. The best time to visit is between January 15 and March 15, which is the height of the camellia season. Open daily.

Savannah: Forsyth Park
South of Gaston, between Whitaker and Drayton streets.

If you need to take a break from visiting the charming historic houses of Savannah, stop by the city's largest park (dating from 1851), with its magnificent central fountain. Here, too, is a fragrance garden for the blind (open by appointment).

Savannah: Owens–Thomas House and Garden
124 Abercorn Street. Telephone: (912) 233-9743.

This historical site is one of the best examples of English Regency style in America. The garden, designed circa 1820, is walled and charming, and is planted with fig and banana trees, in addition to flowers and grape vines. Open daily, except September. Fee.

HAWAII

Honolulu: Foster Botanic Garden
180 North Vineyard Boulevard. Telephone: (808) 538-7258.

In the heart of Honolulu's downtown you'll find 20 acres of rare tropical trees, orchids, and other garden pleasures. The famous "Prehistoric Glen," the recipient of various awards, should not be missed. Free guided tours or self-guiding brochures available. Open daily, 9 A.M. to 4 P.M.

Kauai: Pacific Tropical Botanical Garden
Lawai. Telephone: (808) 332-8131.

To visit this one-of-a-kind tropical botanical garden—chartered by Congress and devoted to research and education—you must take a guided tour or make special arrangements. Fee.

Oahu: Koko Crater Botanic Garden
Oahu Island. Telephone: (808) 538-7258.

Some 200 acres within the crater of a volcano are in the process of being developed as a dryland botanic garden featuring desert plants from around the world. This unusual setting will particularly interest serious botanists and horticulturists. For further information, contact Director, Foster Botanic Garden, 180 N. Vineyard Boulevard, Honolulu, Hawaii 96817.

IDAHO

Boise: Ann Morrison Memorial Park
South Capitol Boulevard.
In the midst of Idaho's capital you'll find these 153 formally landscaped acres. Don't miss the illuminated fountain. Open daily, dawn to dusk.

ILLINOIS

Belleville: National Shrine of Our Lady of the Snows
9500 West Illinois, Route 15.
These 200 acres of both small and large individual gardens are especially known for their reproductions of religious sites. As you wander around the extensive grounds you'll see the Lourdes Grotto, Annunciation Garden, Resurrection Garden, and Agony Garden, among others. No fee, but donations accepted.

Chicago: Garfield Park
300 N. Central Park Boulevard.
This large urban park contains 4 acres of conservatories (dating from the early 1900s), featuring mostly cacti and succulents and ferns. The 16 acres of surrounding park include an extraordinary formal garden, complete with many (at least 30) geometric flower beds with thousands of annuals. A large pool contains over 100 water lilies for your pleasure. Open daily.

Chicago: Grant Park
Congress Parkway.
With the impressive Chicago skyline as a backdrop, this park boasts an elegant rose garden in the style of Versailles, a fountain with two large pools graced by more roses, and many colorful flowery displays. Open daily.

Chicago: Lincoln Park
2400 N. Stockton Drive. Telephone: (312) 742-7736.
This park is another Chicago garden landmark. Included is "Grandmother's Garden" (dating from 1893), with its thousands upon thousands of annuals and perennials. The five conservatories on the grounds feature a Palm House, Fernery, Orchidarium, and Tropical House. Watch for special exhibits. Open daily, 9 A.M. to 5 P.M.

Chicago: Marquette Park Rose and Trail Gardens
3540 West 17th Street.
Here you'll find a colorful display of more than 4,000 roses (80 varieties), pleasant walkways, pool, and flowering shrubs and trees. One of the many flower beds is dedicated to topiary animals. Bring the children!

Danville: Dr. Fifthian's Herb Garden
116 North Gilbert Street. Telephone: (217) 442-2922.
This garden was designed by the Architect's Office of Colonial Williamsburg in the 1960s. Located on the grounds of the Vermilion County Museum, it's a sure delight for colonial history buffs as well as gardeners. The garden is free, although there is an entrance fee for the museum.

Evanston: Shakespeare Garden
Northwestern University, Sheridan Road.
The Shakespeare Garden on this pretty campus is planted with flowers and herbs mentioned in the plays and sonnets. Open daily, year-round.

Glencoe: Chicago Horticultural Society Botanic Garden
775 Dundee Road. Telephone: (847) 835-5440.
This most comprehensive—and large (300 acres)—botanic garden contains many demonstration gardens, greenhouses, nature trails, and other features. Among its many offerings is a Garden for the Disabled, which has won prestigious awards. Open Monday to Friday, 8:00 A.M. to 4:30 P.M.

Winnetka: Hadley School for the Blind
700 Elm Street. Telephone: (847) 446-8111.
A Discovery Garden features plants with unusual textures, fragrances, and shapes. There are special fountains to attract birds and provide sound as well. Open daily, by appointment.

INDIANA

Indianapolis: Holliday Park
6349 Spring Mill Road.
A long allée of trees and attractive seasonal flower gardens form the setting for a sculpture garden. Open daily.

Indianapolis: Indianapolis Museum of Art and Eli Lilly Botanical Garden
1200 West 38th Street. Telephone: (317) 923-1331.
This well-endowed museum complex includes several gardens as well as a 150-acre art park, complete with botanical garden and greenhouse of orchids. Closed Mondays.

Michigan City: International Friendship Garden
Pottawattomie Park. Telephone: (219) 874-3664
There are 65 different gardens here, representing different nations. Among them are a Persian Rose Garden, and Dutch, Polish, English, German, Italian and Indian gardens. Open daily, May through November. Fee.

New Harmony: New Harmony Historic Site, The Labyrinth
Telephone: (812) 682-3271.
A nineteenth-century settlement of Harmonists built a series of formal gardens as part of their historic community here. Among the gardens (replanted by the state of Indiana and moved slightly) is a maze of concentric circles made of privet hedge and flower borders. The original garden was planted between 1814 and 1824; the replanted maze is one of the best in the nation, covering 140 feet across.

IOWA

Cedar Rapids: Shakespeare Garden
Ellis Park. Telephone: (319) 398-5080.
This formal 1.4-acre English garden features many of the plantings mentioned in the plays of Shakespeare. A bust of the bard, by French artist Roubilac, graces the grounds. Open daily, May through September.

Des Moines: Des Moines Botanical Center
909 East River Drive. Telephone: (575) 283-4148.
A domed conservatory with a collection of plants from around the world is surrounded by formal flower beds and many acres of parkland. Here, through demonstration sites, you can appreciate the evolution of the Iowa landscape from forests to prairies.

Des Moines: Arie Den Boer Crab Apple Arboretum
408 Fleur Drive.
Located within a 150-acre city park, this arboretum features one of the largest collections of crab apple trees in the world. There are also many rare trees, a formal garden, and 180 varieties of hosta. Open daily.

KANSAS

Lucas: S. P. Dinsmoor's Garden of Eden
Corner of Second and Kansas streets. Telephone: (913) 525-6395.
Within the rolling grasslands of Kansas you'll find this curious and unlikely sculpture garden. Created in the early 1900s by Samuel Perry Dinsmoor, a Civil War veteran, it includes some 150 figures (both human and animal) and 30 trees, all made of concrete. The sculptures on one side of this rather overgrown 1/2-acre site narrate the Old Testament, from Adam and Eve to Cain and Abel; on the north side, separated by a painted concrete American flag, they represent contemporary American political life in cartoonlike form. (Apparently Dinsmoor took a dim view of the politics of his day.)

The figures are informally—but dramatically—placed around the garden. Many are perched atop cement "branches," sword and staff in hand. Dinsmoor wanted to make the figures of God and Satan particularly compelling: he placed electric lights within them, so that their blazing eyes would mesmerize the viewer. The sculptures are rough-looking, but contain a surprising variety of facial expression.

Considered a "mecca for tourists" when it was first built (Dinsmoor's personal tally indicated over 23,000 visitors by the mid-1920s), this Garden of Eden still draws many visitors. Open daily year-round.

Topeka: Reinisch Rose Garden
Gage Park. Telephone: (913) 272-6171.
This 10-acre marvel has the well deserved reputation for one of the country's best rose collections—more than 7,000 rose bushes in all! Surrounding the main part of the Rose Garden is a grouping of 25 rose beds that tell the surprisingly long history of the rose. (Did you know, for instance, that during Napoleon's time imperial gardeners worked frantically to develop new roses to excite the very demanding Napoleon and Josephine, and started hybrid roses?) You might wish to coordinate your visit with the popular annual Rose Show held in April.

KENTUCKY

Lexington: Ashland
East Main Street and Sycamore Road. Telephone: (601) 266-8581.
Ashland, dating from the early 1800s, was the home of Henry Clay. Designed by Benjamin Latrobe and Pierre L'Enfant (the brilliant architect/designer of Washington, D.C.), it is surrounded by a delightful garden, replicating an eighteenth-century parterre. Both house and garden are open daily. Fee.

LOUISIANA

Lafayette: Around the World Tropical Gardens
U.S. 167S and Ridge Road. Telephone: (318) 555-1212.
As their name indicates, these gardens represent worldwide collections. Within a pleasing 32-acre setting—both outdoors and in greenhouses—you can see exotic plants from Latin America, Africa, Asia, and the Pacific, as well as some native examples. Closed on Mondays. Fee.

Many: Hodges Gardens
U.S. 171 (12 miles south of Many). Telephone: (318) 586-3523.
This extensive (over 4,000 acres) "garden" was created within an abandoned rock quarry. Its many shrubs and flowers and other natural features are surrounded by a vast pine forest. Open daily. Fee.

New Iberia: Avery Island Jungle Gardens

Avery Island. Telephone: (318) 365-8173.

Located on a salt dome, these gardens are known for their live oaks, camellias, azaleas, iris, as well as their rare plantings from around the world. A Chinese garden and a bird sanctuary where egrets and herons can be seen are not to be missed. Open daily, 9 A.M. 5 P.M. Fee.

New Iberia: Live Oaks Gardens

Highways 675 and 14, Jefferson Island. Telephone: (318) 365-3631

This 25-acre island, once the refuge for a pirate named Jean Lafitte, is now the site for a grouping of fine English gardens. Here the visitor can enjoy a variety of camellias, roses, magnolias, and rock gardens, or wander along trails through wildflowers, tropical forests, and flowering vines. Open daily. Fee.

New Orleans: Longue-Vue Gardens

7 Bamboo Road. Telephone: (504) 488-1875.

This fine city estate includes 8 acres of English gardens, wooded areas, wildflowers, and small cloistered gardens surrounding a Spanish court inspired by the Generalife Gardens of Spain. Open daily except Monday. Fee.

Saint Francisville (Baton Rouge Area): Rosedown Plantation

SR 10, off U.S. 61. Telephone: (504) 635-3332.

This historic 1835 antebellum plantation reflects plantation culture both in its elegant mansion and surrounding grounds. Elaborate seventeenth-century–style gardens in the French mode contain some of the original planting of azaleas, gardenias, camellias, and other flowers. There are water features, medicinal gardens, and kitchen gardens. Open daily, March through November 9 A.M. to 5 P.M., and December through February, 10 A.M. to 4 P.M. Fee.

MICHIGAN

Ann Arbor: Matthai Botanical Garden

University of Michigan, 1800 Dixboro Road.

Within the university grounds is this remarkable botanical garden. Its 60 acres are devoted to roses, medicinal plants, and many varieties of ferns. There is a tropical plant conservatory, as well as a research greenhouse. For those who like to walk further, there are inviting woodsy and marshland trails. Open daily, 9 A.M. to 5 P.M.

Detroit: Belle Island Conservatory and Park
Detroit River (Mac Arthur Bridge). Telephone: (313) 224-1097.
This park, designed by the famed Olmsted landscape architectural firm in the 1880s, is situated on the Detroit River, just a short distance away from the center of the city. Included are wooded areas (with animals roaming about), a horticultural conservatory, individual gardens, and an extensive canal system ideal for canoeing. Open daily.

Detroit Area (Bloomfield Hills): Cranbrook Gardens
380 Lone Pine Road. Telephone: (810) 645-3149.
Forty acres of formal gardens surrounding a main house include sculpture courts, fountains, cascades, terraces overlooking the lake, sunken formal gardens, and even a Greek theater. Open May through October. Fee.

East Lansing: W. J. Beal–Garfield Botanical Garden
Michigan State University, West Drive. Telephone: (517) 355-9582.
This botanical garden, thought to be the oldest botanical garden continuously operated in the country, has more than 5,500 plants, many displayed in a landscape setting. Open year-round.

Mackinac Island: Grand Hotel
Mackinac Island. Telephone: (906) 847-3331.
This is a resort hotel with extensive and beautiful Victorian gardens that display thousands of colorful plants. There are also a daylily collection, English gardens and a gazebo garden.

Tipton Area: Hidden Lake Gardens
Route 50, west of Tipton. Telephone: (517) 431-2060.
This huge site covers 670 acres and is notable for some of its odd natural settings, including a glacial pothole, and its rare collections of dwarf conifers and rare shrubs. There are conservatories for tropical, arid, and temperate plants as well. Open year-round.

MINNESOTA

Minneapolis: Kevin Oshima Bonsai Garden
St. Mary's Point, St. Croix Beach. Telephone: (612) 436-7920.
This is a Japanese bonsai garden, visited by appointment only. Open year-round.

St. Paul: Como Park Conservatory
1224 North Lexington Parkway. Telephone: (612) 489-1740.
This 3-acre glass conservatory is home to a wonderful collection of tropical plants, ferns, and palms. Beyond the conservatory, within Como Park, are outdoor gardens offering brightly colored plantings. The conservatory is open daily, 10 A.M. to 4 P.M.

MISSISSIPPI

Jackson: Mynelle Gardens
4736 Clinton Boulevard. Telephone: (601) 960-1894.
This landscaped garden features an Oriental garden, Asiatic magnolias, camellias, and Mississippi favorites. There are also trails for the handicapped. Open year-round, 8 A.M. to 5 P.M. Fee.

Natchez: Stanton Hall Gardens
401 High Street. Telephone: (601) 446-6631 or (800) 647-6742.
Dating from 1851, this live oak landscape features azaleas, camellias, caladiums, and other pleasures. Open daily, 9 A.M. to 5 P.M. Fee.

University: Rowan Oak
University of Mississippi. Telephone: (601) 232-7318.
The house and garden of the Nobel Prize–winning author William Faulkner is open to the public. Here you'll find his home, Rowan Oak, and the hedge-bordered rose garden he created. Open during university sessions. Closed Sundays.

Centralia: Chance Gardens
319 Sneed Street. Telephone: (314) 682-5521.
Named after its creator, Bishop Chance, this lovely site began as a pastime backyard garden in the 1930s. The main cultural influence is Oriental, both in the careful use of stone, wood, and water as well as in the well-tended plantings. Adding to the Oriental theme are the entry, reminiscent of a Japanese torii gate, a delightful Japanese-style pergola with a red roof, a wishing well, and an arched bridge. There are water lilies and lotus flowers and tastefully planted flower beds of iris. Open year-round.

MISSOURI

Columbia: University of Missouri, Botany Greenhouses and Herbarium.
Hitt Street and College Avenue. Telephone: (314) 822-6650.
There are two sites of interest for the garden enthusiast at the university: on College Avenue is the Learning Garden with 2,000 flowering plants and shrubs and trees and a rock sculpture, and on Hitt Street is the Paleobotanical collection, featuring 10,000 fossil plants and 108,000 dried specimens, lichens, and fungi. Open Monday through Friday, 8:00 A.M. to 4:30 P.M.

St. Louis: Missouri Botanical Gardens
4344 Shaw Boulevard. Telephone: (314) 577-5100.
A unique feature of this grand municipal park is its famous Climatron, a giant steel-ribbed transparent structure that houses an extraordinary collection of tropical plants. This futuristic greenhouse—the first of its kind using Buckminster Fuller's principle of the geodesic dome—is fascinating in and of itself. It contains a two-level massive indoor jungle, where you can experience many of the wonders of the tropics all at once. In addition to the many plants, you can admire the pond, waterfall, and stream.

Equally impressive (although perhaps not as dramatic) is the park's famous Shaw's Garden, considered by many to be on a par with Kew Gardens in London. This most comprehensive botanical center encompasses acres of wide varieties of plantings, more greenhouses, and centers of study for the most serious of horticulturists. Open year-round. Fee.

Also found at this site is the Seiwa-En, the largest Japanese garden in the United States. It features water gardens, Japanese bridges in different styles, and numerous plants from Japan.

St. Louis: The Jewelbox Floral Conservatory
1501 Oakland Avenue, Forest Park. Telephone: (314) 531-0080.
Inside this charming construction are display flowers and trees and outside are water lily ponds and perennials, including rose gardens. Open daily year-round, 9 A.M. to 5 P.M.

MONTANA

Bozeman: Montana State University
There are 20 acres of plantings here and two greenhouses. Open daily.

NEBRASKA

Bancroft: Sioux Prayer Garden
Corner of Elm and Washington streets, off I-29. Telephone: (402) 648-3388.
This small garden is a living symbol of the Sioux "Hoop of the World." Open April through November.

Lincoln: Sunken Gardens
2700 C Street.
These water gardens are set in a natural hole; there are three pools and a waterfall and 30,000 plants to enjoy. Open daily.

Nebraska City: Arbor Lodge State Historical Park
Second Avenue. Telephone: (402) 873-3221.
It's hard to imagine that this 65-acre site was once a treeless prairie plot. During the 1850s Sterling Morton (who would become secretary of agriculture under Grover Cleveland and founder of Arbor Day) created his estate here and brought in many trees from the east. Today there are formal gardens, as well as gardens featuring wildflowers and grasses. Open daily (mansion open April through October).

NEW MEXICO

Carlsbad: Living Desert
Living Desert State Park. Telephone: (505) 887-5516
These extensive (250 acres) desert gardens, arboretum, and zoo show the botanical and zoological life of the desert. Open year-round; winter 9 A.M. to 5 P.M. and summer 8 A.M. to 9 P.M.

Columbus: Pancho Villa State Park
Telephone: (505) 531-2711.
A large botanical garden of desert plants commemorates the 1916 raid of Pancho Villa. Open year-round.

NORTH CAROLINA

Asheville: University of North Carolina Botanical Gardens
W. T. Weaver Boulevard. Telephone: (704) 258-6444.
Plants native to North Carolina are featured in these 10-acre botanical gardens; of special note are the prize-winning garden for the blind and the wildflower trails.

Asheville Area: Biltmore House and Garden
U.S. 25, South of Asheville. Telephone: (704) 274-1776
This is one of the nation's showplaces; the palatial chateau that belonged to George Washington Vanderbilt is surrounded by an estate of 12,000 acres on the side of a mountain. Of particular interest are the gardens, which were designed by Frederick Law Olmsted. The magnificent settings include an Italian garden complete with pools, a 4-acre espaliered English garden, a large shrub garden, a spectacular azalea, laurel and rhododendron collection, a rose garden, and—of particular interest—Olmsted's distinctive blending of naturalism and formality of design. Open year-round except holidays. Fee.

Chapel Hill: North Carolina Botanical Garden
University of North Carolina Campus. Telephone: (919) 967-2246.
This botanical garden has an unusual specialty: it is the finest outdoor collection of carnivorous and insect eating plants in the nation. Its 70 acres also include a large collection of plants native to the area. Tours are available. Open daily year-round.

Durham: Duke Memorial Gardens
Duke University Campus. Telephone: (919) 684-3698.
This delightful botanical garden lies in a quiet valley adjoining the Duke University campus. Its wrought iron entrance gate opens onto 50 acres of individual flower gardens, walkways, ponds, and woodlands. Curved terraces of brightly colored perennials lead to inviting nature trails. This is a popular spot with college students, botanists, and tourists.

Manteo (Roanoke Island): Elizabethan Gardens
Telephone: (919) 473-3234.
This 10-acre garden is a memorial to the intrepid Elizabethans who tried to colonize Roanoke Island in 1585. Adjacent to the site of the

Lost Colony, it is planted in formal arrangements including a knot garden and sunken garden and a great lawn typical of the Elizabethan era. Open daily, year-round. Fee.

New Bern: Tryon Palace Restoration Complex
1618 Pollack Street. Telephone: (919) 638-5109.
These formal gardens adjoin the capitol and governor's palace from the royal colony and the Revolution, dating from 1770 on. Featuring authentic plantings of the colonial era, they include kitchen and herb gardens, espaliered fruit trees, magnolia and laurels, and ornate parterres, all set into geometric areas bordered with brick paths. There are about a dozen historic homes to see in New Bern during springtime. Guided tours. Fee.

Salisbury: Poets' and Dreamers' Garden
Livingston College Campus. Telephone: (704) 633-7960.
This garden honors famous poets and dreamers with special plantings. Among the thematic areas are an international garden, a Shakespeare garden, and a biblical garden. Open year-round.

Winnabow: Orton
Telephone: (919) 371-6851.
This is an unusual scroll garden in a lagoon setting, suggestive of the antebellum era. Once a rice plantation, it now consists of flooded rice fields on a small peninsula; the formal arabesque shaped gardens, edged in evergreen hedges, are viewed from platforms above the water level. Open daily year-round. Fee.

Winston-Salem: Reynolda Gardens
Reynolda Road. Telephone: (910) 725-5325.
These beautiful gardens are located next to Wake Forest University, on what once was a private estate. Four acres of formal gardens feature rectangular flower beds, clipped boxwood hedges, grassy plots, and rows of weeping cherries. A grouping of stately Japanese cedars leads to a conservatory and well-tended greenhouses, which are used for horticultural research by the university. Beyond the main gardens are more than 100 acres of natural woodlands with nature trails, streams, ponds, and waterfalls. Native shrubs and trees are often labeled for identification.

NORTH DAKOTA

Dunseith: International Peace Garden
Off U.S. 281. Telephone: (701) 263-4390.
This 2,300-acre site along the U.S.–Canadian border has been dedicated to the preservation of peace. Its formal landscaped areas contain formal gardens, an arboretum, and a "floral clock." Open April through November. Fee.

OHIO

Akron: Stan Hywet Hall and Gardens
714 North Portage Path (south of Exits 11 and 12 of the Ohio Turnpike). Telephone: (216) 826-5533.
Here you'll find a 65-acre garden setting including the Dell, a woodland wildflower area that is magnificent, and an English walled garden and Japanese garden with waterfalls. All these gardens can be visited from early spring through fall, and you can tour the Hall itself, a fine example of Tudor architecture. Open Tuesday through Saturday, 10 A.M. to 4 P.M.; Sunday, 1 P.M. to 5 P.M. in season. Fee.

Cincinnati: Krohn Conservatory
950 Eden Park Drive. Telephone: (513) 352-4086.
In these 20,000 square feet of conservatory gardens you'll find specialty plantings of orchids and cacti. Open daily 10 A.M. to 5 P.M.

Cleveland: Cleveland Botanical Garden
University Circle, 11030 East Boulevard. Telephone: (216) 721-1600.
This beautiful extensive center includes a fine Japanese garden on a hillside, a rose garden, a garden designed for reading and quiet reflection, and a medieval-style herb garden with its "knot." Open Monday through Friday, 9 A.M. to 5 P.M., Saturday noon to 5 P.M., Sunday 1 P.M. to 5:00 P.M., but grounds open dawn to dusk daily. Fee.

Cleveland: Rockefeller Park and City of Cleveland Greenhouse
750 East 88 Street.
Gardens representing 19 nations and a greenhouse of tropical plants are featured here. There is a large Japanese garden and a "talking" garden for the blind. Open Monday through Friday, 9:30 A.M. to 4:00 P.M.; Sunday 8 A.M. to 5 P.M.

Coshocton: Roscoe Village

Hill Street. Telephone: (800) 877-1830.

This restored nineteenth-century village on the Ohio and Erie Canal includes several gardens of historic interest. Among them are the vegetable, herb, and flower gardens planted by the town's first doctor, who used species that were popular in the mid-1800s.

Mentor: Holden Arboretum

9500 Sperry Road. Telephone: (216) 946-4400.

This giant (over 3,000 acres) preserve is among the largest in the country. Founded in 1931, it contains woodlands, fields, and many walking trails. Featured are wildflower gardens, flowering fruit trees, nut trees, hollies, rhododendrons, azaleas, lilacs, and many, many birds.

Newark: Dawes Arboretum

7770 Jacksontown Road S.E. Telephone: (614) 323-2355.

This impressive, 980-acre arboretum has over 2,000 different trees, a lakeside setting, the Dawes homestead, and a Japanese garden. Open daily.

Perintown: Cincinnati Nature Center

4949 Tealtown Road (20 miles east of Cincinnati).

Extensive plantings of pink amaryllis in among the 75 acres of forest with great trees and woodland spring daffodils are highlights here. Open Mondays, 9 A.M. to 5 P.M.; members and their guests are invited to visit on weekends.

Perrysburg: Wildwood Park

5720 W. Central Avenue, Perrysburg (Toledo area).

Some 35 acres of this vast natural prairie and woodland estate surrounding a Georgian manor house are formal gardens of boxwood and other plantings. Open daily, 8 A.M. to dusk; house open for tours Wednesday through Sunday, 12 noon to 5 P.M.

OKLAHOMA

Oklahoma City: Garden Exhibition Building and Horticulture Gardens

3400 Northwest 36th Street. Telephone: (405) 943-0827.

Here you'll find 26 acres of plantings, including iris, roses, and azaleas, among crape myrtle and other trees. Open daily 8 A.M. to sundown.

Pawhuska: Chinese Gardens
10th Street between Prudom and Leahy avenues. Telephone: (918) 287-9924.
This small town, with ties to the Osage Indian Reserve, offers an unusual Chinese garden with carvings and plantings brought from China almost a century ago. Open year-round.

Tulsa: Tulsa Municipal Rose Garden
21st Street and South Peoria Avenue. Telephone: (918) 749-6401.
What makes this gracious garden especially appealing is its unusual terraces of roses. The six terraces are connected by stone steps: the upper level begins on a gentle incline, and the garden continues gradually to the lowest level—the street level—some 900 feet below. Within these spaces are trellises with bright climbing roses and pools surrounded with more blossoms. Color schemes have been carefully planned so you can enjoy brilliant hybrids, as well as more traditional combinations. Open year-round.

Tulsa Area: Philbrook Art Center
2727 South Rockford Road, 3 miles from downtown Tulsa. Telephone: (918) 749-7941.
Formal gardens in the Italian Renaissance style (the villa houses the Art Center) cover a 23-acre hillside site. Open year-round.

OREGON

Portland: Crystal Springs Rhododendron Garden
S.E. 28th Avenue, near Woodstock Blvd. Telephone: (503) 796-5193.
This spectacular display of rhododendrons (2,500 plants) is on a 4-acre island in Crystal Spring Lake. Visit in springtime for the full glory of the rhododendrons in bloom on this woodsy island setting. Open year-round.

Portland: Ira's Fountain
Southwest 3rd Avenue. Telephone: (503) 222-2223.
This city park features a contemporary design incorporating a series of man-made waterfalls; the prize-winning landscape design is by architect Lawrence Halprin. Open year-round.

Portland: Japanese Garden
Washington Park, Southwest Kingston Avenue. Telephone: (503) 223-1321.
Many consider this among the finest gardens of its kind in the country. It consists of five different types of traditional Japanese garden design. Surrounding it are an extensive rose garden and an arboretum featuring some 600 species of trees. Fee.

Portland: Rae Selling Berry Garden
11505 Southwest Portland. Telephone: (503) 636-4112.
Among the 2,000 plants, including 6 acres of rhododendrons at this site, are some rare plants from the Himalayas. Some species are endangered. Open year-round with guided tours.

Portland Area: Gardens of Enchantment
Oral Hull Park for the Blind, 43223 Oral Hull Road, Sandy. Telephone: (503) 668-6195.
This garden, especially designed for the blind, includes plants to be enjoyed through touch and smell and taste. Markers are in Braille. Open year-round.

SOUTH CAROLINA

Aiken: Hopeland Gardens
Whiskey Road and Mead Avenue. Telephone: (803) 648-5461.
These 15 acres of gardens include a touch and scent trail for the blind, pools, and waterside plantings. You can also visit their Thoroughbred Hall of Fame. Open daily, 10 A.M. to sunset.

Charleston Area: Cypress Gardens
Off S.C. 52, 24 miles north of Charleston on I-26. Telephone: (803) 577-6970.
Once part of an eighteenth-century plantation, these spectacular gardens can be visited by boat or on foot along miles of canals and foot trails. Featured are cypress trees, camellias, azaleas, and roses. Open daily, February through May. Fee.

Charleston Area: Mateeba Gardens of Historic Ashley Barony
Ashley River Road (S.C. 61) between Charleston and Summerville.
This exquisite garden, "a fairyland of flowers," features ancient moss

draped live oaks along a dark water lagoon, azalea displays and extraordinary views. Open February through May. Fee.

Charleston Area: Middletown Place
Route 61, 15 miles northwest of Charleston. Telephone: (803) 556-6020.
Once a rice plantation, this famous historic landmark is known for its fabulous gardens, the oldest landscaped gardens in America. It features the Middleton Oak, supposedly 1,000 years old, as well as world-renowned camellias (the first camellias planted in America were brought here). Beautiful terraces and butterfly lakes grace this lovely site. Open daily. Fee.

Charleston: Magnolia Plantation and Gardens
Highway 61. Telephone: (803) 571-1266.
These magnificent gardens, in the Drayton family over 300 years, include one of the major magnolia collections in the nation. The seventeenth-century garden, managed by the ninth generation descendant of its founder, includes acres of floral and landscape highlights. Its topiary gardens feature a living "zoo" of plant animals, a recreation of the Hampton Court maze made of camellia shrubs, and a formal biblical garden of Old Testament plants that includes a parterre shaped like the Star of David and another shaped like a cross.

Murrells Inlet: Brookgreen Gardens
1931 Brookgreen Drive. Telephone: (803) 237-4218.
This extraordinary site is located within a property of over 9,000 acres that comprised four rice plantations during colonial times. Situated between the Atlantic coast and the freshwater swamps along the Waccamaw River, it includes a remarkable sculpture garden—the oldest and largest in the country. The collection contains 547 works by 241 artists—and is still expanding. Among the many artists represented are such masters as Anna Hyatt Huntington (note especially her *Fighting Stallions*, the largest sculpture ever cast in aluminum), Paul Manship, and Carl Milles.

A magnificent 250-year-old live oak allée leads to enclosed formal gardens, whose pathways wind around in the shape of an enormous butterfly. In this outdoor gallery the sculptures are beautifully set amid terraces, pools, fountains, and the lush plantings typical of the region. Nearby is the elegant and symmetrical dogwood garden, surrounding a powerful work by Adolph Alexander Weinman. In addition to the outdoor sculpture sites are indoor galleries. Particularly enchanting is the Moorish-style Small Sculpture Gallery, where some 150 works are on display.

Nature lovers won't want to miss the wildlife park, adjacent to the sculpture gardens. Included are a cypress bird sanctuary, otter pond, alligator swamp, phlox glade, and other delights.

Brookgreen Gardens are open year-round, from 9:30 A.M. to 5:30 P.M. There are picnic facilities, a terrace cafe, a museum shop, and other amenities. Fee.

Orangeburg: Edisto Memorial Gardens
U.S. 301. Telephone: (803) 534-6376.

This is a beautiful riverside series of gardens—110 acres of camellias, daylilies, azaleas, and flowering shrubs; don't miss the roses. Open daily.

Sumter: Swan Lake Iris Gardens
36 Artillery Drive. On U.S. 15, east of Columbia. Telephone: (803) 773-9363.

These gardens are named for their magnificent swans and 6 million Japanese iris, a sight to behold in late spring. An Iris Festival is held in late May. Open daily.

SOUTH DAKOTA

Brookings: McCrory Gardens
East 6th Street (Highway 14). Telephone: (605) 688-5136.

Part of South Dakota University's Horticulture/Forestry Department, these gardens feature almost 500 varieties of flowering annuals, 500 woody shrubs, and a ground-cover juniper collection. Open daily from dawn to dusk.

TENNESSEE

Chattanooga Area: Rock City Gardens
Lookout Mountain.

Situated among spectacular rock formations high atop a mountain,

Rock City Gardens seem more like an unusual geological phenomenon than "gardens." Millions of years of erosion have formed these dramatic natural "sculptures" and the surrounding channels, which seem as if they had been carved from the rock. In the 1920s artist Freida Carter and her husband bought 10 acres of the land and set out to plant native trees, flowers, and shrubs. In this extraordinary setting are more than 400 different kinds of plants, including some that are quite rare. Walking through the gardens is an adventure, as paths wind around cliffs and giant boulders and through natural caves.

Knoxville: Blount Mansion Garden

200 West Hill Avenue. Telephone: (423) 525-2375
A beautifully restored eighteenth-century garden surrounds the Governor Blount Mansion that was once capitol of the territory of the United States south of the Ohio. The garden follows the design of Alden Hopkins, the resident landscape architect for Colonial Williamsburg. Open all year: Tuesday through Saturday, 9:30 A.M. to 5:00 P.M.; Sunday, 2 P.M. to 5 P.M. Fee.

Memphis: Memphis Botanic Garden

750 Cherry Road. Telephone: (901) 685-1566.
This is an 88-acre botanic garden that is particularly noted for its specialized collections of flowering plants indigenous to the South. Among the displays are camellias, magnolias, iris, and roses. There is also a Japanese garden. Open year-round.

Memphis: Dixon Gallery and Gardens

4339 Park Avenue. Telephone: (901) 761-5250
Here you'll find 17 acres of gardens and natural woodlands. There are formal plantings, sculpture, a camellia house, and an art gallery. Open Tuesday through Saturday, 11 A.M. to 5 P.M.; Sunday, 1 A.M. to 5 P.M. Free on Tuesday.

Nashville Area: The Hermitage

U.S. 70, 13 miles east of Nashville. Telephone: (615) 889-2941.
The gardens here were designed by Rachel Jackson, wife of Andrew Jackson, who built the Hermitage in 1819. Flowers, shrubs, and trees are all of the period. Open every day from 9 A.M. to 5 P.M. Fee.

TEXAS

Austin: Japanese Oriental Garden

Zilker Park. Telephone: (512) 477-8672.
The creation of Isamu Taniguchi, this fairly new garden covers 3 acres of hilly area with elegant landscaping in the Japanese style. Open year-round.

Austin: National Wildflower Research Center

4801 La Crosse Avenue. Telephone: (512) 292-4200.
An extensive new botanical center for wildflowers and plants indigenous to the Southwest, this 42-acre site has both wonderful flowers and interesting architectural features, including a working aqueduct and observation towers that collect rainwater. Its pesticide-free environment is home to thousands of flowers and shrubs, as well as butterflies and hummingbirds. The Center also includes demonstration gardens in which various types of desert, wetland, traditional, and natural plantings are arranged to encourage the individual gardener to use wildflowers and native species. A great place for wandering, the Center is open year-round.

Dallas: Civic Garden Center

Second Avenue and Martin Luther King, Jr Boulevard. Telephone: (214) 428-7476.
Here you'll find tropical conservatories, a Xeriscope Garden and Braille display garden.

Dallas: Dallas Garden Center

Forrest and First avenues, State Fair Park. Telephone: (214) 428-7476.
This is a lush tropical garden with orchids and other exotic plants from all over the world and conservatories covering 6,000 square feet. A waterfall and a catwalk high above the tropical plantings are among the features of this special garden complex. There are also an herb and scent garden for the blind and 7 acres of formal and informal outdoor gardens. Open every day except Christmas.

Dallas: Fountain Plaza

This unusual water landscape in downtown Dallas features a series of fountains and descending cascades surrounded by large potted plants. Combining formal and freer elements, the intriguing design echoes the flow of rivers.

Dallas: Samuel Grand Park Garden

6200 East Grand Avenue (off I-20 at Samuel Boulevard). Specialties here include 30,000 azaleas (late March–April for best viewing), 600 rose bushes (best seen in April and May and October and November), and a large collection of iris and other spring flowers (visit in April and May). Open daily.

Dallas: Thanksgiving Square

Pacific, Bryan, and Ervay streets. Telephone: (214) 651-1777. This park and its nearby chapel were designed by Philip Johnson. Included is a delightful water garden. Open daily, year-round.

Fort Worth: Fort Worth Botanic Garden

3220 Botanic Garden Drive. Telephone: (817) 870-7686. This not-to-be-missed site is especially known for its wonderful Japanese garden, which includes over 7 acres of waterfalls, ponds, tea houses, a Meditation Garden, and many exotic plantings. You can enjoy the greenhouses with their unusual plants, as well as a variety of individual gardens: a Rose Garden, Water Garden, Fragrance Garden, and Test Garden, among others. Open daily, except Mondays. Fee for Japanese Garden only.

Fort Worth: Fort Worth Water Garden

13th and Commerce Streets. Telephone: (817) 870-7016. This unusual site in the heart of the city uses water in imaginative ways.

Galveston: Moody Historical Gardens

1 Hope Boulevard. Telephone: (409) 744-1745. Presently still in the planning stage, these gardens, designed by the late Sir Geoffrey Jellicoe, one of the twentieth century's leading landscape architects, will inhabit 126 acres of wetlands between an old abandoned airfield and the Gulf of Mexico. The gardens will represent the history of landscape, beginning with the Garden of Eden, through the gardens of ancient Greece and Rome, Japan, and China, all the way to Thomas Mann's *Magic Mountain*. Visitors will travel on this mythic journey by boat. This should certainly be one of Texas's—not to mention the country's—most unusual "gardens."

San Antonio: Breckenridge Park

1500 North St. Mary's Street. Telephone: (512) 299-3132. Originally created from an abandoned quarry, this interesting park contains pools, a pavilion, stone walkways, spiral steps, and terraced flower gardens. Open daily.

San Antonio: Courtyard of the Spanish Governor's Palace
105 Military Plaza. Telephone: (210) 224-0601.
This peaceful enclosed oasis includes a tiled patio, vine-covered walls, exotic banana plants, and a central fountain. Recently restored, it is considered a prototype for courtyards in the southwest.

San Antonio: San Antonio Botanical Center
555 Funston Place. Telephone: (512) 821-5115.
A specialty of these 33 acres of formal and informal gardens is a Garden for the Blind. In addition, there are many exhibits of native Texas plantings. Open Wednesdays through Sundays. Fee.

Tyler: Tyler Rose Park
West Front and Boone streets.
A 22-acre rose garden is one of the attractions of this public garden, and the fine camellia garden and a conservatory of tropical plants are not to be missed either. Open daily, sunrise to sunset.

Weatherford: White Shadows
This singularly beautiful garden in the middle of Texas was the creation of English artist Douglas Chandor. Noted for his portraits of Eleanor Roosevelt, Winston Churchill, and Bernard Baruch, among others, he set out to design a garden in the 1930s that would survive the harsh climatic extremes of his newly adopted land. The result is a fanciful arrangement of fountains, stone sculptures, grottos, and Chinese-style pavilions set amid imposing rock formations, lagoons, acres of flower beds, expanses of the greenest of lawns, and boxwood hedges. The style is eclectic and fascinating, combining Western and Asian influences with unusual imagination. Fee.

UTAH

Salt Lake City: International Peace Gardens
9th West and 10th South streets.
This is a garden with a theme: Each of its 14 individual gardens features the culture and heritage of a different country. Open daily, May 1 through September 30, from 8 A.M. to 5 P.M.

Salt Lake City: Perception Garden
Memory Grove Park, at City Creek Canyon. Telephone: (801) 581-0755.
This Braille garden features beds of plants designed for fragrance and touch. There are broad walks and fountains and a large park dedicated to war heroes. Open daily.

Salt Lake City Area: Red Butte Garden and Arboretum.
University of Utah at mouth of Red Butte Canyon. Telephone: (801) 581-5322.
Here you'll find 16 acres of plantings from around the world, set within 150 acres for hiking to the nearby mountains.

WASHINGTON

Seattle: Carl S. English Botanical Garden
Hiram Chittenden Locks, Market Street and 26th Avenue, N.W.
Maintained by the Army Corps of Engineers, this unusual garden with a worldwide selection of plantings extends from the locks down the banks of the Lake Washington Ship Canal. Open daily year-round.

Seattle: Washington Park Arboretum
Lake Washington Boulevard East.
This well-known Japanese Tea Garden contains a pagoda, tea house, stone lanterns, and flowering plum and cherry trees. There are also nice collections of azaleas, rhododendrons, magnolias, and lilacs. Visit in spring.

Spokane: Manito Park
17th and Grand Avenue.
There is a lilac garden here, a Japanese garden, a rose garden, and other formal gardens, as well as a conservatory. Open daily, 9 A.M. to dark. Free.

Tacoma: Rhododendron Species Foundation
Federal Way. Telephone: (206) 838-4646 or (206) 927-6960.
A woodland area that has more than 10,000 plants from all over the world, with a specialty of rhododendrons. By appointment year-round, but particularly recommended in springtime.

Wenatchee: Ohme Gardens
3 miles north of U.S. 97.
Alpine gardens on a rocky bluff here feature spring flowering perennials, rockeries, pools, and a great river view. Open daily, April through October 31, from 9 A.M. to dusk. Fee.

WEST VIRGINIA

Charleston: Sunrise Cultural Center
746 Myrtle Road.
On these 16 acres you'll find a formal garden, a demonstration garden of iris that will be of particular interest to iris lovers, and a continual-bloom garden. There is also a rose garden. Visit Tuesday through Saturday, 10 A.M. to 5 P.M.; Sunday, 2 P.M. to 5 P.M.

WISCONSIN

Bailey's Harbor: The Ridges Sanctuary
Door County (northeast lakeshore area), 175 miles north of Milwaukee. This 800-acre sanctuary on the shores of Lake Michigan is an unusual area of sand dunes, watery hollows, and uncommon wildflowers. Visit during wildflower season.

Milwaukee Area, Hales Corners: Boerner Botanical Gardens
Whitnall Park, 5879 South 92nd Street. Telephone: (414) 425-1132. This lovely 450-acre park is set atop a hill and features a collection of 400 crab apple varieties as well as a large rose garden, unusual herb garden, and many native flowers and shrubs.

Madison: Olbrich Botanical Gardens
3330 Atwood Avenue. Telephone: (608) 246-4550.
This is a truly delightful midst-of-city garden, including a glass pyramid conservatory of rare rain forest plantings. The outdoor gardens, particularly the large and elegantly designed sunken herb and perennial gardens, are especially pleasing to the eye—and informative too. Carefully labeled, and beautifully kept, these 14 acres of different kinds of gardens show how much a small city with enthusiastic volunteers can accomplish. Open daily, year-round.

Milwaukee: Mitchell Park Conservatory (The Domes)
524 S. Layton Boulevard. Telephone: (414) 278-4383.

Here, in three geodesic-domed conservatories, you'll find temperate, tropical, and arid climate plantings, and outdoors some 60 acres of perennials, roses, and a sunken garden. Open daily except Mondays, 9 A.M. to 9 P.M. Fee.

Phillips: Fred Smith's Wisconsin Concrete Park
State Highway 13, south of Phillips; for information, write Price County Tourism Department, Phillips, Wisconsin 54555.

This unusual sculpture site is populated with human and animal figures made mostly from recycled material. Created in the 1950s by Fred Smith, a German immigrant farmer, the 3-acre sculpture garden is a celebration of America, from its frontier heroes and historic personages, to anonymous folks of the north woods. Represented are the legendary Kit Carson on his rearing horse and Paul Bunyan flanked by wolfhounds, as well as Abraham and Mary Lincoln. Scenes of Americana—a frontier wedding, farmers plowing with oxen and horses, and lumberjacks sawing down trees—are shown in narrative vein.

Smith was able to achieve unusually varied effects, considering his somewhat limited materials. The primitive-style figures (some 200 strong) are made of cement. Most are decorated with shards of brightly colored glass, salvaged from a nearby tavern. Smith also incorporated found bottles, mirrors, automobile taillights, and other objects to enliven his populist sculptures.

After some restoration and additional landscaping (needed after a series of devastating windstorms severely damaged the site), Fred Smith's park continues to fascinate art lovers and other tourists. Open year-round during daylight hours.

WYOMING

Cheyenne: Cheyenne Commercial Solar Greenhouse
Route 30. Telephone: (307) 635-9340.

You might enjoy a visit to this vast vegetable garden, the largest solar greenhouse operated commercially in the country. It provides food for many needy people and also has community plots for outdoor gardening. Open every day except Sunday.

CHOOSING AN OUTING

ARBORETUMS

Maine
Merryspring

Maryland
Salisbury State University

Massachusetts
Arnold Arboretum
Smith College

New Jersey
Frelinghuysen Arboretum
Rutgers University
Willowwood Arboretum

New York
Bayard Cutting Arboretum
George Landis Arboretum
Planting Fields Arboretum

Pennsylvania
Barnes Foundation
Hershey Gardens
Morris Arboretum
Tyler Arboretum

Rhode Island
Blithewold Gardens and
Arboretum

Washington, D.C.
United States National
Arboretum

ARTISTS' GARDENS

Maine
Celia Thaxter's Garden

Massachusetts
Chesterwood (Daniel Chester
French)

New Hampshire
Aspet (Augustus Saint-
Gaudens)

New York
Garden of April Gornik
Madoo, Garden of Robert
Dash
Noguchi Museum (Isamu
Noguchi)

Pennsylvania
Cedaridge Farm
(Impressionists' Gardens)

ASIAN GARDENS

Maine
Abby Aldrich Rockefeller
Garden
Asticou Azalea Garden

Maryland
Breezewood
Brookside Gardens

Massachusetts
Naumkeag

New Hampshire
Fuller Gardens

New Jersey
Sayen Gardens

New York
Martin Lee Berlinger's Clove
Valley Gardens
Brooklyn Botanic Garden
Hammond Museum and
Japanese Stroll Garden
John P. Humes' Japanese Stroll
Garden
Innisfree Garden
Noguchi Museum
Pennsylvania
Fairmont Park
Washington, D.C.
United States National
Arboretum

*COLONIAL- AND FEDERAL-
PERIOD GARDENS*

Delaware
George Read II House and
Garden
Maryland
William Paca Garden
Massachusetts
Adams National Historic Site
New Hampshire
Strawbery Banke
New York
Abigail Adams Smith Museum
and Garden
Elizabethtown Colonial
Garden
Pennsylvania
Historic Bartram's Garden
Rhode Island
Shakespeare's Head and
Stephen Hopkins' Garden
Virginia
Agecroft Hall
Gunston Hall
Kenmore

Monticello
Mount Vernon
Pavilion Gardens of U.V.A.
Williamsburg's Gardens
Washington, D.C.
Old Stone House Garden

CONTEMPORARY GARDENS

New Jersey
Grounds for Sculpture
Sayen Gardens
New York
Battery Park City Esplanade
Donald M. Kendall Sculpture
Gardens at PepsiCo
Long House Foundation
Gardens
Madoo, Garden of Robert
Dash
Noguchi Museum and
Sculpture Park

*GARDENS LAID OUT OR
INSPIRED BY FAMOUS
LANDSCAPE DESIGNERS*

Connecticut
Glebe House (Gertrude Jekyll)
Harkness Memorial State Park
(Beatrix Farrand)
Maine
Abby Aldrich Rockefeller
Garden (Beatrix Farrand)
Maryland
Hampton National Historic Site
(Andrew Jackson Downing)
Massachusetts
Castle Hill (Frederick Law
Olmsted)
Codman House (Ogden
Codman, Jr.)
Glen Magna (Frederick Law
Olmsted)

Naumkeag (Fletcher Steele)
Smith College (Frederick Law
Olmsted)
New York
Fort Tryon Park (Frederick
Law Olmsted and Calvert
Vaux)
Frick Gardens (Russell Page)
Donald M. Kendall Sculpture
Gardens at PepsiCo (Russell
Page)
Montgomery Place (Andrew
Jackson Downing)
Springside (Andrew Jackson
Downing)
Rhode Island
Hammersmith Farm (Frederick
Law Olmsted)
Wilcox Park (Frederick Law
Olmsted)
Virginia
Monticello (Thomas Jefferson)
Pavilion Gardens, University
of Virginia (Thomas
Jefferson)
Virginia House (Gertrude
Jekyll)
Washington, D.C.
Dumbarton Oaks (Beatrix
Farrand)
National Arboretum (Russell
Page)

*GARDENS OF NOTABLE
AMERICANS*

Connecticut
Gillette Castle (William
Hooker Gillette)
Nook Farm (Mark Twain and
Harriet Beecher Stowe)
Delaware
Nemours (Alfred I. du Pont)

Winterthur (Henry Francis du
Pont)
Massachusetts
Adams National Historic Site
(John Adams)
Longfellow House (Henry
Wadsworth Longfellow)
New Jersey
Georgian Court College
(George Jay Gould)
Ringwood (Cooper Hewitt
family)
New York
Cedarmere (William Cullen
Bryant)
Clermont (Livingston family)
Eastman House (George
Eastman)
Kykuit (Rockefeller family)
Vanderbilt Mansion Gardens
(Vanderbilt family)
Pennsylvania
Historic Bartram's Garden
(John Bartram)
Longwood Gardens (Pierre S.
du Pont)
Virginia
Gunston Hall (George Mason)
Monticello (Thomas Jefferson)
Mount Vernon (George
Washington)
Stratford Hall Plantation
(Robert E. Lee)

*GARDENS THAT CHILDREN
WILL ESPECIALLY ENJOY*

Connecticut
Gillette Castle
Maryland
Ladew Topiary Garden
Massachusetts
Berkshire Botanical Garden

349

Stanley Park
New Hampshire
Lost River Nature Garden
New Jersey
Ringwood
New York
Donald M. Kendall Sculpture
Gardens at PepsiCo
Petrified Sea Gardens
Storm King Art Center
Pennsylvania
Appleford
The Henry Foundation for
Botanical Research
Rhode Island
Green Animals

GARDENS WITH WATER VIEW

Connecticut
Cricket Hill
Gillette Castle
Harkness Memorial State Park
Laurel Ridge
Maine
Asticou
Celia Thaxter's Garden
Hamilton House
Thuya Lodge
Maryland
London Town House and
Garden
Massachusetts
Castle Hill
Hammond Castle
Nantucket Cliffside Walk
New Jersey
Georgian Court College
New York
Battery Park City Esplanade
Bayard Cutting Arboretum
Boscobel

Clermont
Kykuit
Montgomery Place
Untermyer Park
Rhode Island
Blythewold
Hammersmith Farm
Newport Mansions
Virginia
Agecroft
Mount Vernon
River Farm

GARDENS WITH "GARDEN ROOMS"

Maine
Asticou
Massachusetts
Sedgwick Gardens at Long
Hill
New York
Wethersfield
Pennsylvania
Cedar Ridge Farm
Meadowbrook Farm
Virginia
Agecroft Hall
Pavilion Gardens at U.V.A.
Virginia House
Washington, D.C.
Gardens of the National
Cathedral
Dumbarton Oaks

GARDENS WITH SCULPTURE

Maryland
Salisbury State University
Massachusetts
Butler Sculpture Park
Chesterwood

New Hampshire
  Aspet
New Jersey
  Georgian Court College
  Grounds for Sculpture
  Ringwood
New York
  Battery Park City Esplanade
  Griffis Sculpture Park
  Kykuit
  Long House Foundation
    Gardens
  Nassau County Museum of Art
    Sculpture Gardens
  Noguchi Museum and
    Sculpture Garden
  Old Westbury Gardens
  Snug Harbor
  Storm King Art Center
  The Donald M. Kendall
    Sculpture Gardens at
    PepsiCo
  Wave Hill
Pennsylvania
  Morris Arboretum

HILLTOP GARDENS

Connecticut
  Gillette Castle
Maine
  Hamilton House
  Thuya Lodge
Massachusetts
  Castle Hill
  Nantucket Cliffside Walk
  Tower Hill
Pennsylvania
  Chanticleer
Vermont
  Hildene
Virginia
  Monticello

*INFORMAL ENGLISH-STYLE
GARDENS*

Connecticut
  Caprilands Herb Farm
  Glebe House Museum
  Harkness Memorial State Park
  Laurel Ridge
Delaware
  Rockwood Gardens
  Winterthur
Maine
  Celia Thaxter's Garden
  Thuya Lodge
Maryland
  London Town House and
    Garden
Massachusetts
  Berkshire Botanical Garden
  Glen Magna
  Sedgwick Gardens at Long Hill
  The Vale
New Hampshire
  Aspet
  Moffatt-Ladd House
New Jersey
  Cross Estate
New York
  Clermont
Pennsylvania
  Joanna Reed's Garden
Rhode Island
  Hammersmith Farm
Virginia
  Virginia House
Washington D.C.
  Dumbarton Oaks

ITALIANATE GARDENS

Connecticut
  Harkness Memorial State Park

Massachusetts
Codman House
Glen Magna
Sedgwick Gardens at Long
Hill
New Jersey
Georgian Court College
New York
Vanderbilt Mansion Gardens
Virginia
Maymont
Washington, D.C.
Dumbarton Oaks

ORIGINAL AND ECCENTRIC GARDENS

Connecticut
Caprilands Herb Farm
Gillette Castle
Maryland
Ladew Topiary Garden
Massachusetts
Castle Hill
Hammond Castle
Naumkeag
New Jersey
Ringwood Manor
New York
Long House Foundation
Madoo, Garden of Robert
Dash
Petrified Sea Gardens
Pennsylvania
Cedaridge Farm
Grey Towers
Virginia
Oak Ridge

PALATIAL GARDENS

Delaware
Nemours

Winterthur
New Jersey
Georgian Court College
New York
Kykuit
Old Westbury Gardens
Vanderbilt Mansion Gardens
Pennsylvania
Longwood Gardens
Rhode Island
Newport Gardens

PRIVATE GARDENS

Connecticut
Garden of Susan and Robert
Beebe
New Hampshire
Mr. Jacquith's Garden
New York
Martin Lee Berlinger's Clove
Valley Gardens
David and Helga Dawn Rose
Garden
Garden of April Gornik
Madoo, Garden of Robert Dash
Pennsylvania
Meadowbrook Farm
Joanna Reed's Garden

ROCK GARDENS

Maryland
Breezewood
Massachusetts
Stanley Park
New Hampshire
The Fells
New Jersey
Leonard J. Buck Garden
New York
Stone Crop Gardens
Clermont

Pennsylvania
Henry Foundation

ROMANTIC GARDENS

Connecticut
Gillette Castle
Maryland
Hampton Court
Massachusetts
Glen Magna
Hammond Castle
New Hampshire
Barrett House
New Jersey
Cross Estate
Ringwood Manor
New York
Clermont
Lyndhurst
Montgomery Place
Wave Hill
Pennsylvania
Cedaridge Farm
Virginia
Oak Ridge
River Farm

ROSE GARDENS

Connecticut
Bellamy–Ferriday Garden
Elizabeth Park
Massachusetts
Stanley Park
New Hampshire
Fuller Gardens
New Jersey
Lambertus C. Bobbink
Memorial Rose Garden
Colonial Park
Deep Cut Horticultural Center

New York
David and Helga Dawn Rose
Garden
Lyndhurst
Mills Memorial Rose Garden
Pennsylvania
Hershey Gardens
Rhode Island
Rosecliff

SPECIALTY AND THEMATIC
GARDENS

Connecticut
Caprilands Herb Farm
Cricket Hill (peonies)
Laurel Ridge (daffodils)
Maine
Asticou (azaleas)
Maryland
Lilypons (water lilies)
McGrillis Gardens (shade)
Sherwood Gardens (tulips)
Massachusetts
Heritage Gardens (rhododen-
drons)
Newbury Gardens
New Hampshire
Rhododendron State Park
New Jersey
Doris Duke Gardens
Frelinghuysen Arboretum
Rutgers Gardens (hollies and
bamboo)
Sayen Gardens (daffodils)
New York
Brooklyn Botanic Garden
New York Botanical Garden
Highland Park (lilacs)
Donald M. Kendall Sculpture
Garden at PepsiCo (iris)

Rhode Island
  Kinney Azalea Garden
Vermont
  Olallie (daylilies)
  Hildene (peonies)
Washington, D.C.
  United States. National
    Arboretum (bonsai,
    conifers)

TOPIARY GARDENS

Delaware
  Nemours
Maryland
  Ladew Topiary Garden
  William Paca Garden
New York
  Wethersfield
Pennsylvania
  Longwood Gardens
Rhode Island
  Green Animals

WALLED OR INTIMATE
GARDENS

Maine
  Hamilton House
  Woodlawn, Colonel Black
    House
Massachusetts
  Codman House
  Isabella Stewart Gardner
    Museum
New Hampshire
  Fuller Gardens
  Moffatt Ladd House
New Jersey
  Cross Estate Garden
New York
  Clermont

The Cloisters Gardens
The Frick Gardens
Pennsylvania
  Joanna Reed's Garden
  Wyck
Vermont
  Great Woods Garden of
    Goddard College
Virginia
  Agecroft Hall
  Pavilion Gardens of University
    of Virginia
  Virginia House
  Williamsburg Gardens

WILDFLOWER AND
WOODLAND GARDENS

Connecticut
  Larsen Sanctuary
Delaware
  Winterthur
Maine
  Hamilton House
  Merryspring
  Robert P. Tristram Coffin Wild
    Flower Reservation
  Wild Gardens of Acadia
Maryland
  Cylburn Garden Center
Massachusetts
  Garden in the Woods
New Hampshire
  Plainfield Wildflower
    Sanctuary
New Jersey
  Leonard J. Buck Garden
  Sayen Gardens
  Skylands
  Willowwood
New York
  Root Glen

Pennsylvania
  Bowman's Hill
  Brandywine Conservancy
  Chanticleer
  State Wildflower Preserve
Vermont
  Vermont Wildflower Farm
Washington D.C.
  Franciscan Monastery Gardens

GARDENS WITH WATER

Maryland
  Brookside Gardens
  Lilypons
  London Town House and
    Garden
  William Paca Garden
Massachusetts
  Stanley Park
New Jersey
  Waterford Gardens
New York
  Frick Gardens
  Stone Crop Gardens
  Wave Hill
Pennsylvania
  Brandywine Conservancy
  Longwood Gardens
  Meadowbrook
Virginia
  Virginia House
Washington D.C.
  Dumbarton Oaks
  Kenilworth

ESTATE AND FORMAL
  GARDENS

Connecticut
  Bellamy–Ferriday Garden
Delaware
  Nemours

Maine
  Hamilton House
  Woodlawn, the Colonel Black
    Mansion
Maryland
  Hampton National Historic Site
  William Paca Garden
Massachusetts
  Castle Hill
  Naumkeag
  Sedgwick Gardens at Long
    Hill
New Hampshire
  Fuller Gardens
New York
  Boscobel
  Eastman House
  Old Westbury Gardens
  Sonnenberg Gardens
  Vanderbilt Mansion Gardens
  Wethersfield
Pennsylvania
  Appleford
  Longwood Gardens
Rhode Island
  Newport Mansions
Vermont
  Hildene
Virginia
  Agecroft
  Gunston Hall
  Hillwood Museum
  Mount Vernon
  Oak Ridge
  Stratford Hall

CONSERVATORIES AND
  BOTANIC GARDENS

Delaware
  Rockwood

Maine
  Wild Gardens of Acadia
Maryland
  Brookside Gardens
  Cylburn
Massachusetts
  Berkshire Botanical Garden
  Garden in the Woods
  Sedgwick Gardens at Long
    Hill
  Smith College
  Tower Hill
New Jersey
  Deep Cut
  Doris Duke Gardens
  Frelinghuysen Arboretum
  Skylands Botanical Garden
New York
  Brooklyn Botanic Garden
  Buffalo and Erie County
    Botanical Garden
  Cornell Plantations
  New York Botanical Garden
  Queens Botanical Garden
  Sonnenberg Gardens
  Wave Hill
Pennsylvania
  Fairmount Park Horticultural
    Center
  Henry Foundation
  Historic Bartram's Garden
  Longwood Gardens
  Phipps Conservatory
Virginia
  Lewis Ginter Botanical Garden
    at Bloemendaal
  Norfolk Botanical Gardens
Washington D.C.
  Hillwood Museum
  United States Botanic Garden

Also by Marina Harrison and Lucy D. Rosenfeld

ART ON SITE
Country Artwalks from Maine to Maryland   *$16.95*

ARTWALKS IN NEW YORK   *$15.95*

A WALKER'S GUIDEBOOK
Serendipitous Outings Near New York City   *$13.95*

WALKS IN WELCOMING PLACES
Outings in The Northeast for
Strollers of All Ages and the Disabled   *$14.95*

Also available from Michael Kesend Publishing, Ltd.:

A GUIDE TO THE SCULPTURE PARKS & GARDENS OF AMERICA
by Jane McCarthy & Laurily K. Epstein   *$18.95*

To order, please send a check for the listed price to:

Michael Kesend Publishing, Ltd.
1025 Fifth Avenue
New York, NY 10028

Add $4.50 for shipping and handling plus 50¢ for each additional copy
with the same order.
Or, phone 1 800 488–8040. Credit cards accepted.
For quantity discounts, contact the special sales department at:
Tel: 212–249–5150
Fax: 212–249–2129